THE

FINANCIAL ECONOMY

OF THE

UNITED STATES ILLUSTRATED,

AND

SOME OF THE CAUSES WHICH RETARD THE PROGRESS OF CALIFORNIA DEMONSTRATED:

With a Relevant Appendix.

BY

JOHN ALEXANDER FERRIS, A.M.

"No danger is too appalling, no toil too excessive, no sacrifices too costly, where humanity is to be benefited and the nation to be served."—LONDON TIMES.

"THE Constitution which at any time exists, until changed by an explicit and authentic act of the whole people, is sacredly obligatory upon all."—GEORGE WASHINGTON.

JUSTICE is an attribute of the DEITY, and the foundation of all permanent prosperity; it cannot be disregarded by nations, or individuals, without certain retribution.

SAN FRANCISCO:
A. ROMAN & CO., 417 AND 419 MONTGOMERY STREET.
NEW YORK: 17 MERCER STREET.
MDCCCLXVII.

PRINTED BY TOWNE & BACON,
No. 536 Clay Street,
SAN FRANCISCO, CALIFORNIA.

To the Friends of our Constitutional Currency—
Gold and Silver Coin;
To the Advocates of Justice and Right,
Wherever they may be found,
In the United States;
To all who Recognize the Importance of Moral Principle
In National Legislation and Jurisprudence,
And all who desire the Permanent Prosperity
Of the American Republic in General,
And of the Pacific States Especially,
These Papers are Inscribed,
With subservient regard,
BY THE AUTHOR.

CONTENTS.

PAGES

PREFACE .... xi–xiv

NUMBER I.

THE EFFECT UPON GOLD—AS MONEY—BY INFLATING ALL THE CURRENCIES OF THE WORLD EQUALLY.

Money should possess intrinsic value to exchange for value; secured on stocks or property, not an accurate measure of value; should exist in a country proportionately to the requirements of the same; rapidity of circulation does not compensate for inadequate supply; money adapted to the purposes of its design—currency no repletive substitute. Currency often circulates at the par of gold when far below gold value; effect of sudden inflation, in equal proportions, in all countries; irrepressible conflict between gold and paper................. 15–23

NUMBER II.

AMOUNT OF CURRENCY NEEDED IN THE UNITED STATES.

The currency of the nation should be governed by Congress, for national defense. Issues of State Banks should be suppressed. Currency should never be any form of credit. Congress should not allow banks to circulate currency of less value than coin; American mines ample to supply all healthful demands of the nation for money; possibility of making our entire currency equal to gold coin; currency and population of the country in 1860; yield of the Pacific mines in eighteen years; amount of currency required in 1860 24–35

NUMBER III.

PAGES.

DOES CALIFORNIA NEED THE NATIONAL BANKS?

Gold the staple of the State—no currency should be tolerated which cheapens gold, or lessens the demand for it as Money. Yield of California Mines, $50,000,000 yearly—Population not over 400,000. Laudations of a uniform Paper Currency. No uniform currency can exist unless the equivalent of gold coin. The Currency of California desired by all honest men in the old States. Losses which would result from introducing the National Bank Currency—the system would work interminable mischief.. 35-38

NUMBER IV.

THE LEGAL TENDER ACT EXAMINED.

Justice, one of the Fundamental Principles of the Constitution. The Legal Tender Act of Congress makes the word dollar a meaningless term—destroys it as a standard. The half of a quantity cannot be equal to the whole of it. The States have the same right to charter Corporations to coin money as to charter them to issue Bills of Credit. When Currency falls below the par of gold, it is issued in dead loss to the country at large. Congress has no power to enact a new system for raising funds, when the Constitution provides a definite system for the same object. The Mint Laws of Congress are in full force. The Act would establish a tender far inferior to gold coin in value. A Double Standard, varying in value, an impossibility. Congress has power to borrow and tax without any limitation, except public necessity. Has no right to use means not delegated. to accomplish a purpose, where express powers are delegated to effect such purpose. A hypothetical case in illustration of the Act (pp. 49-51). Congress fixes the value of coin by prescribing its weight and fineness. California being admitted into the Union with a hard-money Constitution, Congress is estopped from forcing on her any other currency. Opinion of Daniel Webster on Legal Tender. The depreciation of the Legal Tenders proceeded *pari passu* with their issue. The Act had no power to keep them at the par of gold. The tendency of the Act is to create a moneyed oligarchy which will govern the nation, and if it is to remain a permanent enactment, to ruin our Form of Government.. 38-74

PAGES.

NUMBER V.

The Constitutionality of the Specific Contract Act Defended.

The Law gives to Courts the power to enforce payments of Contracts in the identical currency which the parties specify. Some of its provisions enumerated. The gold and silver coin of the mints the only legal tender. What is legal tender by the Constitution cannot be made illegal by Congress. The Act is a State Law, furnishing the legal mode for collecting the only legal tender money known to the Constitution; of course is most thoroughly constitutional, and above the power of Congress...... 74–82

NUMBER VI.

The Right of the Federal Government to Control the Currency.

The Constitution gives Congress the power to coin money and regulate the value thereof. This power was given to insure a pure currency. States prohibited from coining, also from issuing Bills of Credit. All issues of money under the control of the Federal Government. Congress cannot regulate the value of coin without regulating the currency also. The regulating the value of coin is with Congress, which has power to make all laws necessary and proper for the execution of the trusts reposed by the Supreme Law. Currency does affect the value of coin, therefore Congress is bound to rule currency. Federal or State Stocks are no proper basis for the issue of currency. Gold should never be cheapened by paper currency. Congress is bound to provide for the general welfare of the country—nothing of more importance to this welfare than sound currency. Currency should be coin, or represent it. Unlimited liability of stockholders no proper basis for the issue of currency. The specie basis, dollar for dollar, the only proper regulation of currency.......................... 82–96

NUMBER VII.

Resumption of Specie Payments.

Specie payments cannot be resumed, while Congress allows a legal tender of inferior value. Congress, the Courts, and the People must recognize and maintain the difference in value between Treasury notes

PAGES.

and gold coin. The volume of currency must be reduced—Value of Legal Tenders results from being convertible into Bonds. Every dollar of paper currency should represent a metallic dollar in the Treasury. No part of the business of Congress to provide currency for speculation or gambling. Specific Contract Law of California should be enacted by Congress, for the benefit of the Union. Gold must be monetized by withdrawing currency from circulation. National bonds are not a proper basis for the issue of currency. The profits from circulation should be suppressed by Congress. Losses on the sale of Government bonds abroad by reason of a depreciated currency. Reform of the currency possible and practical. The reform needed in the National Bank system is to change the basis from Government Bonds to gold coin (p. 127). *How to resume specie payments* (pp. 124–129). $68,000,000 may be applied yearly, in gold coin, to change the basis of the National Bank Circulation from bonds to gold. Banks must keep gold and currency accounts while the system is in transit. The values of each currency must be recognized. Specie in the banks a national shame, not amounting, in some, to half per cent. of their immediate liabilities. National Banks clamoring for more circulation, and *that their issues be made a legal tender*. Currency cannot be pure unless entirely so. Every inflation lessens its value. Government should pay off the debt to the banks first, and hold the gold for security of Bank issues instead of Bonds. The rise in our National Securities abroad would pay for a prompt return to specie payments. 96–142

NUMBER VIII.

THE TARIFF OF THE UNITED STATES—ITS EFFECT UPON THE VALUE OF GOLD FOR USES ABROAD.

Equal Taxation is what the Supreme Law contemplated —the Tariff acts unequally—oppresses some States and aids others—the present Tariff extremely onerous on California—Estimated yield from 50 to 75 per cent. on goods imported. *It takes one-third from the value of gold for uses abroad* (p. 143). Is equal to a fine of one-third the value for the purchase and importation of foreign goods. More onerous on California than other States, because gold is *always* marketable in the marts of the world, while other articles are not. Helps New England immensely, and crushes California equally (p. 145). Prices of

PAGES.

Foreign Goods (pp. 144–145). What California has paid and is paying for the Union (p. 147). Losses enough to build four railroads from the State to the Missouri.................................... 142–149

NUMBER IX.

The Effect of Demonetizing Gold upon its Domestic Value.

The Acts of Congress have a blighting effect upon the value of coin. The Tariff bolsters a rotten Currency in direct proportion to the amount imposed. Domestic goods are advanced directly by the tariff on foreign goods. How the Losses on Currency are balanced (pp. 154–155). The reduction of the value of Gold in the domestic markets is an intolerable grievance (p. 158). "The Balance of Trade," by C. H. Carroll, Esq. (p. 159). The permanent interest of the Union and the Pacific States identical —upon the matter of Currency. Every State entitled to all the immunities of the Constitution. Secretary McCulloch bears witness that goods were higher with gold at 47 premium than when it stood at 185. This immense loss to California comes from Demonetizing Gold. The Legal Tender Act and the National Bank Act may now be discussed from a peace stand-point. The organizing of Government or State Stocks into Currency, makes an annual national loss equal to the entire product of our gold and silver mines (pp. 168–169).................. 150–170

NUMBER X.

Bank Circulation.

The Principle of Circulation explained. Circulation is twofold—outside, or bills paid out; and inside, or deposit account. Coin will not remain in the country beyond the demands for Money. Banks should not be allowed to receive Profits upon Circulation. The People must blame themselves for the Sins of the Banks, for they exist by sufferance. Supply would follow demand for Banks, even if their issues were limited to specie basis, dollar for dollar. Savings' Banks recommended. When Currency has displaced Coin, the good and bad circulates together at the nominal par of Gold. The gain from Circulation is similar to that from transporting passengers in a dangerous vessel—it is made at the imminent risk of the public (p. 175). Interest may be justly paid for Real Capital — not for Credit. Banks

PAGES.

should not be the Custodians of the Specie upon which their circulation is issued—the specie should be deposited in the Federal Treasury............ 170–179

NUMBER XI.

GOVERNMENT CIRCULATION.

Congress cannot legally issue any permanent form of Circulation which lessens the value of Coin. Its only right to rule currency, comes from the necessity of keeping it at par of coin. The Gains from Circulation are insignificant, compared with the damages of an inconvertible currency. The Legal Tenders should be funded and annihilated. The Honor of the Country at stake. Government should never disgrace itself by so flagrant an act as the issue of an inconvertible currency................ 179–182

NUMBER XII.

THE SALES OF GOLD BY THE SECRETARY OF THE TREASURY.

Sales of Gold from February to May, 1866. Profits, in currency, on sales. Different views as to the policy of sales. Importing business done largely on foreign account. Sales made for Currency and at currency prices. Importance of keeping gold at its proper relative value to currency. Whatever it rules under this is dead loss to the country. To bring the value of all currency up to coin is desirable, but to drag the value of coin down to currency is national loss without reducing prices generally. Gold should never be sold to force down its own value. The best use to make of gold for the good of the country. By the sales of gold, Congress recognizes the difference in value between gold and Treasury notes. A real difference of value being admitted by the Legislature, citizens should have equal rights with the Government to deal in such values, and these dealings should be protected by law, not prohibited or made contraband.......... 182–188

NUMBER XIII.

WHO OWNS THE GOLD TAKEN FROM THE GOVERNMENT LANDS?

Unjust censures of the miners—their excessive toil and losses of health and constitution. The farm-laborer will endure his work three or four times as long as

PAGES.

the miner. The yield of the mines belongs to the miner as justly as the farmer owns the crops which he sows. The Fisheries have Bounties—their claims less national than those of the miner. The mines must be worked—the Credit of the Government depends largely upon them — Government should rather foster the mining interest with bounties than hamper it with taxes or excises. The mining interest should be faithfully represented in Congress... 188–191

NUMBER XIV.

THE INDEPENDENT TREASURY.

Removal of Deposits from the United States Bank. The pet Banks made the Fiscal Agents of the Government. Mania for Speculation from redundant currency. Specie Circular by President Jackson. The Bank of England refuses to Discount for American Bankers. Suspension of Specie Payments by all the Banks. Honorable Silas Wright on the Suspension. The New England System of Banking. The New York Safety Fund system. The last United States Bank and the Charter by the State of Pennsylvania. The General Banking Law of New York. Argument of the Hon. Silas Wright for an Independent Treasury. Argument of Hon. Thomas H. Benton, for the same. Benefits of the Independent Treasury should extend to the people. Government cannot receive the full advantages of the Bill, unless Congress suppresses the issue of all currency not equivalent to coin. Gold at paper prices (p. 204). Opinion of Daniel Webster on the Equality of Currencies. The only way to make currency equal to coin, is to limit the issues to the coin deposited for its redemption................ 192–207

NUMBER XV.

THE DUTY OF CALIFORNIA IN RELATION TO THE LEGAL TENDER ACT.

The Maintenance of State Credit an indispensable Duty. A Prompt Payment of Interest upon the Debt necessary. The debt should be kept from increasing. The State Policy should be to keep up the value of gold. Reducing the Value of Gold, a direct thrust at the vital interest of the State. Such reduction would increase the State debt, without increasing the means to discharge it. An Illustration by Dr. Smith. His position proves that a paper circulation could be of no use to this State. If the Treas-

PAGES.

ury notes are lawful money by Act of Congress, the coin of the Mints is legal tender on all debts, by the Constitution. Opinions of eminent Senators on legal tender. It is not necessary to cut off California from the use of the coin of the mints for currency. If legal tender be forced upon the State permanently, the public debt will be greatly increased. Resolutions of the California Legislature. The Gordian Knot of the currency question finally settled, for the State, by the enactment of the Specific Contract Law.............................. 207–221

NUMBER XVI.

PAPER CURRENCY—TESTIMONY OF STATESMEN, FINANCIERS, ECONOMISTS, PHILOSOPHERS, AND PHILANTHROPISTS UPON THE SUBJECT OF PAPER MONEY.

Any element which makes price without value, is subversive of sound economy. It is the very essence of paper money to make such price. Prices without value create bankruptcies. The policy of such money would be suicidal to California. An Illustration of its Operation (p. 227). The difference in Prices of Commodities, under a gold or paper currency, is an index of the amount of bankruptcies which a country assumes by an inflated currency. Paper Money to California would be as noxious as tares and darnels among the wheat of her farmers. 221–228

NUMBER XVII.

BANK DEPOSITS AND INSCRIPTIONS OF CREDIT IN BANKS.

The quality of Bank Deposits—those resultant from notes discounted not Deposits Proper. Undrawn Loans should not be reported as Deposits. Deposits rule prices as much as Bills in Circulation. The Deposit Account, through the discounting power, may Monetize all kinds of Property. Such Inflations are constantly being balanced by Bankruptcies in the body politic. Deposits should be equal to coin in value. The System of California Banks. To change it to that of the Eastern States, would involve a loss to us of $20,000,000 annually....................................... 229–234

PAGES.

NUMBER XVIII.

PAPER MONEY TRIED BY THE DOCTRINE OF ETHICS.

Quotations from the Scriptures, proving the Abomination of all kinds of False Measures. Every one has a Right to his own Property. Defrauding by False Measures of Value equally heinous as by False Measures of Quantity or Capacity. The latter is a Crime by our laws, the former is upheld by Legislation. Gold and Silver are almost universally cited in the Bible to illustrate Values. The Cost and Difficulty of obtaining these Metals. They were given to Mankind for the purpose of Correct Standards. False Money makes all Business partake of the hazards of Gambling. The Perversion of Currency an effect of Avarice. The Laws of God are Irreversible, and a part of these Laws are the Laws of Nature and Science. False Standards of Value condemned by Political Economy, the Federal Constitution, and Divine Law. The Spoliation of False Money. Double Standards, varying largely in Value, and yet held as equivalents in law, must work interminable mischief. We cannot atone for Unjust Laws by stamping on our coin "In God we Trust." The Proof of such Trust would be more satisfactory in doing away with all Unrighteousness in Measures.. 235–260

NUMBER XIX.

ENLARGEMENT OF THE POWERS, USES, AND BENEFITS OF THE INDEPENDENT TREASURY.

Relevant Opinions of Eminent Writers. The Regulation of Currency should reach the Deposit Accounts of Banks. The Failures of 1857. Our Foreign Debt in 1850 and 1860. This Indebtedness to be ascribed largely to our Currency. The Author's Bill, of 1860, for Reforming the Currency and Deposit Accounts. Recapitulation of the Measures proposed in the Bill (p. 285). The Power of Congress to Regulate the Value of Money is Nullified, through the emission of Bills of Credit by the Banks. The Rights of Persons considered. Opinions of Mr. Webster and Adam Smith upon the Duty of Government to restrain Private Rights. The National Banks, being the Creatures of Congress, may be Moulded and Governed by any needed amendment of the Law. The Advantages of Treasury Exchange for Domestic Uses. Government Banking, on a Gold Basis solely. Whatever form of Paper Issues are to Circulate as Currency, Government should

PAGES.

Suppress every species of it which is not secured, dollar for dollar, by Coin in the Treasury. The United States have the means to Saturate the Currency with Gold and Silver. The Silver Coin of the Mints a better Basis for Currency than anything else except Gold. The immense Saving to the Country, if a similar Bill could have been the Law of the Land when California came under our National Flag.................................. 261–293

NUMBER XX.

THE PACIFIC RAILROAD.

Subsidies to the Work by the Government. The great necessity of its Speedy Construction. May be Finished by January, 1872. Its great Addition to the Wealth of the Country. It has cost FOUR BILLIONS OF DOLLARS to bind the Union, North and South—would it be unreasonable to expend $200,000,000 to Bind it East and West? What California has Paid and is Paying for the Government. Expenses of the Pacific Coast are National—not Chargeable to California. The Railroad is needed, as a Measure of National Defense, as much as our Navy or Army. Causes which retard the Progress of California not to be attributed to a Gold Currency. These are: first, her Isolated Position and Distance from the large Populations of the World; secondly, the Want of Correct Knowledge of her Resources; thirdly, the Want of a Certain Market for her Agricultural Products, and reasonable Freight Charges, when shipped to other countries. But the Great, Overshadowing Drawback to her Prosperity is, that she has lost a large fraction of the value of her staple—Gold. The Tariff has virtually confiscated a large per centage for uses abroad, and, in connection with the Currency, made Prices without Value upon Domestic Manufactures. The Immense Losses of California since 1848, amounting to $693,000,000 (see pages 299–300). These Losses have resulted from the Neglect of Congress to do its duty in the matter of Currency. As a small return for this Unequal Taxation which has been imposed, it is proposed that Government shall aid the Pacific Railroad $100,000,000, and the roads in California $100,000,000. The excellence of the Scheme is that it will be a National Defense; that it will be an act of justice to California; a lasting bond of interest and union to the nation; and will increase the direct value of the country many fold the amount of the subsidies................. 294–301

CONTENTS OF THE APPENDIX.

(A.)

PAGES.

A SCHEME FOR A LAND BANK IN ENGLAND.

The Project Explained by the Historian Macaulay. The Wonders which would follow its Organization in England. The "blessed effects" that were to be produced by issuing enormous quantities of notes on landed security. If a person held real estate worth £2,000, he ought to have his estate and £2,000 in paper money. The absurdity of the Scheme set forth. The Principle of issuing Bills on Land compared with issuing upon Government Bonds. Neither of these Schemes are any proper basis for the issue of Currency.................. 302–305

THE POSSIBILITY OF A METALLIC CURRENCY 306–307

(B.)

AMERICAN BANKING.

The Difficulty of Teaching the People that "Paper Money" is no Element in the Nation's Prosperity. The multiplication of Bank Notes adds not a dollar to the Wealth of the Country. The issuing of "Paper Money" should take its place alongside of Astrology and Divination. The system totally useless and radically absurd...................... 307–308

Returns of the National Banks. Immediate Liabilities over $900,000,000. Specie on hand, $8,170,835. Who could wish to see such a system of Banking adopted in the Pacific States 309

(C.)

EXTRACTS FROM ELLIOT'S DEBATES IN THE FEDERAL CONVENTION UPON THE SUBJECT OF EMITTING BILLS OF CREDIT BY THE UNITED STATES 310–312

PAGES

(D.)

LEGAL TENDER NOTES.—HAS CONGRESS THE POWER TO MAKE NOTES A LEGAL TENDER?

OPINION OF JUDGE SHARSWOOD, OF PENNSYLVANIA .. 312–331

(D.)

JUDICIAL OPINION.

Judge Alexander, of Maryland, has filed the Opinion that Congress has no Power to make Greenbacks a Legal Tender 331

(D.)

Legal Tenders declared Unconstitutional by the Court of Appeals of the State of Kentucky 331–333

(D.)

ILLUSTRATIONS OF LEGAL TENDER, BY S. NEWCOMBE. 333–334

(E.)

THE SUPREME FOLLY OF PREFERRING PAPER TO GOLD CURRENCY IN CALIFORNIA............... 334–336

(E.)

THE MASSACHUSETTS ANTI-SPECIE DECISION.—THE OPINION OF THE COURT IN FULL........... ... 336–338

(E.)

UNITED STATES DISTRICT COURT, NEW YORK.—RULING OF THE COURT 338–339

PUNISHING TRADE FOR THE SINS OF PAPER........ 339–342

THE TARIFF AND MIXED CURRENCY................. 343–345

ALPHABETICAL INDEX........................... 347

PREFACE.

EVERY intelligent being should try to leave the earth some better on account of his having trodden its surface. If each individual who attains to an age of thirty years, *could* give to posterity one original, useful and truthful idea, how rapidly would the world increase in wisdom! "Knowledge is power," and in a republic it is the only power which can long perpetuate its existence. Wealth, too, is power; and every proper effort put forth by individuals or the government to diffuse affluence among all classes of society, by favoring the industries of the whole country as equally as possible, must result advantageously to the republic. For, as the national authority can not be used more efficiently to promote the opulence of the country, than when it is exercised in making such laws as are in harmony with the laws of science,—which are the laws of nature, — so the same authority can not be exerted in legislating in conflict with such laws, without wide-spread ruin; and, if persisted in, the total demolition of the government.

Our monetary and fiscal interests are second in importance only to the republic itself. If we have demonstrated our power and prowess in fighting battles and achieving works of destruction, we need wisdom and discretion in our councils to repair such immense sacrifices; and, while the work of reparation is advancing, to adopt such measures as will not essentially change our form of government, by passing the wealth of our country into few hands, and leaving the masses of the population in a condition of vassalage.

No scheme of personal aggrandizement, put forth by any class of citizens, can despoil the masses of the people, and change the ownership of property from the many to the few with such rapidity, as for the laws of the country to be at variance with the principles of truth and justice, and lend their aid in destroying our standards of value. Such enactments create bankruptcy beyond any and all other causes combined, and corrupt the morals of the people directly as they induce their insolvency. The effect of general financial ruin — changing the ownership of property to comparatively few hands, would as efficiently destroy the republic, and change the nature of the government, as though it were subjugated by military power. The result, though not so sudden, would be equally certain.

These papers were written at different times — a few of them have been published before — but their contents are as applicable at this present as when they were produced. While the subjects have been treated in their general scope upon the weal of the nation, the special bearing upon the interest of this State, as a gold producing community, is kept in constant view. So far as they discuss propositions of a legislative nature, without any reference to the manner such subjects are treated, it will be no self-praise to assert that the propositions themselves are of the highest importance to the State and nation. Hence, the subjects should command the special attention of our delegation in Congress, and our future State legislators.

Since the power of our Government is essentially in the people, it is matter of moment that they also understand, for themselves, the natural laws which govern the relation of values to each other.

There are some of the elementary principles of financial economy—such as the true relation of real money to other forms of wealth—how a false currency deranges our business operations, and turns all the proceeds of industry, measurably, into gambling—the action of such disorganizing agent in subverting the morals of society and striking at the vital interests of the people, both material and moral — these and their corollaries, are subjects which need to be put forth in all manner of plain propositions—to be iterated and reiterated with "line upon line, precept upon precept, here a little and there a little," till all can understand them; and this repetition must be kept up for cycles and centuries, for generations to come, till the power and prestige of false money shall be driven from the pale of honesty, wisdom, and all enlightened civilization.

B

To the States of the Pacific Coast the matter of currency is a specialty, the importance of which can not be over estimated. It is not to their gain that the uses of coin should be substituted in any manner by paper issues, or that the uses of metallic currency should be economized. And the State which will not, in its legislation and its judicial decisions, adhere to the principles of its own and the Federal Constitutions, while those principles are promotive of its highest interest, will be justly liable to the certain retribution which must follow such perversion of truth, justice, natural law, and the behests of morality.

If the Pacific States, with such an excess of metallic currency, cannot move the industries of a population considerably below one million, then it would seem hopeless to try to bring prices, through the Union at large, to the basis of a gold currency.

This, however, has been done in these States, and successfully, for the past seventeen years; and the ability to continue the policy increases every year in the direct ratio as the general wealth of the Coast advances. In instituting comparisons between the Pacific and Atlantic States, we forget or ignore the fact that our towns do not count a score of years, while some of the Atlantic cities have been peopled for centuries. Time will demonstrate, not only to the old States, but to the civilized world, if we persevere in the use of a metallic currency, the wisdom of our system, and the aggrandizement which it will achieve beyond any other currency upon earth.

No. I.

THE EFFECT UPON GOLD—AS MONEY—BY INFLATING ALL THE CURRENCIES OF THE WORLD EQUALLY.

The attributes of money—its functions among the peoples of earth—its relative value to commodities—whether it should possess intrinsic value, or be a credit leaning upon some other form of wealth for its efficiency—whether it should be gold and silver only, or these metals mixed with paper promises in quantities and proportions to be regulated by law:—in the United States, whether the regulation of money is an exclusive prerogative of the Federal Government, or may be exercised by the State Legislatures—whether either Congress or the State Legislatures have any right to change the relative value of coin to commodities by the circulation of paper as money, or by instituting any other legal tender than gold and silver coin:—these are inquiries of vast importance to the nation; and since our Government is derived from the people, their decision must be made by themselves, be the same for weal or for woe.

The financial world is divided into two great classes upon the nature of money. These may be properly styled bullionists and currency makers. The bullionists hold that nothing but the precious metals should be money, and that currency and money should be the same thing. The currency makers hold that currency secured upon property, State stocks, merchants' and traders' notes, bonds, and mortgages, is as good as the gold. The redemption of the currency in gold, being guaranteed and secured by property or stocks pledged, makes the currency as good as gold, according to these cambists.

The eminent French economist, M. J. B. Say, holds

this opinion of money as it ought to be: "The precious metals are so well adapted for the purposes of money as to have gained a preference almost universal; and, as no other material has so many recommendations, no change in this particular is desirable."

Money being not only an instrument of exchange, but a measure of value, must possess intrinsic value to make this measure accurate, for values cannot be measured except with equivalents. That the quantity of real money in a country, in proportion to its commodities and exchangeable properties, and also in proportion to its industrial interests, should bear a certain relation to the amount of such commodities and interests, to make a prosperous condition in such country, is admitted by all economists. The amount, however, of real money needed for such prosperity is a point upon which there exists a wide difference of opinion. Money, in its circulation through the body politic, may be aptly compared with the circulation of the blood through the human system. A strong, athletic man, possessing a frame of the weight of two hundred and thirty pounds, needs a large amount of the vital circulation to keep his body in healthful condition. This circulation must also be adapted in quantity and quality to the requirements of his system. Rapidity of circulation can not supply the place of quantity of vital fluid; nor can any process of transfusion of blood from the veins of sheep, of oxen, or even of the human race, take the place of the vital fluid which nature has given him, or afford a substitute which shall possess the needed quality of the human blood. Man needs just the right quantity of healthful circulation; he needs it of the proper quality adapted to his nature; and he needs the velocity of this circulation adapted with the same unerring wisdom as its quality. If the circulation be too rapid, it denotes deranged and febrile action, and may induce insanity. The wants of the body politic are quite analagous to those of the body natural in respect to circulation, quality, and quantity. The quality of circulation in each of these bodies must be sound and healthful, the quantity sufficient for the needful effect, and the velocity of motion neither too rapid nor too slow. All of these attributes are necessary, in each of these forms of circulation, to produce a sound and healthful action. Adaptation is one of nature's uniform laws; and when men can find this principle attached to any gift of God to his creatures, in so unmistakable form as the adaptation of gold to the uses and purposes of a sound and valuable currency, they should give up all hopes of improving, or even attempting to improve, the works of a beneficent Providence. The air we breathe, as chemists inform us, contains 21 parts of oxygen, and 79 parts of nitrogen, or azote. Suppose the proportions were inverted, and the atmosphere were made up of 79 parts of oxygen, and 21 parts of nitrogen; would such a substitute sustain animal life? Not for one hour. The principle of circulation in the body politic being analagous to the circulation of the blood in the body natural, it cannot be tampered with in either case with impunity. Its quantity and quality must accord to the requirements of each respectively.

The amount of money needed in a nation or a state, to move its industries, to distribute its productions, and make just its exchanges between and among its own people, as well as its dealings with other nations through the channels of commerce, is a question that is fraught with difficulty to solve in theory, or by any given rule. Still, if money were left to act in its normal condition, without any diluting of its value by paper issues, or by substitutes of bank credits, each civilized country of the globe, with open commerce, would take its fair and just proportion of the gold and silver of the world, upon the principle of supply and demand, with as much accuracy and justice as all other exchanges of its commodities and properties are made.

Money would be a miserable substitute for bread to a hungry man; he could not eat it, and he might perish with hunger possessing thousands of dollars, if he happened to be in a wilderness where bread was not to be found. In like manner the merchant, who possessed flour in an over-stocked market, might find it utterly impossible to sell his flour for money, and his notes might go to protest, and he be ruined from such cause. The flour would be adapted to the wants of the hungry man, and the money to the wants of the merchant who owed debts. Every form of property has its use, order, place, position, and proper state. Houses cannot circulate as money; nor can ships and railroad cars be deposited in banks. We need just the right number of houses, ships, steamboats, etc., to do our business; and we need just the right amount of money to move the proper business of the country. It would be a forced operation to try to make a steamboat perform the offices of money, as much as to try to make money perform the services of the boat. It is this blending and confusing of articles of entirely separate qualities, striving to make them subserve unnatural purposes, that has made such wide difference in the minds of men upon the matter of money. Equivalents may and do exist, and yet each form of property have its specific, distinct and separate functions.

Because a man owns a house or a ship worth $50,000, this is no reason why he should have the right to mortgage this property and issue currency, or money, upon it. He may receive the rents upon his house, the freight-money upon his vessel—and let that satisfy his avarice. So, if he holds government or state debt, let the coupons for interest be his just gain. He has no right to use such form of debt to monetize it, and thus receive double gains.

It is, then, the substitution of a new form of money, commonly called currency, which is not money in fact, and can never be money by all the artifices of man; it is this substitute for money which banishes and demonetizes the sterling gold, and leaves in its place nothing but promises, which, if ever performed, must entail on the people the most fearful losses and ruinous sacrifices of their estates.

Nearly a century ago the learned Doctor Adam Smith published his work on the Wealth of Nations. In Book II., chap. ii., on page 122, he maintains this position: "The whole paper money of every kind which can easily circulate in any country, never can exceed the value of the gold and silver of which it supplies the place, or which (the commerce being supposed the same) would circulate there, if there was no paper money." What latitude the learned doctor, if he were living, would claim for this position, by reason of having qualified it with the term "easily," we are left to conjecture. One thing is certain: the "universal Yankee nation" does not quail at anything which *can be done*, whether it be fraught with dangers and difficulties or not, if they think they can make money by it. If it cannot be done "easily," they will do it by the hardest.

The idea of difficulty and danger is to them only an incentive to action. Whether the Doctor would admit that, *with difficulty and danger* more paper money might circulate in a country than the amount of gold and silver which would circulate in such country if there were no paper money, we are not certain. But one thing he would have no reason to doubt, that the experiment has been most perseveringly tried in the United States, to solve this difficult problem; and, although the currency-makers professed to keep their issues at the par of coin, I apprehend that it would be difficult for the Doctor, or any one else, to make them believe that their circulation did not exceed the coin which would circulate if these issues were all withdrawn.

Adam Smith's rule of circulation, as he gives it, applies to all commercial countries with an open commerce. He admits that gold and silver will be sent abroad, and the channel of home circulation filled with the precise amount of paper money which such paper displaces of gold circulation.

The United Kingdom, the nations of Europe, the United States of America, and the British Provinces in North America and elsewhere, are competent to fix the prices of gold and silver for the whole world. Nay more; they are not only competent to do this, but they exercise this power. Now, suppose all these nations dilute their currencies one-half, by substituting paper money, upon the theory of Dr. Smith, one-half of the precious metals would leave these countries. After the gold was sent from them, or was driven to the arts for a market as merchandize, by being demonetized through the action of the substitute—paper money—these countries would then be left with currencies of one-half coin and one-half paper. Again, suppose that the currencies of these countries, (which we will regard as equally diluted, say one-half with paper) were not greater than the normal volume of currency which belonged to each of them, and not more than they possessed in coin before the paper was issued; would they not be circulating, for the time being, an amount of currency twice as large as would be circulating if their paper were suddenly withdrawn from the currency? If such paper were suddenly withdrawn from circulation in all these countries, how long would it take for the channels of trade and commerce to replace the gold and silver which the paper had displaced? The precious metals being banished by paper, or manufactured into articles of merchandise, it would take many years to fill the vacuum which the paper issue had caused, with gold and silver. Hence, during all these years there would be in circulation a currency much larger than would have circulated during this time in gold and silver if the paper had not been issued.

The increase of currency increases the demand for it. Money is a universal agent; and he who possesses it can, at once, convert it into any other form of wealth which is equivalent to the same. Not so with other forms of property. The owner of real estate and merchandise may be compelled to hold the same for years, or sell at large sacrifice. Hence this insatiable desire among our people to monetize property, debts, and credits. But so long as the real dollar is made only of gold and silver, and is the only constitutional legal tender in existence in the Union, all attempts to monetize paper, property and credits can only work confusion and mischief in the nation. If paper be monetized and made a legal tender, it demonetizes gold and silver. These metals will only be valuable as merchandize, to be wrought up in jewelry and the arts. However, while foreign nations recognize the value of the precious metals as money, the acts of our Congress in demonetizing gold, by monetizing and making a legal tender of paper, will not deprive gold of its value abroad, but it will most certainly drive it from the country.

Beyond doubt, gold would not exchange for or purchase one quarter of what it commands of other forms of wealth, were it not recognized by other nations of the globe as money. M. Say writes thus upon this subject: "The adoption of any specific commodity to serve as money considerably augments its intrinsic value, or value as an article of commerce." "A new use being discovered for the commodity, it unavoidably becomes more in request; the employment of a great part, the half or perhaps three-fourths of the whole stock of it on hand, in this new way, cannot fail to render the whole more scarce and dear.

"The employment of the precious metals in manufacture makes them scarcer and dearer as money, in like manner as their employment as money makes them scarcer and dearer in manufacture."

If the monetizing of silver and gold gives to these metals three-fourths of their value — and beyond doubt such is the fact—it is apparent what blighting effect it must exercise upon the State of California, to monetize paper and make it legal tender. There is an "irrepressible conflict" going on between paper and gold: one or the other must ultimately come off victorious, although the contest may last for many years.

The world contains gold and silver enough to do the business of all nations; and, even if it did not, no permanent advantage can be gained from supplementing coin with promises to deliver it, by corporations which do not possess it.

All economists admit that the circulation of bills of credit as money will expel an amount of coin from the country equal to the amount of paper which circulates at the par of gold. The gain, then, would seem to result from the theory that the nation which dilutes its currency the most with paper, saves the most by this violent and unnatural expedient of paper issues. Upon this hypothesis, all the printing presses of the world might be started in making promises to pay gold coin. These promises could not be fulfilled, because the world would not possess the coin to pay them. To introduce a condition impossible to be fulfilled into the currency, and try to make the promise good by extravagant pledges of other forms of wealth, is to crush the people between the upper and nether millstone, without any good cause to justify such cruel infliction. An impossible promise should never circulate as money or currency; and all promises to pay coin, which circulate as money, beyond the coin in the country, are impossibilities. The more property or wealth that is pledged for the convertibility of paper issues into coin, the more ruinous and oppressive is such a currency to any people ; but if the pledge be coin itself, there is no such result. A golden eagle of the United States mint is good security for the issue of ten dollars in paper ; but a mortgage upon property worth five hundred dollars would not redeem that bill, in coin, if the coin was not in existence. I have supposed an extreme case to illustrate the action of the principle. If property-money is as good form of money as gold coin, through the action of printing-presses we may monetize and pledge all the wealth of the country, and have a promise-dollar circulating for every dollar of wealth of any form we possess. The absurdity of the position is too apparent to need illustration. The genuine coin is good, but falsehood in money is as obnoxious as it is in moral principles.

Suppose that at a given time all the currencies of the world had been gold and silver coin, of the same standard of fineness, and coined in ounces and aliquot parts of an ounce. These currencies would be sufficient to move the industries of the world, because their value would depend upon the laws of supply and demand. Their values, and the values of commodities, would be adjusted to them almost with mathematical precision. At least, they would be as nearly accurate as it would be possible to make equivalents. This adjustment would be self-constituted, and would continue reasonably perfect, so long as legislation did not interfere with it, or impose upon the people some substitute for money. Again : suppose that on a given day the nations of the world should issue an addition of fifty per cent. to their currencies, in the form of bills of credit, secured upon bonds, mortgages, government stocks, ships, steamboats, farms, houses, live stock, mechanical implements, merchandise, wares, or any form of wealth, except gold and silver, which had heretofore been the only form of money that had been recognized by the world ; what effect would the uttering of such additional form of paper money have upon the wealth of nations, and the prosperity of the world ? Its first effect would be to advance all prices of merchandise and commodities fifty per cent. Next, it would enable the debtor portion of the world to pay their debts with two-thirds the value which it would have required to do the same under a metallic currency. The creditor would be compelled to receive one-third less by such tyranny. The value of metallic currency would be reduced one-third, the world over, by such addition. Its effects upon instituting and perpetuating vast national debts, if there were no other reason against it, would be amply sufficient to condemn it in the minds of all judicious and honest men. I can see immense losses that would result from such expansion, but no practical use. The great difficulty in the whole matter lies in the fact that such promises are all false; and being so, they are unworthy the toleration of a wise, an honest, and opulent nation.

The constant action of a paper currency is to drive gold out of the country, by its expansion, and when the evil of driving this coin away is seen, by panics and ruin on all sides, its tendency is to bring the gold back again slowly, by unlimited sacrifices of the property of all the debtor portion of the people. It is a forced operation, in driving money away by high prices of goods; and it is only through the ruinous operation of sacrificing property that it returns. National, State, municipal, and private debts are generally — other things being equal — in direct ratio to the expansion of the currency. If there were really the advantage resulting from the issue of bills of credit to circulate as money which is claimed, does not every nation possess the power of issuing currency? It would become a race of nations, striving which could issue it most rapidly. (See Appendix, A.)

No. II.

THE AMOUNT OF CURRENCY NEEDED IN THE UNITED STATES.

In a subsequent number, it is maintained that every system of banking which has heretofore been instituted in the old States was not only in conflict with the Federal Constitution, but was an essential failure in practice, and a subversion of sound morality.

The state banks grew up from a necessity for some public depositories for public and private funds, to promote the facilities of exchanges, for discount of mercantile paper, and for objects of general convenience and utility. In all their purposes they were praiseworthy institutions, with the exception of issuing bills of credit. In this regard they placed themselves upon the ground of direct opposition to the organic law of the nation, and, as I maintain, in direct opposition to the laws of justice and morality.

When the civil war was fully organized, the Federal Government was found in the humiliating position of supplicating favors of these, comparatively, impotent currency makers. Much credit has been ascribed to the State Banks for the ready manner in which they contributed to help the Government, by advancing loans upon national bonds and other securities. The lesson of the war, however, has taught the Government that any reliance upon such institutions as these—whose very vitality consisted in the credits which the people gave them, rather than in the benefits which they distributed to their proper localities—was only deferring the day of reckoning, to be met at last by more gigantic indebtedness on the part of the Government.

It is now seen that the government of the currency belongs to the National Legislature, not only by the

Constitution, but by the principles of national defense. We do not want our currency built upon so sandy a foundation as that, when war comes, the suspension of cash payments by those institutions which have been allowed to print and circulate their promises to pay dollars, and to receive from the people interest upon these promises, shall be protected by the law. And, least of all, we do not want the Federal Government to be humiliating itself by asking favors of any such unlawful associations. The issues of the State Banks should be immediately, imperatively, and totally withdrawn from circulation. If it be necessary, Congress should enact that after a notice of six months it should be a felony to circulate any State Bank bills, and the penalty should be equal to that of uttering and passing counterfeit bills. At all events, the legislation should be so stringent as to stop it at once and for ever.

The State Bank issues have all been upon a wrong basis. The excuse for them was that Congress had neglected to do its duty in regard to the currency, and the States were compelled, of themselves, to do something in the premises. Let this excuse suffice for the past. The matter has now been taken in hand with a will by Congress, and let them have the full ruling of the business; and then with our National Legislature will rest the responsibility of giving to the people a currency equal to gold. Let Congress not be subject to any side issues with State Banks; let State Banks which issue bills for circulation be driven at once to the wall. No State can issue bills of credit; consequently, no State can charter banks to issue such bills. A State Legislature has the same right to charter banks to coin gold and silver, as it has to allow them to issue bills of credit. The supreme law is as much against the one as the other. The grand achievement in regard to the currency, thus far, has been to bring it under the action of one Federal Legislature, instead of thirty-six State Legislatures. For while it is impossible to get so many Legislatures to agree upon any general system, it is not only possible but hopeful that Congress will ultimately bring wisdom out of the former chaos, and give us, as is easy for them to do, the most perfect system of currency on earth.

The system of the National Banks is subject at all times to revision and amendments. As it now stands, it recognises the old heresy in currency—that Government bonds are a good basis upon which to issue the currency of the nation. This heresy is what underlies all the evils which result to the country by teaching the doctrine that issues of paper to circulate as money may be founded on other securities than gold and silver, and still be fully equal to them. The currency of the country should never be any form of credit. The evils of a false currency are wrought and brought upon a people while they are totally blind to its action. Government should never wink at the fraud of banks imposing upon the people a currency which they cannot at all times convert immediately into gold, at its face value, dollar for dollar.

While it is the duty of the Government to regulate the currency, they should regulate it with a will; they should regulate it upon the principle that a dollar should always mean, in law, in justice, in equity, and in fact, one hundred cents. Hence, if a bank would issue one hundred thousand dollars in paper promises, and the Government sees fit to allow those promises to circulate as money, the Government should have on hand one hundred thousand dollars in gold to redeem those paper promises.

The great failure, then, of the National Bank Act, is that, instead of requiring a deposit of gold, dollar for dollar, for the issues and circulation of the banks, it allows a deposit of Government bonds, or debt of the nation, which is monetizing debt and driving the gold out of the country. It is not wisdom for the Congress to institute any system of currency which will sack the nation of its gold; I care not what substitute it may introduce to supply the hiatus of such displacement. So long as real dollars are made of gold, and so long as the reality is better than a counterfeit, so long will gold dollars be better than any promises to pay gold, which are only secured by the pledge of Government stocks.

Some men, who are almost insane upon the advantages of a paper currency, insist that it is entirely *a matter of indifference to the public* how the payment of currency is secured, if the security is such as will at all times insure prompt redemption. This is another great heresy in currency. If the currency of the country, by law, be gold coin, and the substitution of paper money banishes this coin to other nations by the course of trade and commerce, then the security for the redemption of bills issued by the banks depends upon their power to grind their customers in the dust. When panic seizes the public from any cause, the property of dealers in bank must be sacrificed at any amount of loss to enable the banks to withdraw their circulation. Now if their circulation was based on gold, dollar for dollar, banks would never fear a panic; such a thing would be impossible. Is it better, then, that the Government should insist that the whole of the circulation of banks should be secured dollar for dollar on gold, and thus place the monetary position of the currency at once and forever above and beyond the power of panics; or have every five or ten years a general breaking up of all business, financial as well as mercantile, commercial and manufacturing, leaving the failures to be balanced in bankruptcy ten times the amount of the failures in the currency? It is estimated that every dollar of failure in the currency produces ten dollars of bankruptcy in the general business of the country. But, says one, your system would be a decided improvement upon any and all systems of currency, except for a very weighty reason, to wit, that it is impossible. You can never get gold enough to make it the basis of all the currency of the country, dollar for dollar.

If such were the case, it would be wasting time to contend for the principle, even as one of moral reform. It is useless for an individual to oppose popular prejudices and errors, no matter how great evils these errors are working to the nation, unless he has a plan of reform which is possible and practicable.

I announce the broad principle that *it is possible* and *practicable*, and not only so, but, with proper legislation of Congress, comparatively easy, for the whole currency of the United States to be based on gold alone, dollar for dollar. And now to the task of demonstrating this position to my countrymen.

In this connection it becomes necessary to inquire—what amount of currency is required in the United States to move and continue the industries of the people, and to distribute their products and commodities? This query can be easily solved by the statistics of the nation. The census of the United States for 1860 gives the aggregate population of the States and Territories at 31,420,891. The annual report made by the Clerk of the House of Representatives, in January, 1860, of all the Banks in the United States, gives the following summary:

BANKS OF THE UNITED STATES.

In January, 1860, there were 1,392 Banks and 170 branches.

Their aggregate Capital was	$421,880,095
" " Circulation	207,102,477
" " Deposits	253,802,129
" " Loans	691,945,580
" " Specie	83,594,537
" " Stocks	70,344,343

From the amount of loans it will be correct to deduct the deposits, because the Banks retained these in their hands out of the loans — that is, they charged interest on about $230,000,000 more than they circulated of bills. From the above report, we see that the aggregate capital of all the Banks and branches of the United States, in 1860, was less than $422,000,000; that their whole circulation was a little over $207,000,000; that their deposits were nearly $254,000,000; that their loans were about $692,000,000, and that their specie was less than $84,000,000. The liabilities of the Banks in 1860 were as follows:

For Circulation	$207,102,477
For Deposits	253,802,129
Aggregate liability to the public	$460,904,606

The liability to shareholders we are not now considering. From this last amount, above stated, we will deduct the specie held by the Banks, $83,594,537, and this leaves the amount $377,310,069 as the whole sum which the Banks had in circulation in 1860 beyond their specie. By adding the specie in the hands of the people, we have the whole amount of money needed to move the industries of the United States, in 1860, containing a population of about thirty-one and one-half millions. The amount held by the people is something which cannot be got at with accuracy. My opinion is, that $100,000,000 would be a high estimate for the specie in circulation and in hoards, in 1860; but we will call it that for the nonce. We have, then, for the currency of the United States in 1860:

From the Banks	$460,904,606
Specie with the People....................	100,000,000
Total currency of the United States in 1860,	$560,904,606

Deposits are here considered currency, as much as bills in circulation.

And now the question comes up: Can the United States furnish for the uses of all its great and growing interests, this vast amount of specie to move its industries? and can it increase this currency as fast as its popnlation shall increase, so that its entire moneyed operations shall rest upon a thorough specie basis for the ages of futurity? I answer the question positively and categorically—IT CAN BE DONE. With proper legislation on the part of Congress, this achievement, so needful to posterity, to the honor, to the morality of the people of the United States—and perhaps I might add, to the permanence of the American Government—can be accomplished with comparative facility.

The circulation of the Banks, added to their deposits, gives the whole currency of the country, except the specie in the hands of the people. These deposits and circulation amounted to, say in round numbers, $461,000,000 in 1860. But as the Banks held at that date $85,500,000 in specie, it needed about $377,500,000 in coin to make the currency of the country equal to the specie standard, dollar for dollar.

I presume every candid man will admit that the volume

of currency in 1860, with our population at thirty-one and one-half millions, was fully up to the healthful demands of the people for currency, and fully up to the amount of the normal quantity which would circulate in specie if bank notes had been entirely prohibited at that time in the United States. If these premises be correct, $561,000,000 in specie would have been an ample supply, in 1860, to move all the industries of the United States, and to distribute their products and commodities. Was it possible to have had $561,000,000 in coin in the country in 1860? I answer: It was not only possible, but it might have been achieved with the greatest ease, with proper legislation to save it.

It is a rule in the commercial world that every nation, under a free commerce with other countries, will secure to itself its proper relative proportion of the gold of the world, for its own business. Fortunately for ourselves, however, we need not rely upon commerce for our own supplies. The country yields gold in great abundance, ample for the legitimate business of our people, and ample to move all her industries. The necessity of looking to commerce for our gold is not imposed upon us; if it were, I fear we should be a poverty-stricken community, so far as relates to a gold currency.

Free trade is a boon which Americans are not to know for a distant future. We are bowed down with immense Federal, State, county, city and private debts; and our commerce must suffer severely from the imposts of customs, and the necessary expense of collecting them. This, however, is a collateral branch of the currency question which I will not now consider.

Our country is rich in the precious metals, and the currency may be all in specie from the yield of our own mines, without the importation of a dollar from other countries. I do not suppose that the business demands of our country for currency, aside from the wants of the Federal Government, should be any greater than they were in 1860, when all our industries were in active operation, north and south, east and west, through the vast extent of the United States.

The treasure shipments of gold from the port of San Francisco from 1848 to 1863, inclusive, were, by manifest, $784,652,194.

(See "Hunt's Merchants' Magazine," Vol. XXXI, p. 227. Vol. LI, p. 150.)

Shipment treasure from San Francisco in	1864, ..	$56,707,201
" " "	1865,....	45,308,228
" " first quarter "	1866,....	9,582,544
		$896,250,167

The above amount has been shipped from San Francisco since 1848, as shown by the Custom House. It is very safe to assume that, during the past eighteen years, at least one hundred millions more have gone forward in the trunks, belts and purses of passengers and returning miners. Government has forwarded several millions, which are not included in the above figures. With these statistics before us, it will call for no great stretch of our imagination to believe that California and the Pacific States have yielded, in the last eighteen years, the vast sum of one thousand million of dollars in gold and silver. Assuming that we had on hand, in 1848 one hundred and forty millions in specie, and that the yield from commerce and all the mines east of the Rocky Mountains, in the past eighteen years, has been sixty millions of dollars, then we have used, wasted, and expended (except the amount we have on hand at this time) twelve hundred millions of dollars in eighteen years. Probably we may have one hundred and fifty millions in specie, in the United States, in 1866. The balance, ten hundred and fifty millions, has been used, spent, exchanged for tops and whistles, gewgaws and flaunts, satins and laces, diamonds and jewelry.

The statistics of the United States' mints show that the actual coinage has been more than eight hundred and sixty millions of dollars in the past eighteen years. If, then, it only needed an addition of three hundred and seventy-seven and one-third millions of dollars in coin to the amount which was in the country in 1860, to make our entire currency of specie, and the mines of the Pacific Coast have yielded one thousand millions of dollars in the past eighteen years, and commerce, with the yield of the mines east of the Rocky Mountains, has brought sixty millions more in the same time; and it is further proved by the statistics of the mints that more than eight hundred and sixty millions of dollars have been coined since 1848,—these premises being established, it follows that, in eighteen years, the Pacific mines alone have yielded enough for the whole currency of the country, estimating that at five hundred and sixty-one millions dollars for a population of thirty-one and a-half millions; and an excess for shipment, to balance exchange and imports, of four hundred and thirty-nine millions of dollars. From these figures it may be deduced that the average rate of yield of gold and silver from the mines of California has been sufficient to supply the entire demand of the people for currency, in ten years and two months mining; and this would still allow the product of eight years mining to be exported, and leave the volume of currency entirely filled with specie.

In further corroboration of my position, that the yield of our mines is far in excess of the requirements of our people for currency, I will cite from Hunt's Merchants' Magazine, vol. 54, page 221. Here the production of gold is enumerated in quinquennial periods; and it will he interesting to the careful inquirer to see the amount which has been added to the world's stock since 1848.

This writer makes the production of gold from the Pacific States, for eighteen years, from 1848 to 1865, inclusive, $1,056,500,000; the product of silver for the same time, $53,000,000. Therefore, we have a yield of $1,109,500,000 in gold and silver, for the eighteen years after the discovery of gold in California; say from 1848 to 1865, inclusive, from the States of the Pacific. The same writer makes the yield of gold in the world, for the same time, eighteen years, $3,341,500,000; and of silver, $1,620,500,000, being an aggregate addition of $4,962,000,000 to the stock of the precious metals of the world from 1848 to 1865, inclusive. The gold and silver mines of the world have yielded, in eighteen years, nearly $5,000,000,000; and the gold and silver mines of the Pacific States alone have yielded, in the same time, $1,109,500,000. The idea that the United States cannot get gold enough to do the business of the country, is, with these statistics before us, too absurd to require further proof.

We have demonstrated that, in 1860, our population of 31,500,000 only needed $562,000,000 to move all of their industries; that they only needed, at that time, $377,330,000 more in specie than they possessed to make the whole circulation and deposits of the country rest upon a specie basis; that the mines of the Pacific States have yielded in eighteen years more than one billion dollars; that the mines of the world have yielded in the same time about five billions of dollars; that, as a commercial nation alone, we ought to receive gold enough for our currency from our trade with other countries, even if we possessed no gold mines. I shall, therefore, assume that it is possible to have our whole currency of gold, or paper representing gold, dollar for dollar. In another paper I purpose to show how this may be achieved, and the legislation needed to endow the people of the United States with this colossal legacy.

It is manifest, however, that the greater the value of gold, in comparison with other forms of wealth, the less amount will it require to subserve the wants of the people as currency. If one dollar of gold, under a purely metallic currency, were equivalent to two dollars in gold under a mixed currency, then, obviously, gold would be doubled in value, by dispensing with the paper or credit money which is mixed in with the circulation. But the business of the country, and of the world, might be done just as well, and have the relative value of gold to commodities four times its present ruling. That such would be the case in the United States, if the substitute of paper money were dispensed with, is beyond all doubt. The gain which the champions of paper money claim as the result of an inflation of the currency, is based upon the fact that other nations of the globe have not debased their currency to the same extent; therefore, we may receive permanent advantage by vilifying our medium of exchange.

Immediate specie payment, it is contended, is a thorough panacea to the evil; and if banks can stand this test, they ought not to be hampered with any further restrictions. The reason is illogical, unsound, and a gross financial heresy. When the prices of commodities are advanced to harmonize with the inflation, the call for currency is made upon the basis of this inflation. And in the United States—a country which mines $75,000,000 yearly in gold and silver—it would be strange indeed, if the banks could not turn the corners by sinking the gross annual product of the mines, and being allowed by law to issue $300,000,000 of paper, (which is nearly tantamount to the issue of so much counterfeit) the value of which depends not upon its intrinsic qualities, but upon the wants of the people, it having expelled the coin from the country; and, as the people must have some form of currency, and this is the only form within their power of attainment, with the necessities of the people for currency, the yearly sacrifice of the yield of the mines, and the advances in prices of commodities—all combining to make a perpetual call for currency; it would show most thorough rottenness if our banks could not maintain specie payments, similar to that sustained by the State Banks before the war.

The truth is, that although specie payments nominally are better than the present system of open bankruptcy, by which those institutions are making so much profits out of the people, this is by no means the measure to bring things upon a proper basis. Because the requirement of the people is fully equal to $400,000,000 in gold coin, that is no reason why corporations should have the right to issue three hundred millions of paper, which banishes that amount of gold, and by such banishment institutes an imperative demand for the paper issue. Counterfeit coin would circulate as well if it were fortified with equal legislative acts.

The real touchstone, and the only one which a wise and honest people should ever allow, is this: that paper money shall only be issued dollar for dollar of the deposit of gold coin in the United States Treasury, to secure the issue; then paper money would be honest and right.

The American mines are amply sufficient to cover all the wants of the nation for currency, dollar for dollar, in gold.

Do we lack the wisdom, the honesty, the efficiency, or persistent exertion necessary to found our monetary interests upon this basis?

By printing promises to pay dollars which do not exist, we are constantly lessening the value of real dollars; and it is a form of extortion that should never be tolerated by a wise and honorable government.

No. III.

DOES CALIFORNIA NEED THE NATIONAL BANKS?

The National Banks are an experiment, upon a grand scale, how far it will be possible to cheapen and vilify gold by the issues of paper money without inflicting upon the nation the certain evils of a general bankruptcy. That the issue of paper money does lessen the purchasing power of gold, there can be no doubt. California is a gold-bearing State. Gold is her staple commodity. It is not the part of wisdom for her to seek any substitutes for this metal, any more than it would be wise in Pennsylvania to seek some substitute for fuel in the place of her coal. If coal is extensively used, it helps Pennsylvania; if gold is extensively used, it helps California. The same wisdom which would induce Pennsylvania to dispense with the use of coal as a fuel, and for manufacturing purposes, would induce California to reject the best money on earth—her gold—and adopt a system of paper currency. We are sending this gold away at the rate of about fifty millions of dollars per annum. We do not send away our gold to purchase gold again, but to purchase other forms of wealth; therefore it is clear as the noonday sun in his splendor, that it is not gold that we want, but other forms of wealth. We *can command these other needed forms of wealth just as far and just as fast as we can pay for them, and no* farther. To say, then, that we cannot command those other forms of wealth to the extent of our necessities or desires, is merely to plead our own poverty. The idle vagabond desires wealth; but what right has he to possess it? Will the National Bank discount his paper without being fortified with proper security? It is folly to suppose it.

Since California is sending away that form of money in vast sums monthly, which is acknowledged by all the civilized world to be the best money on earth—money which passes current in all nations—it is not money which California needs. To argue different from this would be to attempt to prove that an inferior and viler medium of commerce is really better and superior to a perfect medium, which is receivable the world over in all commercial exchanges. The population of California is not more than 400,000. The mines yield a million of dollars per week, and to say that with this yield she cannot have a sufficiency of currency to move all the industries of this population is simply absurd. If there be any lack of prosperity or gain in this State, it must be attributed to some other causes than the scarcity of the best money on earth. We do not want our gold cheapened, or shorn of its purchasing power. In adopting the National banks, and substituting the shadow for the substance, we are inflicting upon ourselves prices in commodities without real values.

We hear on all sides the laudations of a uniform currency, and California is considered by some fanatics as the foe to her own progress, because she does not adopt the system of the National Banks. The difficulty in the case results from the fact that it is impossible to have a uniform currency until it all comes to the gold value. It is plain to the most simple understanding, that a hundred bushels of wheat, measured in a standard half bushel containing sixteen quarts, would be worth more than a hundred bushels of the same quality of grain measured in a half bushel containing only twelve quarts. The values would be as different as the difference in quantity. What gain could result from making such difference in the measures? The price would vary directly as the quantity varied, the quality of the grain being the same. Precisely so with measures of value. And what gain would result to this State from putting aside the best money on earth to adopt the paper money, varying thirty per cent. and more from the gold standard?

Such a currency as California now possesses is what all honest men in the old States desire; and to make it uniform with any other currency, such currency must be its equivalent.

Suppose that California reckoned in British sterling; would this be any hardship to the old States? Surely not. The relative value of the respective currencies would be adjusted as accurately as at present. The whole difficulty results from the dollar of the mint being worth more than the printed promise to pay a dollar, which is false. No legislation can make them equal, and of course uniform currency is out of the question, because the metallic dollar rules a large fraction above the value of the National bank note dollar. The panegyrics bestowed upon the new-fangled currency are hypocrisy or lunacy.

The champions of the National banks argue that in one year more their issues will be at the par of gold. Whether they will be or not is a matter of opinion; but it is a matter of certainty that we do not want them, at all events, until they make their dollars worth one hundred cents each.

To illustrate this practically, we will assume a hypothetical case. Suppose that it takes $10,000 in gold to move an operation, and that this loan is needed for one year. In our present banks this sum would be had, on good security, for 15 per cent. per year. The cost, then, to move this operation would be stated thus:

Loan in gold coin............................	$10,000
Interest one year 15 per cent....................	1,500
Amount to be reimbursed in one year............	$11,500

Now suppose the same operation is to be moved with the National bank paper, which the advocates of it say will be at par in one year, and how will the account stand?

$10,000 in gold coin equivalent to greenbacks....	$14,300
One year's interest on do. at 15 per cent. is......	2,145
Amount to be reimbursed in one year...........	$16,445

In case the loan was made in gold, the borrower must pay only $11,500; but if made in paper, he must pay $16,445 in paper.

Now if these paper champions are right in the assumption that National bank paper will be at par in one year, and they ought to be willing to assume all the sequences of their own premises, then the borrower in the gold bank would save $4,945 in one year, on this operation, more than he would to get his loan at the National bank. Is it supposable that under these circumstances the National banks could loan money here? None but speculators, gamblers, and bankrupts, would think of making an operation with them. The good paper would all go to the old and tried institutions, where the dollar is worth one hundred cents, and where the deposit is sure to be paid in a currency as good as when received. The National banks in California could only work interminable mischief, so long as their dollar is not at the par of gold. As regards loyalty and patriotism, the cry is perfectly fatuous. So long as the Constitution of the United States forbids the issue of bills of credit, and prescribes that nothing but gold and silver shall be a tender in payment of debts; so long as all our public officers are sworn to uphold, support, and defend this Constitution; and so long as the solemnity of an oath is binding on the consciences of men, so long will California be in the direct line of her duty to uphold the Constitution and cling to her gold currency. (See Appendix B.)

No. IV.

THE LEGAL TENDER ACT EXAMINED.

Is Congress vested with proper power and authority by the Constitution to make Treasury notes a legal tender?

In the preamble to the Constitution these words are written: "We the people of the United States, in order to form a more perfect union, establish justice, insure domestic tranquility, provide for the common defense, promote the general welfare, and secure the blessings of liberty to ourselves and our posterity, do ordain and establish this CONSTITUTION for the United States of America." One of the cardinal points enumerated in this list of the motives and reasons why the people of the United States formed a Union is to ESTABLISH JUSTICE. Justice is one of the columns upon which our National edifice is built. It underlies all Acts of Congress, all acts of State Legislatures, all decisions of courts, all treaties with foreign nations, and all municipal and international law. The Constitution of the United States is, by the very terms of it, the supreme law of the land. In article six, paragraph two, it is written: "This Constitution, and the laws of the United States which shall be made in pursuance thereof, and all treaties made, or which shall be made under the authority of the United States, shall be the supreme law of the land, and the Judges in every State shall be bound thereby, anything in the Constitution or laws of any State to the contrary notwithstanding." It is plain that all State law which conflicts with the Federal Constitution is illegal; and it is equally clear that all Acts of Congress which conflict with the supreme law of the land are alike invalid. The Federal Constitution is the supreme law of the land, and to this all Legislative enactments

—both Congressional and State—must be most strictly concordant.

Section eight of the Constitution confers upon Congress the right "to coin money, regulate the value thereof, and of foreign coin, and fix the standard of weights and measures"; also "to provide for the punishment of counterfeiting the securities and current coin of the United States."

Congress has enacted laws which govern the operations of the United States mints, and regulated the weight of the several kinds of coins, with the amount of pure gold and silver, and the amount of alloy which the respective coins shall contain. The Statute of January, 1837, makes the weight of the eagle 258 grains; the half eagle, 129 grains. The alloy is one-tenth, leaving the amount of fine gold in the eagle 232.2. The fractional coins of gold are also alloyed one-tenth, so that of 1,000 parts by weight of United States gold coin .900 shall be of pure gold and 100 of alloy. Hence the gold coin of the United States is called 900 fine. The same act which establishes the weight and fineness of the eagle gives its denominational value, and makes it a legal tender for ten dollars; also the half eagle a legal tender for five dollars. No one can call the justice of this act in question. It is as necessary to the general welfare of society that the meaning of the word dollar should be fixed by Act of Congress and invariable as that a half bushel should contain sixteen quarts, that the yard should be thirty-six inches, that the pound weight should be sixteen ounces, that the gallon should be four quarts, and that the foot rule should be twelve inches. Indeed, if there is any difference in point of utility to a commonwealth, it is more necessary that the standards and measures of value should be kept with scrupulous exactness, than that the standards and measures of quantities, weights, lengths, and capacities should be matters for the strictest scrutiny and legal adjustment, and for this reason: If you change the size of the half bushel by law, such act affects the commodities measured by that standard, but it would not relate to commodities measured by the yard, or by the pound weight. But change the value of the dollar by any Legislative enactment, and you change the value of everything that is measured by the dollar. Fixity and uniformity of value is one of the indispensable requisites of national coin. Without these requisites anything and everything that circulates as money—be it currency, circulating medium, bank notes, or anything which the wit of man can devise, —all else, and everything else, which does not possess this uniformity of value, is a fraud upon the country and hostile to the permanent welfare of the body politic. It is this uniformity in the value of gold coin which makes it so peculiarly fitted and adapted for the precise wants of a nation in the matter of its currency. No doubt supply and demand have their efficient bearings in fixing the value of gold as they have in adjusting the value of commodities and property; but gold seems to make business for itself wherever it goes, being essentially and intrinsically valuable, which function the substitute—paper money--does not possess. Not possessing this value in itself, it is impossible to galvanize it with any permanent vitality, or even utility, by Legislative enactments. Gold, by its uniformity of value for long periods of time, seems to be almost miraculously designed by the Creator to serve mankind in the matter of a sound and reliable currency. A gold currency builds up all forms of useful industry, while a paper currency converts these industries into legalized gambling. The value of gold, however, cannot be tested by comparing it with the fluctuations in price of any one article or commodity. If all the commodities and wealth of a people rise in value when measured by gold, then gold is really depressed; if all the commodities and wealth of a people sink in value, then gold has advanced. The value of gold when tried as a standard by all the commodities and wealth of any people who use this metal as money, making a fair allowance for short and bountiful supply and demand of commodities, and of the prices of these commodities for a series of years together, this gold value will be found nearer a constant level than any other commodity in existence.

We often hear our Eastern friends crying out that gold is high, gold is rising, gold is falling, etc. Such is never the case to any extent. Greenbacks go up and down, but gold is fixed and constant in value. To prove this, I will state that during the four years of war, from 1861 to 1865, gold was almost uniformly of the same value in New York as in London, Paris, Hamburg, Amsterdam, Bremen, and other European cities. To corroborate it, the statistics of the rates of exchange on those cities can be easily examined. While greenbacks in New York stood at $110 for $100 coin, exchange on London ruled at 109½, when purchased with gold. While greenbacks stood at 120, 150, 200, 250, 280 for $100 gold coin, exchange on London, when bought with gold, ruled at 109½ to 110½. During all the war it scarcely varied three per cent. from this ruling when paid for in gold coin.

The rate of exchange between the various commercial cities of the world fixes the values of the respective coins of each nation, and brings them upon a strict equality. Hence the absurdity of all legislation to fix the values of coin any different from their real values. When exchange on London, in New York, is sold at 109½, the value of one ounce of pure gold in New York is exactly the same as one ounce of pure gold in London. It is reckoned on the value of the old Spanish dollar, and the pound sterling is equal to $4.44.4 of the Spanish dollar. Silver coin is only a tender up to five dollars, by the Act of Congress. The standard fineness of our gold coins was fixed by the Act of January, 1837, at 900 fine gold; expressed, 900–1000. The weight of the eagle being 258 grains; alloy, 25.8 grains, making it of fine gold 232.2 grains. The weight of the sovereign is in grains 123.274; alloy, one-twelfth—10,273; fine gold in the sovereign, 113 100.01 grains. Our dollar, not being equal to the old Spanish dollar, brings the pound sterling, or the British sovereign—which is a coin of the exact value of the pound sterling—worth in our currency $4.86.6. When exchange is at 109½ on London it is at par, as will readily be seen by this formula—As 232 2-10 : $10 :: 113 100.01 grs. : $4.86.6. Again—As 100 : 4.44.4 :: 109½ : 4.86.6. And as 100 : 109½ :: 4.44.4 : 4 86.6. Here, then, is mathematical demonstration that gold has ruled almost exactly the same in New York as in London for and during the civil war;

and if gold has been high or low in New York, it has been at the same price in Europe.

The practical effect of the law of Congress making a legal tender of paper money was simply to make the word dollar a meaningless term. That which before was in law a coin of the United States mint of the requisite weight and fineness, as prescribed by the laws of the mint, containing so much gold or silver, was subverted into a promise of the Government to pay, and this promise was notoriously and professedly false; for the same act which created the Treasury notes, and ordained that they should be a legal tender on all debts except on duties, imports, and interest on bonds and notes, prescribed that these promises of the Government should be redeemed by the issue of bonds, bearing interest at the rate of six per centum per annum, and redeemable at the pleasure of the United States after five years, and payable twenty years from the date thereof. (See Loan and Treasury Note Bill of 25th February, 1862.)

The Government issues these Treasury notes in sums as low as five dollars, bearing on their face a promise to pay the sum named in the note, but in fact only redeemable by funding on twenty years. Is it reasonable to think that such an issue of convertible paper could stand in the markets of the country at the par of gold? Every one knows that the Act has most signally failed, so far as keeping the Treasury notes at the par of gold was purposed to be achieved by it. Since the passage of that Act, Treasury notes have ranged from 95 down to 35 cents on the dollar. We have witnessed the absurdity of the dollar standing at all prices from 95 cents down to 35 cents, and ascending again from 35 cents to 70 cents, at which point it stands at this writing. We all know that the half of a quantity cannot be equal to the whole of such quantity; and yet we are constrained to adopt the absurdity that the legal tender paper dollar of the Government, when it is only ruling at 50 cents on the dollar, is legally equal to the mint coin of the country, which is equal to one hundred cents on the dollar. Is not such a result a total subversion of reason, equity, justice, and the Federal Constitution?

The Loan and Treasury Note Bill of February, 1862,

declares the Treasury notes "lawful money, and a legal tender in payment of all debts, public and private, within the United States, except duties on imports and interest" upon the public debt. This provision most effectually bars all redemption, in coin, of the said notes, unless the Government chooses to pay in coin; and it also bars all attempt on the part of the holders of Treasury notes to convert them in any other manner than as the Government may prescribe. The holder may present a note at the Treasury for payment in dollars, and the Treasurer, instead of paying in dollars, can tender another note of the same tenor, and the tender will be, according to this Act, good. Inasmuch as one note can be redeemed with another of the same amount and tenor, there can be no demand on the Treasury for these notes, except through converting them into Government bonds. The notes, then, will not vary much from the gold value of the bonds, into which they are convertible. The provision also demonetizes gold, in effect, for all purposes except duties and interest. On the 11th July, 1864, it required 285 Treasury note legal tender dollars to pay for 100 gold dollars: or, stated conversely, 35 dollars in gold coin would purchase 100 dollars in Treasury notes. This great difference in the commercial values of the two currencies the Congress would reconcile by enacting that the Treasury note should be the absolute and legal equivalent of the gold dollar in the business relations of citizens. The only gain which the Legal Tender Act ever effected for the Government was of a very ephemeral nature. It coerced the creditor to receive pay of the debtor in a currency greatly depreciated, when measured by gold. This made a demand for legal tender, as a kind of money to pay debts. But, although it extorted from the creditor a very considerable fraction of his dues by allowing the debtor to pay in a kind of tender of much less value than the contracting parties had agreed for, it was impossible to exert this influence over general values. Whoever had property for sale marked the price up, to cover the loss or depreciation on greenbacks and currency. This form of forced loan, as some choose to term the legal tender of Congress, is a direct spoliation of private rights on the part of the Government, for it is not intended to ever compensate for such losses—although the supreme law ordains that "private property shall not be taken for public uses without just compensation," and that all duties, imposts, and excises shall be uniform and equal. But where is the equality or consistency in compelling the creditor portion of a community to surrender the obligations of a solvent debtor upon his paying only one-half or two-thirds of it? A law of Congress compelling such injustice can never be made consistent with right reason, or the supreme law.

There is a class of our population who consider that the failure of the act to keep the treasury notes at the par of gold is not the fault of the legislation, but the action of brokers, speculators, and enemies of the Government. Such, however, is not the case. No man understands the uses and offices of money but he who has made it a special study. Congress had the power, and, in view of the necessities and exigencies of the country, it was the duty of that body to put such an excise upon the circulation of State banks as would have coerced them to withdraw all their bills from the market. The amount of this circulation was known. It was illegal and unconstitutional in its inception, and has ever remained so down to this day. No State can issue bills of credit, and by consequence no State can charter banks to issue bills of credit. A State has the same right to charter corporations to coin money that it has to charter corporations to issue bills of credit. The Federal Constitution positively forbids both. The Federal Government, if the State banks' issues were withdrawn, could have issued an amount equal to their issues, at the par of gold. It needed no coercive legislation, like that of making treasury notes a legal tender, to give them easy and quick circulation. Every dollar of paper money which circulates in any country at the par of gold, drives one dollar in gold out of circulation; and every dollar of paper money which is issued and put in circulation, after the paper circulation falls below the par of gold, is issued in dead loss to such country. For example, if the United States in 1860, when every branch of industry was flourishing, required a circulation of $600,000,000, and could circulate this amount at the par of gold, what would be the effect of suddenly expanding this circulation to $700,000,000? The banks would immediately suspend cash payments; gold would rise when measured by currency; the one hundred millions added to the currency would immediately mix with former issues, and seek a natural level in raising the prices of commodities. What six dollars would buy before the expansion would require seven dollars to buy afterwards, and the purchasing power of the $700,000,000 would be exactly the same as was the purchasing power of the $600,000,000. Nothing would be gained, but simply to unfix the definite meaning which should always be attached to the dollar. The direct loss resulting from such issue, would fall upon the holders of the old circulation of $600,000,000, and the new issue of $100,000,000, in the following proportions:

Loss on the $600,000,000 of the first issue,	$85,715,285 72
Loss on the $100,000,000 of second issue,	14,285,714 28
Loss by the general inflation............	$100,000,000 00

The *direct* loss on the issue is thus shown to be the full amount of the over-issue. The *indirect* loss is, that the general prices of commodities would advance about sixteen two-thirds per cent., and every one must buy and sell at these advanced rates, thereby introducing and perpetuating prices at sixteen two-thirds per cent. above gold values, to be paid by the people until this over-issue should be withdrawn from circulation; all time-debts, contracted to be canceled at a future day, would be made payable with the risk that the relative values of currency and gold might be greatly different at the maturity of such contract. The indirect loss it is very difficult to estimate. My own imprsssion is, that the circulation issued in any country beyond the business requisitions of such country, or beyond the normal specie volume, (and by the specie volume is meant the amount which would circulate in such country in specie, if all bills of credit were prohibited) sinks its face value in every ninety days which it circulates. In other words, the community at large carry this circulation as a dead weight, and the loss to them is the whole amount of such circulation every ninety days. The losses are created through the prices which such circulation makes, beyond the specie values, in general commodities. If the masses could see the untold evils which such circulation brings upon them, they would blow it higher than the moon.

Can any sane man, then, maintain that it was wise, expedient, necessary, fit, proper, right or judicious, to issue a form of currency that was dead loss to the government and people jointly, and which loss was carried for a few years in a joint capacity, but which finally must fall upon the people entirely, to be paid with immense losses in interest account, expenses of collection, and in the dollar worth its metallic equivalent?

But if such over-issue be made a legal tender, how will this qualify it? If it be made a tender by law, the creditor class of the community must lose in precisely the same proportion as the debtor class would gain. The making treasury notes a legal tender some would justify on the ground that it was the *only way* which Congress had to raise funds for the war. Such is not the true state of the case. Congress had power to excise the State bank circulation enough to coerce its total withdrawal from use. Then it could have issued, to the amount of the State bank circulation, the treasury notes, and they would have stood at the par of gold, without any coercive legislation to make them legal tenders. Whenever they fell below the par of gold, they would be issued in dead loss to the nation. It was neither expedient, good policy, wisdom, justice, or fair dealing, to issue them when they fell below gold.

The losses of such issue would fall on those who held the former issues and on the Government, in the shape of advanced prices, which it must pay for all commodities and materials needed for the war.

In estimating the actual losses of such issues, it is not unreasonable to say that they have more than doubled the expenses of the war. We cannot roll back the wheels of time, and amend what has been done amiss; but when we assume for granted that the manner in which our finances have been managed was the very best, or the only way they might have been managed successfully, we assume much more than is necessary to admit. If we have gone through the war with the paper dollar worth from thirty-five to ninety-five cents on the dollar—on the average perhaps as low as sixty cents—how much easier could we have achieved the same end if we had kept the currency dollar worth one hundred cents all the time?

Obviously, the raising of funds by issuing circulation, or treasury notes, without suppressing the State bank circulation, was the most expensive manner of getting money which could have been adopted. But it is not alone the government loss which we have to consider in view of this experiment. The loss to individuals has been immense. The damages of doubling the prices of commodities, in a country like ours, can scarcely be computed. Every man feels it: every one loses by it sooner or later.

Congress had no power to enact a new system of raising money, where the Constitution had already provided one. It is claimed that Congress might make a paper legal tender on account of a "war necessity," to provide the means of carrying on the war. The Constitution gives to Congress the right to "borrow money on the credit of the United States." It also gives to Congress the power to lay and collect taxes, duties, imposts, and excises; to pay the debts, and provide for the common defense of the United States." (See Section eight of the Constitution.) Let it be observed, there is no limit to the amount which Congress may borrow, nor to the rate of interest it may pay, nor to the amount of taxes it may impose upon the people; only they must be uniform throughout the United States. The most latitudinarian constructionists of the Constitution admit "*that there can be no implied power conferred on Congress by that instrument, where an express power is given by it for the same object.* Congress has the express power to raise money by borrowing, and by imposing taxes, duties, imposts, excises, etc., to any amount the country may need "to pay debts, *and provide for the common defense and general welfare* of the United States." Article ten of the amendments reads thus: "The powers not delegated to the United States by the Constitution, nor prohibited by it to the States, are reserved to the States respectively, or to the people." Certainly the Constitution does not give to Congress the right to make paper money legal tender; and it positively prohibits the States from issuing bills of credit. And, since it gives to Congress positive power to levy taxes, make loans, pay interest, impose excises without limit, for national defense, these powers may be exercised lawfully; but implied powers cannot be presumed, for the very reason that others are given. A power cannot be implied to effect a given purpose, where an express power of a different nature has been conferred, by the instrument itself, to effect the same purpose.

If upon a fair construction of the Legal Tender Acts, tried by the Constitution of the United States, it shall be apparent that their just and proper execution will treble or quadruple the national debt, then we have not only the right to conclude that these Acts were not necessary and proper; not needful, essential, or adapted to the proposed end; but that they were not judicious, expedient, wise, or requisite. Because they were adopted, and because the wealth of the nation, added to an immense national debt, has enabled us to pass through the trial, does not prove this to be the only way, or that taxation, loans, and excises would not have answered the same purpose with much smaller debt than now oppresses the people.

But Treasury notes are not legal tender, because Congress has no power delegated to make such a tender, and because the Constitution provides other ways for raising money—to wit, by borrowing, taxing, imposts, excises, etc. This brings us to another view of the subject.

The Legal Tender Act has been sought to be justified on the ground that it is a forced loan from the citizen to the Government, which the "necessities of war" compelled Congress to impose. The necessities of war, I presume, would be accounted as national; in other words, the wants of the nation compelled Congress to enact the Legal Tender Bill.

Let us make a case for illustration. Suppose that on the 11th of July, 1861, two worthy citizens completed a bargain and sale of a farm of land, valued at $10,000 in gold coin. This farm was sold by Mr. White to Mr. Brown, at $10,000, payable in three years with interest, and the deed was duly executed to Mr. Brown of the farm, and a mortgage upon the estate, in turn, was executed to Mr. White, to secure the payment of the purchase money. Let it be fully understood that, at the time the bargain and sale was made, the parties intended and agreed that the price of the farm was to be $10,000, and that each of these dollars, at the time of making the bargain, was worth one hundred cents. At the maturity of the undertaking, when the mortgage note of Mr. Brown fell due, 11th of July, 1864, Mr. Brown counts down to Mr. White $10,000 of United States Treasury notes, commonly called greenbacks or legal tenders, worth thirty-five cents on the dollar, in gold coin. Mr. White objects to receive them, because the dollars for which he contracted were worth one hundred cents each. Mr. Brown very coolly replies: This is legal tender on all debts—it is all you can claim—it is all I shall pay. Mr. White gets $3,500 value for $10,000 value he has given, making a clear loss of $6,500 to one of the parties, and an equal gain to the other. Mr. Brown avers that it was no part of his undertaking to guarantee the currency; that it is the province of the Legislature to determine what shall be a dollar, or its legal equivalent; and that it is merely a fortunate turn of the times which has enabled him to make this gain; that it is all a fair, *bona fide*, legal, and just transaction. By the compulsory and coercive action of the Legal Tender Act, Mr. White has lost nearly two-thirds of the claim which he held against Mr. Brown, for the sale of his farm. It is a positive, direct loss to him. And is the Government aided by any such loss? If it is, I cannot see it. But, *if it is aided,* then of course it should pay for such aid. The advocates of the tender say it is a forced loan. Well, *if so*, is it not to be paid? If it is a forced loan, and never intended to be paid, it is very like the loans which the highwayman forces from the traveler when he demands his purse or his life. Mr. White must make this loss *to sustain the credit of the national legal tender.* This is the only good which the most zealous advocate of the tender can claim, for its spoliations of private property. If it be put on the ground of a loan to the Government, should not the Government pay for this loan? Nor is the case met at all by answering that Mr. White may make his loss good by victimizing some other citizen. Mr. White may not be a debtor—he may not owe a dollar—

and if he does, he may be too honorable to pay his debts in dollars worth but thirty-five cents each, when he has received equivalents of dollars worth one hundred cents each. But if the Government is not aided by this loss of Mr. White, then is the Legal Tender Act not only useless, it is an action of the National Legislature of most wanton cruelty and tyranny, in thus intervening to impair the validity of private contracts. And nothing can be needed more in point to illustrate that the Act is not adapted to the objects and purposes for which it was made. If the Act is constitutional, and a just and proper exercise of the powers delegated to Congress, then the Government has taken from Mr. White $6,500 to sustain and support the credit of the legal tender notes ; and although this money did not go directly into the National Treasury, yet as it was *necessary* that Mr. White must lose that amount of his debt *to sustain the credit of the legal tenders*, it follows as a necessary consequence that the Government is justly holden and bound to compensate this loss, upon the ground that the Constitution declares "private property shall not be taken for public use without just compensation." The parallel to this hypothetical case has occurred in millions of instances in the United States in the past five years. Through the force of the Legal Tender Acts, probably billions of dollars have been taken from one class of citizens for the gain of another class—direct losses to the creditor interest, and direct gains to the debtor interest. Another feature of the failure I would state, that the Treasury notes were only worth thirty-five cents on the dollar to Mr. White ; he could only get that for them in gold, or in property at gold prices. How, then, does this loss of Mr. White sustain the credit or power of the legal tenders ? The object of the bill is absurd, and its practical workings demonstrate its fatuity.

Admitting, for argument's sake, that the paper is legal tender : who must bear the loss on this legal tender ? I say unhesitatingly, the nation. It is a corollary inevitable that the loss upon the legal tender shall be borne by the nation, and not by individuals, *if the Legal Tender Act, making paper tender, shall ultimately be decided by the Supreme Court of the United States to be a real and bona fide good tender in payment of debts.* Such a decision would quadruple the national debt.

Upon what grounds would the nation be liable for this loss? First, upon the grounds of justice. The creditor's money is taken from him by the power of law; and the preamble to the Constitution asserts that the same was ordained and established, among other reasons, to "establish justice." If the Constitution of the United States was made to establish justice, what right has Congress to pass laws to subvert it? If it is a national necessity to subvert the Constitution, which makes nothing but gold and silver a legal tender in payment of debts, it is a bounden duty of the Government to make good to its citizens all it takes from them in this manner by forced loans, as some choose to call the legal tender. Whether these loans be forced or not, they should be paid, if the national exigencies require such sacrifices from its citizens. But the suggestion of calling the legal tender a loan is totally absurd, so far as its losses fall upon the people, for Government never intends to pay them. Still I maintain that it must pay them to be consistent and honorable to its citizens, provided that the Supreme Court of the United States shall *ultimately rule* that the Treasury notes are in reality a *valid legal tender on all contracts between citizens.*

The issue of the notes is defended on the ground that it was a war necessity, or a national necessity. The making of the notes legal tender on all contracts between citizens is defended on the ground that, without their being a legal tender, they would not possess the functions of money: therefore, it was a national necessity to make them a legal tender on private debts as well as government debts. If it were a national necessity to make them a legal tender on private contracts, as an inevitable corollary it is a *national liability* to pay to private citizens all the damages for despoiling them of their property. I argue this from the express words of the Constitution. Article five of the Amendments to the Constitution provides that "private property shall not be taken for public use without just compensation." If treasury notes are issued and made legal tender from a national necessity, they despoil the creditor for the benefit of the debtor, discharging the debtor from his legal obligations by such tender, and the creditor loses one-third, one-half, two-thirds, or whatever discount the paper may rule at in the markets of the country, at the time the debt happens to be paid. This is taking the creditor's property to sustain the currency of the legal tender for the benefit of the government, and comes fully up to the case specified in the Constitution; that is, that private property is taken for public use by the action of the bill making treasury notes legal tender; and hence the injured parties have a right to just compensation for such loss, by the very words of the Constitution.

The same article provides that property shall not be taken without due process of law. The legal tender act does take property without process of law; therefore, the same is unconstitutional.

Furthermore, the Constitution provides that no bill of attainder, or *ex post facto* law, shall be passed by Congress. Again: Section eight of the Constitution provides that taxes, duties, imposts, and excises shall be uniform throughout the United States. What uniformity of the public burdens is attained by a law which takes from the creditor one-half or two-thirds of his debt for the benefit of the debtor directly, and for the benefit of the Government very indirectly? Surely this imposes a most grievous tax on the creditor portion of the people, for a very indirect benefit to the Government, without equality, uniformity, right, or equity. One of the cardinal objects in forming the Federal Constitution, as expressed in the preamble of the same, was to establish justice. The Legal Tender Act above referred to totally subverts justice, and thus perverts the very object of making the Constitution. It also impinges the duty of the Government in this regard, that Government is as much bound to defend the citizen's property as his life; and no one should be so lost to a perception of right as to suppose it is for the general welfare that the creditor should be compelled by law to give the debtor a large fraction of his debt for the support of the Government, without any restitution by that Government. The legal tender act, making treasury notes a tender, takes the property of the creditor citizen and gives it to the debtor citizen, in exactly the amount which the prices of the treasury notes rule in the market under the prices of gold coin. This is a forced loan! It is a forced loan, indeed, with a vengeance! A loan upon which the Government never expects to refund the losses to the person from whom it is distrained. Borrowing and lending are terms which imply volition—free action—free moral agency. Spoliation and appropriation are acts of injustice which should never be legitimated by any government.

The Constitution of the United States is in full force and virtue in regard to the provision which makes nothing but gold and silver a legal tender in payment of debts. The laws establishing the United States mints and their coinage are in full force and virtue. These laws prescribe the amount of fine gold in the eagle, the half-eagle, and the quarter-eagle, and the gold dollar. By these laws these coins are the legal tender of the United States. The mint laws are in perfect harmony with the Constitution. They have never worked injustice, oppression, or robbery to the citizen. No one has ever found fault with them for any of these reasons.

Now, if the mint laws are in perfect harmony with the Constitution of the United States, and the law making Treasury notes legal tender is diametrically opposed to the gold tender prescribed by the Constitution, then are the mint laws constitutional and sanctioned by the supreme law of the land, and the law making Treasury notes a legal tender is unconstitutional; and, as has been most fully demonstrated by its operation in practice, most unwisely conceived, and all of its tendencies are towards disorganization of society, destruction of business, and universal demoralization. We cannot have two kinds of legal tender dollars varying from forty to sixty per cent. in value from each other. Either the gold dollar must go the wall or the paper dollar.

The operations of the people of the United States are of such immense magnitude, that they cannot afford to be wrong on this subject. The dollar should have a definite and specific meaning attached to it in law and in business operations, as the half-bushel or the pound weight. Without such definite meaning, the word dollar becomes entirely useless as a measure of value, or as a national standard. If this definite meaning is to be detached from it—if it is not to mean the legal gold coin of the country, the sooner we commence to reckon in pounds sterling, in francs, in roubles, in ounces and decimals of an ounce, the better will it be for the welfare and happiness of the body politic. It is complete lunacy to cling to the system of promising dollars, and swearing that these promises, to be redeemed twenty or forty years hence, are equal to the real substance in hand. No legislation can ever make them equivalents; no decisions of courts can permanently impose such fatuity upon the intelligence of the American people. The first thing needed, if the American people are determined to demonetize gold, is to amend the Constitution making gold coin a legal tender in the payment of debts. Then they can make their currency of oyster shells, cowries, soap, tobacco, nails, Indian wampum, eggs, or whatever the wisdom of these paper champions may choose to institute. But, whatever the currency is, let us have the real article itself; not the promise of it, payable some scores of years hence, or never; or, at any rate, long after the generation now living have finished their earthly career.

Either the laws of the United States making the gold coin of the mints legal tender are unconstitutional, or the laws making Treasury notes a legal tender are unconstitutional. These laws are entirely conflicting, and cannot be made consistent with each other. And, although it is not the province of the Courts to make law, but to interpret it, it is their bounden duty to pronounce a law unconstitutional when they believe it such, as all judges are sworn to support and defend the organic law.

At a session of one of the Courts in Indiana, the legal tender of treasury notes being under review and trial, the presiding justice argued with singular force against the constitutionality of the tender; he was thoroughly convinced of the illegality of it, yet he gave judgment in direct conflict with his own opinion and argument, on the ground that it was a law of Congress, and a question for the ultimate decision of the Supreme Court of the United States. If our Courts should usually evade their obvious duty in this manner, how could the people get from them justice or the proper ruling of law?

Very few men have time or money to spend in getting the opinion of the Supreme Court of the United States upon a question of law. Upon this point, Chancellor Kent says: "It has accordingly become a settled principle that it is the right and duty of the judiciary to declare null and void every act of the Legislature in conflict with any provision of the Constitution." [Kent's Commentaries, vol. 1. p. 650.]

It results from these premises: That the legal tender act conflicts with the Constitution, in that it subverts justice by robbing the creditor-citizen for the benefit of the debtor-citizen; the Constitution having been made to establish justice, as its preamble sets forth.

That it conflicts with the Constitution in impairing the obligation of contracts; since it causes the creditor to take a kind of money, which is not an equivalent, from the debtor.

That it conflicts with the Constitution in that it is an unequal system of taxation, which requires the creditor to surrender to the debtor a considerable amount of his claim, for the general credit of the Treasury notes, without any return from the Government; whereas the Constitution says, that "private property shall not be taken for public use, without just compensation," and that all taxation shall be uniform throughout the United States.

That it is *ex post facto* in its terms, and retrospective in its action on contracts.

That if it shall be sustained by the Supreme Court of the United States, as a necessary corollary to it, the Federal Government must be bounden for all the damages to individuals which result from it, since private property cannot be taken for public use without just compensation, by the letter of the Constitution.

Congress can exercise no powers except such as are delegated; and, more especially, Congress cannot exercise powers which are not delegated, to achieve any purpose where distinct and explicit powers of another nature are delegated to achieve the same purpose. The making of Treasury notes a legal tender is not delegated by the Constitution for any purpose; but the imposing of taxes, excises, duties, etc., is a power granted to Congress, without limitation; also the borrowing of money on the credit of the United States is another delegated power to Congress, without limitation. These modes of raising money by Congress, being delegated for the public good, are lawful and right. Therefore, the raising of money by legal tender treasury notes, not being delegated, is wrong, and subversive of the whole tenor of the Constitution upon the subject.

"No State can coin money, or make anything but gold and silver a tender in payment of debts."

Congress has power "to coin money, and regulate the value thereof, and of foreign coin." The word "thereof" used in this sentence means the identical coin which the Constitution empowers the Congress to make. The only way they can fix the value is to enact the precise amount of fine gold and silver which the coinage of the mints shall contain. Congress can make the counterfeiting of the national coin a felony; and it can suppress the issue of all paper money, on the ground that paper money unfixes the value of the national coins, vilifies and degrades the issues of the mints, lessens the purchasing power and the exchangeable power of gold, by the action of such form of currency in making the prices of all commodities and property. But as the States cannot coin money, they must depend on the coin of the mints; and as nothing but gold and silver can be made a legal tender by the States, it follows inevitably that it is the duty of Congress to enforce the mints to make such coin as the Constitution prescribes to be a legal tender; which being gold and silver, it follows that the coinage of no other metals can be made a legal tender by Congress. The power of Congress is subordinate to the Constitution, derived immediately from it, and all acts in conflict with it are, if there can be degrees of comparison in illegality, superlatively illegal.

Congress has no power to coin brass, zinc, pewter, lead and iron, making these a legal tender, so long as the States cannot make anything but gold and silver a tender.

Therefore, the Constitution of the United States must be amended before Congress can coin money of such metals and make them legal tender. The States never delegated to Congress the right to coin any different metals than such as the Constitution required as legal tender;

and these are specified in the Constitution as gold and silver. A different ruling from this would constitute a tyranny equal to King James' base coin. This monarch supposed he could release himself from his financial difficulties by the simple process of calling a farthing a shilling. The right of coining, says Macaulay, "was undoubtedly a power of the prerogative; and, in James' view, the right of coining included the right of debasing the coin. Pots, pans, knockers of doors, pieces of ordnance, which had long been past use, were carried to the Mint. In a short time lumps of base metal, nominally worth near a million sterling, intrinsically worth about a sixtieth part of that sum, were in circulation. A royal edict declared these pieces to be legal tender in all cases whatever. A mortgage for a thousand pounds was cleared off by a bag of counters made out of old kettles. The creditors who complained to the Court of Chancery were told by Fitton to take their money, and be gone. But of all classes the tradesmen of Dublin, who were generally Protestants, were the greatest losers. At first, of course, they raised their demands; but the magistrates of the city took on themselves to meet this heretical machination by putting forth a tariff regulating prices. Any man who belonged to the caste now dominant might walk into a shop, lay on the counter a bit of brass worth three pence, and carry off goods to the value of half-a-guinea. Legal redress was out of the question. Indeed, the sufferers thought themselves happy if, by the sacrifice of their stock in trade, they could redeem their limbs and their lives. Some persons, who refused the base money, were arrested by troopers and carried before the Provost-Marshal, who cursed them, swore at them, locked them up in dark cells, and by threatening to hang them at their own doors, soon overcame their resistance. Of all the plagues of that time, none made a deeper or more lasting impression on the minds of the Protestants of Dublin than the plague of the brass money." The making of paper money a legal tender is an act of injustice of the same nature as King James', making his base coin a tender.

No National legislation, which is in conflict with the principles of justice and morality, can be for the permanent interests of any people. If we build our whole national wealth on a column of fraud and injustice, we may expect to see it fall with a most terrific destruction. Justice can neither be subverted by an individual or a nation without certain and irreversible retribution.

The Legal Tender Act is against the Constitution, the supreme law of the land, the laws of trade, the laws of science, and the laws of God. For these reasons, the sooner Congress shall repeal the Acts making such notes a tender, or the Supreme Court shall declare them unconstitutional, and the notes are funded, the sooner the nation will be released from its present system of legalized gambling and injustice, specie payments be again resumed, and the nation assume right and honesty to be the proper foundations for permanent happiness and prosperity.

There remains for examination one point of great importance, which I have never seen brought forward for the consideration of any court, or the judgment of public opinion. In admitting California into the Union of the States, the Constitution was thoroughly examined by the Congress or its competent committees, accepted by this august body, and every article of that Constitution was virtually ratified and agreed to by the Federal Legislature, when she became a member of the Confederation. Section thirty-four of the Constitution of California reads: "The Legislature shall have no power to pass any act granting any charter for banking purposes; but associations may be formed, under general laws, for the deposit of gold and silver; but no such association shall make, issue, or put in circulation, any bill, check, ticket, certificate, promissory note, or other paper, or the paper of any bank, to circulate as money." Sect. thirty-five reads thus: "The Legislature of this State shall prohibit by law any person or persons, association, company, or corporation from exercising the privileges of banking, or creating paper to circulate as money." These provisions in the Constitution of California, rejecting every form of paper money, are in perfect harmony with the Constitution of the United States—the supreme law of the land. California has a perfect right to adhere strictly to the letter of her Constitution, and to maintain her system of hard currency against any acts of Congress upon the subject; and all such acts are doubly unconstitutional: first, because they are opposed to the Federal Constitution, which prescribes that nothing but gold and silver shall be a tender in payment of debts; and secondly, because the Constitution of California, in perfect accord with the Constitution of the United States, ordains that paper money shall not circulate in the State, and the statutes of California make any such circulation a felony. This Constitution is ratified by Congress, in every article, in the admission of the State. Congress can not go behind this. Federal legislation conflicting with the Constitution of California, where that Constitution is in harmony with the supreme law, is estopped, is null and void; and to enforce a paper circulation would be to oppress California with useless tyranny and unlawful exaction. It is very plain, then, that Congress has no power to impose paper money upon California in any form whatever. If Congress has this power, it has the power to vote any other provision against the Constitution of California; and, for anything I can see, to vote her out of the Union again, and make territory of her domain. It is a privilege and immunity of the citizens of California to use a gold currency. The supreme law of the land, the Constitution of the State, and the admission of California into the Union, all unite to guarantee and defend her in this privilege, this immunity.

Article four Section two, of the Constitution prescribes that "The citizens of each State shall be entitled to all the privileges and immunities of citizens in the several States." The privilege and immunity granted by the Constitution of the United States, by the Constitution of California, and by Congress itself, in admitting the State into the Union with a hard-money Constitution, not being matters which it is possible to rescind or repeal by subsequent acts of Congress, it follows that this State does most fully, rightfully, and constitutionally have and enjoy this privilege and immunity of using gold for money, and rejecting all forms of paper money; and the corollary seems irresistible, that all the States and citizens of the several States have the same privilege and immunity as California; since what is Federal law and constitutional in one State must be constitutional in every other. Any different decisions or rulings from this must involve the absurdity that the gold coin of our mints is not a legal tender in the United States ; and that Congress has the right, without any amendment of the Constitution, to demonetize gold and silver in all the States, and to impose upon them a disorganizing and irredeemable issue of paper money, to terminate in chaos and general bankruptcy.

If the Supreme Court of the United States shall rule that the Treasury notes, as they are called, are a legal tender, on contracts payable in gold coin, at their face, it will be an impossibility to call them in or fund them. Gold will be virtually and efficiently demonetized by the highest judicial decision that can be rendered in the Union. The banks will hold the legal tenders in reserve instead of specie ; prices of all commodities will keep on advancing ; the poor and middling classes of our population will be ground to death and dust by this tyrannical, and, now, worse than useless enactment, and the whole country sold in worse than Egyptian bondage, to these new dispensers of the money of the nation—the national currency makers. On the contrary, if the national legislature shall immediately repeal the legal tender quality of this form of money ; or if the Supreme Court shall rule that investing paper money with any such quality as legal tender is in conflict with the supreme law of the land, this form of money will immediately go out of circulation and the country return again to cash payments and honest dealings. The learned Doctor Adam Smith, in treating of the fraud in raising the denomination of coin—and his work has been written for nearly a century—has the following pertinent remarks :

"The raising of the denomination of the coin has been the most usual expedient by which a real public bankruptcy has been disguised under the appearance of a pretended payment. If a sixpence, for example, should, either by act of parliament or royal proclamation, be raised to the denomination of a shilling, and twenty sixpences to that of a pound sterling, the person who, under the old denomination, had borrowed twenty shillings, or near four ounces of silver, would, under the new, pay with twenty sixpences, or with something less than two ounces. A national debt of about one hundred and twenty-eight millions—near the capital of the funded and unfunded debt of Great Britain—might, in this manner, be paid with about sixty-four millions of our present money. It would, indeed, be a pretended payment only, and the creditors of the public would really be defrauded of ten shillings in the pound of what was due to them. The calamity, too, would extend much further than to the creditors of the public, and those of every private person would suffer a proportionable loss; and this without any advantage, but in most cases with a great additional loss to the creditors of the public. If the creditors of the public, indeed, were generally much in debt to other people, they might in some measure compensate their loss by paying their creditors in the same coin in which the public had paid them. But in most countries the creditors of the public are, the greater part of them, wealthy people, who stand more in the relation of creditors than in that of debtors, towards the rest of their fellow citizens. A pretended payment of this kind, therefore, instead of alleviating, aggravates, in most cases, the loss of the creditors of the public; and, without any advantage to the public, extends the calamity to a great number of other innocent people. It occasions a general and most pernicious subversion of the fortunes of private people; enriching, in most cases, the idle and profuse debtor, at the expense of the industrious and frugal creditor; and transporting a great part of the national capital from the hands which were likely to increase and improve it, to those who are likely to dissipate and destroy it. When it becomes necessary for a state to declare itself bankrupt, in the same manner as when it becomes necessary for an individual to do so, a fair, open, and avowed bankruptcy is always the measure which is both least dishonorable to the debtor, and least hurtful to the creditor. The honor of a state is surely very poorly provided for, when, in order to cover the disgrace of a real bankruptcy, it has recourse to a juggling trick of this kind, so easily seen through, and at the same time so extremely pernicious."

"An augmentation, or a direct raising of the denomination of the coin, always is, and from its nature must be, an open and avowed operation. By means of it, pieces of a smaller weight and bulk are called by the same name, which had before been given to pieces of a greater weight and bulk. The adulteration of the standard, on the contrary, has generally been a concealed operation. By means of it, pieces are issued from the mint, of the same denomination, and, as nearly as could be contrived, of the same weight, bulk, and appearance, with pieces which had been current before of much greater value. When king John, of France,* in order to pay his debts, adulterated his coin, all the officers of his mint were sworn to secrecy. Both operations are unjust. But a simple augmentation is an injustice of open violence ; whereas an adulteration is an injustice of treacherous fraud. This latter operation, therefore, as soon as it has been discovered, and it could never be concealed very long, has always excited much greater indignation than the former. The coin, after any considerable augmentation, has very seldom been brought back to its former weight ; but after the greatest adulterations, it has almost always been brought back to its former fineness. It has scarce ever happened that the fury and indignation of the people could otherwise be appeased." (See Smith's Wealth of Nations ; Book V, p. 396.)

Now fraudulent, unjust, and tyrannical as is this form of national deception, of raising the denomination of coin, or of increasing its alloy, while the sovereignty still makes it a tender on debts previously contracted, such injustice is even surpassed by making paper promises, which are irredeemable in the exact kind of money which they declare upon their face a legal tender at anything beyond their value in the open markets of the country, in the gold coin of the mints. And for this reason : An adulterated coin will soon be detected by the assayers, and must pass at its value or go to the melting pot for refining. But a promise of the Government to pay coin, which everybody knows is false, can only be kept in circulation by acts of legislative tyranny. Our forefathers, in making the Constitution of the United States, never

* See Du Cange Glossary, voce Moneta ; the Benedictine Edition.

intended to invest the Congress with any such power for dominating the people. On the contrary, they most scrupulously and carefully provided that the national coin alone should be the only lawful tender of the States. If any impartial examiner would know the intentions of the framers of the Constitution of the United States, let him examine the Supplement to Elliot's Debates in the Convention upon the Constitution, vol. V, p. 435.* The vote against the power of Congress to emit bills of credit was nine to two. Hence the framers of the Constitution, by a decisive vote on the subject, prohibited Congress from emitting bills of credit, and inserted in the organic law that no State should emit bills of credit. In binding the future acts of Congress and State Legislatures in the matter of bills of credit, these men, who had learned by a most disastrous experience the intolerable evils of a vitiated paper currency, intended to prevent its further emission by a positive provision in the organic law.

But, whatever good may be passed to the credit of the Legal Tender Act for its action in time of war—and men of long study in the matter of currency will always differ in opinion as to its having been a measure founded in wisdom—in time of peace, all sound, practical economists will condemn it as an act not only unconstitutional, but of most oppressive tyranny.

In considering the expediency, the fitness, the adaptation of such a measure as making paper a legal tender upon all money contracts—of subverting the principles of justice—of the supreme law—for the temporary aid which such digression from the principles of right might bring to the country in times of great financial distress; in deciding upon such expediency and the means to effect the end, if we would make a just comparison of the good and evil of the measure, we must duly weigh all the disadvantages resulting from the change of values in their transition from a gold basis to an elastic paper basis, to remain on this expanded basis for years, thence till these values again return to the specie standard.

The damage to a people producing and distributing the annual amount of more than six billions of dollars in value, by reason of having a currency inflated fifty per

* See Appendix C.

cent. is a matter of immense importance—perhaps $500,000,000 a year. The experiment has abundantly demonstrated that the main object of the making the paper legal tender—to keep it at the par of gold—has been a most marked failure. From the incipient issue of Treasury notes, their depreciation, when measured by gold, has proceeded *pari passu* with such issue. If they are really constitutional tender upon all debts, the Government is justly and equitably holden for all losses which the creditor portion of the country has had to sustain by reason of such law, which bound them to receive the Treasury notes, promissory dollars, and which promises were only an imposition—the reason for this distraint upon the creditor's property, by the action of the Statutes at Large, being to sustain the credit of the legal tender notes. This being a fair and just exposition of the case, the Government assumed this arbitrary interference, to take the wealth of one citizen from another citizen, by allowing him to pay a debt at half its value, and compelling the other citizen to accept this payment in full for his claim. And this revolting spoliation is done under the sanction of law; the excuse for it being that it is necessary to do it to support the credit of the legal tender notes. If this be all so, then the Government takes the property of one class of citizens and gives it to another from a national necessity—the necessity of supporting the credit of the legal tender notes. Now the support of the credit of the legal tender notes being a national necessity, the nation is bound to impose taxes equally, and not to invade private rights wantonly. To protect the rights of citizens, the supreme law says (Article five, amendments) that "private property shall not be taken for public use without just compensation." And what compensation does the creditor get, who gives up a note and mortgage for gold, on the payment in a currency which is only worth half or two-thirds the gold? If the Legal Tender Act is in harmony with the supreme law, then is the Government bound in honesty and justice to pay up the loss on such claim. The losses on such claims between citizens would not be less than one billion of dollars, and this would be justly and properly passed to the debit of the legal tender law.

The time when specie payments will be restored is in the indefinite future. It may take place sooner or later, but if it be put at four years from the close of the war, (April, 1865) or in April, 1869, the damages to the people will not be less than two billions of dollars, resulting from the Legal Tender Act.

But how could the Government have done different? It could and should have suppressed the State bank issues at all hazards and consequences. This would have allowed the issue of about $160,000,000 of bills at the par of gold. It could have issued $200,000,000 more of bills, and made them receivable for taxes, licenses, excises, postage, and all salaries of government officers. It could have issued, upon the principle of bank circulation, by reason of the extravagant demand for currency during the war, perhaps 200,000,000 dollars more, redeemable in five-year bonds, after the end of the war. For the balance needed, it had unlimited powers of borrowing and taxation given in the Constitution. These issues would have kept quite as near the par of gold as the legal tender has done—this, too, without working the incalculable mischiefs and injuries which are justly chargeable to that measure. For these reasons I think the Legal Tender Act was not wise, judicious, adapted to the end proposed; nor was it the only or best means of raising the national credit.

But however statesmen and economists may view the matter in the light of necessity—as a measure that was needed—its use is no longer called for. If the Supreme Court decide that it was an error of Congress—that the legal tender clause of the Treasury note bill was unconstitutional—the bills will be funded at the treasury and canceled. This will end the matter finally, and the best way it can be ended, save that Congress itself shall repeal the legal tender quality of all the acts making paper a tender between citizens. On the contrary, if the Supreme Court shall hold to the Constitutionality of the tender, and Congress does not repeal the same, I see no way that we can get rid of the evils which will be consequent upon such legislation for the indefinite future. It may be twenty or fifty years before we return to specie payments again. Our gold is bound to go from us, so long as our national legislation shall tolerate any form of money, and make it lawful tender, which is of less value than gold; and the test of this value will be—not the ruling of courts—not the Statutes at Large—but equivalents tried and adjusted by the commerce of nations, the laws of trade, and the ruling of the world. If Congress and the Supreme Court heed these principles, our monetary affairs will soon be getting better. On the contrary, if they oppose them, they resist equity and the right, and the longer the opposition continues the more difficult will be the return to truth, honesty, justice, and prosperity.

In deciding upon the fitness and propriety of the Legal Tender Act to achieve the purposes for which it was intended by Congress, we must look at its operation not only during the civil war, but until it shall be repealed by Congress, or pronounced unconstitutional by the Supreme Court.

It must be admitted, that all the good it has done is measured by the difference in the price of greenbacks as they have ruled through the war at their gold prices, and what they would have ruled at, measured by gold, if the State Bank circulation had been stricken out of existence, and if the balance of the greenback issue, in excess of the State circulation, had been secured by making them receivable for taxes, excises, debts due to and from the Government of all kinds, except duties and interest upon the national debt. My own opinion is, that they would have held their relative position to gold nearly the same as they have done, with that act in full force. *If this be so, or any where near correct*, the entire action of the measure has done incomparably more mischief than all the good that can be passed to its credit. But the din of arms has, long since, ceased, and the enormous act still disgraces our Statutes at Large. Furthermore, it has been the entering wedge—"*the first step which costs*"—the example of a great and potent nation, using it's utmost legislative power, and probably far exceeding its constitutional right, to fasten upon the people an irredeemable currency by arbitrary enactments. Already does the tocsin sound the alarm, and the National Banks are crying for more circulation, more power, more privileges.

Not satisfied that their notes are allowed to be circulated as money, and receivable for taxes, excises, public lands, and all other dues to the United States, except for duties on imports; and also for all salaries and other debts and demands owing by the United States to individuals, corporations and associations, within the United States, except interest on the public debt, and are also receivable in redemption of the national currency—not satisfied with these immense privileges, they are already asking that they be made a legal tender on all contracts between citizens. These banks would never have thought of such extravagant demands from Congress had not the Legal Tender Act paved the way for such apathy on the part of the people. Money is power, and this power attaches even to false money, so long as it is in good credit. The war was waged to put down the rebellion and save the Government. One of the bulwarks of our republican institutions has been the moderate equality of wealth and general distribution among its citizens. That while we had but few exceedingly wealthy men, we had scarcely any paupers. The Legal Tender Act has done more than anything else to break down this support of the Government, and to crush the laborer and the medium class of citizens between the upper and nether millstones. Its tendency is directly to create a money oligarchy, making the rich richer and the poor more and more abject. If we have put down the war by the Legal Tender Act, and the Legal Tender Act has instituted a system to grind the poor and medium classes in the dust; to build up an oligarchy of wealth upon the taxation and toil of the medium classes of society, it needs no great stretch of reasoning powers to see that this oligarchy is destined to rule the nation absolutely. That part of the national debt which foreigners do not purchase at half or two-thirds of its face, will pass into the hands of the aristocracy of wealth, to be a source of power and profit to them, and to build up their claims to such form of government as shall best subserve their purposes. With every succeeding year the profits and wealth of this class increases, and with that increase the medium classes are rendered more obsequious, and more pliant to the will of their superiors.

The system of taxation grinds heavily, but it is only yet in its incipiency.

I know that some think the national debt will soon be paid off; but its rapid reduction does not seem possible, except by most blighting taxation.

The public debt in August, 1865, was..	$2,757,253,275 65
" " 1866, ..	2,633,099,276 38
Reduction,........................	$124,153,999 27

But to reduce the debt $124,000,000, as above, there has been collected $556,000.000, as appears by the official report of United States receipts and expenditures for the fiscal year ending June 30th, 1866, as follows:

RECEIPTS.

	1865.	1866.
From customs.......	$184,928,260 60	$179,046,630 64
From public lands....	996,553 31	665,031 03
From direct tax......	1,200,573 03	1,974,754 12
From internal revenue	209,464,215 25	309,226,812 81
From miscellaneous..	32,978,284 47	65,125,966 46
Total.............	$329,567,886 66	$556,039,195 06

EXPENDITURES.

Civil, foreign and miscellaneous.........	$44,765,558 12	$41,049,965 96
Pensioners and Indians	14,258,575 38	16,253,300 44
War................	1,031,323,360 79	284,449,701 82
Navy...............	122,567,776 12	43,519,632 21
Interest.............	77,397,712 00	133,074,737 27
Total..............	$1,290,312,982 41	$518,347,337 70

"The internal revenue increased $99,762,597. The miscellaneous includes the premium on gold sold; or in other words, the buying up by the Treasury of its own paper at a discount. The result is a surplus of $37,691,857."

Surely it does not seem to be an easy reduction of the debt, if the people must be taxed $556,000,000 to pay off $124,000,000.

We shall continue to roll the wealth of the country into

the hands of the few, so long as we have two kinds of dollars, held by Congress and the Courts to be equal, but in truth and in equity, differing in value from one-third to one-half. We shall continue to pass our national debt into the hands of foreigners, and of our wealthy citizens, at fearful sacrifice, so long as we cling to this falsehood of making two currencies legally equal, which vary in fact from thirty to fifty per cent.

The Legal Tender Act is a carcinomatous cancer upon the body politic which is eating its way towards the vitals, and will, if not amputated, destroy the government. It never was adapted to the purposes for which it was enacted, even in time of war; but in time of peace, its tendency is to pass the whole wealth of the country into the hands of a few, and to make the great majority their vassals. It is as anti-republican in principle and practice as can possibly be conceived. To return to our figure: there are but two surgeons in the United States competent to perform the operation of its amputation. These are Congress and the Supreme Court. Will either of these incumbents use their power for good, and save the country?

The Constitution of the United States was made "TO ESTABLISH JUSTICE." (See Preamble.) The Legal Tender Acts of Congress do positively and unequivocally SUBVERT JUSTICE. Therefore, they are diametrically opposed to the design, spirit and letter of that instrument. Furthermore, justice is an attribute of Deity; hence, these acts are opposed, not only to the supreme law of the land, but they are opposed to the will of the Creator; and no nation can hope for permanent prosperity whose laws and whose courts are framed and administered in known violation of the Divine Law." * (See Appendix C.)

A cogent argument against the justice of a law is a

---

* Deuteronomy xvi, 19, 20. Thou shalt not rest judgment; * * * That which is altogether just shalt thou follow, that thou mayest live, and inherit the land which the LORD thy GOD giveth thee.

Isaiah lv, 1, 2. Thus saith the LORD: Keep ye judgment, and do justice: Blessed is the man that doeth this, and the son of man that layeth hold on it.

powerful argument against the constitutionality of such law; if the argument for such law is founded on any constrained interpretation of the Constitution, rather than a positive grant. This results from the fact that the Constitution was made to *establish justice*, not to evade it, or subvert it. Whatever is expressed in the Constitution is, beyond doubt, the prerogative of Congress to exercise; but whatever is merely implied, must certainly be subject to express grants and conditions. The right to make a legal tender of paper is implied, say its advocates, as a war necessity. This implication must certainly be subject to the written law of the instrument itself. The written law guards everything with scrupulous exactness in Amendment ten. It takes from the States the power to impair the validity of contracts, and the said Amendment takes from Congress itself any such power. It declares that private property shall not be taken for public use without just compensation. It ordains that no State shall make anything but gold and silver a tender in payment of debts; pass any bill of attainder, *ex post facto* law, or law impairing the obligation of contracts. It also provides that Congress shall have power to lay and collect taxes, duties, imports and excises; and provides that these shall be uniform throughout the United States.

The Legal Tender Law, to be justified on the ground of necessity and not of a grant, nullifies the following express conditions of the Constitution:

First. It is a direct subversion of Article ten of the Amendments.

Secondly. It takes private property for public use without just compensation, by compelling the creditor to accept a depreciated form of currency of the debtor.

Thirdly. It subverts the Constitution, in that it allows States to make a legal tender of Treasury notes—that instrument declaring that no State shall make *anything* but gold and silver a tender.

Fourthly. It is *post facto* in its scope and compass, in that it makes the legal tender receivable upon all dues between citizens.

Fifthly. It institutes unequal taxation, the creditor class suffering, and the debtor class gaining thereby.

Sixthly. It subverts one of the cardinal objects of the

Constitution—the principle of justice. Now, let any honest judiciary in the United States weigh these six positive provisions of the Supreme Law in the balance, and place against them the naked presumption or implication of a right to pass a law directly conflicting with them, and how would a court sworn to support this instrument rule?

The framers of the Constitution were men of sound common sense, and in the preamble of the Instrument they set forth that the Constitution was made TO ESTABLISH JUSTICE. If a law is *manifestly* and *enormously* unjust, Congress must show by the Constitution an express, positive, clear grant in that instrument to pass it. The powers of Congress are delegated, marked, and defined. Whoever thought of questioning the right of Congress to use and exercise its delegated powers? One of these powers is, to "establish uniform laws on the subject of bankruptcies throughout the United States." Another is to declare war, grant letters of marque and reprisal, etc., etc. If the discharge of bankrupts be a delegated power, to be governed by the act of Congress, it is a very different matter from the discharge of solvent men from their debts. It may be, and probably is, the moral duty of every man to discharge his debtor, upon giving him up all he possesses. If this be sound morality, and I firmly believe it, then it is not in conflict with strict justice; for the high behests of justice must ever comport with moral principle. It is, therefore, not only delegated to Congress, but it is an imperative duty to release the debtor portion of the community who are honest, unfortunate, insolvent, and who surrender their property.

In the case of declaring war: this, too, is a delegated power which Congress has by the Constitution. Now, to infer that, because Congress has these powers delegated, and because these delegated powers do in their exercise relieve the debtor from his obligation, or impair the validity of contracts, therefore Congress may use *powers that are not delegated*, to release a solvent debtor from his obligation, or from a large fraction of it, is such a preposterous subversion of the Amendment ten of the Constitution, as, if generally carried out, would defeat the whole purpose of the Constitution and the Union of the

States. There is not a subject matter provided for in the supreme law that Congress might not subvert with as much propriety and right as the spoliation made upon private property by enacting the legal tender laws.

The question of *Constitutional power* is answered by the instrument itself. "The powers not delegated to the United States by the Constitution, nor prohibited to it by the States, are reserved to the States respectively, or to the people." The power to make Treasury notes legal tender has never been delegated—the inference is irresistible—it does not exist in the Congress.

If the Legal Tender Act of Congress, making Treasury notes a legal tender upon all debts between citizens, subverts justice instead of establishing it; if it inflates the currency so as to make general prices above their gold values; if it banishes the gold coin from the country, and leaves in its place the promises of the Government to deliver coin, which promises are notoriously false; if it has augmented the national debt by a very large fraction of its total amount; if it has been demonstrated by experiment that it was and is a total failure to keep the price of the notes at the par of gold; if it has injured the monetary credit of the United States at home and abroad; if it has been a fruitful source of occasioning and facilitating the sale of our bonds to foreigners at two-thirds or less of their face value, or what they are the promises of the Government to pay; if it has been the cause of most exacting taxation on the part of the Government, which must continue to grind the people indefinitely for the future;—then surely it is not a measure which is judicious, equitable, adapted to the purposes for which it was enacted, or which will promote the real interest of the people of the United States. But in addition to all these disabilities and pernicious consequences of the act, if it works individual wrong and losses larger to the people even than to the Government; if it has laid the foundation for a moneyed oligarchy which can rule the people; if it is a device which will essentially contribute to make the rich more wealthy, and the poor and middling classes more dependent and more abject; if it is a measure which is promotive of the rapid passage of the wealth of the country from the hands of the many into the power and control of the few ; if these are the scope and the tendency of the legal tender, then it is in fact the most dangerous bill which has been enacted by any Congress.*

In reckoning the advantages and injuries of the measure, we must commence at its first fruits, and continue our researches through all its history till it is repealed by Congress or pronounced unconstitutional by the Supreme Court. To me it seems that where thousands may be passed to the credit of the measure millions should be carried to its debit. The expediency of the measure has been the ground upon which many of the courts have ruled its constitutionality. But nothing can be expedient in a national point of view, any more than an individual, which essentially conflicts with justice, equity, right, and science. No legislation can successfully oppose such principles ; no tribunal can bind men to disregard them. A successful demolition of these would destroy any government upon earth. (See Appendix D.)

* Let it never be forgotten that large accumulations of wealth in few hands' *are inimical to the very existence of a republic.* Even the general and reckless squandering of our resources, for which we are justly reproached, may work less permanent mischief than would the same amount of wealth accumulated and permanently distributed among a small class of the community.—*Bankers' Magazine.*

No V.

THE CONSTITUTIONALITY OF THE SPECIFIC CONTRACT ACT DEFENDED.

The Specific Contract Law of California is one to enable the Judiciary of the State to compel contractors to fulfill their specified engagements. Its opponents do not found their resistance to its conservatism and justice in any of its provisions, except that it shields with the sanction of the law contracts made payable in United States gold coin. They are not opposed to the Specific Contract Law, because it makes it impossible to discharge a contract for one thousand bushels of wheat legally, by the delivery of one thousand bushels of rye, or one thousand bushels of oats. They do not contend for the defense of such an injustice. The essence of their opposition to the law is that, after the party has received one thousand dollars in gold coin or its equivalent in other property, and executes a note to pay for this value in United States gold coin at a future day, such note, contract, or obligation ought of right to be canceled and discharged in full by the payment of one thousand dollars in legal tender notes, as they are called.

The Specific Contract Law does not prevent any debtor from making his election in what sort of currency he will pay, at the time the debt is contracted for the loan of money, for the purchase of property, for the delivery of goods, wares, and merchandise; but after he has made his election in what form of currency he will pay the debt; after he has borrowed gold and promised to pay in gold; after he has bought goods and commodities on time and promised to pay in gold; the law will not allow the creditor, under these circumstances, to pay in any other currency than the identical one specified in the contract.

For the convenience of such as have not the Specific Contract Law at hand, I will cite some of its provisions:

"In an action on a contract or obligation in writing, for the direct payment of money, made payable in a specified kind of money or currency, judgment for the plaintiff, whether the same be by default or after verdict, may follow the contract or obligation, and be made payable in the kind of money or currency specified therein.

"If it (the writ of execution) be issued on a judgment made payable in a specified kind of money or currency, as provided in this act, it shall also require the sheriff to satisfy the same in the kind of money or currency in which said judgment is made payable, and the sheriff shall refuse payment in any other kind of money or currency; and in case of levy and sale of the property of the judgment debtor, he shall refuse payment from any purchaser at such sale in any other kind of money or currency than that specified in the execution. The sheriff collecting money or currency in the manner required by this act, shall pay to the plaintiff or party entitled to recover the same, the same kind of money or currency received by him; and in case of neglect or refusal to do so, he shall be liable on his official bond to the judgment creditor in three times the amount of the money so collected." [See Statutes of California, April 27th, 1863, p. 687.]

I presume no one will contend that the Specific Contract Law is in conflict with the Constitution of the United States. The Constitution, the supreme law of the land, determines that "no State shall make anything but gold and silver coin a tender in payment of debts."

Now the States must make something a tender in payment of debts; and, as the Constitution will not allow them to make anything but gold and silver coin such tender, it follows that they are obliged to make the gold coin of the mints such tender. Does the Specific Contract Law conflict with this? Not in the least. It is, on the contrary, in perfect union and accord with it. The law compels the Courts to give judgment for such form of currency as the contracting parties have agreed upon; that execution shall issue for such form of currency, and that the sheriff shall sell property or collect the execution in such form of currency. It is plain, then, that the law is not unconstitutional in coercing gold payments. While gold coin remains a legal tender by the supreme law, it is obvious that every citizen has the right to receive it and pay it, to contract for it and insist upon its payment. Any State or Federal legislation conflicting with this is not only unconstitutional, but tyrannous and obnoxious in the extreme.

The Constitution of the United States also provides that "no State shall pass any law impairing the obligation of contracts." If a contract between parties be for gold, the debtor must pay in gold. If the contract between parties be for wheat, the identical kind of grain must be delivered; and if the parties contract for greenbacks, then it is right that greenbacks should discharge the obligation. Contracting parties have the right themselves to agree upon what form of currency shall discharge a debt, contract, or obligation. But for this power which individuals have to stipulate and specify in positive terms what shall be payment in full of a contract or undertaking, it is not so manifest that a note written for a given amount of dollars, payable in currency, could be discharged lawfully in any other payment than gold coin, so long as the Constitution positively makes nothing but gold and silver coin a tender for debts. But since the Constitution of the United States will not allow any State law to impair the obligation of contracts, it follows that any currency which the parties themselves agree upon is a constitutional act, which may be properly and legally enforced by State law. To bind men legally to perform exactly what they promise in good faith, is the object and purpose of the Specific Contract Act.

If there be any unconstitutional principle involved in the Specific Contract Law, it is not in allowing the Courts to give judgments payable in gold coin, where the engagements of the parties call for that form of money in payment, but in allowing the Courts to give judgments payable in any other money than gold coin, even where the specification of the parties calls for currency, greenbacks, or United States Treasury notes, which Congress have enacted to be legal tender. But since parties may legally contract for any form of currency, instituted and made under an act of Congress, which has not been pronounced unconstitutional by the Supreme Court of the United States, it follows that, until gold and silver be pronounced by the Supreme Court of the United States unlawful currency, it is not unconstitutional for State Courts to enforce all contracts, expressly made payable in such currency, in the constitutional tender—gold and silver. And until the Supreme Court of the United States, or the Act of Congress by legislation, shall make the Treasury notes—commonly called greenbacks—unlawful currency, it will not be unlawful for the State Courts, under such a law as the Specific Contract Law of California, to coerce the payment of judgments in the currency allowed by Congress and agreed upon by the contracting parties themselves.

The Constitution of the United States says: "No State shall make anything but gold and silver coin a tender in payment of debts." As the States are positively prohibited from coining money by the Constitution, they have no resources for constitutional currency except the Government mints. The Treasury notes are called lawful money; but they certainly are not *constitutional* tender, and it is fatuous so to regard them. To carry out the ordinances of the Constitution, the mint laws have been enacted by Congress. Section ten of the Act of 1837 reads thus:

"*And be it further enacted:* That of the gold coins, the weight of the eagle shall be 258 grains; that of the half-eagle shall be 129 grains; and that of the quarter-eagle $64\frac{1}{2}$ grains. And that for all sums whatever, the eagle shall be a legal tender for payment for ten dollars; the half-eagle for five dollars; and the quarter-eagle for two and a-half dollars." (See United States Statutes at Large, vol. 5, page 138.)

This is the enactment of Congress, now in full force and virtue; and the acts making the Treasury notes lawful money, do not repeal any of the mint laws making the gold coin of the mints legal tender on all sums whatever. Hence, the Specific Contract Law of California, enforcing payments in gold coin where the parties contract for such form of currency, is sanctioned by the Constitution of the United States, by all the mint laws which apply to gold coin, by the Constitution of California, by the laws of right and equity, and by every principle which should influence the actions of the Government and the morals of just men.

Hence, the Specific Contract Law is in agreement with the Constitution of the United States, inasmuch as it coerces the payment of the gold coins of the mint, which are legal tender by the Constitution, upon all contracts made payable in such coin.

It is in harmony with the laws of the mint, which make the gold coins of the nation a lawful tender on all debts; which laws are now in full force and virtue.

It is in agreement with the Constitution of California, which positively forbids the making, issuing, or putting in circulation any bill, check, ticket, certificate, promissory note, or other paper to circulate as money, or creating paper to circulate as money.

It is in agreement with the most obviously implied conditions on the part of Congress towards the State of California, when the same was admitted into the Union with a hard money Constitution, and when the State Constitution was accepted by Congress, thereby ratifying and binding the Federal Government as well as the State itself, to all the provisions of that Constitution. It is in agreement with the conditions that California should ever have and hold the right to adhere to the Constitutional currency, which is only gold and silver.

It is in agreement with the Constitution of the United States, inasmuch as no State may impair the validity of contracts. And where parties themselves agree and stipulate upon the specific form of currency that shall fulfill a contract, the State has no right to make a law to impair the validity of such contracts. The law is also in agreement with the Constitution of the United States, inasmuch as all of its provisions are founded on the principles of justice and equity to all men; and one of the cardinal reasons for making the Constitution of the United States, as declared in the preamble to that instrument, was to establish justice. California should never repeal the Specific Contract Law, but every State in the Union should enact it. This would monetize gold again in the old States, make a domestic market for our staple, and would expedite and aid in the resumption of specie payments by the Government and the banks more than any other legislation which the State Legislature could enact.

To ostracize gold as currency, the provision which makes it legal tender in the Supreme Law must first be amended. But even if we have two kinds of legal tender dollars—the metallic dollar, worth one hundred cents, and the "promise dollar," worth half or two-thirds as much; should the citizen be proscribed by law, from electing to contract for, and make his obligations payable in the metallic dollar?

It would be a matter of grievance of no ordinary nature if California should find herself opposed by the Federal Government, upon a constitutional principle of such plain and unequivocal right, as the use of metallic currency; or, if the Supreme Court should rule that the statute authorizing the use and collection of this form of the national currency—gold and silver coin—the only constitutional currency known, is unconstitutional legislation. If both currencies are made by the Federal Government, the gold dollar worth thirty to fifty per cent. more than the paper dollar, shall this inequality of value be held as just equivalent, in our business relations, by the inflexible enactments of the Statutes at Large? To say it shall be so, reflects upon the honesty and wisdom of our people and Government.

It seems to be impossible that the Supreme Court of the United States should ever rule that a State law, coercing the payment of contracts in United States gold coin, is unconstitutional, while that Constitution, which is the Supreme law, ordains that "no State shall make anything but gold and silver coin a tender in payment of debts." The Specific Contract Law is an Act to enforce practically one of the cardinal provisions of the Supreme Law.

The United States present to the civilized world, in the nineteenth century, the anomaly of a Government making two kinds of currency—the one a metallic currency—a currency of gold and silver—the other, the Government promises to pay or deliver this metallic currency, which are not true in fact—the promises being fundable in a public stock, payable twenty or forty years from date—Congress legislating that the promises shall be received where the coin is due, as its just and full equivalent, dollar for dollar. I cannot believe the Supreme Court of the United States will ever rule, that laws for the collection of coin of the United States mints, passed by any State Legislature, are to be held as unconstitutional. [See notes "*A*," "*B*" and "*C*," following; also see Appendix E.]

Note "*A*." IMPORTANT PRINCIPLE RECOGNIZED IN A LEGAL TENDER CASE.—S. P. Johnson, presiding Judge at Erie, Pennsylvania, lately rendered a decision in reference to legal tender notes, in which he says: "The plaintiff had deposited $620 of gold with defendants, and taken a certificate of deposit, payable in gold, dated May 1st, 1862, and claimed the market value in gold at the same time suit was brought. By arrangement of the parties, the premium on gold was fixed at 50 per centum. The defendants claimed the right to pay the certificate of deposit in legal tender Treasury notes, under act of Congress of 25th of February, 1862, and tendered plaintiff notes for the par value of the certificate of deposit. Judge Johnson held that a debt not payable in money, but expressly payable by a return of the deposit *in kind*, is not a debt within the act of Congress aforesaid, and therefore the plaintiff was entitled to recover the market value in gold. The Court also held that the certificate of deposit containing the express promise to pay gold was a waiver of a right or privilege of paying in lega tender notes; that although debts are payable in legal tender notes, the right or privilege to pay with such notes may be waived as well as the right to exemption, stay of execution, trial by jury, and many other statutory and constitutional rights which have long been held liable to be waived by the acts or agreements of parties interested."

"*B*." THE PRINCIPLE OF THE CALIFORNIA SPECIFIC CONTRACT LAW.—In the Court of Common Pleas at Baltimore, recently, a case was decided which involved the validity of a special stipulation to pay in gold. A piece of land was rented so long ago as 1791, with the stipulation that the annual rent should be paid in golden guineas. Upon legal tender notes being offered in liquidation they were refused, and the Judge of the Court above named sustained the refusal, and maintained the right of the lessor to demand gold. He held that so long as the laws of Congress recognize two kinds of currency as legal tender, the Court should recognize the validity of a contract for payment in either one alone. If paper currency was to be placed on a level with gold and silver when the laws of trade make a fundamental distinction between them, a legal fraud would be accomplished. Contracts which specify that payment is to be made in gold are still binding. This was the reasoning of the California Legislature, which only furnished the legal machinery to enforce such contracts.

[From the Philadelphia Ledger, Oct. 27th.]

"*C.*" INTERESTING DECISION.—During the current week a very important case was decided in the United States Circuit Court at New York. The point in the case was the use of the word *cash* in the ship's charter, the plaintiffs in the suit claiming that the phrase used meant *coin*. The Judge, in his charge to the jury, presented the true points which should control the verdict of the jury in all cases of this kind. He said the question was not what says the Legal Tender Act, but what was the intent of the parties to the contract? Did they intend that the freight should be paid in legal tender notes, or in gold and silver coin? Law must sustain and enforce contracts; not furnish the means of evading them. This is the only proper rule in regard to the interpretation of contracts, and it does not speak well for our Judiciary, that they have not, from the first, laid down the rule precisely as the Judge has so correctly done in this case. Every contract must be interpreted in accordance with the general current meaning of the words used at the time the contract is made. Any alteration in the meaning of words which may have taken place since the making of the contract, whether by universal consent or in consequence of legislation, should have no effect on the fulfilment of the contract. Measures and currencies may change in the meantime, but every contract must be carried out in accordance with the measures and currencies in use at the time of making the contract, because equity forbids that a law shall be retroactive in its effects. Had this been held as the rule of law from the time of the passage of the Legal Tender Act, it would have been better for the currency, and for public morals. There is nothing truer than that laws should be made and regarded as for enforcing contracts in good faith, and not treated as a means for their evasion.

No. VI.

THE RIGHT OF THE FEDERAL GOVERNMENT TO CONTROL THE CURRENCY.

The American system of Federal and State Governments is complex, and unless it be executed in the manner designed by its makers, will necessarily be coming into frequent conflicts in its administration. The dangers of consolidation and disunion are to be carefully avoided. If we are to have a Constitutional Government, we must make up our minds to respect and abide by that instrument.

So far, then, as an individual holds firmly to the doctrines of the Constitution, he is both a Constitutionalist and a States' rights man—the Constitution being the supreme law of the land, and by consequence as much the law of every State as though it were engrossed in each State Constitution.

Witness the preamble to that instrument, which is in these words: "WE THE PEOPLE OF THE UNITED STATES, in order to form a more perfect Union, establish justice, etc., etc., do ordain and establish this Constitution for the United States of America." Hence the Constitution for the United States of America was formed by the representatives of THE PEOPLE of the United States acting in concert, and not acting as separate States. The ratification of the Constitution subsequently by the States, through the action of their respective conventions, did not take from that instrument its binding force as the Constitution of the people, instituted in their joint and sovereign capacity.

This Constitution provides the way for its own amendment, and under this power the following amendment has become a part of that instrument. Article ten: "The powers not delegated to the United States by the Constitution, nor prohibited by it to the States, are reserved to the States separately, or to the people." Article one, section eight, prescribes the powers of Congress. Among these the power is delegated "to coin money, regulate the value thereof, and of foreign coin, and fix the standard of weights and measures." It would seem that the makers of that instrument intended that it should be very precise upon this point.

An objection is made by the States' rights men to the regulation of the currency under this authority, to coin money and regulate its value, that "the Constitution has not the word currency in it, and that the power to regulate the value of coin, domestic and foreign, does not include or imply the power to regulate currency: that currency may be cash or credit, or a compound of each, mingled in any given proportions ; and that it is no part of the duty of Congress to rule the credits of the country." The delegation of the exclusive power to Congress to coin money and rule its value, and the value of foreign coin, by the Constitution, was made to insure to the people a pure currency, and one of sterling value in itself. For this reason the States are prohibited in the same instrument from coining money. No matter how pure the States might make coin, the right to make it does not belong to them. It is a vested right in the Federal Government, solely and exclusively. It is equally clear that Congress has the sole right to fix the value of coin. Now the only power that the Government has to fix the value of coin is to keep it pure, according to the legal standard ; to prevent its being counterfeited, which the Constitution expressly provides for ; and to make all the issues of money under the authority of the Government. Gold and silver coin must take its place in the marts of the Union, and its relative value to other wealth must be measured by supply and demand. But all issues of coin by States or individuals are most clearly illegal and prohibited. And further, every spurious or false issue of anything to circulate as money is illegal, robs gold of its value, and conflicts with the spirit and letter of the Constitution.

Now, would it be held by sensible men, that banks had the right to coin brass or copper planchets, and circulate them as money among the people, even though they professed to keep on hand gold and silver for their redemption? Such issue would certainly be counterfeit coin, and expressly against the provision that nothing "but gold and silver shall be made a tender in payment of debts." But suppose the banks should not only issue such bogus coin, but issue it in quantities five or ten times as much as they kept genuine coin to redeem; is it not manifest that such issues would be a theft from the value of the genuine coin, provided such bogus coin circulated as money and discharged the functions of money? *Would it change its nature by calling it currency?* Should the powerful protection which the Constitution was intended to guarantee to the people, upon so cardinal a point as the money of the country, be frustrated by the substitution of a name for false money by calling it currency, and the power to regulate the value of coin be thereby destroyed? This applies to any form of false money, or substitute for money, which is not issued by authority of Congress, be the same of copper, brass, leather, or paper. The common mode of counterfeiting and uttering false currency now, is with paper—it is done by banks, and done by the ægis of State legislation. The former practice was for each bank to get a special charter under which to do business, and this charter allowed such bank to emit bills of credit to circulate among the body politic as money, claiming the attributes of money, and discharging the functions of money. The makers of this circulating medium screen themselves from liability on the ground that it is currency, not money; that, being currency, it is only credit, and it is not competent for Congress to regulate private credits; that the dealings between individuals are subject to their own control, and Congress cannot recognize them. Undoubtedly such construction is true as relates to all forms of barter and exchange of property between individuals; but money, which is always currency, and currency which should always be money, or at least represent money, is a manifest exception to the rule.

The regulation of currency belongs to Congress, from the fact that it cannot regulate the value of coin unless it also regulates the currency; and as to the regulation of coin, no one disputes its authority. Congress, then, having the power to regulate the value of coin, has this further power: "To make all laws which shall be necessary and proper for carrying into execution the foregoing powers, and all other powers vested by this Constitution in the Government of the United States, or in any department or officer thereof." (See Article one, section eight, paragraph eighteen of the Constitution.) It follows, then, that Congress can legally govern the *currency* absolutely and beyond all doubt.

Even if the Constitution did not prohibit the issue of bills of credit by the States, (which necessarily prohibits the States from chartering banks to make such issue) this last recited paragraph from the Constitution would give to Congress the absolute authority of regulating the currency. All that is necessary to show in the premises is, that currency does affect the value of coin; that it does banish coin from circulation; and, this demonstrated, it is as much the bounden duty of Congress to govern it as it is to punish the utterance of bogus coin. And most wisely is this power vested in Congress, for it is necessary that it should be lodged in the same Legislature as governs the minting operations of the nation. All the protection which the bullionists claim for silver and gold, from Congress, is that its coinage shall be according to the standard fineness, and that the value of such coin shall not be impinged by the utterance of any form of currency which does not represent coin in the hands of safe custodians, and dollar for dollar for such issue.

If the exchangeable value of gold, in comparison to other wealth, be reduced by the bountiful yield of the mines, the owner of gold has no reason to find fault at such depreciation. Such bounty is the gift of Providence, or the rewards of toilsome industry. The same reduction of price follows an excessive crop of wheat. Again, if gold is depressed by commerce, or the nominal laws of trade, this loss is at the risk of the holder of gold. But inflating the currency with paper issues, (no matter how such issues are secured, unless it be in coin) is the very essence and substance of the principle which the makers of the Constitution sought to empower Congress to avert, by the clear and stringent provisions in that instrument. This opens another view of currency, which few seem to understand, or if they understand it they do not consider it of sufficient importance to enlarge upon the theme.

What possible difference can it make whether the issue of currency is secured on gold, on mortgages of real estate, on State stocks, on Government bonds, or any other good security? To the security of paper issues on gold, dollar for dollar, as a bullionist, I do not object. It is right, expedient and very convenient. To the security of currency on bond and mortgages there are weighty objections.

And, first: It opens the door for any man who possesses real estate, houses, stores, farms, etc., to receive the rents, issues and profits of such estate; and by pledging it for security, to receive stamped paper to issue as currency. Thus he receives revenue from his estate as such, and interest from all the currency he can circulate. This, if it was a correct principle, would enable him to "eat his cake, and have it also." Precisely the same result is attained by pledging stocks and issuing currency upon them. The owner of the stocks receives pay for his coupons for interest, and also the interest on the "bills of credit," which he circulates as currency.

And, secondly: If bonds and mortgages on real estate are a good security for the utterance of currency, we may convert all of our real estate into currency by such alchemy; and after we have done it, what have we gained by it? What would currency be worth under such inflation? And yet, if this principle be sound, why should one man be allowed to issue currency on the pledge of real estate, and his neighbor, who can offer equally good mortgages, be excluded from such profits? Why should there be any limit to the issue of currency to any one who can give what is called good property security for the redemption of the currency which he issues? Why may not all of our State stocks and Government stocks be made the basis of bank issues, and the amount of issues be limited only by the power of circulation? The power of circulation is almost boundless, provided all the banks expand their issues in a proportionate amount to their capitals.

While they are under suspension of specie payments they may play this game *ad libitum;* and they seem to think nothing of the suspension of payments, for they claim that their bills are equally good whether they pay specie or not. To a great extent this is true, for they are never, even when panting under their greatest plethora of gold, able to redeem in coin more than one dollar in six of their immediate liabilities. Hence the value of their promises depends upon the property of their debtors which they can sacrifice in an emergency, and not upon the specie which they retain in reserve. It is a useful reflection to contemplate how this system of organizing Government and State stocks, bonds and mortgages, into currency, affects the vital interests of the people. Money is a universal agent. The man who possesses it in necessary amount, can convert it into any other form of wealth. This universal agency makes it the grand medium which is constantly being sought for. All property is seeking to be exchanged for it, at least as often as once in thirty years, and nearly all the property of the country is in the market every five years, while one-half of the whole wealth of the country may be said to be constantly seeking to be converted into cash. The settlement of estates, and the embarking in trade, commerce, industrial pursuits, manufactures and the varied modes of gain which each succeeding generation has to institute, necessarily requires a large amount of capital, and this capital is sought in the form of currency. To obtain this capital, the erroneous principle of organizing Government and State stocks into currency has been adopted. It is erroneous, in that it does not add a single dollar of real capital to the country; but, on the contrary, is constantly increasing the demand for currency by banishing real money from us, and creating false prices for every species of property. Men cannot get *real money* so fast as they desire to amass wealth, and their covetousness leads them to make a currency from property security, and endow it with all the attributes of money, or, at least, try to do this, and contend most manfully that they have done it to all intents and purposes. Still to do it in fact has been an impossibility, and must remain such. It is totally impossible to make paper equal to gold by securing it on property or on stocks ; and, therefore, paper should never be transformed into currency, unless its security be on gold. Its action on the public weal is after this manner. The currency being reputed strong by the pledge of stocks and mortgages, and easily manufactured by the banks, the bills promising on their face to pay real dollars on demand, they acquire a credit and circulation among business men, and are received as cash and equivalents of value in the exchanging of property. Every dollar of such currency which circulates drives one dollar of gold from circulation, and bank paper and credits become the measures of value, and gold is but merchandise.

Gold should never be made an article of merchandise among any people, by reason of its having been cheapened in price from the use of paper currency. The whole necessities of the people for currency should be fully saturated with gold, before the owners of gold are compelled to seek a market for it as merchandise. In other words, gold should never be depreciated but by its own superabundance—by its excess over and above the wants of the people for currency. That no such superabundance of the article exists in the United States is patent from the fact that our specie, in 1861, is only one hundred and eighty millions of dollars all told, while our currency is more than six hundred million of dollars. This shows a deficit of gold in the currency of fully four hundred and twenty millions of dollars. The only argument that has any shadow of plausibility in favor of a paper currency built upon credits, stocks, bonds, and mortgages (that is, making money out of anything but gold and silver) is based upon the supposition, that it is impossible to get gold and silver enough in the currency to do the business of the country ; and hence that all our industrial pursuits must languish if we resort to a purely gold currency. No such impossibility exists, if the people will have a gold currency. The whole currency of the United States, in 1861, was only six hundred and twenty millions of dollars. California has yielded two hundred million of dollars over and above this last sum—say, eight hundred and twenty millions—since the Treaty of Guadaloupe Hidalgo was signed. The whole banking capital of the United States is less than five hundred millions of dollars. Why may it not be *all* gold? Every second the clock has ticked for the last twelve years, California has sent out of the Golden Gate more than two dollars of gold, on the average. Australia has yielded nearly an equal amount; and if we had no gold fields at all, our commerce ought to yield us an ample supply of coin. Whence, then, the impossibility of having a currency of gold in the United States, equal to six hundred millions of dollars? I make the following estimate of the yield of the gold and silver mines of the United States for the next ten years:

The mines of California, $40,000,000, ten years,	$400,000,000
Other mines in the United States, west of the Rocky Mountains, $35,000,000, ten years,..	350,000,000
Now in the United States (1861)............	180,000,000
	$930,000,000

If the above estimate is correct, we may have a currency of more than nine hundred millions of dollars, in the next ten years, in coin; provided we institute proper national legislation to demonetize paper money.

There is another way that is plainly constitutional, and competent for Congress to regulate the currency of the country. Section eight, Article one of the Constitution provides that "The Congress shall have power to lay and collect taxes, duties, imposts, and excises, to pay the debts, and provide for the common defense and general welfare of the United States." Here, then, Congress has power to excise anything it may choose to, bank notes and the issues of banks, as well as any other kind of property, not excepted. Why may not this excise be made so high as to drive all bank notes out of circulation, except such as are willing to be regulated by Congress, and will pledge such security with the Federal Government for their redemption, as they may require? The latter clause of the section gives the power to Congress in this, that it shall "provide for the common defense and general welfare of the United States." Is there a more essential point of general welfare to the Union than a sound currency?

The same arguments which Mr. Webster has used to prove that Congress has the right to regulate the currency, by reason of its having the right to "regulate commerce with foreign nations, and among the several States," will apply to the same power, vested in the same Congress, to provide for the general welfare of the United States. Hence, Congress has the power to regulate commerce, and by consequence, the currency which governs commerce; and also to regulate the currency as an indispensable means of discharging its duties and functions upon the subject of money, which is due to the Union at large by its vested right "to provide for the common defense and general welfare of the United States."

To say that Congress has the constitutional right to fix the value of coin, which of course must mean its exchangeable value for property, and still that it has no right to suppress the issue of paper which does not represent coin, is absolutely to nullify its right over *both coin and currency*. Currency, as it now exists in the United States, is constantly unfixing and changing the value of coin; *and such must inevitably be the case while currency represents anything else than coin.*

From this it results that currency should always be coin, or represent it. It should not represent property of any kind, save the precious metals; for if it does, it opens the way to virtually monetize such property as the currency represents. It should not represent debts, State stocks, or any other form of debentures or securities, whether of the Federal or State Governments; for this opens the way to monetize such securities, and thus *unfixes the value of coin;* partially demonetizes gold, and makes it an article of merchandise, and most materially depreciates its value.

Unlimited liability of stockholders has been exalted by some as a *ne plus ultra* for governing issues; and that banks whose solvency is thus guarded may be left to their own discretion in all their business. The truth is, no system of issue is correct, just, wise, discreet, economical, or of any permanent practical use to a country, but the one which strictly limits such issues to the gold coin deposited for their redemption. Every system which tries to evade this, is a struggle to perform impossibilities; and although it may support itself for a long time, and make profits to the shareholders, these profits are extorted from the people in high prices of commodities, in plunging them needlessly and ruinously in debt, in sapping the vital interests of every form of industry, to build up and continue such mode of subtle exaction. Impossibilities should never be allowed to disgrace a national currency.

Suppose a brilliant of immense value existed in the star Aldebaran: would the promise of the Bank of England to deliver this jewel be good? Would the joint promise of the Banks of England and France to make the delivery, ensure it? If the endorsement of the Dukes of Bridgewater, Bedford, the Rothschilds, Barings, Hopes, and all Threadneedle and Lombard Streets were added, would these command the jewel? It might command the wealth of these corporations and individuals, but the jewel would be just as far from the earth after the promise as before.

To govern the currency belongs to Congress; and it should not allow any impossibility to be engrafted into the system. The more stringent the bond to perform an impossibility, the more intolerably does the condition grind upon the Commonwealth. It is the duty of Congress to suppress all issues of banks not based upon an equal amount cf coin; and issues so secured can never oppress the makers of the same, or the people.

The clause in the Constitution which declares that "nothing but gold and silver shall be a tender in payment of debts" gives to the Government virtual control of the deposit account of banks, and is broad enough for Congress to legislate to compel banks to possess money before they can discount bills, or manufacture currency; and that they shall not discount bills, or utter currency, except they possess the gold to cover such credits and such issue of currency. If banks were compelled to pay gold on their discounts, the power of discount banking would be limited to the cash on hand. All intelligent examiners pronounce the deposits of banks currency as much as their circulation.

Mr. McDuffie, in his "Report of the Committee of Ways and Means, April, 1830, says: "The power to coin money and fix the value thereof is expressly and exclusively vested in Congress. This grant was evidently intended to invest Congress with the power of regulating the circulating medium. Coin was regarded, at the period of framing the Constitution, as synonymous with *currency*, as it was then generally believed that bank notes would only be maintained in circulation by being the true representative of the precious metals." In proportion as we monetize property and credits, we demonetize gold, and make it but an article of merchandise. Here is the first starting point from truth, from right, from justice: to wit, that bank notes promise dollars and pretend to guarantee the payment of dollars in coin, and base that promise upon the security of stocks. These stock pledges give them a credit; and this credit, conferred upon them by the public, with the fact that real wealth exchanges hands through the potency of this credit, keeps them in circulation, and they thus displace real money, exercise its functions, and leave the whole money credits of the country resting on a shadow instead of a reality.

The banks issue their promises to pay dollars, and exact in exchange for these the promises of their dealers and customers to pay dollars. The names must be considered solvent for three or four times the amount of the paper discounted, and thus they have their talons in the vitals of the people. When times come stringent they shield themselves behind this bulwark of the people, and say, you may crush us by your calls for specie, but before we die we must pass over your dead bodies. Then comes the stern fiat of the banker: "No expectation of forbearance or indulgence should be encouraged. Favor and benevolence are not the attributes of good banking. Strict justice and the rigid performance of contracts are its proper foundation." Undoubtedly this rule is correct where banks deal solely in gold—in real cash—when they give dollars to their dealers, as a currency, to pay dollars. But after making currency of stocks, mortgages, and all forms and varieties of credit, the rigid exacting of dollars in payment for such currency is but the essence of tyranny; and the wonder is that our people do not see the injustice and resolve to abate the abomination.

Is it not manifest that every one who goes in debt, or purchases property, does so under the belief that the currency is sound, not inflated? A rotten currency does not come into our calculations, and indeed it ought not to, for it is the duty of the Government to guarantee that the currency is sound, and convertible at any time, *and under all circumstances.*

But, says one, if the normal amount of our currency, with a population of thirty millions, be six hundred millions of dollars, may we not keep two-thirds of that currency in credit, and one-third gold, and make prices rule the same under the mixed currency as they would under a gold currency, thereby saving interest upon four hundred millions of dollars by the substitute of credit? Perhaps the answer to this query may be more satisfactory to many minds if they extend the case a little farther, and say: Why not make the whole currency of credit, but let that credit be secured on property or stocks? If by substituting credit for two-thirds of the necessary amount of currency which the nation requires for its prosperity, we can save interest upon that sum, why not make it all of credit, and save interest on the whole?* The difference between possessing a currency of gold or one of credit to a nation, is precisely analagous to the difference between erecting a valuable edifice upon an unstable and insufficient foundation, and building that edifice upon a rock.

Money being the measure of all values, except moral worth, and also the equivalent of all forms of wealth, it is the needful agent for which all properties are seeking to be converted. Hence it underlies everything, and becomes the foundation of all business operations, of all credits of a monetary nature, and is the measure of the permanent prosperity of a country, as well as of its immediate power. Wherever it remains, civilization, enlightenment, power, opulence, advancement, prosperity, and happiness are diffused among the masses of the population. It builds up business upon a firm basis, and

* The profundity of this logic is well illustrated by a facetious anecdote of a farmer, who was boasting to his hired man, a Hibernian, that he had bought a valuable stove, which would save one-half his wood. The Irishman replied, "Troth, why don't you get another one, and save all the wood."

gives to the patient toil of industry a just and sure reward. Unlike its competitor in the circle of currency—paper money and credit—it gives stability to prices, banishes the uncertain, gambling, fitful, and bankrupt operations which necessarily result from using a false currency, and is not less salutary to the people in a moral point of view than in its universally beneficent influence upon every branch of honest industry. Such, then, is the difference to a people between a currency of intrinsic value and one of credit. Under the former, the normal action of gold makes prices on a real basis according to supply and demand; under the latter, the prices of all property are in chaos and confusion, and debtors are not only liable to failures, but failures are the necessary consequences of such currency. Is it well, then, that our medium of exchange should be two-thirds credit, so long as we are competent to make it all gold with proper national legislation? *No currency inferior to the best one attainable is true economy.* [*This article was written in* 1861, *when the State banks dominated.*]

NO. VII.

RESUMPTION OF SPECIE PAYMENTS.

The organic law of the land has made gold coin the legal tender in payment of all debts. The law of Congress, in violation and in direct subversion of this law, purports to have made United States notes, or Treasury notes, commonly called greenbacks, a legal tender in payment of all debts. The practical effect of this legislation has been to make money of paper and to demonetize the coin of the Government mints. It is obvious that human nature is not so constituted as to pay debts with dollars worth one hundred cents each, when a law of Congress is in full force and virtue which allows such debts to be paid in the promises of the Government, and while these promises are to be had at seventy-five cents on the dollar, or less, in any sums which are needed. So long, then, as these promises to pay dollars are maintained by the Government and by the Courts to be legal tender, so long, it is obvious, the country will not return to specie payments.

The Legal Tender Acts relating to paper money must be either repealed by Congress, pronounced unconstitutional by the Supreme Court, or the issues of the paper must be retired by funding the bills, and canceling them, before the country can return to specie payments upon any sufficiently sound basis to continue such payments.

The first step toward a return to a specie foundation, is for Congress and all the Courts to recognize the difference in value between these paper promises and the gold coin of the mints. This difference would adjust itself almost with mathematical exactness, if it were not interfered with by tyrannous legislation. But for the mints of the country to make one kind of dollars worth one hundred cents, and the Congress to print another kind of "promise dollars" worth, say seventy-five cents each, and the Courts and Congress insist that the promise dollars are as good and lawful equivalents as the gold dollars of the mints, is making an interminable labyrinth of fraud, injustice, extortion and disorganization, which can never be readjusted upon any proper basis until we go back to first principles, and let citizens settle their business matters on the grounds of equitable values, without the coercion of law, or acts of Congress to shield one class of the community in robbing the other.

The Legal Tender Acts passed by Congress in 1862, and since that date, have only instituted legalized frauds of the debtor upon the creditor. The excuse for this unparalleled and outrageous invasion of the constitutional rights of our citizens is upon the principle that such infringement of private rights was required for the public good; that these Legal Tender Acts have been a necessity imposed by the existence of the war. But the war ceased in April 1865, and the Legal Tender Acts are still held to be in full force and virtue. How much longer the people will be willing to submit to the extortion of paper money, in time of peace, is a matter that no one can predict with accuracy.

Certain it is, however, that we can never return to specie payments with such a mass of currency in the shape of greenbacks and national bank issues. As I stated before, the first step towards a return to specie payments is for the Government, the Administration, the Congress of the United States, the Courts of the

---

NOTE.—The difficulty of returning from a wrong position, after such step is once thoroughly inaugurated, is well illustrated by comparing the hopes of honest men to retrace such measures. The following is from the Washington correspondent of the New York *Post:* "Mr. Lincoln was rejoicing with his friends last evening over the altered aspect of our conflict with the rebels. A distinguished financier present remarked that 'if these successes had occurred three months ago the Legal Tender Bill would have been unnecessary.' It is safe to add that one week ago the bill would have been voted down in the House, with the present aspect of our affairs. The friends of the legal tender claim that it is only needed for three months, till the taxation bills are in operation. Even Mr. Chase made this statement in the committee room."

country, from the Supreme Court of the United States and the Supreme Courts of the respective States, down to the Courts of the Justices of the Peace of the townships—all to recognize the difference in value between the paper legal tender—"promise dollar"—and the real legal tender—gold dollar. That such difference in value does really exist, I need not, after the experience of the past four years, attempt to prove. The truth of the demonstration has burnt itself into the pockets, if not into the very living, of the people. To this end the laws of the United States, and the laws of the States, must respect and enforce contracts made between citizens upon a gold basis. The Specific Contract Law of California, allowing a judgment to be entered for gold coin of the United States, where the contracting parties have stipulated for such form of payment, should be passed by every State Legislature. This would make gold coin money again, and make a healthful and proper demand for it. As it now stands, gold, with the organic law declaring that "no State shall coin money; emit bills of credit; make anything but gold and silver coin a tender in payment of debts," with such plain constitutional doctrine, gold coin has become almost a contraband article. California adheres to the organic law of the Union and of the State, and compels her Courts by State law to give judgment for gold, where the parties contract for gold; and this law alone is what has continued to California the blessings of a sound and uniform gold currency.

If the State of New York should enact the Specific Contract Law of California, it would not be one year after the passage of such act, before we should see one-half of all contracts and bargains would be made payable in gold coin of the mints, or its equivalent. In two years nearly the whole business of the country would be done on a gold basis, and gold would again rule the prices of commodities. This would monetize gold again—make it what our forefathers designed it should be—the money of the country.

Is it supposable that the National Banks will redeem in gold so long as greenbacks are legal tender? Most assuredly they will not. They will not redeem their issues in the gold dollar when they can redeem in greenbacks, worth only seventy-five per cent. of the gold coin. The consequence is that the greenback dollar makes the prices of all commodities less; and what keeps up the price of the greenback? The current rate of our national debt in the markets of the country, and in foreign markets. The greenback being convertible into bonds of the Government, is directly dependent upon the value of the bonds for its own value. This, I contend, shows the absurdity of the Legal Tender Act. The value of the greenback is not derived from the fact that it is a legal tender; but from the fact that it is convertible into a Government bond. So far as these bonds are sold in London, Paris, Hamburg, and other foreign cities, so far they are a fund equal to gold to draw upon, for the time being; whatever future liabilities and sacrifices they may entail upon the country notwithstanding.

The Legal Tender Acts never kept the greenbacks up to the value of gold, or anything approximating to it. Hence it has been almost an entire failure, for the intent of it was to keep the paper dollar up to the value of gold. The Government five-twenties sell for gold abroad. Would they not sell at as high a rate abroad if our currency were gold? No sane mind can doubt it. The only use then of the Legal Tender Act is to keep the country in all the trouble and perplexity into which that act has so needlessly engulfed the people.

Without keeping the Government paper any where near the value of gold, and thus failing in the very cardinal point of its institution, the act remains in force, in time of peace even, demoralizing our people and rearing a moneyed oligarchy, which can become wealthy by dealing in dollars only worth two-thirds or three-quarters of the real mint dollars; but whose wealth is most surely drawn from the losses of the people, and at immense sacrifices. Such is the system of finance and currency which our Government has fastened upon us in time of war, and which in time of peace they do not seem inclined to reform. The issuing of greenbacks in such quantities has made a demand for currency directly in proportion to the volume of the issue.

With the relative value of currency to commodities at double its present ruling, the country could advance in all its material interests just as well with half the present volume, as to allow it to remain at its present inflation, imposing upon all kinds of business the chances and sudden reverses of the gambler.

The currency must not be contracted, says the speculator, because it will ruin everybody. To this I reply, that the bankruptcy which the currency has created must fall upon some one in every instance, and continuing this bankruptcy in circulation, as real cash, is but a manifold multiplication of the evil. Let the bankruptcy come at once, then, and let us be done with it. I suppose that it is now a fixed fact that the system of the national banks, as they are called, is to have a trial. Their issues are now far in excess of the amount of paper money which inflicted the country previous to the war; this, too, with but a mere pittance of their issues being apportioned to the Southern States. We are not so deeply in debt as Great Britain, and our annual excises and taxes need not be greater than theirs; for, *as yet*, we have not to provide for all the pomp and equipage of a monarchical government.

The circulation of the United Kingdom, including the Bank of England, the private and Joint-Stock Banks of England, Scotland, and Ireland—that is, the whole paper circulation of the United Kingdom, in April, 1864, was only £35,578,850; or, in our currency, less than $173,000,000. The coin and bullion held by these banks was, then, £18,369,610; or. in our currency, a little over $89,000,000. Thus, the circulation of the United Kingdom, in 1864, was $84,000,000 above their constant specie reserve. The revenue of the United Kingdom for the year 1863, was £70,433,620 5s.; the expenditure for the same year was £67,810,987 11s. 10d. sterling. The revenue for 1864 was £70,373,944 sterling; equal to $342,439,611.50, our currency. It is not necessary to compare this with the revenue of our own country during the four years of war between the North and South. The revenue through the war was derived mainly from the issuing of bonds and Treasury notes of various descriptions. Our revenue, surely, need not be larger than that of Great Britain, now that the war is ended; and even if it be so large as three quarters of that of the United Kingdom, a considerable sum of that can be laid aside as a fund to redeem the national debt. If Great Britain, with a paper currency of $173,000,000, can and does collect an annual revenue of $342,000,000, and move all of her industries and commerce, her manufactures and agriculture, her mines and railroads, her stock operations, and her general fiscal concerns involving moneyed capital, —I say, if she can, and does perform all this upon so small a paper circulation of bills of credit as $173,000,000, and even this comparatively insignificant circulation, covered by a constant specie reserve of more than half the last-mentioned sum, held by the issuing banks, if these premises and statistics be all historical truths; what amount of paper currency does the United States need to collect her revenues, and to move her industries? The population of the United Kingdom and the United States is almost equal. The debt of Great Britain is about $1,000,000,000 larger than that of the United States.

Great Britain, with a national debt larger than our own, and a revenue beyond any needed for our country, actually makes all her collections and disbursements with a paper currency of only $84,000,000 in excess of the constant specie reserve of her banking institutions. Great Britain might just as well have her entire paper circulation secured, pound for pound, on gold in the banks, as to make this small amount rest upon credit and circulation of money.

What other nations have done, in permanent utility, towards founding their paper circulation upon a basis of gold, the United States are competent to do. Commerce alone ought to give our country all the gold which it needs for currency; and in the counting of such needs I reckon these requirements upon a gold basis, whether they be five hundred millions or double that amount. But if it required $1,000,000,000 to move the industries of the people of the United States, even this sum, with commerce and the mines of the country, might be easily amassed, under a proper organization and administration of our fiscal affairs; so that every paper dollar in circulation should represent a gold dollar on deposit in the Treasury of the United States.

To effect this salutary change—this national reform in our currency—this moral reform in the ethics of our finances, we must give up at once and for ever the profits of circulating false money. The people, the Government, the nation, the States, the banks, must all be willing to make money on honest principles. The profits resulting to banks from making money out of circulating "promises" to pay dollars, which they do not possess, should be dealt with by Congress with most marked severity. Whenever the moral sense of the people shall put the circulation of paper promises by the banks upon the same ground as the utterance of counterfeit money, unless such circulation is based, dollar for dollar, upon specie, then we may hope for a thorough reform in the money of the country, which is the measure of the value of every man's property.

It is useless, however, to find fault with existing institutions, unless we have something better to offer. Our people are wedded to paper money, and they think it impossible to do business without it. An experience of sixteen years in California convinces me that the principle of circulation of paper money is a financial heresy fraught with most fatal consequences to the prosperity of the country at large. We have banks of discount and deposit here—institutions which discharge all the proper functions of banking and exchanges, discounting notes, drawing drafts, giving certificates of deposit, and rendering every facility to business operations which it is right and legitimate to perform; this, too, without corrupting themselves or the public by vitiating the currency with bills of credit.

The Bank of California has a paid-up capital of five millions of dollars in gold coin. This, with the other banks in San Francisco, will make the banking capital equal to ten millions of dollars. Is there another city in the United States, old or young, with a population of 120,000, that can boast of a bank possessing a capital paid up in gold coin, of five million dollars? It is also a matter of certainty that bank capital will increase, so long as there is a healthful demand for its use. But there is a wide difference between a healthful and speculative demand. The former is bounded by legitimate wants; the latter is like "the horse leech, which cries—Give, give." The one is content with reasonable gains; the other could scarcely be satisfied with the wealth of the universe.

While money possesses power it will be desired by all; but the healthful demand for it is only that which can return a just and reasonable reward for its forbearance. The highwayman who replenishes his purse by despoiling the traveler; the gambler who stakes his all upon the turn of a card; the speculator, who soon becomes reckless by his repeated adventures; have each a strong desire to possess money, to amass wealth. The business of all such is illicit, and it is no part of the duty of Government to furnish the means for them to continue their operations. And yet probably not less than half the call for currency in the country arises from such demands. The return which such call for money makes comes from unjust and fraudulent means. Government, instead of fostering and supporting it, should frown it down.

California has passed through the war adhering to her gold currency; making, what the Constitution of the United States prescribes that all the States shall do, "nothing but gold and silver a tender in payment of debts;" and living up to the requirements of her own Constitution, which forever interdicts the issuing of paper money in the State, to which Constitution Congress has affixed its seal of approbation by admitting California into the Union of States, with a fundamental law forever repudiating paper money in any and all forms. The present regime of banks in California is nearer perfection than any that ever existed in the United States, and comes nearer the ideas of the makers of our Federal Constitution than the best devised modes of Congress or the wisdom of State legislation has ever yet emanated. Its cardinal merit is that it allows of no issue of bills of credit. Californians believe that they have the right to do their business upon the currency which the Constitution makes the legal tender of all the States, and which was specially guaranteed as a right to them by Congress when the State was admitted into the Union, with a Constitution coercing the use of hard money, and interdicting the use of paper money under the severest penalties. Congress has just as good right to *expel* California from the Union as to *compel* her to use or adopt any form of paper money.

This is a digression from the direct argument before me; still it is relevant to the case in this regard, that whatever one State can do, others may do with equal facility, if protected by proper legislation. California recognizes the real nature of money, and maintains that no form of credit, however sound, however secured, should be allowed to enter into the money of the Union. But in the matter of currency California has the right to use the coins of the national mints as her money, and her own Constitution and the laws of the State make it a felony to circulate paper as money. It would be strange indeed, if California jurisprudence should be found in conflict with that of the Federal Government upon so plain a principle of law as the carrying into practical effect one of the organic elements of the Federal Union, which ordains that "no State shall coin money, emit bills of credit, make anything but gold and silver coin a tender in payment of debts."

To coerce the observance of the Supreme law, the State of California has been compelled to pass a law making it obligatory upon the Courts to give judgments payable in United States gold coin; and for sheriffs and constables to collect such judgments in coin where the contracting parties have covenanted and specified for such form of payments. Precisely such a law as this is needed to be passed by Congress, allowing citizens of the United States to specify and make contracts payable in gold coin; and compelling all Courts, both State and Federal, to respect these contracts, and to give judgments payable in such gold coin; and compelling marshals, sheriffs, and constables to collect the executions issued on such judgments in gold coin. Such legislation would be most salutary to the people, for the reason that it would begin the process of monetizing gold coin once more. In direct proportion as gold is made money again by Congress, so far will a demand for it be induced by the wants of trade and the industries of the people.

No doubt it would be better for Congress to repeal the Legal Tender Act at once, and let the legal tenders be funded. This would demonstrate the injury which the legislation has wrought, and the bankruptcies would come at once and be ended. If, however, we cannot at once and forever banish from our national statutes so inconsistent, so unjust, so mischievous, so disorganizing, so unconstitutional an act as is each of those making paper promises a legal tender for debts, then let Congress enact the Specific Contract Law of California for the benefit of the Union at large, and allow gold to be no longer a contraband article, which, however strongly citizens may bind themselves to pay it, is most effectually proscribed by the ruling of the Courts, inasmuch as they cannot give judgment, and distinguish between the value of the various kinds of money in use, without Federal or State laws allowing such discrimination.

The first step towards a healthful return to specie payments is to monetize gold again; once more make it money through the length and breadth of the land; encourage citizens to make contracts payable in gold coin. This will make a domestic market for gold, and in a fair field fight, where odious and oppressive legislation are not instituted to banish this honest currency from the keeping and esteem of the people, where it is left free to make the prices of property and wealth in the country; it will either drive paper from circulation, or at least, compel such paper to come up to its own standard of value.

But the legislation of Congress upon gold has been almost vindictive. It has been treated as though it were the most thorough foe to all sound and virtuous government. A greater fallacy than this could not well seize upon the minds of a sane people. Our whole industries and wealth depend upon the principle of fixity and uniformity of value in our measures of value. In proportion as we possess a sound currency, we have stability in our opulence; and in proportion as our currency is unsound, so far have the other nations with whom we are in commerce and communication a lever power to grind us to powder. In this connection I would remark that, beyond doubt, the old State bank systems of issuing bills of credit to circulate as money were, one and all of them, not only unconstitutional, but, as conducted, decidedly hostile to American industries. Soon after the Southern revolt burst upon the country, the Secretary of the Treasury was forced to the humiliating necessity of supplicating these unconstitutional and, of course, illegitimate creations of the State legislatures, for the requisite funds to prosecute the war. But what could they do for the Government? Only exchange credits with it. They had no real money to lend. Their entire means were only about five-sixths credit and one-sixth cash. Was it not disgraceful that a nation with such immense resources should be supplicating favors of such impotent State corporations? And yet these institutions, weak as they had been demonstrated to be by the experience of the times, suspending cash payments every decade, or oftener; failing outright in numerous instances, and in their failures carrying with them multitudes of the business men of the nation, whose circumstances would have been completely sound and solvent, but for the bankruptcy in the currency which the issues of these illegitimate institutions had induced; these institutions Congress had suffered to exist, while it had ample powers to control and reform the currency, and bring it upon a strictly specie basis.

That the whole currency of the country, in 1860, was less than $620,000,000, is a statistical fact. That the gold mines of the country have yielded over one billion of dollars, since 1849, is equally true.

If the system of State banks had been a proper one, (and every one can see that a score or two of State legislatures, more or less, could never agree upon any system good, bad, or indifferent) if the old system had been a proper one, we should have had five hundred millions of dollars in gold coin in the country when the revolt first broke out. This would have enabled the Government to carry the war through on a gold basis, thereby lessening the expenses of the war and the national debt at least one-half. For, with five hundred million dollars in gold coin, the whole of the expenses of the war could have been managed so as to keep the prices of commodities upon the gold basis. The power of issuing bonds would have remained the same as now; and this power the Government could have availed itself of to any extent. It follows, that one-half of the war debt is directly chargeable to the impotent system of State banks, which was in full operation in 1860.

Thus, the people of the United States must pay a tribute of one billion and a-half of dollars, or half of the national debt, for their experience and practice in State banking, in addition to all the other evils which it has brought upon them, by driving the gold from the country, and substituting promises for the reality—the shadow for the substance. The losses which these illegitimate issues induced, in time of peace, were abundantly sufficient to sweep them from existence with an honest and enlightened people; but the fearful increase of national debt, and the extreme difficulty in raising funds in any way, to prosecute the war, should for ever banish them from any recognized legal existence, by the Federal Government.

Still, it was necessary to have banks of some kind; the grand error was in allowing them to issue bills of credit, in contravention of the direct provisions of the organic law. When Congress passed the Independent Treasury Bill, separating the funds of the nation from the pet banks, taking immediate charge of the nation's treasure in the National Treasury, and ordaining that its receipts and disbursements should thereafter be made in the coin of the National Mint, it enacted one of the most wise, conservative and salutary laws that has ever appeared on the Statutes at Large. But while the law of the Independent Treasury worked well for the Government, the people had a right to participate in its salutary provisions.

The Independent Treasury Act should be more extended in its operations, so as to secure a gold currency to the people as well as to the Government. I purpose to devote an article to this subject hereafter.

The National Currency Act, as it is called, purports to secure the issues of the banks upon the bonds of the Government. The great advantage of having the currency under the governance of one legislature instead of many, is that it may be governed in wisdom and justice, and not in caprice, favoritism, tyranny, and folly. I am not disposed to underrate the advantages of having the currency of the country under the government of Congress instead of the State Legislatures.

The aggregate capital stock of the State banks in 1860 was, according to the national statistics, $421,880,095. I believe that the old system of the State banks was so imperfect that it gave to foreigners an advantage of at least twelve per cent. upon all the goods we imported, so that every decade the nation lost a sum equal to its whole banking capital, which it might have saved under a proper system and regulation of its currency and monetary interests. The advantage, therefore, of transferring the governance of the currency from the State Legislatures to the National Congress will depend entirely upon the question whether Congress will govern this controlling interest of national prosperity upon the principles of science, justice, equity, right, and sound policy. Will Congress recognize and act upon the great moral principle that it is as necessary for a government to do right to ensure permanent prosperity, as for an individual? With these premises, I proceed in the discussion of the subject.

Are national bonds a proper and just basis upon which to issue a national currency? I maintain that they are not such a basis, and that in addition to all the evils and injustice which they work to the United States in their domestic relations by making false prices to property—prices not corresponding with values—and thus allowing one class of citizens to be preyed upon by another class—they absolutely sink to the nation the nominal face of such securities, in their commerce and trade with other nations, at least as often as once in ten years. Or to state it in simpler form, the losses entailed by such a system of banking upon the nation are equal to $50,000,000 a year in gold. This immense sum is absolute loss annually to the country, and absolute gain in gold value to the countries with which we have a commerce. Large as is this amount, however, it is only the foreign loss, or loss which goes out of the country. The domestic losses are ten times that amount; but these all fall in the country, and although they work ruin and disorganization in society, there are not wanting men who justify such extortions on the ground that what is one man's loss is another's gain.

The issues of paper money, by swelling the volume of the currency beyond its normal standard, or what it would stand at if such paper were not issued, make the prices of all forms of wealth in the country correspondingly above their normal value, when measured by gold coin. It is this excess of price in our country, above the prices of other countries which use a currency less inflated, that stimulates imports to such an extent. These imports cannot be paid for in local money—paper money—but they must be settled by exports, or money of the world—gold and silver. Since our exports are far less than our imports, our gold must go to pay these balances, and it is drawn from us at prices greatly enhanced upon the imports by the action of a currency based upon credit, with very little regard to the coin of the country. Every one who carefully studies the relation of values to each other will see that where the shadow is deemed equal to the substance in any country, or where the promise to pay a dollar, which does not exist, is counted as good as the actual coin in hand, such fallacy in reasoning and in practice must ever keep the people which believe it and act upon it most dangerously depleted of their real wealth in coin. It makes wealth in merchandise disproportionately higher than wealth in gold. This is one of the great objections to making national bonds the basis of currency instead of gold. The currency put forth upon such a basis may be a source of great profit to the banks, but it is a source of continual bankruptcy, extortion, injustice, and poverty to the country which will tolerate such imposition and exaction upon its vital resources. No nation should ever tolerate a currency which needs redemption in times of panic, in times of short crops, in years of scarcity, in years of immense losses by fires, marine risks, or from other causes. When any of these calamities fall upon the land, the monetary interest of the country should be so founded and fortified that it would remain firm and unshaken as the mountains of granite, upholding the people by its potency, not driving them mad by its weakness. Fire, floods, and pestilence should never affect the currency of a country. But, as our schemes of finance and currency exist, any great national calamity is sure to induce a monetary panic. And why is this? Why should the controlling interest, which is at the foundation of all our wealth, and which ought to be so potent for good in all times of national trial, invariably be the first one to tremble and seek aid from the people when overwhelming calamities fall upon the land? Because it is instituted upon a false basis. The currency maker issues promises to pay dollars which do not exist. These promises circulate as though they were based on coin. The issuers—the banks—hold the promises of their customers, who are the people; and whenever panic comes these promises must be redeemed. This grinds the people between the upper and nether millstone. Now if the currency were of gold, or paper based on gold dollar for dollar, there would be no need of redemption by the people. Such a thing as a monetary panic would never be known.

That a currency based on Government bonds instead of gold does drive the gold from the country, is sufficient reason for an intelligent and honest people to banish it, and eschew it as a moral pestilence. It is held that commerce will give to every nation sufficient coin to do its own business. But if commerce alone will do that, what right have the people of the United States, with mines yielding seventy-five millions of dollars of the precious metals annually, and only requiring six hundred millions of dollars to move all their industries, to dilute their currency with paper issues? What excuse is there for such a country to tolerate any form of deception or falsehood in the money which it issues?

The people of the United States must be content to stand before the judgment of the civilized world, either as profoundly stupid and ignorant in the matter of currency, or as grossly dishonest and lache in the plainest principles of justice. In this position they must remain, so long as they allow any kind of currency to circulate among them not equal in value to gold coin, and while the laws of Congress make such form of currency a legal tender.

But the country is in this very difficult dilemma, the paper champions contending that all the paper issues are needed, because these issues have advanced the prices of property to correspond with the excessive volume of their issue. And so are we to go on for ever, with two dollars of gold legal tender worth three dollars of paper legal tender, (the Government itself recognizing and acting upon this difference of value, by selling gold legal tender at 130, and putting it into the treasury) and the laws of Congress and the ruling of the Courts stultifying and conflicting entirely with the unbending laws of value, and ruling against honesty, right, justice, and reason, that two-thirds of a dollar shall be equal to a whole dollar?

When the American Constitution was trodden under foot by Congress, in making a legal tender of the Government issues of paper, the only excuse for the enormity was, that it was a "war necessity." Even its votaries required this excuse to quiet the stings of conscience which upbraided them for the passage of the Act, after they had sworn to support and defend the supreme law. But at this day we are beginning to hear loud calls for Congress to make the issues of the National Banks a legal tender on private contracts. It is the first step in wickedness which costs: let that be made, and the next is more easy. The first step was taken when Congress made the issues of Treasury notes legal tender. Will it, now that the war is past, and there is not the excuse of the mad excitement of arms to trample on private rights, repeal the legal tender quality of paper money, and return to the specie basis?

The legal tender of the paper issues of Government, between citizens, should be repealed immediately. Government coercion, to fix their value equal to gold in time of peace, however much individuals may differ about such a stretch of power in times of war, is the very essence of tyranny. Besides, they cannot be funded until they are shorn of this legal tender quality. Men possessing money would prefer it in that shape rather than in bonds payable ten or twenty years after they are dead. The Government cannot come to specie payments till the Legal Tender Acts, making paper as good as gold, are repealed.

Before specie payments can be resumed on a firm basis, the Government issues or the National Bank issues must be withdrawn from circulation. As a matter of right, no doubt, the profits of circulation would belong to the Government rather than the banks. But we ought to look at the matter for all futurity. I am decidedly opposed to the Government, now that it has after ninety years gotten the control of the currency into its own hands, taking any course, or looking to any expedient, which shall not be a thorough and complete system making every paper dollar that circulates as money based upon a gold dollar in actual possession. To give to Congress the function to issue a paper legal tender, irredeemable, and beyond the power of the people to coerce the same, would be the destruction of the Government. So powerful, may I say, so just a Government as the United States, should never set so base an example as the issue of an irredeemable paper currency.

The people seem determined that the National banks shall have a fair trial; and, as yet, Congress has them in leading strings, if the lobby-house is not too powerful for the Senate and the House of Representatives. Congress has power to alter or repeal the National Bank Act. This power, I trust, it will ever retain. If Congress does its duty in the premises, and coerces these banks to a system of redemption in gold coin, it will be infinitely better for the country, than to issue paper legal tender of its own, which is irredeemable, for the petty gain upon the circulation of such paper, with the unbounded injury which must result to the body politic from such issues of Government.

What amendments are needed in the National Bank Act to make it a boon to the people of the Union? The fundamental principle—the basis of the Act—is wrong in theory, and subversive of right and equity in practice. No greater financial heresy was ever devised than to make debt, whether individual, State, or Federal, the basis for the issue of currency. If a paper currency is a national necessity, it should be governed by the National Legislature; and it should be governed with as much absolutism and the same scrupulous exactness which is enforced by the laws of the mint, in regard to the coinage and alloy of the national coins.

The impress of the United States mint upon the national coin is a guarantee to the public that such coin is of the proper weight and fineness; and under this guarantee the coins of the mint are a legal tender, as prescribed in the mint laws of the Statutes at Large. If these coins were alloyed with base metal in excess of the requirements of the statute, they would be almost destroyed as money. The laws are ample for their protection and purity, and for the punishment of counterfeiting these coins.

It was contended by the great statesman of Massachusetts, the late Daniel Webster, that Congress derived its right to regulate the currency through its right to regulate commerce. [See works of Daniel Webster, vol. four, pp. 338–363.] With all deference to the argument of this learned statesman, to me it appears that Congress derives its right to govern the currency of the country in a much more direct manner than incidentally, because it has the right to regulate commerce. In Section seven, page five, the Constitution delegates to Congress the power "to coin money, regulate the value thereof, and of foreign coin, and fix the standard of weights and measures." Let it be observed, the regulating the value of coin, and the measures of value, was placed in immediate *juxtaposition* in the Constitution with the fixing the standard of weights and measures, thereby demonstrating that it was as positively the duty of Congress to regulate the value of coin—the standard of values—as it was to fix the standard of weights and measures, which were to measure merchandise.

I maintain that the words in the Constitution, "to coin money, regulate the value thereof, and of foreign coin," does give to Congress the right to fix the value of coin; and since it gives the right to fix the value of coin, so far as this, to say what weight of the precious metals and what weight of alloy the coins of the country shall contain, and also gives the right "to make all laws which shall be necessary and proper for carrying into execution the foregoing powers, etc., etc.," (Par. 18 Constitution) with the powers to punish the counterfeiting of the national coin, etc., etc., it follows that Congress has the power to regulate the currency of the country *solely, thoroughly and entirely, upon the basis of gold and silver values.* If a national paper currency be a national necessity, Congress derives no power to issue such currency to banks or individuals, unless such currency shall be not only by reputation at the par of gold but equal to it *by actual deposit of the gold in the national treasury*, to cover such issue of paper dollar for dollar. The bills would then be not bills of credit, which are properly and most positively forbidden by the Constitution to be issued by the States, and which were equally positively intended to be forbidden to the Federal Government by the framers of the Constitution, (for proof of this position I would refer to Elliot's Debates, Madison Papers, vol. 5, p. 435, the vote of the Convention stood nine against, to two in favor of the issue of bills of credit by the Federal Government) and further, the Federal Government being one of delegated powers, and strictly confined to such matters as are so delegated, by the very terms of the Constitution, it follows that it has no right to issue bills of credit to circulate as money, any more than the several States have such right. But if a bank deposits gold with the Treasury, and wishes to receive paper of an equal amount, such paper cannot work mischief, being radically and essentially different from the old bills of credit which are described in the Constitution, the meaning of which it is very important to establish, and fortunately it has been done by the Supreme Court of the United States. Upon this point we will quote the authority of Chief Justice Marshall, as reported in Marshall's Constitutional Opinions, page 397, etc., in the case of Craig et al. vs. The State of Missouri :

"What is a bill of credit? What did the Constitution mean to forbid? In its enlarged, and perhaps its literal sense, the term 'bill of credit' may comprehend any instrument by which a State engages to pay money at a future day; thus including a certificate given for money borrowed. But the language of the Constitution itself, and the mischief to be prevented, which we know from the history of our country, equally limit the interpretation of the terms. The word 'emit' is never employed in describing those contracts by which a State binds itself to pay money at a future day, for services actually received, or for money borrowed for present use; nor are instruments executed for such purposes, in common language, denominated 'bills of credit.' To 'emit bills of credit' conveys to the mind the idea of issuing paper intended to circulate through the community, for its ordinary purposes as money, which paper is redeemable at a future day. This is the sense in which the terms have been always understood. At a very early period of our colonial history, the attempt to supply the want of the precious metals by a paper medium was made to a considerable extent; and the bills emitted for this purpose have been frequently denominated 'bills of credit.' During the war of our revolution we were driven to this expedient; and necessity compelled us to use it to a most fearful extent. The term has acquired an appropriate meaning, and 'bills of credit' signify a paper medium, intended to circulate between individuals, and between Government and individuals, for the ordinary purposes of society. Such a medium has been always liable to considerable fluctuation. Its value is continually changing; and these changes, often great and sudden, expose individuals to immense loss, are the sources of ruinous speculations, and destroy all confidence between man and man. To cut up this mischief by the roots, a mischief which was felt through the United States, and which deeply affected the interest and prosperity of all, the people declared in their Constitution, that no State should emit bills of credit. If the prohibition means any thing, if the words are not empty sounds, it must comprehend the emission of any paper medium, by a State Government, for the purpose of common circulation."

Here the learned Chief Justice Marshall includes and makes a paper medium, for the purpose of common circulation, the very kind of "bills of credit" which the Constitution intended to prohibit. Hence, no State can lawfully issue these. And hence, no State can lawfully charter banks to issue "bills of credit." For the same learned authority decides in the case of the Providence Bank vs. Billings & Pittman, on page 406: "That can not be done circuitously which may not be done directly." Therefore, if States cannot issue bills of credit, they cannot charter banks, companies or associations to issue such "bills of credit."

A bill issued and intended to be circulated as currency, if such bill were fully covered by a deposit of gold coin in the treasury of the United States, could not properly be called a bill of credit. Hence, such bill would be free from the charge that it was issued in conflict with the Constitution. If such form of money be absolutely necessary in the Union, it follows that it is absolutely necessary that it be kept at the par of gold; and it can never be at the value of gold, strictly speaking, unless it represent gold in the hands of some trustworthy custodian.

Another view of the case, and one of immense importance, is that credit money—paper money not representing coin—promises of banks to pay coin which they do not possess, materially diminishes the value of gold. Congress has full power to regulate the value of coin, and of course it has full power to stop the circulation as money of everything which conflicts with the value of gold coin. The value of gold coin is its exchangeable power for other forms of wealth. If gold coin would purchase twice as much of other forms of wealth if the circulation of bills were prohibited by law, then it is most obviously the duty of Congress to suppress the circulation of paper money, or make it on the par with gold coin. While we have two kinds of dollars—the one the gold dollar, worth one hundred cents, the other the promise of the Government or the banks, reputed worth sixty-six cents—all kinds of business will be but varied forms of gambling.

Nevertheless, such are the evils upon us, and how can we rid ourselves of these agencies which are devouring our substance? Without the power in Congress to make laws to suppress and punish the counterfeiting of the national coins, it would have no power to fix the value of coin, no power to keep the national coin at its normal or natural relative value to other forms of wealth; because if a large fraction of the coin in circulation were counterfeit, or alloyed with base metals beyond the requirements of the mint laws, it will be readily seen what effect such frauds would have upon the coin of full weight and standard purity. So long as such base metals are circulated in place of good coin, the genuine coin must be greatly reduced in value. In like manner, for Congress to fix the value of the coin of the mints, it is as absolutely necessary that it possess the control of the currency of the country, whether it be paper or anything else, as it is to possess the power and authority to suppress all counterfeiting of the coin.

The issue of promises to pay dollars which do not exist, where these promises circulate in place of real dollars, has the same effect upon the value of gold coin as the counterfeiting of the coin. From these premises we infer that the issue of currency should be governed and regulated by Congress with the same absolute authority as the coining of gold. Any addition to the currency, whether it be base coin, paper money, or anything else, does, if it circulates, directly act upon the value of gold as money.

Since Congress has the right conferred by the Constitution *to coin money and regulate the value thereof*, and to make all laws which shall be necessary and proper for carrying into execution the foregoing powers, and in furtherance of this duty it does establish United States mints, prescribing fixed and absolute rules for the governance of the same, enacting laws to suppress and punish the counterfeiting of the national coin; and since, to regulate the value of the national coin it is indispensably necessary to regulate or suppress every form of currency which acts upon the value of coin; and since the issue of all forms of currency which circulate as money does directly affect the value of gold coin—it follows that Congress not only has the right to regulate the issues of currency, (provided that any right exists in Congress under the Constitution to issue such currency, and of which I am more than doubtful) but it is the bounden duty of that body to do this, and to prohibit, under penalties as severe as those of counterfeiting the national coin, any and all emissions of paper to circulate as money which are not at all times instantly and immediately convertible into gold coin at the face of such issues. This is the only regulation of the value of money that Congress is charged with by the Constitution. Such regulation of the paper issues is just as necessary as suppressing counterfeits. Given, then, the premise, that a paper currency is a national necessity, it is as much the bounden duty of Congress to regulate such currency, and coerce its par with that of gold, or suppress its circulation altogether, as it is to punish and suppress the counterfeiting of the national coins. It cannot protect the value of gold coins in any other manner, and it is bound to fix and protect the value of gold coin, so far as this, at least, that paper shall not be allowed to circulate as money which conflicts with or lessens the value of gold coin. According to the definition of the term "bills of credit" as used in the Constitution, by Chief Justice Marshall, they are radically different from a bill which circulates with the gold for its redemption always in a safe and trusty depository. Congress may then, if paper money be a national necessity, allow its issue to an equal amount with the gold which banks may deposit in the national treasury for its redemption. Such issue of paper might be called, instead of bills of credit, gold bills—bills representing gold coin on deposit in the treasury of the United States, which can be used for no other purpose but the redemption of these bills. Such bills would not interfere with the value of gold, because, while they were circulating, the gold coin for their redemption would be locked up in the treasury of the United States, and when the gold was drawn out and put in circulation, the bills would be locked up in the treasury. This would involve the necessity of making the treasury, or a branch of it in New York, a sort of clearing house for all the banks of the country. This part of my subject is sufficient matter for a separate chapter, and I will not go into it at present.

An objection is often raised to the issue of gold bills like this. Is it supposable that banks will open an office of discount and deposit, pay a president, cashier, and tellers, to do business upon a purely gold basis? In reply I would state, that I believe supply would follow healthful proper business demand, in banks and their capital, as in all other sound business matters. There are various ways for banks to make money, but this hackneyed, American mode, I might call it, of making money from circulation of notes, should at once and for ever be stopped by the action of Congress. It would be infinitely better for the public to allow banks to raise their rates of discount, than to allow them to dilute the currency with paper issues. A high rate of interest does not so thoroughly disorganize and demoralize a people as a false and rotten currency. It would be a thousand times better for the interests of the country to allow banks to raise their rates of discount to twelve per cent. upon loans, and insist that these discounts should be made in gold or its equivalent, than to allow them to debase the currency by paper issues which are not covered by deposits of gold, dollar for dollar.

If the currency were gold coin, or its undoubted equivalent, it would be worth double what it now is. One dollar would move the industries and wants of the people as much as two dollars under our present *regime*. Therefore, borrowers could as well afford to pay twelve per cent. for such a currency as they now can afford to pay six per cent. for the present diluted article. But rest assured that competition would bring down the rates of interest, on first-class securities, as certainly as it does in merchandising. California has adhered to her gold currency, and the rates of interest have fallen from five per cent. a month to one—and many loans have been made at ten per cent. a year. It is this nefarious tampering with the value of gold, by issuing paper as a substitute for money, that drives our gold abroad, and fastens upon us the burdens of high rates of interest. But for this, our country would as surely retain gold enough for currency as it would retain wheat enough for bread. Californians came to the country poor, and have had to struggle to amass their capital. But they have so many of them achieved it, that they now begin to compete for the strongest notes in the market. This competition is a direct inducement to offer low rates of interest for capital, upon undoubted securities. It would act the same at the East, if they would adhere strictly to the gold principle.

With proper national legislation, in a few years, with the mines of gold and silver which we possess, the monetary interests of the country would become so strong that no nation on earth could compete with us. In proportion as this wealth increased, banks would be compelled to lessen their rates of interest, from competition, if for no other reason.

But our national banks are not, as at present organized, at all adapted to save the wealth of the country, or to inure to its permanent prosperity. On the contrary, their organization is such as will sack us of our gold without any just equivalent. The Government pays the banks a bonus of $18,000,000 yearly in gold, being the interest coupons on the bonds deposited for security for the redemption of the bills which they are allowed to issue. This sum is paid to work the most subtle and mischievous iniquity in the country which could possibly be devised. So long as this system is allowed to exist, so long will foreigners get the whole product of the gold and silver mines of our country for nothing. This position may be hard to demonstrate, but it is of such importance that it claims our closest attention. That money goes from one country to another, to purchase articles of utility or luxury which cannot be produced in the country which purchases, or which cannot be produced at so cheap a rate as such articles can be imported, is apparent.

While commodities of equally good quality can be produced at home, at the same prices as it costs to import such goods from abroad, the real money of the country—gold coin—will not be sent away to purchase such goods. It is the difference in real price—money price—which stimulates imports; and it is the essential nature of paper money to produce this difference in price. The issue of paper money beyond the normal amount of currency required in a country, does not *immediately* expel the gold from the country, but it inflates the prices of all commodities, and this inflation brings foreign goods into competition with our own manufactures. The foreign goods are sold for such currency as the country deals in, the prices being made by such currency, but the remittances are all made in gold, or its equivalent. The use of paper money then seems to be this, to inflate prices so that foreigners shall get the whole of our gold product for nothing. Absolutely for nothing! If the wealth of the country is so great that we can give to other nations, outright, the whole annual product of our gold and silver mines, without bankrupting ourselves by such unprecedented liberality, still the question is open to all inquiring and patriotic minds. Is it wisdom or justice to allow this fearful drain upon our vital resources, when we are entirely competent to stop it? The profits of this nefarious system enures to foreigners in the first place, and to the national banks in the second place, directly and most thoroughly by the losses of the people.

If Congress had studied to prepare a system of currency which should sack us of our gold, giving us in place of it inflated prices on goods without corresponding values, it could not have done it more efficiently than by instituting banks to issue currency upon the security of national bonds. Nor is this the only way by which it inflicts upon us national robbery. Foreigners are purchasing largely of our national debt, and the price of the bonds is graduated by the value of our currency at home.

The financial article of the *Alta California* of 7th August has the following sensible remarks:

"The United States in a time of profound peace ought to be able to borrow, if borrow it must, on better terms than one per cent. per month. California can do that. The idea that United States bonds should stand among the lowest on European exchange markets, and that a class of papers and trumpeters should deem it evidence of "loyalty" to shout over it, is somewhat humiliating to Americans that were wont to see United States stocks at twenty-two premium at home and abroad. It certainly makes the blood boil to take up the last London Stock Circular and compare quotations as follows:

	Interest.	Price.	Equivalents.	Higher than U. S. Stocks.
United States bonds	6	65	65	..
Virginia State	5	52	55	..
Brazilian	5	71	55	16
Egyptian	7	80	77	3
Peruvian	4½	67	50	17
New Granada	2	39	22	17
Portuguese	3	42	33	9
Russian	5	80	55	25
Sardinian	5	63	55	8
Spanish	3	30	33	..
Turkish	6	78	66	12
Dutch	4	85	44	41
French	3	62	33	29
British Consols	3	86	33	53

Thus, Brazil stock is 16 per cent. higher than United

States; Peruvian, although at war, 17 per cent. Even Sardinia gets better terms. The Turk sells his 6 per cent stock at 78; while Mr. McCulloch boasts that he sells his at 66, and a shout goes up when they are sold at all. Certainly, this is not a pleasant picture to contemplate—the more so when we remember how heavy the reckoning is to be. Thus, the six per cent. stock is due in five to ten years hence, in gold. For one bond sold we get $700, and are to pay as follows:

Principal in ten years	$1,000
Ten years' interest at $60 per annum	600
Total to be sent out of the country in gold	$1,600
Amount received in goods	700
Interest and bonus in gold, 9½ per annum	$960

"That is a pretty round rate for the United States to pay, when Russia borrows at 6, Holland at 4½, the Turks at 7½, etc., etc. The money so borrowed by the United States comes to us in the shape of goods which are consumed, and the Treasury policy of selling gold is to give a premium on the operation. The nation is thus eating out its own vitals on credit."

To reform the currency is to lay the ax at the root of the mischief. Is such reform possible in relation to the existing National banks? The power is with Congress, if it will use it, for the weal of the nation, and for the deliverance of the people from this odious tyranny. It can be done by bringing matters to a deadlock at once, and balancing all off in bankruptcy; or it can be done gradually, by leaving this bankruptcy upon the people's shoulders, to be met by them or not, as they shall feel able to struggle under the load. Congress has the power and authority to coerce the National banks into specie payments, and it cannot be too soon in commencing to put forth this power.

The National banks purport to be a new system; but, in fact, are an extended experiment of the New York Banking Law on a grand scale. The system of issuing currency on state stocks was the old New York General Banking Law. This was a most signal failure in 1857—a time of profound peace, most unexampled heavy crops, and after the receipt of about $450,000,000 in gold from California. In August, 1857, the rates for money in New York and Boston were four per cent. a year; in October they were four per cent. a month. It was computed that the monetary failures in the currency of that year made one billion of dollars of failures in the general credits of the country, all of which might have come out sound and right if the currency had been well founded. However financial minds may regard the failures of 1857, after such a deluge of gold as California had poured into the coffers of the eastern banks, all will agree that the test of the Southern revolt proved them utterly impotent.

The United States was supplicating favors of unconstitutional corporations, which could by possibility only exchange credit with them—the whole being one vast pile of credit upon credit, which, but for the continued yield of California's mines, must have ended in one vast maelstrom of ruin and bankruptcy, both national and individual.

And does the United States want to try over again such a demonstrated system of impotence and poverty? The issues of the National banks are founded on Government bonds, instead of State; and does this difference radically change their nature? If an emergency to the Government should arise as trying as the one out of which we have but just survived, would the National banks be in any more potent position to aid the Government than the State banks were in 1861? The impotence of the State banks is a lesson to the people, that in addition to all the charges which were brought against them by the bullionists and hard money men of the nation, they had so thoroughly monopolized the circulation as to expel the gold from the country, and through the nefarious and poverty-stricken policy which they had instituted, the Government had been compelled to issue greenbacks—the State banks still keeping the volume of their issues up to the utmost point of circulation—and the joint issues of the banks and Government so inflating prices as to make the cost of the war double what it would have been under a gold currency, so that the tribute which the people must pay by reason of having and allowing such an impotent system as the old State banks is equal to $1,500,000,000.

A lesson of experience, taught at such high rates of tuition, one might suppose would be amply sufficient, *satis superque*, to satisfy the most incredulous of the baneful national effects of such a currency. And yet, as instituted, the National banks would be equally powerless to aid the Federal Government, in times of great distress, as the State banks were in 1861.

The reform necessary in the National banks is, to monetize gold, to make gold coin—which is the constitutional currency—the real money of the nation. Unless they are willing to do this, to act heart and hand with the Government in achieving so important an object, the sooner their doors are closed the better for the country at large.

Nor should it be deemed satisfactory to resume specie payments upon a similar principle of the old State banks, keeping barely specie enough to turn the corners. The principle of allowing banks to make money upon circulation should be at once and efficiently put down by Congress. Anything short of this is dodging the real question. With the yield of our gold and silver mines, nothing short of the coin, or paper issued upon the coin dollar for dollar, should ever satisfy the people. We can have it if we will. I will now attempt to show how it can be done.

The power being in Congress to amend the Act creating the National banks, let that power be exercised in the following manner. First, The coupons of interest, attached to the bonds which are pledged to the Government for the security of the redemption of the bills, will amount upon $300,000,000, the sum allowed to be issued of currency by the national Banks, to $18,000,000 annually. These coupons are largely of the Five-Twenty Bonds, and are payable in gold coin. Here, then, is a basis of $18,000,000 a-year to operate upon to lift the banks out of the slough of despondency into which this credit money system has plunged them. This eighteen millions of dollars yearly should be used by the Government, and the Treasury department should have the authority to carry out the necessary arrangements to perfect the scheme, in the following manner. The gold should not be paid by the Treasury upon these coupons, but should be retained in the Treasury for the uses and purposes as follows. Allowing that the coupons are due for one year in gold coin to the banks which have pledged them, and the Treasury has the coin to pay the coupons, instead of paying the coin I would have a new emission of gold bills, to the amount of the coupons due, and let these gold bills be secured by the gold in the Treasury, which is collected and ready for their payment. Then for one year's coupons—$18,000,000—the United States would be ready to issue to the banks $18,000,000 of a currency of gold bills.

But as fast as the Treasury issued these new gold bills it should be obligatory upon the banks to return an equal amount of the old circulation, previously issued, which was secured upon the national bonds, and as fast as the old circulation was called in by this process it should be canceled, and the bonds pledged for its redemption should be returned to the bank which hypothecated them as security. In this manner $18,000,000 a year would be withdrawn from circulation of the old issue, which was secured by the Government bonds, and $18,000,000 of new circulation of gold bills, secured upon gold coin in the Treasury of the United States, dollar for dollar, would be substituted for such issue. This the examiner will readily perceive would be getting out of the difficulty at the rate of $18,000,000 a year. But this is by no means the rate at which we can or ought to be satisfied. Secondly: assuming that the banks have issued the full quota of currency allowed by the law—$300,000,000—their annual profits will be, moderately stated, at $30,000,000. This sum should be used by imperative legislation of Congress to help on with the good work of coercive return to specie payments. This profit account, which I have above assumed to be $30,000,000 in currency, would equal about two-thirds the amount in gold, or $20,000,000. I would make it obligatory by law that the banks should not make their dividends of profits annually, but convert these profits into gold coin for the following uses. The gold coin resulting from the conversion of their annual profit account into the same, should be paid into the Treasury of the United States, and thereupon the United States treasurer should issue gold bills to the bank or banks making such deposits, so fast only, however, as the said bank or banks should return their old circulation, which should be canceled, and the bonds pledged for their redemption should be returned to the bank or banks making such gold deposits. In this way the further sum of about $20,000,000 yearly would be withdrawn from the circulation of the old issue, which was secured upon bonds, and a new issue of $20,000,000, secured upon gold coin in the Treasury of the United States, dollar for dollar. This, the examiner will see, would help, with the former conversion of the coupons, at the rate of $38,000,000 yearly. After these bonds were returned to the banks, they could sell them for currency, and make their dividends out of the same. This, however, is not all the means and force which I would apply to the resumption of specie payments. Its importance is such to the nation, that no temporizing policy should be adopted in regard to it. Thirdly: a large amount of the debt of the nation is funded; and the Government can pay it off at pleasure after five years from date, as fast as its means will allow. After paying the interest upon the Government bonds, yearly, in gold, I would have the whole excess of the receipts of gold from the customs applied to the *payment of the bonds* held by the Treasury as security for the redemption of the issues of currency by the banks. This might reach sixty millions a year; but, to be within bounds, I will assume that it is only half that sum, or $30,000,000 a-year. The first part of the national debt paid off, I would have applied upon those bonds deposited with the Treasury as security for the bank circulation. Every three months I would have the department give notice to the banks, that the Treasury was ready to redeem so many millions of dollars of those bonds in gold coin; and after such notice was sent to the banks, the interest coupons should cease to draw, and should be virtually canceled. *But the gold coin I would have retained in the department.* In place of it, however, I would have the department issue to the banks gold notes of an equal amount, dollar for dollar, to the coin reserved in the Treasury; only so fast, however, as each bank should call in and return to the Treasury for cancelation its old issues which were secured by the bonds; which bills should be canceled by the department, and thereafter the new issues of gold bills should be secured by an actual amount of gold in the Treasury, dollar for dollar.

Here, then, I have given an easy way of returning to specie payments, at the rate of $68,000,000 a year; this, too, without oppressing the banks or the people in the least. By the application of the debt of the Government in the interest coupons, the profits of the banks, and the surplus income of the custom-house in gold, beyond the demands for interest on the national debt, specie payments may be restored on a sound basis.

To simplify the subject and give a synopsis of it at once, I will recapitulate the means and sources for specie payments.

Interest upon $300,000,000 national bonds, pledged by the banks, yearly coupons,..	$18,000,000
Yearly profits of the banks in currency, $30,000,000, to be converted by them into gold and pledged for gold bills..........	20,000,000
Redemption of bonds by the Government, from gold received from customs' duties, yearly,..............................	30,000,000
	$68,000,000

Here, then, we have resources, which, if faithfully applied, will enable the banks to resume specie payments at the rate of $68,000,000 a year; or, in four years and a-half every dollar of their issues of bills of credit may be withdrawn, and in place of them may be issued bills of substance—GOLD BILLS—secured by a deposit of gold in the National Treasury, dollar for dollar. The scheme neither oppresses the Government, the banks, or the people. It, however, cuts off all profits from the circulation of bank notes, further than such circulation is based on gold. It rids the Government of the obnoxious position into which it has placed itself, by creating monopolies to circulate paper money, (which has ever been the bane of the country) and actually paying these monopolies an immense bonus for the mischief which they most thoroughly achieve, by expelling the real money from the country, and making all the business industries depend upon a basis of gambling. It rids the Government of the charge of issuing "bills of credit," for it makes the issues all gold bills.

While the scheme is in transition from a system of credit to a system of gold basis, it will necessitate the keeping of double accounts by the banks; one a currency account, the other a gold account. Some of the banks' customers will keep their accounts in gold, others in currency. Each dealer might elect in which kind of money he would account with the banks. But in either case *the law of the land should protect both the banks and their customers*, that no unfairness could be exercised on either side. Hence the Congress of the United States should immediately enact the Specific Contract Law of California, for the benefit of every citizen of the Union, making it imperative upon every contractor to pay in *such kind of money as he specifies.*

The scheme, when established, will make it necessary for the banks to redeem at a branch or branches of the Treasury in New York, Boston, and other commercial cities of the Union. That the scheme will lessen the amount of bills in circulation, and increase the actual circulation of gold coin, is too plain to need illustration. The expenses should be borne largely by the Government, for all losses of bills by fire, floods, by shipwrecks, by hoards of persons deceased which will never come to light, these will all be direct gain to the Government.

Hence I have shown that it is not only possible to return to specie payments, but comparatively easy; and to return so that the circulation shall not only be reputed as equal to gold coin, but actually be equal to it, by the deposit of gold in the Treasury to cover the issue. The United States guarantee the circulation of the National banks. This is reason enough for exacting the deposit of coin for the redemption of such circulation. Therefore the legislation needed to coerce the reform should be instituted at once, and put it in process of a gradual perfecting of the national currency; and this reform may proceed, without oppressing the banks or the people, at the rate of the yearly product of the gold and silver mines of the country. And so long as the work of reform is deferred, so long will the product of these mines go to foreign countries in pure loss to the United States.

It may be thought by some that to lock up hundreds of millions of dollars of gold coin in the Treasury would be so much actual loss of capital to the nation, and that such a hoarding of gold would be wholly useless. This objection is entirely without foundation. The gold, when not in circulation, would be represented in circulation by the gold bills. Nothing would be lost to the nation. As well might one say that the granite foundations upon which the treasury buildings are erected, or upon which the Capitol stands, might as well be of wood, or some some cheaper material, which would sustain these edifices for a few years and then crumble to dust, because such material was cheaper than a lasting foundation, as to say that the currency need not be so valuable as gold, because a cheaper form of circulation may be instituted.

The whole fabric of our credit system rests upon the currency. It is this that lies under and supports the whole. If the currency be gold, or rests on gold, dollar for dollar, the foundation will not rot or settle, and the superstructure will not fail by reason of the foundation. But if the foundation of the whole system be liable to decay, and is utterly impotent to sustain the weight of the edifice which we are building thereon, when such foundation fails it spreads ruin throughout all the works which rest upon it. A sound currency will not remedy an unsound credit; but a vicious and diluted currency will destroy general credits in a tenfold proportion to the amount in circulation, making the bankruptcies under a system of false currency ten times more than they would be if it were sound. And this for the reason that every dollar of currency which circulates as money sustains ten dollars of the general credits of the country, and every dollar of the currency which fails drags down with it ten dollars of the general credits. In this view of the matter, is it possible to make the currency too sound for the vital interests of the body politic?

If it were necessary to make the sacrifice, every citizen who carries a gold watch should be willing to substitute a silver one; nay more, every one should be willing to take the gold out of his mouth and send it to the mint, to achieve so salutary a national reform as a perfect gold currency. These sacrifices, however, are by no means called for. We have gold enough for our currency if we have the wit to save it for so wise purpose. Seven years' saving, with what we now possess, would make ours the model currency of the world. Shall we make it such, or continue to give away our gold, and content ourselves with the shadow?

But another objection is, that we should have no banks upon a strictly gold basis; that the expenses of their management would not justify such institutions. I deny the premise entirely, and in confirmation of my position I point to the existing fact that San Francisco, with a population of only 120,000, and with all her banks established and doing a sound business, has lately raised the capital stock of the Bank of California to $5,000,000, and that these institutions are all doing a prosperous business, upon a strictly gold basis, without any issues of currency whatever. Experiment is the touchstone by which to try theories. To say that business would not be done if it had to be done with real money instead of a fiction, is the same sort of argument as to urge that people would not travel on our magnificent steamers if they could travel at a cheaper rate on such vessels as would very likely explode and kill them. The United States are now old enough, and their mines are rich enough, to set an example of the best currency on earth.

The people of the United States, having used a paper currency so long, are not aware of the advantages which a gold currency would give them. The paper money champions have ruled for more than half a century; let the bullionists now try it for a few decades; they cannot make matters worse. For a gold-producing country to economize the use of gold as currency by substituting promises to pay the coin which are not based upon its possession, is a saving of exactly the same nature as though a man should trust his life and money on board some extra hazardous and unseaworthy vessel, or some steamboat whose boiler is ready to collapse at any moment a little extra pressure is needed to be put upon it, rather than select the most thoroughly built and substantial vessel upon which to risk his life and property.

This policy is also a voluntary surrender to other nations of our real money, with which a beneficent Providence has so bountifully favored us, and substituting the promise for the reality—the shadow for the substance.

We need only $620,000,000 in gold to move all of our industries and distribute our products. Probably we have on hand $120,000,000, which reduces the amount needed to $500,000,000. This can be amassed, with proper national legislation, in six or seven years; and after this national saving, we need retain the yield of our mines only as fast as our population increases; the balance may be exported to pay for imports. But until the volume of currency be entirely filled with gold and silver coin, our gold should not be exported. Its remaining in the country, however, should not result from any coercive legislation, like imposing an export duty, but from its imperative necessity as coin for domestic uses—thus making it really more valuable at home for currency, than to send abroad for merchandise. As fast as we demonetize paper money, our gold is bound by the laws of trade and commerce to remain with us, and to fill the place of the paper.

The currency of the United States should not be of such worthless material, as that, to purify it, we must contract its volume, and thus bring ruin upon our industrial pursuits. This, however, is the practical effect of contracting or calling in the currency, when banks are moving on under pretended specie payments. The remedy which strikes at the heart of the disease—the medicine which will give immediate relief to the body politic—is to save every dollar of the yield of our gold and silver mines, and with this sink one dollar of our "bills of credit" leaning on the national bonds. The remedy is easy, and if persisted in, the result will be a return to complete solvency in currency. If we sustained the whole business of the country in 1860, upon a currency of $620,000,000, it is entirely possible, with the yield of our mines, and without a dollar return from commerce, to have our monetary basis strictly founded upon gold. To effect this salutary change we must recognize gold as money, and make a home market for it to the extent of our domestic wants of currency.

A pure currency may be well compared to a virtuous woman. If a woman harbor the thought that she may step aside from a course of purity, and secretly practise for a while the ways of the wanton, and again return to the paths of innocence and virtue, she is at once on the highway to ruin. Every step in vice makes reform more hopeless.

> ——— *Facilis descensus Averni:*
> *Sed revocare gradum superasque evadere ad auras,*
> *Hoc opus, hic labor est.*—Virgil.

> "Avernus' gates are open night and day,
> Smooth the descent, and easy is the way:
> But to return to Heaven's pure light again,
> This is a work of labor and of pain."

Precisely so it is with the practice of vitiating the currency. It commenced with small beginnings. First, the idea that one hundred dollars of specie might be made one hundred and one by issuing that amount of currency; then it was raised to one hundred and ten; then to one hundred and fifty; then to two hundred; and the preposterous principle has been extended and extending, till the banks scarcely hold a small portion of their immediate liabilities in specie. On the 10th of October last, the banks of Boston owed for deposits and circulation $68,588,709, and held of specie only $250,638, or less than forty cents specie on one hundred dollars of immediate liabilities.

The New York City banks, holding large deposits belonging to the country banks, which ought to be immensely strong in specie, owed on the 13th October, 1866:

For deposits	$225,858,897
For circulation	30,176,908
	$256,035,805
They held in specie	5,576,062

or less than two and a-quarter cents on the dollar upon their immediate liabilities.

The National banks of Chicago have had their specie

reserve as low as one-fourth of one per cent. to their immediate liabilities.

Twenty-five cents in specie for one hundred dollars of liabilities! If this is not totally ignoring a specie basis, it must be admitted that it comes so near an entire repudiation of coin as not to be very wide from it in practice.

After the principle of allowing issues of bills of credit beyond the amount of specie on hand, dollar for dollar, is once admitted, recognized, and legalized, there is no predicting where so nefarious a scheme will terminate. The calls of the currency makers are incessant; their demands are aggressive and bold; their arguments are plausible to those minds which have not compassed the subject; and in their greed of gain, they make no hesitancy in sacrificing the permanent welfare of the country to their unbounded avarice. Already do they insist that the National Currency Act should be amended, allowing a further issue of $100,000,000 of promises to pay, which are not to be covered by specie. Already do they protest against assorting the notes, clearing houses and every form of redemption. And, what is most outrageously insolent and presumptive, they are clamoring that their diluted issues should be made legal tender between citizens as well as for taxes and excises. The only way to stop all this contempt of right, justice, and equity, (which these currencymakers impose upon the majesty of the people, by insisting that their issues shall pass as good coin, making the prices of all forms of wealth in the land) is to limit the issues of currency to the amount of gold coin which banks deposit in the Treasury to redeem such issues. For, as a woman cannot be virtuous unless she is entirely so, in like manner a currency cannot be pure unless it is kept up to the legal standard of such purity.

It is not a function of Congress to create currency of any kind, further than the coinage of the mints. The right to regulate the currency is incidental to the right of "coining money and fixing the value thereof." It is impossible to keep up the purchasing and exchangeable value of gold coin and let the power of issuing bills of credit run riot. Therefore Congress has power either to suppress *in toto* all forms of circulation of bills of credit in the United States, or to make this circulation conform to such rules as will render it impossible to interfere with the normal value of gold coin.

My own opinion is, that the power of Congress is reached when it suppresses every form of issue of bills of credit. I use the term bills of credit here in the same sense in which it was understood by the Convention which made the Constitution. But, without contending for strict construction, which is so scouted in these days of latitudinarian interpretation, it must be apparent that, in times of peace at least, justice is a principle which cannot be trampled upon by any legislative body without a fearful retribution. If paper money, therefore, be a national necessity, it is the bounden duty of Congress to see to it, that this form of money shall be equal to gold coin at all times and under all circumstances—panics and commercial crises not excepted. This can only be done by limiting the amount of issues of paper to the specie on deposit to redeem such paper. Nor will it do to trust the banks to hold this specie and give them the power of issuing bills also. The specie must be locked up with some safe custodian while the bills circulate, and the bills must also be locked up with the same care while the specie circulates.

Again: it is no function of Congress to furnish currency for speculators, stock gamblers, usurers, faro and monte dealers, and all the thousand forms of parasites which prey upon the gains of honest industry. Strike out these classes, which are of very small use to the production of real wealth among any people, and it would not be difficult to find capital enough from the yield of our gold and silver mines to move all the industries of the country.

Paper money is extolled by its advocates for its legerity and portability. A person, say they, may carry hundreds of thousands of dollars in his pocket, and no one suspect that he has more than enough to balance his daily bills. Grant all this; still would it not be vastly better that these bills should be based on gold coin, dollar for dollar, than that they lien on Government Stocks payable twenty or forty years ahead? If they lien on gold, they do not lessen the value of gold; if they lien on stocks, they do most materially lessen the purchasing power of gold.

And they do make it utterly impossible for Congress to coin gold "*and fix the value of it.*" Therefore they do render it impossible for Congress to discharge one of its imperative functions to the people, which is to fix the value of gold coin—at least to fix it so far as that bills which they issue shall represent gold and nothing else. In short, the bills which Congress issue, or authorize to be issued, either by the Federal Government directly or to banking corporations to circulate as currency, should not be bills of credit, but bills of substance—bills resting on gold, not on debt, national, state, or private.

All of these unspeakable advantages are waiting for our acceptance and appropriation. The National banks will be a boon to the people if they make them such by purging them from the unjust principle of issuing promises to pay dollars which they do not possess. As a bludgeon in the hands of the Government to break down the old systems of the State banks (which were always so impotent to help in time of need, and yet so potent as to drive all the gold from our country to foreigners, the loss of which gold was a damage to the country of a billion and a half during the war of 1861–5), the National banks have served a good purpose. The government of the currency is now under the legislation of Congress; and this advantage is worth $500,000,000 to the country, provided Congress will coerce, by imperative legislation, the system of the National banks on to the principle of the gold and silver basis—dollar for dollar.

But if Congress will not do this; if the sworn delegates of the American people will hold their sessions in the city of Washington, and by their legislative action throw aside all their scruples of moral principle, all their oaths of office, to support and defend that Constitution, one of the cardinal objects of making which was "to establish justice," and which does most positively prohibit the States from issuing "bills of credit," or of making anything but gold and silver coin a tender in payment of debts; if, regardless of these sacred injunctions of the Constitution and the oaths of office to support and defend it, the Congress shall so far prove recreant to its trusts and duties as to allow and encourage by legislative acts the issue of bills of credit by the National banks, thereby driving our gold to other countries and radically changing the substantial basis of our monetary system, as established by the wisdom of our forefathers, then we have nothing to hope of good from them. One rotten system will have been broken down to give place to another which, if possible, exceeds it in impotence to do good and in power to work mischief.

The National banks will be a boon to the country if Congress brings them and holds them to a strict specie basis. As at present organized and conducted, they are worse to the prosperity of the country than the old State banks, which held to specie payments, in name at least. If they are not compelled to specie payments they will work nothing but ruin in the republic.

It is so easy to do this—to do it and have it rest upon a basis so different to what our currency has ever rested heretofore, as I have proven above, that I will not despair of favorable action by Congress in the premises. The National banks will be useful to the country in direct proportion as they approximate to a specie basis ; they will be disorganizing, mischief making, spreading the evils of Pandora's box through the country, in direct proportion as they reject the specie basis and substitute for it a basis of debt.

Whenever Congress shall take from the government circulation—commonly called greenbacks—the legal tender qualification, or the Supreme Court of the United States shall decide that this circulation is not a tender between citizens, then will the first step have been taken toward the Government resuming cash payments. Then the greenbacks can be funded ; but while they remain money, and legal tender too, it will be nearly impossible to fund them. This act is indispensable, and must be a condition precedent to the resumption of specie payments by the Government, unless we remain in a state of bankruptcy through the present generation. The Government must resume before the banks will think of the measure. But it is in the power of the Government to coerce the banks into resumption gradually, if it has the nerve to do it.

All the coupons of interest upon the bonds held by the Government for the security of the circulation of the banks, should be retained by the Government in gold; the old circulation should be withdrawn from time to time, and new circulation issued to the amount of these coupons, the new circulation would then be based on gold. All the profits of the banks should be converted into gold, this gold deposited in the Treasury of the United States, and an equal amount of the old circulation called in and canceled, and new circulation based on gold coin be issued to the banks. The bonds could be returned to the bank in an amount equal to the amount of this lastnamed new circulation. Lastly; the Government should, from time to time, appropriate every dollar of its surplus revenue from customs, after reserving enough to pay the interest upon that portion of the debt which is payable in gold coin, to taking up and canceling the bonds which have been deposited to secure the circulation of the National banks. This should continue until the entire capital of the banks becomes gold coin in the Treasury of the United States, and their entire circulation of bills will then be gold bills—bills of substance—not bills of credit, which are forbidden by the organic law of the Federal Government.

Some may object to making the first payments of the national debt to the National banks: but, beyond doubt, the Government has the right to pay off first that portion of the debt where the advantages of such payment shall inure most signally to the benefit of the people. War, debt, the legislation of Congress, and the necessity of the times, if you will, have brought on the suspension of cash payments. This suspension has raised prices, so that the people are ground, as it were, beneath the upper and nether millstone. The Five-Twenties of the Government will soon be due. The Government can, if it chooses, pay them at any time after five years from their date. When the Government shall pay them, such payment will, of course, stop interest. The interest and happiness of the people are certainly relevant matters for national legislation. Besides, this changing of the basis of the National Banks from *Government debt to gold coin*, will bring these institutions into harmony with the supreme law of the land. And, if we are to have any constitutional Government hereafter, it is meet that Congress should make

M*

its laws to conform, at least so far as is possible, to the organic law. The National banks when brought on to this basis, having all their circulation secured, dollar for dollar in gold coin, will be very different institutions from the old State banks. In case of war, or any great national calamity, they would have the sinews to stand by the Government in time of need. They would have something more than credit to lend.

It will not be possible for the Federal Government to render the people a greater boon, than to pay off that portion of the public debt held by the Treasury department for security of the circulation of bills of the National banks, and hold the gold as security in lieu of the bonds. In this way the interest will stop running on the bonds, while the banks will be coerced into specie payments. The advantages will be felt both by the Government and the people. It will require an assorting and clearing house to be attached to the Treasury department in the cities of New York, Boston, and, in time, in other commercial cities of the Union. All the banks should be required to redeem their notes in gold as fast as they were returned to the Treasury. This would make a domestic requirement for gold coin, exactly equal to the amount of gold bills in circulation. The bills, however, would not be sent to the Treasury for redemption only as gold was required for shipments abroad. The mines of the country will yield $75,000,000 a year, and, through the customs, the Federal Government will receive the whole of this amount, and probably $50,000,000 more of the gold in the hands of the people. This will leave a large excess of gold in the Treasury, after paying the coin interest on the public debt, to be applied to paying off the bonds, and making the basis of the circulation coin.

The preceding measures only reach the reform and purity of the bills in circulation. Some may say it is not radical enough—that it ought to reform the deposit account in banks as well as their circulation. There is no doubt but the liability of banks, in proportion to their constant specie reserve, should be rigidly enforced by legislative enactments. But it is not well to attempt too much at once. The reform of the "circulation without" is sufficient to begin upon. The preceding chapter is in the right direction of reform so far as it goes. Besides, when the outside circulation is made entirely pure, the deposits will be made corresponsively more sound. This will be proper matter for another chapter. So far as reform of the currency in circulation goes, the banks ought not to object to it, while there remains to them the power to work such efficient mischief through the deposit account, or their internal circulation.

There remains one point of great importance for consideration, which is this: Is it safe to trust the Federal Treasury with such an immense amount of gold coin? Immense trusts must devolve upon every generation. Man is mortal; and however much of wealth he may amass in life, it must all descend to future generations. Our lives, liberties, and properties, we trust in the hands of statesmen, jurists, legislators, and generals. These are quite as important trusts as our monetary interests. In deciding this question we may inquire—Are the moral qualities of our people on a par with those of other nations? If they are, the trust may be made. No doubt the Federal Government would be as legally responsible for any embezzlement of funds left in the Treasury for the redemption of bank bills, as it would for embezzlement of gold left at the mints for coinage. The bank of England has often on hand £20,000,000 in coin and bullion, besides all its bills of exchequer, bank-notes, rest, government deposits, and private deposits. The bank of France had on hand recently £26,000,000 sterling in specie, besides all its other trusts. I believe neither of these institutions have suffered any severe losses by embezzlements. It is safe to say that the trusts in the Treasury of the United States, if they held the gold to cover the entire circulation allowed the national banks, would not be equal to the trusts in the bank of England or the bank of France. The deposits of gold to secure the circulation of the bills would of necessity be divided among the sub-treasurers of various commercial cities, probably not less than four or five in number. The New York branch would be the largest—that being the commercial and fiscal centre of the Union. The Federal Treasury holds in gold frequently for customs' duties collected, seventy-five to eighty millions of dollars; and there has never been any large direct robbery of the Treasury. The trusts which a deposit of gold would require, to cover the circulation of the banks, in the Treasury, would not exceed the trusts of the bank of England or the bank of France, or of the actual trusts which have already been committed to the Treasury.

The treasure could be under the keeping of a dozen officers, each holding separate keys, which could not be reached by any one of them without possessing all of the keys, and which would require the combination of all these officials in crime, to commit an embezzlement.

The general banking law of New York was a demonstrated failure in 1857. The Government should not desire to renew upon a grand scale the old New York system, nationalizing it, and preparing it for a gigantic swindle on the vitality of the people. Every dollar of gold which goes from the mines of California to the old States, should be the means of retiring from circulation one credit dollar, which is now based upon the national debt. To effect this salutary reform, our legislators in Congress should amend the National Currency Bill. With the coupons of interest attached to the national bonds which are held in the Treasury to secure the circulation of the banks, and which the Government must pay semi-annually to these institutions, with the profits of the banks converted to gold, and the excess of gold which the customs will put into the Treasury; from these three sources the Treasury may, in less than five years, have gold enough to secure the entire circulation of the National banks, dollar for dollar. Neither the people, nor the banks, nor the Government, need be at all oppressed or burdened, to effect all this salutary reform quite speedily.

This reform will immediately make a domestic market for about $68,000,000 of the yield of our gold mines; and it is as certain as the laws of gravitation, if we allow the "promised dollar" to circulate, and continue to usurp the uses and functions of the gold dollar, that the whole annual yield of our mines in the precious metals will go from us to other countries in dead loss. We shall get it in goods advanced in prices enough to cover it. We shall get it balanced in extra prices, not in real values. We shall get for it only price without corresponding values. The present organization of the National banks is upon a system which gives to other nations, virtually, the whole product of our gold and silver mines.

What would be the effect upon the credit of the United States abroad to have three hundred millions of gold coin in the Treasury? Certainly it could not be other than most salutary. With such an amount of gold coin on hand, would British Consols, paying only three per cent. interest, stand at eighty-nine, while American Five-Twenties paying six per cent. interest, stood at sixty-eight? Such a disparity in value would be impossible. The rise in our National stocks abroad, if we must part with them to balance our imports, would pay for the change of our monetary basis from credit to gold, four times over; besides all the domestic advantages of an honest and just currency.

When, however, we do return to specie payments, we want it based upon an entirely different principle from any that has heretofore existed in the United States. If the National bank system is to be no better than the Suffolk bank system of New England, and the general banking law of New York, as these existed before the war, keeping only from five to twenty per cent. of their immediate liabilities in coin, it will prove a vast delegation of power to corporations to work untold mischiefs in the body politic. I mention these two systems because they have been considered the best that have ever been devised, to circulate currency without keeping means to redeem it—shirking all the losses of such business upon the people, keeping them out of their sight, and making them suppose that banks were the very soul of justice and beneficence to the nation. Congress should wield the whole power of the Government against any and every form of currency which banishes the gold from the country. This cannot be done in any way but to make the banks insure their issues, dollar for dollar, by deposit of gold coin. The National banks should be made national in fact as well as in name. This can only be done by bringing them into *accord with the organic law.* They are in conflict with this law so long as they issue bills of credit; the Government acts in conflict with this law so long as it prepares bills of credit for these institutions to circulate as money. Neither the action of the Government in the premises, nor that of the banks, can be in harmony with this law, until they change the form of this circulation from bills of credit to bills of substance, and make the issue of bills no larger than the actual deposit of gold in the Treasury for its redemption. Under these restrictions, the issue of bills will be adjusted as accurately to the wants of the people, as the houses in a large city are constructed to meet the demands for such dwellings. Banking business should be as open as farming, merchandising, or manufacturing; but *the issuing of currency is an attribute of the sovereignty*, and should be guarded as closely as the coining of gold and silver.

No. VIII.

THE TARIFF OF THE UNITED STATES—ITS EFFECT UPON THE VALUE OF GOLD FOR USES ABROAD.

The subject of equal and just taxation is one which in practice is almost an impossibility. To tax every citizen his exact proportion in relation to his means and the necessities of the Government, would be a problem as difficult as to square the circle, or to achieve a human devised successful perpetual motion. Nevertheless an equal taxation is what the supreme law contemplated when it was ordained that "all duties, imposts, and excises shall be uniform throughout the United States." How can all imposts be made equal? To exact a fixed tariff rate of ten, twenty, fifty, or any other per centage upon all kinds of importations, *ad valorem*, would by no means make a tariff which would tax all alike; for a tariff of any sort only collects imposts of those who use the goods—that is, the consumers. The tariff, however, is an encumbrance to free trade and commerce which acts very unequally upon various States of the Union, oppressing some with most grievous burdens, and aiding others by the losses which these imposts necessarily create.

And although it is impossible to make a tariff which shall bear equally upon all the nation, yet all very obvious, patent, glaring, and clearly demonstrated great inequalities in any such law should be amended, if possible; but if not possible, then the State or States upon which the law bears so onerously and so unequally should receive an equivalent in some other form of legislation.

The present tariff, I contend, acts with crushing influence upon the prosperity of the State of California. And why does the tariff oppress California more than other States in the Union? I answer, because it excludes gold—her staple product—from the markets of the world, except upon conditions the most onerous.

The present tariff, it is estimated, will yield from 50 to 75 per cent. upon articles imported. I will take the lesser sum, and I am certain that this will bring my estimates within the bounds of truth. If the tariff yields 50 per cent., then suppose the American merchant buys in London, Paris, Hamburg, or any foreign city, goods valued at $10,000, and pays for these in gold coin. He imports them to New York, and pays at the Custom House $5,000 for duties. This makes his goods cost $15,000 in New York, besides freight, which I will not count at present. To get $10,000 of foreign goods, after paying the European value for them in gold, he must pay $5,000 more in gold coin to the American Custom House. Thus his money is discounted one-third—one-third of the value of his gold—that is, for $15,000 gold he gets only $10,000 in foreign goods. Now if this be not so, I call on any accountant or economist to show the error in the premises. It follows that California is excluded from all the markets of the world with her staple—gold—except at a loss of one-third of its value. It is tantamount to imposing a fine of one-third the value upon gold used abroad in the purchase of merchandise, the forfeiture to be recoverable by the Government when the goods purchased with the gold shall be discharged from the vessel at any American port.

The same fine attaches to other forms of goods shipped by Americans; but the difference between California and other States is this—that her staple, gold, is always marketable abroad at its full value, while it is perhaps not one year in four that the products of most of the States can be shipped. Thus, there is a demand for wheat when the crops are short in Great Britain and on the continent. When there is no demand abroad for breadstuffs, our people do not ship them; therefore the grievance of the tariff does not bear upon other States as it does upon the State of California.

Californians may trade abroad; they may exchange their staple for the goods and wealth of other nations, which are produced under currencies not diluted like our own; but when they bring that wealth to the United States they must pay one-third of it, or fifty per cent. of its value, into the Customs. The corollary to this is positive; it is deducible beyond contradiction that *the gold of California is shorn of one-third of its value by the American tariff for uses outside of the United States.* This is, indeed, a heavy impost to put upon the staple of our State; but it is nevertheless the fact, right or wrong, that gold is shorn of one-third its value by the action of our tariff upon all goods imported.

Californians could get the full value of their gold by abdicating their country, and going abroad to live and spend it; and the difference in the prices of living is such that thousands of our wealthy citizens are residing abroad, purely from motives of economy. Surely it is not well to make laws which will thus drive our wealthy population abroad.*

---

* The Paris correspondent of one of the San Francisco papers gives the following quotations of prices abroad: "We can buy in Paris a good summer silk for 6 francs a yard—a dollar and twenty cents. Black silks which at home are $3 50 a yard, are here $1 90. French cambrics, for which we pay 75 cents, are here 39 cents. Kid gloves, for which we give a dollar, are 50 cents in Paris, and at Naples 20 or 30 cents; $2 50 gloves with us are here $1 a pair. Six months ago, in America, coarse flannel was 50 or 75 cents a yard; here it is 18 or 20 cents. Lace edging, for which a friend paid 33 cents last month at Mudge's, in Boston, I patterned here for 11 cents. Lubin's soap, for which I paid Harris and Chapman $1 25, I found in Genoa for 80 cents, and I am told it is less in Paris. Lubin's extracts, for which our druggists charge $1 50 or $1 25, are here 25 cents. A point lace collar and cuffs, for which at home we pay $25, are here $12. A lace shawl, for which we pay $400, is in Paris $200, and at Brussels, where it is made, $150. Black trim-

While the tariff enables the manufactories of New England to make yearly dividends of forty, fifty, and sixty per cent. upon their capital stocks, in many cases leaving a large reserve undivided, increasing the value of their stock even after making such enormous dividends, the same tariff does virtually and effectually take from the value of gold, for use in the markets of the world, one-third of its value. And is this the equality which the framers of the Constitution meant to institute when they ordained that "all duties, imposts, and excises shall be uniform throughout the United States?" I know how the argument is answered: that the duties are collected upon the merchandise returned to this country, purchased with the gold, and not upon the gold itself. Let us examine the force of this argument: For illustration, we will suppose that a farmer puts thirty bushels of wheat into his wagon, and goes to mill to have it ground. To get to the mill he must pass over a turnpike, and upon this turnpike is a toll-gate at which he must pay, in value, one third the amount of his wheat; would not the farmer lose just one-third the value of his grain by submitting to this tribute, or toll, on the turnpike? Most assuredly he would; and so does the owner of gold lose one-third its value, if

---

ming lace of narrow width, for which we pay 75 cents, is here 30 cents. As for bonnets, which with my last American experience were at fabulous prices, such as from $20 to $80, the ordinary price of a handsome one in Paris is $5, often only $4, with fine French flowers. Those with blonde lace trimmings are $6 or $8, and the most exorbitant milliners charge $14 to $18. Yet ribbons are, from some unknown reason, as expensive in Paris as in America. So are boots and shoes, provisions, rents, and a few other things. Under garments of all kinds can be bought here ready made and elaborately trimmed for what the mere cotton costs at home. One is suspicious of cheap ready made clothes, so often the tears of the poor are worked into them; but as I waited the other day in a large shop of this kind, I observed the neat little sewing girls who brought home their work in a handkerchief, and they looked smiling and prosperous. A French woman lives upon an inconsiderably small sum, and provisions are so subdivided to suit their economy that a few sous procures them a luxurious dinner. Once or twice a week a few lodgers in the attic of some great house club together and order a dinner which is really luxurious, though it is paid for in hardly-earned sous—and this is all they ask."

he expends it for foreign goods, and brings them to the United States.

The necessity for the high tariff under which one part of the country is amassing wealth so rapidly, while the rest of the country is languishing and paying the bills, is said to be for protection. If this be the real reason, are we not all in the same boat? Have not agriculture, commerce, mining, and all sorts of industries, the same right to protection as manufactures? Does not the permanent prosperity of the Union rest upon all of these? Why should one class of industries be selected for protection, and the aid be given this class by hampering and ruining all other classes of national wealth? The system is absurd and ruinous. Everything should bear its just proportion of the nation's load; and everything which is obviously and apparently disproportionately imposed, should be immediately amended. "A house divided against itself cannot stand." The hand cannot say that it has no need of the head or the heart. Every organ of the body has its place, its function, and its usefulness; and so, in the body politic, the great national industries all have equal claims upon the fostering care of the Federal Government. To break down one section of the country and build up another, by legislative enactments which oppose the natural right which a man possesses, to use his money in the nation where it will command the most of the necessaries or luxuries of life, will be a sure way, in the end, to drive our wealthy citizens from the country.

The nearer all the nations of the globe can come to the principle of exchanging the surplus products of their gains, which they do not need at home, for the surplus products of other nations, upon the cheapest rules and without customs, the more true liberty will they enjoy, the more luxuries and the more value will they receive for their industries. With these remarks, I will now try to show what the State of California has done heretofore, and what she is now doing for the common Union.

The yield of the mines of California have been in round numbers, at least, $850,000,000 in gold. This gold has gone forward to pay for goods: upon these goods, if foreign, she has lost the whole amount of the customs' rates.

If the goods were domestic, still they were greatly advanced in price by the action of the tariff upon imported goods; for it is a rule of human nature to ask as much price as can be obtained, with but little regard to cost of production. The tariff, by excluding foreign goods, or enhancing their prices, helps the home producer of such goods to advance his rate of charges upon the excluded or duty-paying article. Under these circumstances, it is within bounds to assume that of the above eight hundred and fifty millions of gold, California has lost one-third of it by the action of the customs upon its value. This makes the sum of $283,333,333 loss to California through the customs. Add to this sum the interest at six per cent. for only eight years, or half the time California has belonged to the Union, and we have one hundred and thirty-six millions loss of interest—making the gross sum of $419,333,333 as a tribute which California has paid to the Union in the shape of loss upon the value of her gold, and interest upon that loss. Surely, this is no trifling tribute for a population of 380,000 to pay for the good of the Commonwealth.

The people of this State suffer under the burden of their taxes, but a large amount of them are out of sight. They pay them in ways which they do not comprehend. At present the mines of California are yielding about $48,000,000 a-year. The custom-house takes one-third from the value of this gold, for foreign use. In a subsequent paper I purpose to demonstrate that quite as large an amount is taken from its value by Federal legislation, for domestic uses as money. Hence we are justifiable in deducting fully one-third the value of all the gold yield of the mines for, and on account of such legislation.

Such being the case, let us see what California pays and loses for the good of the Union:

Annual yield of gold $48,000,000; loss on this gold, as above demonstrated, one-third.....	$16,000,000
Customs collected in San Francisco for the fiscal year just closed	7,134,664
Internal revenue, $7,732,387 currency, equal to	5,154,925
	$28,289,589

Such is the *annual tribute* which California pays for the support of the Union at large, and it is equal to eighty dollars for every one in the State. This, however, is only the national claim. The State, County, and City expenses are some four per cent. further. No wonder then, that with such drafts, occult and patent, upon the resources of the people, they cry out hard times. California has paid in times past to the Federal Government, in losses on her gold through the action of the tariff and interest on these losses, $419,333,333—*enough to build four railroads from the State to the Missouri River.* She is paying to the Federal Government, and losing on her gold through the action of the tariff, more than $28,000,000 a year, enough to build the railroad from California to the Missouri River with a double track the whole distance, and equip it with rolling stock, locomotives, and appointments every five years;—yes, reader, every five years, California is paying enough in gold, adding to it the losses which the tariff makes on her coin, to do all this immense work.

But lest the imposing of an import duty cannot be seen to be the same in effect as an export duty upon the article which pays for the import, I will add a little further upon that view of the case. A duty imposed upon articles which a State neither buys nor sells, cannot directly affect the interest of such State; but a duty imposed upon any article which a State buys or sells does directly affect the interest of the same. The State of Maine would not be much annoyed by a heavy export duty, if such were constitutional, upon diamonds, silks, and laces, because these articles are not produced there. But it would be uproarious, perhaps belligerent, if Congress should impose an export duty of one-third the value upon all the pine lumber manufactured there. It would not satisfy the sturdy lumbermen to tell them that the duty would be added to the value of their deals, and the consumer must pay it. The native sense of the people would teach them that they could neither sell so much nor at so good remunerating prices, with such a duty imposed, as under a free trade. Again: suppose that the duty was not imposed upon the manufactured lumber, but upon goods brought into the State;—goods purchased in Boston with the proceeds of the sales of their lumber, and how would the case stand? Simply thus: if lumber were the only means they possessed of paying for goods, then a duty upon goods would virtually be a duty upon their lumber, and *vice versa*.

The tariff, then, bears onerously upon all those States which have articles for sale in the markets of the world. Under this definition it bears harder upon California than upon any other State. This for the reason that gold is always marketable and in demand in all the civilized world. Wheat and flour, pork, hams, lard, butter, etc., etc., are only marketable abroad when the foreign markets run short of these articles. It is only when these goods bring prices which will pay for shipping that they are exported. But gold is money, and will always bring its value abroad. Cotton comes next upon the list, and it is upon gold and cotton that the tariff bears with oppressive weight. These articles can be marketed abroad, but upon the goods bought with them the imposts of the Customs will take fifty per cent. of their foreign value.

Another objection to the position is this: that the gold of California is paid for largely in goods of domestic manufacture by the old States, and that after it is paid for, it, of course, belongs to the purchaser who has given value for it. The reader will understand me; I am only examining the nature of trade, and maintaining that it stands upon an unequal, unjust, and wrong basis, and that the tariff does largely aid and support this basis. The gold of California is indeed paid for in such domestic goods, but the prices of these goods are advanced greatly by the action of the tariff on foreign goods. Thus, imports must pay fifty per cent. on their value before they can compete with the home-made articles. It is, for these reasons, so plain that he who runs may read. The American tariff takes from gold one-third of its value for use in purchasing foreign goods.

No. IX.

THE EFFECT OF DEMONETIZING GOLD UPON ITS DOMESTIC VALUE.

In a former paper I have shown that the American tariff takes from gold one-third its value for foreign purchases, if those purchases are imported. To Americans, this closes the markets of the world for the article, except at a most ruinous sacrifice. What avenues of trade and commerce are still open to this metal upon a fair business basis? The value of gold is consequent, first, from the labor of extracting it from the quartz rocks; secondly, from the fact that civilized nations have adopted it as their most perfect measure of values—as their most accurate medium of adjusting the balances of commerce—as the most perfect form of money of the world which exists.

If gold were not a universal medium of exchange among civilized nations, as a useful metal in the arts, it would scarcely rule above the value of silver. Indeed, its disuse as money would so lessen its value, that it would not pay for mining, unless found under much easier circumstances of attainment than any which exist in California.

It is not yet known whether coined gold is money in the United States. In other words, the Supreme Court of the United States have not yet decided whether Treasury notes are a legal tender upon all money contracts. If they should rule thus, then will gold be most thoroughly demonetized at home.

Mr. Stevens, of Pennsylvania, in a speech, in 1864, before Congress, made these statements: "By the legislation of Congress, two years ago—whether wisely or not—it was declared, in effect, that gold is no longer money in the actual and practical sense of the word. The money of the nation is that which has been made lawful money by Act of Congress, which has demonetized gold and other coin. He repeated that, practically, what Congress has declared lawful money is the standard of value."

It is to be hoped that a kind Providence will forfend the necessity of any such abominable doctrine being ruled as the supreme law of the land. But while the question remains in abeyance, whether gold or paper is real legal tender, (for both cannot at one and the same time be such upon all contracts, especially if their values be widely different) the acts of Congress do have a most blighting effect upon the value of coin.

The great exponent of the principles of political economy, Adam Smith, in an article upon money (Book II, p. 122, Wealth of Nations) lays down the following proposition: "The whole paper money of any kind which can easily circulate in any country, never can exceed the value of the gold and silver of which it supplies the place, or which (the commerce being supposed the same) would circulate there if there was no paper money."

For my own part, I was never a thorough convert to the doctrine here laid down. But in arguing from it at this time, I will allow it to be strictly orthodox in finance. Granting, then, to the learned Doctor the full force of his reasoning, I contend that the American currency is excluded from his rule by the very terms of it. To make the rule binding, he presupposes that "the commerce is the same." This means a free and open commerce between nations, without any hindrances or trammels of customs. If it means anything different from this, the rule would be such an absurdity that no one of common penetration would admit it. To illustrate the rule by an example: suppose that a certain kind of cloth was worth one dollar in London, and the same kind of goods was worth one dollar and a half in New York, in gold; as Dr. Smith expresses it, "the commerce being the same" between the two countries—that is, no duties on either side—then would that style of goods immediately come from London to New York in quantities to supply the demand. The course of commerce would equalize the currencies. Again: suppose that, instead of free-trade, this foreign cloth, on its arrival in New York, was subject to a duty of fifty per cent., or one-half its value, in that case it would not be sent here for market; for the very good reason that it would cost one dollar and fifty cents a yard in gold, and would leave no profit at all, but an absolute loss to the importer; because the American cloth of the same quality could be sold at one dollar and fifty cents per yard. Therefore, Dr. Smith's rule does not apply to nations with high customs' rates.

My opinion is, that a paper currency can be circulated at the par of gold so long as the borrowers furnish strongly endorsed paper to the issuing banks by which means the borrowers throw themselves into the hazard, and are bound to return the same paper the banks deliver them, or other bank notes of equal quality, or, in default, the specie. This form of discounting may be iterated and repeated till the maker and endorsers of the note are all rendered bankrupt, and the bank notes in the meanwhile be circulating at the par of coin, in countries which have customs' rates.*

Suppose, again, that the natural volume of currency, in gold and silver, for the United States, is $400,000,000. (It would not, with a population of thirty millions, exceed this amount, provided that gold ruled at its normal value.) Then, suppose that the currency be diluted fifty per cent. by the addition of $200,000,000 of paper promises, which would bring the currency up to $600,000,000. With a tariff of fifty per cent. upon imports, this expansion of the currency would not stimulate them at all. Therefore, Americans may substitute fifty per cent. of rottenness in their currency, so long as their tariff rules at that, without commerce interfering to put an end to such abomination. Dr. Smith's rule for regulating currency between nations does not begin to apply till the inflation exceeds the rate of customs.

We will make one more case: suppose the natural gold volume of the country be at $400,000,000, and that the inflation by paper is $200,000,000 more, and that com-

---

* Numberless instances have occurred in the history of British banking, in which the notes of individuals without any real capital, and who were from the beginning in a state of insolvency, have continued to circulate for a long period in company with the notes of the best established houses, and to enjoy an equal degree of credit.—*Edinburgh Review.*

merce has no effect to regulate the currency, or bring it back to sound principles, and the banks or the Government jointly or separately inflate the currency still further, say ten per cent. upon the normal value, or forty millions of dollars; what effect will this have upon imports and gold?* So soon as the charges for duties, freight, and all other expenses are paid, then Dr. Smith's rule begins to come in force.

By the addition of forty millions of fiction to the currency after it reached its normal gold volume of $400,000,000, and after inflating it $200,000,000, which would be rendered powerless to the action of commerce to remedy on account of a high tariff, we should then have a currency of $640,000,000. The forty millions, being in excess of the normal or gold volume of the country, and also in excess of the amount of false currency which was protected by our tariff, would immediately begin to act in the manner laid down in Dr. Smith's rule. This forty millions excess would stimulate imports, because it would bring prices higher on this side than in Europe. It would also be dead loss to the country every time it was turned over here and paid for abroad. If it were turned over twice in a year, that is, sold and settled for, it would be a clean loss to the country of 80,000,000 dollars a year in gold; for in settling our imports we must pay for them in gold or its equivalent. Our gold would go from us without any value, as we make prices of goods on a false basis. However, the injury to the country at large would not be measured by this loss. The inflation in prices would bear upon American goods as well as upon those imported. Now all of this unnatural, abnormal price is devouring our substance, taking our gold without return of value, and only multiplying bankruptcy.

It is useless to add that a high tariff is a direct incentive to smuggling.

The tariff bolsters a rotten currency in direct proportion to the amount imposed. If fifty per cent. be the rate

* I have omitted the charges of freight, custom-house drayage, etc. These all should be reckoned to buoy the rotten currency. I am only examining tendencies.

of the tariff, then fifty per cent. may be added to the normal volume of the currency without commerce having any tendency to check the abomination. Furthermore, all the expenses of freight, boxing, drayage, appraisal of goods, packages, and every form of cost which attaches to the transportation of goods, operates in the same manner as the tariff to protect a rotten currency.

When the currency becomes inflated beyond the protection which the tariff and the expenses of importing give it, then, and not till then, do the salutary rules of commerce begin to operate. Thus we see that a high tariff and a rotten currency work together, and consume the wealth of the nation, while a gold currency and free trade are linked with honesty and the highest prosperity of the country.

Upon all the currency which banks can circulate they make their interest, which goes to swell their dividends. Suppose that their issues are two hundred millions more than they have cash means to meet. They make twelve millions a year upon such over issues; but the people lose ten times this amount. These losses fall upon all the business of the country. They are sustained by the false prices which they create, and the body politic is continually paying them. If a man earns two, five, or ten dollars a day, one-third of it must go to pay for the additional charge which this system imposes. So far as it is paid, it passes into the vast mass of the transactions of the country, and is not recognized. So far as it falls upon solvent men, it is paid till it makes them insolvent. So far as it falls upon insolvent men it must be balanced in bankruptcy. The banks protect themselves by double and treble endorsements and collaterals; the solvent endorsers must pay up; so that upon the honest gains of trade and industry, and the coercive action of securities given to support bankruptcies, the nefarious system of demonetizing gold and monetizing paper is kept up, in a constant round of bankruptcies and changes of property, the result of which is ruin at home, and the possession of our gold without an equivalent by foreign nations with which we hold commerce.

The annual gross products of the United States, estimated in specie are as follows :

Agricultural and forest products..........	$1,700,000,000
Manufactures..........................	980,000,000
Mineral products.......................	75,000,000
Fisheries	13,000,000
Profits from foreign commerce, imports and exports.............................	190,000,000
Earnings from domestic commerce, coastwise, inland, and local.................	1,500,000,000
Average yearly increase in value of domain, roads, canals, dwellings, etc............	2,400,000,000
Total..................................	$6,858,000,000

Probably nine-tenths of these products are consumed in the country; the balance remains in permanent improvements and articles for shipment abroad. In distributing this immense amount, it is easy for shrewd managers of money—which is the medium through which exchanges are largely effected—to keep out of sight the action which inflation of currency has upon all this vast amount of commodities and wealth. If the currency maker can only get a small commission for his medium of exchange, he is coining money out of his tax upon the commonwealth. All the bankruptcies in the currency, and the bankruptcies which a rotten currency necessarily imposes upon the public, must be balanced from the gains and industries of the people and the general products. And every dollar which circulates as money beyond the normal gold amount for the country is an annual tax equal to or exceeding the amount of such circulation, which the people pay in extra prices and successive bankruptcies. These prices and bankruptcies are so inseparably interwoven with the inflated currency that it is impossible to discover them; and the distribution of so vast an annual amount of wealth greatly facilitates this public imposition. But upon the value of gold, this system of using a false currency tells with fearful effect.

If California must lose so much of the value of her gold by reason of the tariff for uses abroad, she ought at least to have its full value for domestic uses. Gold is money at home for the payment of duties on imports, and for interest upon a part of the national debt. Can any one be so oblique in perception as not to discern how demonetizing gold for all other purposes at home strikes at its value? The use of an article constitutes its value. If a substitute for three-quarters of the flour which our people consume could be found, what would be the effect of it upon the value of this article? Flour would fall so low that our farmers could not afford to raise wheat. Iron and Coal are the staples of Pennsylvania. Let Federal legislation be instituted, which would bring into disuse three-quarters of the amount of these staples in the markets of the United States, and see what a hornet's nest would be stirred up among the good people of that Commonwealth.

But, in addition to all other acts of Congress against the value of gold, the Gold Act of June, 1864, was the crowning act of fatuity. Congress has seemed to regard gold as an enemy almost as obnoxious as the leaders of rebellion. Such views of matters which pertain to our fiscal relations are truly unfortunate for the country. If the selection of gold, among all the metals of earth, and by all civilized nations, for money be unwise, then let the organic law, which forbids any and every State making anything but gold and silver a tender in payment of debts, be amended. But while this law stands in full force and virtue, let not Congress stultify itself, and work ruin among the people, by enacting laws which conflict with the supreme law. But even the law which allows gold to be money for the payment of duties is qualified by another act, which allows the issue of deposit certificates for gold coin, and it allows these certificates to be issued for twenty per cent. more than the amount of gold deposited. These certificates are receivable in payment of customs. This amounts to allowing that fraction of the duties to be receivable in deposit certificates which do not represent gold in the treasury.

The Loan Act of 1863, commonly called the "Nine Hundred Million Bill," enacts as follows. Sec. 5. *And be it further enacted:* That the Secretary of the Treasury is hereby authorized to receive deposits of gold coin and bullion with the treasurer or any assistant treasurer of the United States, in sums not less than twenty dollars, and to issue certificates thereof in denominations not less than twenty dollars each, corresponding with the denominations of the United States' notes. The coin or bullion deposited for or representing the certificates of deposit shall be retained in the Treasury for the payment of the same on demand. And certificates representing coin in the Treasury may be issued in payment of interest on the public debt, which certificates, together with those issued for coin and bullion deposited, shall not at any time exceed twenty per cent. beyond the amount of coin and bullion in the Treasury; and the certificates for coin or bullion in the Treasury shall be received at par in payment for duties or imports." The Treasury may issue twenty per cent. more of gold certificates than the amount of gold deposited; and these certificates shall be received as coin for interest on the public debt; then the holders may again pay these certificates into the Treasury for duties. Here is another stab at the uses of gold for money. Why are these certificates issued beyond the gold deposit? Gold is, from all these sources and causes, shorn of fully one-half its normal purchasing power in the markets of the United States. Its uses are substituted by paper certificates, not fully representing it, even for duties and interest on the public debt.

In one respect gold differs from all other forms of wealth in the country. The wisdom of our forefathers made it the legal tender of the Union. They gave it this character in the organic law. While that law remains binding, Congress may have the right to enact most tyrannous legislation against other forms of wealth, and not trample upon the Constitution, which they swear to uphold and defend; but they have no right to touch this form of national money. And yet, to vilify the power and uses of gold has seemed to be one of the cardinal objects of their legislation. This policy, however it may be viewed by other States, whatever may be deemed the necessity for instituting or continuing it, is diametrically opposed to the interests and prosperity of California. The State would have no reason to complain, however, if her staple,—gold—was not protected by the Constitution. Such protection being guaranteed to her by the highest law, it is her right to insist upon this law, and if it be impossible to give her the protection which this law creates as her right, the principle should be acknowledged by Congress, and she should have an equivalent in some other form. It is not the interest of California to economize gold, nor is it for the interest of Pennsylvania to economize the use of coal. So far as their general use goes they stand upon a par. But while there is nothing in the Constitution which would forbid Congress to stop the use of coal in the United States, there are positive provisions in it which will and ought to continue the use of gold as the legal tender on all debts.

No Californian can be true to the interest of the State who does not adhere rigidly to the constitutional principle of gold as the legal tender. And in the long run, no doubt, the same principle holds good in regard to the whole Union. No man can be true to the best, permanent, enduring prosperity of the Union who opposes gold as the proper legal tender of the country, or who would substitute in its place any other form of currency. The losses of California on gold, by reason of the tariff, are sufficiently onerous in all reason. To reduce the value of her staple one-half in the home markets, is not only flatly against the supreme law, but it is a grievance which, if the people could rightly apprehend, would be deemed intolerable. Now that our bonds are going abroad so rapidly to adjust commercial balances, the home market should swallow up the whole product of the mines in gold and silver; and every dollar of metal taken out of the mines should for ever sink one dollar of the paper promises, never again to be put forth as currency unless based dollar for dollar upon gold coin. We should "make hay when the sun shines," according to the adage; and while our shipments of cotton and other produce ought to balance all our imports without a dollar of gold—surely, in addition to these, an annual placing of two hundred millions of our Government bonds abroad, ought to suffice for our most reckless extravagance. The imperative interest and necessities of the country demand that every dollar of the yield of our mines in gold and silver should remain in the country, and retire and cancel a dollar of the circulation built upon the Government bonds. The home market should be constant until we have amassed, in addition to the stocks now on hand, four hundred millions of dollars in gold coin. The policy of the Government should be openly proclaimed, and the people should know that it is the purpose of Congress to make gold worth its normal amount, by suppressing all paper circulation not based on it, dollar for dollar. There is an article in Hunt's Merchants' Magazine, Vol. LIV, No. 2, upon "The Balance of Trade," written by C. H. Carroll, Esq., of Massachusetts. The importance of the principles which he there elucidates cannot be over-estimated. In point of real utility to the opulence of the nation they are far in advance of the uses of the Atlantic cable to America. This writer discusses the subject from a national stand point; and I think he proves satisfactorily that by the "addition of dollars of debt to our currency," we throw away capital and stop an equal amount of production, thus making a double loss. I have frequently discussed this subject from a California stand point during the past decade, and shown that the prices which we paid for commodities, before the war, in the old States, were advanced by the action of paper money forty or fifty per cent,* and that it was possible for prices to be advanced just equal to the tariff upon goods manufactured at home, without any check by reason of imports. Mr. Carroll's article corroborates my views, and is put forth in so plain and logical a manner that I will copy from his paper.

"The community possessing the most capital in relation to population will have the cheapest capital and the lowest general prices, unless their value are disorganized by a false currency, or artificial arrangement and restrictions of trade, and they will have the advantage of all the rest of the world in foreign commerce. With lower general prices they will produce cheaper than other communities, their foreign adventures will cost less and bring greater profits; and these profits will appear in an excess of imports. This is the true balance of trade; it is no

---

* See "Steamer Bulletin," December 5, 1859; also December 20, 1859; also the "Daily Times," March 10th and 19th; April 5th and 20th, 1860; also "Alta California," March 8th, 1861, and August 2d, 1862; also "Hunt's Merchants' Magazine," vol. 43, No. 6, p. 705; "Morning Call," March 20, 1860.

debt, but a balance of profits ; an accumulation of capital in foreign trade.

" England has this 'balance of trade' in her favor ; hence her continued excess of imports, and this excess will continue to increase under the free trade system and limited currency ; while under our high tariff exclusive system and expanded currency we shall have the 'balance of trade' the wrong way in excess of exports, giving England the advantage in international commerce continually.

" A relative of the writer traveling in Europe at this time says he has purchased four suits of clothes for ninety dollars in London which would have cost him two hundred dollars in New York or Boston, as he took particular pains to ascertain the prices here before he left home. This, allowing fifty per cent. for the premium on gold, is obtaining a value of one hundred dollars by our gold measure, for sixty-six and 67-100 dollars in England. Suppose this to be the average rate at which the necessaries and conveniencies of life can be obtained in England, as compared with the United States, then it is not merely possible but probable that a cargo for export may be obtained in England for sixty-seven thousand dollars that would return the value of one hundred thousand dollars, yielding thirty-three thousand dollars profit in the excess of imports over exports ; while a cargo of the same relative value here would cost one hundred thousand dollars in gold, and return simply its cost. Hence England would make a profit of thirty-three per cent. in foreign trade, where the United States would make nothing at all. Yet if the Custom House records even exhibit an excess of exports, it does not follow that there is any absolute loss to this country in the business, since we export overplus products only, and whatever we obtain for them, more or less, is in a national point of view clear gain. That is to say, we support ourselves, pay all our expenses of living and of production, and have these surplus products left. They are of no value, except for export, and the returns they bring us are therefore national accumulation and profit.

" An explication will make this point clear, and show the fallacy of this doctrine of the balance of trade. Let us suppose that by an expansion of currency through banking, or government paper issues, we make general prices here fifty per cent. higher than they are in England; it would follow that the same quantity of labor and capital which would produce a barrel of flour in this country for six dollars would produce the same value in broad cloth, say a yard, in England for four dollars; in other words, there would be this difference in prices for the same value in the respective countries of all commodities. Then suppose England sends us an invoice of 1,000 yards of broad cloth, which is entered in our Custom House records at the aggregate price of $4,000, and, being sold here under our inflation so as to produce the net sum of $6,000, we return an invoice of 1,000 barrels of flour at the aggregate price of $6,000; where and what is the balance of trade? There is no such thing. The 1,000 yards of English broadcloth costs the United States 1,000 barrels of flour, and the 1,000 barrels of United States flour costs England 1,000 yards of broad cloth, neither more nor less. The account is closed. England owes nothing for the difference, because values are exchanged, not prices, and this difference of $2,000 is mere price, the result of an artificial depreciation of the value of money in this country. The two nations gain equally by the exchange, since surplus products are supplied to each other of equal value. Money being the thing tampered with by adulteration, remains untouched in this transaction, as between the two parties to the exchange, and has no more to do with the balance of trade than an equal value of beef, or corn, or wine, which remains untouched in either country.

"But suppose, what is very sure to happen, that England takes $6,000 of gold instead of 1,000 barrels of flour for her broadcloth; then she takes our artificially depreciated commodity, and gets $6,000 of money for a real money value in broadcloth of $4,000, which we raise in price to $6,000 by adulterating our currency. She thus gains $2,000 of *value* that we lose by our own folly. This is a balance of trade that is better missed than found. Its advocates, however, call it national gain. I know what I say when I call it a dead loss; we might as well plunge two thousand dollars of gold into the sea.

"Unpracticed thinkers find some difficulty in comprehending that the dollar is not a fixed value. Make it of gold, or make it a promise to pay gold, interchangeable with gold, and men of whose intelligence better things should be expected fail to discover that an increase of supply depreciates its exchange value, precisely as every other instrument or object of commerce is depreciated in value. The dollar being the currency unit, the depreciation of its value exhibits itself only in the rise of general prices, and more dollars must be given in exchange for other values than before. When we add dollars of debt to our currency, interchangeable with dollars of gold, until six have no more purchasing power than four possessed before, it is inevitable that foreigners will take our dollars and leave our flour, until it gluts the home market insupportably, or its production is reduced to correspond with the demand. Thus we throw away capital and stop an equal amount of production by the same suicidal act—a double loss, like the difference to a merchant between making $2,000 and losing $2,000, which is $4,000 in his stock account.

"Here an objector may say that with an open commerce gold cannot remain one-third cheaper in one country than in another, which is the same thing as saying that general prices cannot remain one-half or fifty per cent. higher. On this point, what is supposed to be scientific teaching differs from the fact of experience, and as science is simply experience classified, the theory must give way where it is contradicted by the well observed fact. The fact is, that under the operation of a currency of debt, which can be made to suit the interest of its producers, general prices can remain fifty per cent. higher in one country than in another, or in all others, for an indefinite period, sometimes for several years, mainly because most of the values of every country are not objects of international exchange, but in a great degree because the makers of such a currency protect themselves by bond and security against its effects. They lend no value, no capital, but promises which create price without value, and throw upon their debtor the obligation to furnish the value and capital to pay the false price and meet such promises. Generally the currency-maker is protected and paid, but the value which is put in his hands to enable him to redeem his obligation he never loaned. It is robbing Peter to pay Paul, and Peter fails. A price that is not a value may be *kited* in the exchanges of domestic commerce for years, but when its ultimate payment in value is demanded somebody must fail, for a value cannot be paid that never existed. It is, as I have on another occasion remarked, like circulating promises to deliver several Kohinoor diamonds, there being but one in existence. The promises may circulate so long as the issues are protected from an absolute demand for payment; but the one diamond being demanded and sent out of the country because its value is greater abroad than where the spurious promises circulate and cheapen it, the several promises for which there is no diamond to respond must be discharged by insolvency. Whether one diamond or millions of them, one dollar or millions of them, or anything else, form the basis of fictitious promises, a currency so constructed must plunder those who become bound with endorsers to save the issuers harmless. But while the issuers are saved, the currency can be maintained so as to inflate prices not merely fifty per cent. but even four hundred per cent. beyond the natural money value, and yet under specie payment, as the experience of France with Law's banking and Mississippi scheme clearly shows.

"Charles Mackay, in his historical sketch of the Mississippi scheme, says:

'The looms of the country worked with unusual activity to supply rich laces, silks, broad cloths, and velvets, which being paid for in abundant paper, increased in price four-fold. Provisions shared the general advance; bread, meat, and vegetables were sold at prices greater than had ever before been known, while the wages of labor rose in exactly the same proportion. The artisan who formerly gained fifteen sous per diem now gained sixty.'

"This four-fold rise of general prices was nothing but a fall of three-fourths in the value of money, and the cheapened commodity. Money rushed out as fast as foreigners could pour other capital into France to exchange for it. Edicts of the Governments, the most despotic, and persecution the most odious, were powerless to prevent this. Plate and expensive jewelry were secretly sent away to England and Holland, and ludicrous devices were adopted to escape the vigilance of the Government. 'Vermalet, a jobber who sniffed the coming storm, procured gold and silver coin to the amount of nearly a million livres, which he packed in a farmer's cart, and covered over with cow dung. He then disguised himself in a dirty smock frock, or blouse, and drove his precious load into Belgium. From thence he soon found means to transport it to Amsterdam.'

"Notwithstanding every effort to the contrary, the precious metals continued to be conveyed to England and Holland. The little coin that was left in the country was carefully treasured or hidden, until the operations of trade could no longer be carried on."

This article shows that a debt currency works a total loss of all the gold we send abroad. We get our pay in extra price of goods instead of real values. If Congress would make Mr. Carroll a present of one hundred thousand dollars for this demonstration, it would be but a small consideration for its value to the nation, provided the wisdom of his argument can be adopted and acted upon by the National Legislature. The gist of the matter then is this: that by allowing the existence of a currency based on debt, we lose the whole value of our gold shipped to foreign countries. This is the loss from a national stand point view. The loss to the gold-producing States is exactly what goods and commodities are advanced beyond the prices they would stand at if gold were the only currency in use. Hence it is, both for the interest of the Union at large in general, and for the interest of the Pacific States in specialty, that the system of debt currency be banished from existence. The permanent prosperity of the Union at large, and of the Pacific States as gold-producing, are concurrent and identical. It is for the interest of the Union to have a currency of intrinsic value, and it is for the interest of the Pacific States that gold and silver be made currency.

There can be no reasonable objection to the Eastern States getting our gold in the course of trade, if they give us a just equivalent for it; but if they get it through the action of legal tender laws, or the law of Congress making the National bank circulation a legal medium of exchange, without possessing the value of the coin of the mints, or without representing it, dollar for dollar, then the Government is imposing upon this State an intolerable grievance. The assumption that gold is obtained cheaply in the State has no relevancy to the premises. As well might Congress make laws to reduce the value of the wheat raised in the North-Western States, because the soil is favorable to the production of that grain, as to take from the value of gold produced in California, because it is reputed to be obtained cheaply. So long as we have a Constitution, each State is entitled to all the guarantees and immunities of that instrument; and if it is proven that gold is not the proper or best money for us, our remedy is in amending that instrument, making nothing but gold and silver a legal tender. Until this is done, California has the right to the whole value of her gold, and what this value would be if gold were the only currency in use, as equitably and justly as she has to what she receives for it now, under the tyrannical acts of Congress against its normal value.

It is enough, in all reason, that gold is shorn of one-third or more of its value, for uses in the markets of the world, by reason of the tariff, without reducing its value by a larger fraction for domestic uses as money.

The Hon. Secretary McCulloch, in his report to Congress, December 4th, 1865, has illustrated this matter of prices of commodities with marked ability and perspicuity. I will quote from his report:

"If the war could have been prosecuted on a specie basis, there would doubtless have been a considerable advance in the prices of those articles which were in demand by the Government; but inasmuch as in the condition of our political affairs extensive credits could not have been established in Europe, the tendency in this direction would have been kept within reasonable check by the outflow of coin to other nations, which would have been the natural result of the advancing prices in the United States. On a basis of paper money, for which there is no outlet, all articles needed for immediate use, of which it became the measure of value, felt and responded to the daily increase of the currency: so that rents and the prices of most articles for which there has been a demand, have been, with slight fluctuations, constantly advancing from the commencement of the war, and are higher now, with gold at forty-seven per cent. than they were when it was at one hundred and eighty-five. Even those which were affected by the fall of gold upon the surrender of the Confederate armies, or by the increased supply or the diminished demand, are advancing again to former if not higher rates. The expansion has now reached such a point as to be absolutely oppressive to a large portion of the people, while at the same time it is diminishing labor, and is becoming subversive of good morals.

"There are no indications of real and permanent prosperity in our large importations of foreign fabrics; in the heavy operations at our commercial marts; in the splendid fortunes reported to be made by skillful manipulations at the gold room or the stock board; no evidence of increasing wealth in the facts that railroads and steamboats are crowded with passengers, and hotels with guests; that cities are full to overflowing, and rents and the prices of the necessaries of life, as well as luxuries, are daily advancing. All these things prove rather that a foreign debt is being created, that the number of non-producers is increasing, and that productive industry is being diminished. There is no fact more manifest than that the plethora of paper money is not only undermining the morals of the people by encouraging waste and extravagance, but is striking at the root of our material prosperity by diminishing labor. The evil is not at present beyond the control of legislation, but it is daily increasing, and if not speedily checked, will, at no distant day, culminate in wide-spread disaster. The remedy, and the only remedy within the control of Congress, is, in the opinion of the Secretary, to be found in the reduction of the currency."

The fact is here eliminated by the highest financial officer of the nation, that goods were higher with gold at forty-seven per cent. premium, than they were when it was at one hundred and eighty-five.

It will be seen at once from these premises, with what

momentous force the demonetizing of gold, by the Congress legislating paper substitutes, has acted upon its domestic value. It is impossible to determine the loss with precision, but it may be very safely put down at fifty per cent., or more. This makes a loss upon gold for domestic uses of one-half at least. We have then these results: Gold is shorn of more than one-third its value for uses in the markets of the world, by reason of the tariff; and it is shorn of one-half its value for domestic uses by monetizing paper. Query: Has California any right to find fault with such infliction?

However, the demonstration that the tariff takes one-third from the value of gold for uses abroad, and the joint action of the tariff, the legal tender acts, and the National Bank Act take fifty per cent. from its value for domestic uses, by reason of the advanced prices of commodities, would have but little influence upon the legislation of Congress, since our delegation in Washington have never deemed the subject of sufficient importance even to speak of it in that august assemblage. The ball must be put in motion by external agencies. Whatever the sins of California may have been, by reason of using three or four months' product of her gold mines during the war as her currency, (while it is acknowledged by all that gold coin is the constitutional currency of the Union) the error, if it were one, can not be amended in time of peace. The war is past, and the fact that California adhered to gold payments through the contest is matter of history. In times of peace, the Legal Tender Acts and the National Bank Act may be viewed in their economic bearings upon the weal of the people from a peace stand point. If the Federal Government deem the weal of her Pacific possessions of too little consequence to merit any special regard by way of fostering legislation, the joint welfare of the Union and these possessions should certainly claim the protection of such legislation. If the interests of the Union at large and those of California are concurrent and identical, these interests should not be sacrificed to favor banking monopolies. That these interests are concurrent is evident, for these reasons. The demonetizing of gold works immense losses to California. Viewed from a national stand point, it works immense losses to the Union at large. The proposition which is before the nation for discussion is this: That the organizing of State or Government debts into currency makes an annual national loss equal to the entire annual yield of our mines in gold and silver.

The National banks have never been under specie payments, or even any approximation to it. Hence we must try the proposition by the old State bank systems. In discussing the subject it is not necessary to go back of the year 1848, which was the year of finding gold in California, and which made the United States essentially a gold-producing country. If her fiscal relations had then been sound and proper, we might now have in our currency at least one-half of the whole yield of our mines. But her legislation was inefficient, and Congress left the subject in entire neglect.

The action of the tariff upon prices is such that the currency of the country may be inflated to the same per centage as the rate which the tariff raises. Thus, if the tariff yields fifty per cent., the currency may be inflated fifty per cent., and the banks continue specie payments nominally all the time, and their circulation pass at the par of gold. Under the old State bank system this process was going on constantly from 1848 down to the time of the Southern revolt in 1861. The constant influx of gold from California enabled the banks to "turn the corners," and keep the ball rolling. The fact being established that banks can circulate, at the par of gold, an amount of currency in excess of the normal specie volume, where a high tariff is enacted, and that such circulation may be continued for a long time, especially in a gold-producing country like the United States, is abundant reason for believing, that the banks did take advantage of this permission to make currency, and did from the year 1848 to 1861 continue their inflation of the currency to the extent which the various tariffs allowed and gave them immunity for such acts of disorganization.

During the year 1857, the United States imported $360,890,141. They exported the same year, in coin and bullion, $69,136,922. These imports were largely on foreign account. The sales were made in the United States for the benefit of foreigners, and the prices were made by the existing currency of the old State banks, nominally at the par of gold, but really and in fact inflated beyond the gold price as much as the respective tariffs and the whole yield of our gold mines could buoy such inflated currency. But to make a liberal allowance upon the imports of that year, suppose that one-half were sold in the country for foreign account, and the other half was imported by American houses. Upon the half which the American houses imported the importers and banks would make the profits—the importers, by the high prices which a vitiated currency enabled them to sell at, the banks, from the profits upon the circulation of some forty to sixty per cent. beyond the normal specie volume. These drains would be taken directly from the people by false prices. The importers would remit enough to cover the cost of the goods, the balance would be their profits. But upon that part of the goods sold for foreign account, how would the trade stand? Suppose that $180,000,000 were sold for foreign account, or one-half the imports for 1857; by the action of the tariff these goods would be advanced say (on the average tariffs from 1848 to 1861) forty per cent., and by the action of a vitiated currency, passing constantly at the par of gold, they would be advanced some forty per cent. more. The nation would lose outright, then, forty per cent. upon the $180,000,000 imported for foreign account, or $72,000,000. This last amount is total loss to the country; it is lost through a false currency entirely, and the loss is almost equal to the gross annual product of gold and silver in the nation. The action under the National Bank Law will be even more onerous to the people than under the State banks. The tariff is much higher, and their monopoly of circulation is raised to three hundred millions of dollars, whereas the old State bank circulation was in 1860 only two hundred and seven millions.

It is impossible to compute the precise damage of the old State bank system to the body politic. That it was immense is beyond all controversy. The National bank system will be no improvement unless the principle of circulation be abandoned, and issues of currency be strictly limited to the gold coin which is held for their security. Is it wisdom for the United States to give to foreigners $72,000,000 a year in gold, for the sake of allowing National banks to make dividends of twenty-five per cent.? This is the question now before the nation, and they must decide it for themselves and posterity. The interests of California and the Union are identical.

No. X.

BANK CIRCULATION.

In every system of banking which has existed in the United States, except the Savings' banks and the banks of California, the principle of circulation has been one upon which these institutions have relied for a large share of their profits. The circulation is of a two-fold nature. It may be called outside and inside circulation;—the outside consisting of bills of credit which banks pay out, and the inside being their deposit accounts. If a bank discounts a note to a dealer, and pays him in its bills, these bills, while they remain out of the bank, are outside circulation. The bank draws interest upon them so long as they are out of its vaults, and the vaults of its redeeming bank. Again: if a dealer gets a note discounted in a bank, and, instead of receiving the proceeds, orders them passed to his credit to be subject to his check, the bank receives interest upon this credit until it is checked for; this is inside circulation. Ninety per cent. of the circulation of the banks of the City of New York comes from the deposit account, or inside circulation. The country banks, on the contrary, depend almost entirely upon their outside circulation. The principle upon which circulation is based is this: a certain amount of money is imperatively required in the channels of business. The banks being the depositories of the money of the country to a great extent, and also having the monopoly of issuing a species of promises to pay money, these promises take the place of real money to just the extent which these institutions can keep them out. While the bills are in the hands of the people they regard them as money, and pay interest upon them as though they were the best form of currency. Some of the paper champions contend that there is the same danger in hard money currency as exists in one of credit ; and that the supply of money might be in excess of the demand if it were coin, as well as paper. This objection to coin, as money, is of no consequence, and for this reason : the precious metals have intrinsic value, and can be used in the markets of the world, and they are certain to be so used whenever any country holds them in excess of their demand. Not so with a money whose vitality is only galvanized by legislative enactment. Such form of money has no value except in the country which institutes it ; and even there, its value exists by its power of working mischief and disorganization. By the action of this cheap form of money the real coin goes to the markets of the world, but the local money—the promises to pay dollars which do not exist—remains in the country which tolerates such imposition. After the real money is driven from the country by the action of this false substitute, the "promise money" being the only form of money remaining, and the necessities of the people for some form of currency to pay debts and as a medium of exchange being constant and pressing, it follows, that the people are compelled to accept such currency as exists. By repeated trials, the banks find very nearly what amount of circulation they can sustain ; and when they are fully certain of this, they make no hesitancy in issuing such amount to their customers : for they find that as fast as it comes in at one end of the counter for redemption, it goes out at the other for circulation. The only question with them is, what amount of circulation can we safely sustain? which, put in another form, is this—How far can we dilute currency without being caught and arraigned for this nefarious business? The advances in the price of property, and the general bankruptcy which the system inevitably inflicts upon the commonwealth, are matters of no concernment to them. How much can we keep out and turn the corners safely, is the extent of their patriotism and the bounds of their political economy.

Bills of credit circulate in the marts of commerce when the issues are not excessive, the good, bad, and indifferent passing with equal facility. The old State banks understood this matter well, and they followed with the scent of a bloodhound the wretch who should presume to infringe their prerogative of supplying the public with promises to pay dollars that never existed; and when caught, the counterfeiter had about the same chance of escape as a lamb would in the jaws of a hungry wolf. What is the difference between the issues of the old State banks and the issues of counterfeiters? Just simply this: that these banks held the law between themselves and destruction, while the counterfeiter knows that for him, there remains nothing but to suffer the vengeance of a violated law. The promises of the banks were all false, except so far as they were covered by specie reserves. This would make about eight dollars of their promises false to two dollars good. But the counterfeit were bad *in toto.* Hence the bank issues were eight-tenths bad and two-tenths good; while the counterfeit was bad entirely. But for a wise, honest, and discreet Government to tolerate either, is a reflection upon its ethics and its efficiency.

Banks should no longer be allowed to receive profits from circulation. It is a dishonest way of making money entirely. Nor is it possible to make money in this way except by inflicting injury upon individuals, or upon the nation, in a far greater amount than the gains which result to the banks by this principle of circulation. If a bank receives interest for money loaned, why should it not loan real money, not promises to pay money which does not exist? However, the blame of the system does not fall entirely on the banks. The partaker is said to be as bad as the thief, in the spoils of dishonesty. If the people will patronize, uphold, protect and defend a system of currency which drives the product of our gold mines to foreign countries, which allows a paper circulation built on debt to usurp the rights of gold and silver as established by our forefathers in the supreme law of the land; if they will do this, there is no alternative—they must suffer the consequences. The objection, that we should have no banks if we restricted the issues of bills to the actual specie reserves kept to redeem such bills, is groundless. Supply would follow proper demand, in banks as in every other form of business, even if they were tied down to the strictest basis of gold valuation upon all their transactions. I am no friend of high rates of interest upon money, but it is very certain that we had better allow higher rates of interest and keep the currency at strict gold equivalents, than to have low interest, and a vile, diluted, vitiated and rotten currency.

If our banks could come more upon the principle of savings' institutions, amassing the small gains of the public in the form of real wealth, allowing low rates of interest upon deposits, and loaning these again at higher rates, they would be more useful, in the long run, to the public; their gains would be amply sufficient to justify their continuance in the right path, and yield to their shareholders good dividends.

That banks can do business upon sound principles, and be very gainful institutions, without circulating notes, is abundantly proven by the California institutions. Some will object to the sequence of this position, because this State produces gold, while other States produce wealth in different ways. It is sufficient answer to this to say that nearly one billion of dollars of gold have gone from California to the old States, and that it only needed proper and salutary legislation on the part of Congress to have had the entire circulation of the banks covered, dollar for dollar, with gold coin in the treasury. It is their own *lache*, or fault, or ignorance, or obstinacy, or pertinacity in adhering to a currency built upon a different foundation, that the currency is not now equal to gold coin. The people are their own sovereigns in this matter, and if they will sow to the wind they must expect to reap in such kind as they scatter broadcast.

Every county or town in the United States with a population of three or four thousand ought to have a savings' bank, not to print and circulate promises to pay dollars that do not exist, but to amass the small increments of gain of the people, to pay a low rate of interest upon these gains, and to loan them again at higher rates upon good securities ; to stimulate the industry, economy, and prosperity of the country in general.

Let Government institute such legislation as shall make the circulation of bills of credit a criminal offence, placing it in the same category as counterfeiting the national coin, and the country will soon be filled with savings' banks, whose capital will be real cash, their loans and deposits consisting of this solely and entirely.

When I can see that it is so easy for my countrymen to have their money in real cash, instead of sending the reality all to foreigners and accepting the shadow to do business upon themselves, I can scarcely treat the matter in proper measured terms. With an annual yield of $75,000,000 from our gold and silver mines, why need we suffer the immense losses which attach to having a currency worth only sixty to seventy cents on the dollar? If no other good comes from the distresses of the people, it is to be hoped that their experience will lead them to study the causes of their impositions, and apply the remedy which will be efficient in the premises.

When the aggregate mass of currency which circulates in any country does not exceed the natural amount which would circulate therein in gold and silver, the currency does not under these circumstances inflate prices. But if the circulation of paper money has driven three-quarters of the gold and silver out of the country, more or less, this three-quarters, represented by paper money, will continue to circulate at the par of gold, even if it is as impotent as burnt flax. It is against the circulation of such trash as good money that the shafts of Congress should be leveled with deadly aim. Let every thing that passes as good dollars, and upon which banks receive interest as for good coin, be currency of sterling value. Nothing is needed but proper national legislation to effect this salutary reform in the currency.

It is just as practicable for the United States to have a currency based entirely upon gold, dollar for dollar, as to have it based upon national debt. The banks, of course, can not make so large dividends ; but they can do well enough and let their circulation be built on gold entirely. Shall the vital interests of the Union be sacrificed by law of Congress, to satisfy the avarice of banking institutions? *A Dieu ne plaise.*

It is contended by many, who ought to see the operation of cause and effect better, that by circulating a currency which is not based upon gold we gain the whole amount of interest upon such currency, and the business is done as well and far cheaper than though we had a currency of coin, or its absolute equivalent.

Soon after the Southern revolt was conquered, the telegraph wires announced the following fearful accident and loss of life:

"CHICAGO, April 28.—A New Madrid telegram says the steamer *Sultana* exploded and sunk yesterday morning, between there and Memphis. Two thousand exchanged Union soldiers from Vicksburg were on board, with about 1,000 civilians. It is said that not more than 700 were saved."

Who supposes, after reading the above account of this destruction of human life, that this steamer was a proper conveyance for passengers or property? My own opinion is, that passengers had traveled at the imminent peril of their lives and property upon that boat for months before this accident happened. That boat is an apt illustration of the workings of a rotten currency. The boat was liable to explode at any time, and destroy all on board. So a currency that is not based on gold may collapse at any unusual pressure, and although it might not be so destructive to life, it would be incomparably more ruinous to property and business in general.

There is no more saved, then, by making a currency upon any other basis than gold, in the business world, than there would be by transporting passengers in a boat which was entirely unsafe. The owner of the boat might make money, but the passengers would be, or would run the risk of being killed outright, or having their property destroyed. And in the case of the currency, the banks which issued it would make money till it collapsed, but the holders and all who leaned upon it, would be swept away in the financial ruin. This principle of rottenness in the circulation (and it commences the moment that issues are made by banks beyond the amount of gold and silver to cover them) is what underlies the whole. How, then, can economists contend that the body politic can gain any thing by diluting the currency, or making it rest upon any thing but coin in equal amount? You might as well say that steamboats can be made too safe as that paper issues of currency can be.

But *in a gold-producing country* to allow the currency to be diluted with paper demonstrates that the people are ignorant, dishonest, or reckless. We should have very little charity for a farmer who raised wheat enough annually to make thousands of barrels of flour, and who had not the wit to save enough of it for his wants, but actually often went hungry himself and allowed his family to do so.

The Americans, by their system of banking, give their gold to foreigners, and leave for themselves the shadow—the promise of gold, executed by corporations which they know do not possess it. For these promises they give their notes, endorsed once or twice over, while the pressure and ruin must fall on the people before the banks are reached. And this currency, men who claim to be sound economists will contend is equal to gold, because it is secured on Government bonds, payable twenty or forty years ahead.

A metallic currency is the only one which never oppresses the people for redemption. It is a perfect antidote to all monetary panics; being value in itself, it needs no redemption. Why cannot our people see this, and lay by enough of the national coin to move all of their industries? The currency will certainly fill up with coin, or its equivalent, if the Federal Government will unflinchingly insist that the dollar shall be worth one hundred cents in gold coin—no more, and no less. To do this, it will be necessary that *all the profits of circulation shall be done away with*, and that banks make no form of currency of less value than the coin of the mints.

Some economists and casuists are so radical as to contend that interest should never be paid for money; but for real cash, I see no reason why its owner may not exact increase for its forbearance, being real capital, as well as for any positive benefit granted by one citizen to another. If one citizen lends another a thousand dollars, and he invests the money in sheep which double its value by increase, in three years, I see no hardship in the borrower dividing his gains with the lender, who has furnished the means for him to make them.

The difference between lending real cash and a substitute is this: that real cash builds up business upon a sound basis, while the "promise money" is destroying regular business, and fostering speculation and gambling. The one is conservative and healthful in its operations, the other is pernicious and disorganizing. Hence, interest may be paid for real money without injuring the commonwealth; but when paid for false currency, it is wholesale spoliation, and works unbounded mischief.

Whenever it comes to pass that all currency shall be coin, or represent coin, *the amount of paper issues will be most essentially lessened;* business will be done more with real cash; and private banks, receiving deposits of coin and discounting and loaning real money, will spring up in all parts of the country. The volume of currency will fill with the coin of the mints, and the monetary affairs of the nation be conducted more like the banks of California—upon gold coin—than upon the impotent and dishonest systems which have heretofore disgraced the American public. But, to achieve such salutary reform, the laws of the land must foster the public desire to return to honest principles, without regard to the profits of banks, and without regard to their opposition. The savings' banks of the country are of vastly greater importance than all the banks of issue.

The principle of securing bank circulation upon stocks is precisely the same as the old New York general banking law—the difference between Government stocks and State stocks of some of the old and wealthy States, being a difference in name rather than in material and essential fact. This principle was a demonstrated failure in 1857, and the civil war proved it entirely powerless to give efficient aid during the progress of the contest. But the consequence of having such an impotent financial system—a system which doubled the expenses of the war—is enough to condemn it for all time to come. And this is the very system, with some few changes, which the Federal Government have re-organized in the National banks.

Now, I maintain that the Government has no right to organize any such system of currency as the one under consideration. The Constitution gives the Government the right to coin money and fix the value of it. Also, it gives the right to punish all counterfeiting of the coin. And, as currency bears the same relation towards genuine coin, and unfixes the value of such coin in exactly the same manner as the circulation of counterfeit coin does, it follows that if a currency of paper is a national necessity, Congress has the right to control such currency.

However, if such paper currency is not "bills of credit," (which the Constitution forbids States to utter, and which in the convention that framed the Constitution was voted should never be issued, by Congress itself) but bills of substance, representing gold coin of an equal amount in the Treasury of the United States, then such form of currency cannot act upon the value of coin to unfix it. This is the only regulation of currency which can keep it at the real par of gold; and the only sure way for the Government to guarantee this is to insist on a deposit of coin in the Treasury, dollar for dollar, to protect the issue.

The guarantee of the Government to pay the issues of the National banks, because they have deposited a portion of the public debt for security, is neither reasonable nor constitutional. Government has no right to issue, or to allow others to issue under its authority, any form of currency worth less to the dollar than the issues of the national mints, or less than the par of gold. Therefore the only power that Congress has over the currency is to keep it at all times, and under all circumstances, at the par of gold coin. If it does not exercise this power over currency, its power to fix the value of coin is virtually nullified, and the people must suffer immensely for the neglect.

In regard to bank circulation, however, there is one point which is material, and cannot be too forcibly impressed upon the minds of the people and our legislators. It is this: that banks should never be the custodians of the specie upon which their circulation is issued; for if they have the right to issue currency, it is clothing them with an attribute of sovereignty; and no matter how strongly they are bound by law not to issue beyond the amount of their specie on hand, they would abuse the trust, so surely as frailty is the inheritance of human nature.

The power of making the prices for all property in the commonwealth is one of immense magnitude, and should never be vested in corporations or individuals. Such power attaches to making currency which is designed to circulate as a medium of exchange; and before such currency should be put forth, the coin should be deposited in the Federal Treasury for its redemption.

No. XI.

GOVERNMENT CIRCULATION.

The principle of circulation being founded upon the laws of trade which require a certain amount of money to move the industries of the nation, it becomes a question of moment whether any part of this circulation should be based upon credits; and if so, whether the gains of these credits should inure to the benefit of the nation, or to the benefit of the National banks.

The regulation of the currency belongs to Congress incidentally only, because the power is expressly delegated to Congress "to coin money and regulate the value thereof" by the supreme law, and because it is utterly impossible to regulate, that is *to rule, to govern, to control*, the value of coin (which is its purchasing power or its exchangeable power, to command other forms of wealth) without ruling and controlling the issues of promises to pay coin which are designed to circulate as money. Congress, therefore, has no power to issue or circulate as money any form of currency which infringes the value of the mint coin, which interferes with its purchasing power, or which drives the coin from the country. It is a common opinion that the Government ought to receive the gains which the banks receive from circulation; but the truth is, neither the Government nor the banks should be allowed to receive gains from any such source. If the Government receives the gains from circulation, the people lose it, many times over, in advanced prices upon all commodities. If the banks receive these gains, the people are equally the losers. The difference of gain, by saving the interest upon three hundred millions of currency, to the Government, would be but a sorry compensation for the damage to the public in advanced prices.

But the principle of establishing a currency which is not immediately convertible, by the Federal Government, is a revolutionary one—demoralizing and disorganizing in the extreme. The way I view it is like this: the National banks are the creations of Congress, and subject to any terms that may be imposed upon them by that body. It cannot be apprehended that the people of the United States, in the nineteenth century, with the lights of sound economical science shining upon them as clear as the sun in his meridian splendor, with gold and silver mines yielding an annual product of $75,000,000, will long remain satisfied with banking institutions founded upon principles which are bound to drive this treasure from the country, to the great damage of the nation, and to the building up of foreign countries, and foreign wealth, at the direct cost of our own prosperity. The people will be very willing to see the remedies applied by Congress, however it may interfere with the exorbitant gains of these institutions. But the withdrawal of the treasury notes—commonly called greenbacks, irredeemable and inconvertible except into national bonds—is more difficult to manage. In my opinion the abomination can only be put down by depriving them of their legal tender character, either by the Supreme Court or Congressional enactment. That they do most materially interfere with the value of gold, is beyond all question. We can never build up commerce, manufactures, agriculture, mining wealth, or any of the great industries of the land, with a currency so widely different in value to the coin which that currency promises. It is for these reasons that I would recommend the annihilation of the legal tenders as fast as possible, and the commencement of specie payments on the part of the banks by compulsory process. The Government should not circulate any form of money worth less than one hundred cents on the dollar, and it should bring the banks upon this basis as soon as possible. When it does this, the superiority of having the currency under the governance of one legislature will be apparent to all; and until it does this, it is derelict in duty to that clause in the Constitution which requires of Congress to fix the value of the mint coin.

The legal tenders should be withdrawn as fast as they can be put into national bonds. But as legal tenders, *so far as the national currency is legal tender*, they might remain such for and during the time it might take the Government to call them in and cancel them. As a tender between citizens, however, they should be immediately and totally shorn of any such power. This would also compel the banks to a speedy resumption of payments.

The National banks owed, at the last official statement, on demand $901,558,020, and held in coin only $8,170,835. What a pyramid of credit to contemplate as our currency! It is high time for Congress to take the matter in hand, and let these currency-makers know that, in time of peace at least, their promises to pay dollars, upon which the public is paying them interest, must have some definite and tangible meaning—that the legal dollar must mean the coin of the mints, and nothing else.

In regard to the government issues being entitled to priority to the National banks—the Government being entitled to the circulation rather than the banks—it is sufficient to answer that the honor of the country is at stake in the matter, and the Government should never disgrace itself by so flagrant an act as the issue of an irredeemable currency; nor should it set such a corrupt example for the imitation of its citizens.

Furthermore, the circulation of the National banks is now fully up to three hundred millions of dollars, being the full amount allowed by the Bank Act. The circulation of the State banks in 1860 was only two hundred and seven millions. The State bank circulation and the deposits acting as circulation, were then extended as far as it was possible to inflate under the existing tariff without general chaos and financial ruin to the country. The Na tional banks can exceed the old State banks circulation $93,000,000, and the power of making an internal circulation, through the deposits, is greater even than under the old State bank systems.

Now, when we consider the baneful effects of any circulation beyond the normal specie volume, and the power and practice of the National banks, which actually circulate nearly one hundred millions more than the old State banks circulated, besides the generally admitted fact that deposits are currency as efficiently to make prices as bills in circulation, it will be seen at once that if the National bank circulation and power to discount upon deposits are to be continued, the question of any further circulation by the Government is not only absurd, but such circulation must be most thoroughly ruinous to our national prosperity. (See pages 64, 65, 73, 97, 109, 153, 155, *et passim.*)

No. XII.

THE SALES OF GOLD BY THE SECRETARY OF THE TREASURY.

The sales of gold, made in pursuance of the order of the Secretary of the Treasury, between the 2d of February and the 23d of May, 1866, amounted to $50,495,000; the premium on the sales was $16,391,418. The aggregate sales during the fiscal year have been about $100,000,000. The premium upon the former sales I have not the statistics to present. These sales of gold are highly condemned by some, and by others are considered judicious and discreet. The public are not always cognizant of the motives which guide the actions of our chief in finance, and the wisdom of the measure must be judged by its result. Whatever may be said in favor of the sales, it is evident that the Secretary was unfortunate in the time of selling; this, for the very obvious reason that gold ruled from twenty-five to thirty per cent. higher than he sold at, within two weeks after he closed his sales. If the sales had been deferred, the premium would have been more than double what was realized.

The importing business in the United States is largely done on foreign account. The wealthy foreign merchants have their business agencies in our commercial cities, and through these factors make sales of their merchandise. The sales are made for currency, and the prices are proportionate to the value of such currency. If, then, after these foreign agencies have sold their goods for currency, the Secretary intervenes, and offers to sell gold at twenty-five per cent. less than its real relative value to such currency, it is a gift outright of that much to these importers. Gold should never be sold by the Treasury to buoy paper or to depress it. The only honest way to make paper equal to gold is to regulate the issues of the paper, and limit these to the amount of gold deposited for their redemption.

Gold, at best, has to labor at immense disadvantage to sustain its value; for the paper circulates at the par of gold, when banks are under nominal specie payments, inflating all forms of prices, while the gold is being shipped abroad to pay for imports. No doubt, it is a worthy motive to bring all of our currency up to the value of gold, but it is a most unwise act to try to bring our gold down to the value of greenbacks, or National bank currency. In the cant of Wall street, the "bulling" of greenbacks for the sake of "bearing" gold is a forced operation—unnatural, violent, and its effects can be none other than abortive to produce any permanent good. The coin of the Treasury should never be used for any such purpose. Gold should never be sold to force down its own value.

To me it seems that the excess of gold taken by the Customs, above what is required to pay the interest on the coin portion of the public debt, might be used in a manner immeasurably more advantageous to the Government and the people than to sell it. (See page 127.)

The Loan and Treasury Note Bill passed by Congress, February 25, 1862, has these provisions:

Sect. 5. All duties on imported goods shall be paid in coin, or in notes payable on demand heretofore authorized to be issued, and by law receivable in payment of public dues, and the coin so paid shall be set apart as a special fund, and shall be applied as follows. First: To the payment, in coin, of the interest on the bonds and notes of the United States. Second: To the purchase or payment of one per centum of the entire debt of the United States, to be made within each fiscal year after the 1st day of July, 1862, which is to be set apart as a sinking fund, and the interest of which shall, in like manner, be applied to the purchase or payment of the public debt, as the Secretary of the Treasury shall from time to time direct. Third: The residue thereof to be paid into the Treasury of the United States. Now, if this bill is not already equal to empowering the Secretary with the authority to coerce specie payments by the banks, a very slight change would make it such.

Let the Secretary be empowered to use the whole excess of gold in the Treasury beyond the amount required for interest on the public debt, in the payment and canceling of the bonds which are deposited as security for the issues of the National banks. Let these payments be made as fast and as often as possible, the Treasury holding the gold as security for the bank circulation in lieu of the Government bonds. This would make the bank deposits with the Treasury the first portion of the public debt to be paid. And, as I have fully demonstrated this subject in an article on the resumption of specie payments, to which I would call the careful attention of that portion of the public who desire prompt specie payments again, it is not requisite to extend the argument. (See pp. 124 to 129.)

While our debt is going abroad so rapidly in payment of imports, we should be using the whole yield of our gold and silver mines in bringing our currency up to the Constitutional requirements, so that nothing shall pass for a dollar which is not worth fully one hundred cents in coin. The excess of gold from the Treasury, applied as above stated, would compel specie payments in two years, and would give an entire specie basis for our whole circulation in four years. And is not this "a consummation most ardently to be wished" by every friend of the nation?

I now purpose to make a special use of the facts above stated, and to add some further premises to them. The Secretary has sold gold and gained by the sales to the country, if currency be equal to gold, $16,391,418. If currency is not equal to gold, he has made nothing by the sales. The law of Congress makes the Treasury notes "a legal tender in payment of all debts, public and private, within the United States, except duties on imports and interest" on the public debt. The Secretary has been purchasing greenbacks at large discounts; or, conversely stated, he has been selling gold coin at thirty per cent. premium. This is tantamount to canceling a part of the debt at large discount. The question then comes up: has the Secretary taken from the people the above sixteen millions and more without an honest consideration, or is there a real difference in the value of the two currencies? Again: the people of California give in their incomes upon a gold basis. The Collector adds to this twenty-five per cent. to bring it equal to currency. And the income tax is collected upon this advanced sum; here, again, the question comes up: are the two currencies equal, or does the Government act arbitrarily in advancing the incomes twenty-five per cent. to make them equal to currency? To my mind it is clear as the noonday sun in his splendor, that there is nothing like equivalents between the gold dollar of the mint and the paper promise of the printing press. And yet some of our learned courts have so far stultified themselves as to decide, that they not only ought to be, but are equivalents; and that it is the action of brokers, gold speculators, and sharpers, that keeps the hiatus between gold and the greenbacks.

In the two cases above cited, I maintain that the Government does make an open, wide, and undoubted distinction between the dollar of the mints and the dollar of the printing presses. This distinction is made because it is matter of fact that it exists. The use I would make of the argument is, that Congress cannot too soon repeal the Legal Tender Act, and allow the citizen to deal with citizen, and to bind each other to the contracts which they may make respectively; and that the laws, if they do not already, should immediately be framed, so that contracts for gold can be coerced by law in any State of the Union.

The wisdom of Congress should never be stultified by enacting absurdities or impossibilities. Legislating values as equivalents, which are not such in fact, can never make them such. What intelligible idea would one get from such positions as these?—White is equal to sour. Benevolence is equal to a burr millstone. No comparison can be instituted between these qualities or entities. Yet Congress assumes to legislate a position almost as absurd—that is, promise is equal to reality—promise shall be the absolute equivalent of gold coin.

A promise is *not even comparable with value,* as an equivalent, unless it be strictly the truth. And what is the corollary?—that the Government issues are only equivalent to gold to the extent that they are convertible. Consequently, the sooner Congress makes our Statutes at Large conformable with the irrefragable laws of value, in the matter of currency, the sooner will order begin to come out of chaos, and the nation be once more in the way of truth and justice.

The sales of gold cannot be used in any way to promote a more permanent and thoroughly useful reform than in paying off the national bonds pledged for security of the bills of credit now circulated by the National banks—the Government holding the gold coin for security instead of the bonds. (See page 127.) This will stop the interest on the bonds; do away with the odious monopoly of the National banks, which are allowed to deluge the country with their issues, receiving interest upon the same and also interest on the bonds, thus taking double interest for the privilege of demoralizing and confusing the whole monetary system of the nation.*

---

* The following monetary article, from one of the leading New York journals, was written in March, 1863. It is, however, as true to-day as it was when published. Is the Government determined, now that peace is again restored, to continue a crusade against gold? I quote from the article: "The recent heavy decline in the

The sinking fund of one per cent. per year would go far towards changing the basis of the bank circulation from bonds to coin if it were scrupulously applied

---

currency price for gold, and the sudden and violent fluctuations during the last week in the price of that 'gold merchandise' which the Bank of England is compelled by the laws of Great Britain to buy at a fixed price, at all times and under every change of circumstances, are events well calculated to make the business community cautious and prudent in all their operations. These changes in the price of gold baffle the usual mercantile calculations of legitimate traders. The position of the State of California may be taken as one illustration of the mode by which the changing price of gold affects trade. For example, the last shipment of gold from San Francisco was over $1,200,000, and if it had arrived one week, or even three days, sooner in New York, the shipment could have been sold for about $250,000 more than it was possible after its receipt here. In other words, California could have paid $250,000 more of its indebtedness to New York had the price of gold not declined from 174 to 150. If the act of Congress to restrain loans on gold and tax its sales caused the decline, then is it evident that Government power and influence are exerted to bring down the price, in this market, of the $50,000,000 annual yield of 'gold merchandise,' which is the chief product from the State of California. Governmental interference with trading operations is no more admissible in gold than it is in flour, or any other merchandise. The principle in political economy that produces these laws is in its very essence evil, and the results can be nothing else but evil. Ordinary intelligence and common sense discern in this legislating against gold-dealing the germ of disunion between California and the Federal Government. The whole course of Government and Congress on this financial question has been sad blundering; and this last 'gold merchandise restriction act of Congress' is not the least of the blunders. Upon what principle of equity or statesmanship do Mr. Chase and his friends commence a stock-jobbing crusade to bring down *artificially* the market price of the 'gold merchandise' which California ships to New York? If the price of gold is brought down legitimately and naturally, by removing the cause—that is, by decreasing the amount of Government paper money in circulation—then California loses nothing; but spasmodic jerks up and down, like those of last week, are devices to rob the people and regular merchants, and enrich the few stock-jobbers who may hold confidential relations with the Treasury Department. There is a cause for the premium on gold, and that cause is said by all sound reasoners on political economy to be an excess of irredeemable paper money. If this opinion is correct, then Mr. Chase is trifling with his fellow-citizens, perhaps to their ruin, if they direct their business operations by his statements, when he deludes them with the hope of reducing permanently the price of gold, unless he means to decrease the paper money in circulation."

to that purpose; and surely it can not be applied anywhere else with such signal advantage to the nation. There are five years due to this sinking fund, even now, which should be equal to $125,000,000 at this time.

The highest financial officer of the nation recognizes the difference in value between gold coin and Treasury notes, and confirms this in the most positive manner by buying and selling, making such difference as the laws of trade indicate. Why should the Statutes at Large, then, try to coerce as equivalents in law what are widely varying in the markets of the world? Such legislation is folly or dishonesty, or both of these principles combined. The "war necessity" plea is at an end. When will justice again resume her even beam, and deal between citizens upon the grounds of equity? The Government recognizes the difference between coin and Treasury notes; why should not the citizen have the same privilege, without the possibility of any legal question arising to frustrate the integrity of his purpose?

No. XIII.

WHO OWNS THE GOLD TAKEN FROM THE GOVERNMENT LANDS?

The miners of California have been considered by some as a class of vagrant outlaws—land pirates—trespassing upon the public domain, and removing the wealth of the country purely for their own aggrandizement. It will be well for the Government and people to know the facts in the premises, before so useful a class of men are thus laconically condemned. Among all the industries of the world there are few occupations more toilsome, more wearing to the health and constitution, than the business of the miner. Ten years' constant pursuit of it are enough to break down the strongest man and unfit him for every other kind of labor. While the farmer lasts forty years, the miner is worn out in one-quarter of the time. Such is the tribute of health and toil which the miner must pay to his business. His fare and style of living are, generally, as rough as his toil. The dangers incident to his occupation are far greater than attach to the ordinary pursuits of men. Government has seen fit, heretofore, to allow the miner to enjoy the fruits of his toil in full. Recently, there has been imposed a small sum as a seigniorage upon the assay of the metals. When we consider the wear and tear of the miner's life, the repeated losses, risks, and disappointments which he must endure in fruitless searches, and expensive preparatory investments, before he can get any return for his labor, it is probable that one-third of his earnings, derived from agricultural pursuits, would secure him better living, better health, longer life, more domestic happiness, and every comfort which makes life desirable, than he obtains in mining, even where his returns seem to be reasonably bountiful. The Government has allowed miners to follow their pursuits and make their own laws. These laws are different in various localities, but seem to be adapted to each precinct, and have served a reasonably good purpose. It would be exceedingly difficult—perhaps I might say impossible, for Congress to adopt any suitable code of mining laws. Each locality seems to have some different exigence to the others. But, beyond all doubt, so long as Congress allows the mines to be wrought as they have been for the past eighteen years, the yield of them belongs, by every principle of right and justice, to the toil of the miner. Whether the policy is right, judicious, and wise, of allowing the mines to be worked as they have been, will be a question that time must determine. But so long as the policy is permitted, so long the gold—the yield of the miner's toil—belongs to him in absolute right, as clear and unconditional as the farmer has to reap the fields which he sows. The hue-and-cry of "trespass upon the public domain," "land piracy," and all other opprobrious epithets, are entirely out of place when applied to the miner. His business is as honest, and perhaps as toilsome and dangerous, as the fishermen off the Banks of Newfoundland, or the whalemen of the Pacific Coast. Congress has heretofore given bounties to the fishermen; and are the fish of greater consequence to the people than their money? The codfish of Newfoundland, the whales of the Pacific, and the gold of the quartz mountains, are each its own peculiar form of national wealth. But as the codfish and whales are not available wealth till they are captured, so the gold of the quartz rock is not available till it is sought, found, quarried, crushed, assayed, and passed through the melting pot.

My own opinion is, that the fisheries have a claim upon the Federal Government, far, far below that of the miners; the relative importance of the product of the two industries being placed upon their exact merits, in a national point of view. In short, I consider money is of much greater consequence to the people than whales and codfish. It is of imperative necessity to the Government that the mines be worked. Our national credit almost hinges upon the product of the mines. Unless they are worked, and efficiently worked, bankruptcy yawns before us more terrific than the maelstrom. The Government itself cannot work the mines to profit. If it were to attempt mining, I make no hesitancy in saying, every dollar taken from the mines would cost the people two. Hence, the policy of allowing the mines to be worked freely seems to be the only certain one from whence the Government can avail itself of their wealth. Through the action of trade and commerce, the customs' duties, and the internal revenue and excises, all of the yield of the mines seems to flow to the Eastern States. These States should not expect to get more than the entire product of the mines from us.

There is, however, a gross misapprehension at the East in regard to the gains of mining. In early days the miner could, with a pick and shovel, gather from and near the surface of the ground his ounce or more of gold for his day's work. But those times are passed, and the gold is now extracted from the depths of the mountains, and from the fastnesses of the quartz rocks. In fact, it may almost be said with truth now, that it takes a mine to work a mine. At any rate, the cost of mining is so great, that it would be more politic for Government to foster it by bounties than to hamper it by taxes or excises. After the gold is extracted from the quartz and coined at the mints, the Customs take it, if not entirely, at least nine-tenths of the whole yield.

Every State opposes, and may properly do so, all national legislation which discriminates unjustly, unconstitutionally, or even harshly against its vital interests. The Legal Tender Act virtually demonetizes gold, and by bringing it into disuse as money, acts with intolerable hardship upon the Pacific States in general, and upon California in particular.

There is no doubt but the joint action of the tariff and the Legal Tender Act reduce the value of gold nearly or quite one-half. I have never heard these opinions suggested in Congress, in all the readings of the speeches of our various delegations. In the most excited political campaigns, I have never heard the question asked of a candidate for member of Congress whether he is in favor of hard currency? Our senators have never been elected to attend to the pressing wants of the State—a proper representation of the monetary interests of California, in the United States Senate, and the constitutional rights which the State has to the whole value of her gold, by reason of our constitutional tender being this metal, through the letter of the organic law. The man who is not thoroughly and uncompromisingly a hard money man, is entirely unfit to represent the interests of California in Congress. If gold were money through all the United States, as the organic law makes it, and paper promises, or bills of credit, were suppressed, California would grow rich $25,000,000 a year faster than she is now doing. The interest of all the Pacific States is identical in the matter of currency. Why has this vast interest never been represented in Congress?

No. XIV.

THE INDEPENDENT TREASURY.

In the year 1833, under the administration of President Jackson, the national deposits were removed from the United States Bank, which had been the fiscal agent of the Government, and were placed within the custody of the *pet banks*. In turn, these *pet banks* became the fiscal agents of the Government. The amount of deposits, at the time of this transfer of funds, was over forty millions of dollars. These *pet banks* were expected and required by the Government to discount freely to the people, in order that they might supply the deficiency of currency which was rapidly being canceled by the winding up of the affairs of the United States Bank. This increased volume of currency, resulting from the lavish discounts of the pet banks, enabled the other local banks to expand their issues in a corresponding ratio. Such excess of currency increased the imports, and enabled the mercantile classes to effect large sales of goods. An astute writer upon the subject has thus graphically described the consequence of this redundancy of the currency: "A perfect mania for speculation in every thing, and especially in real estate in villages and cities, and in the public lands, seized the minds of men, and the current carried along with it many of the most cautious and careful business men in the community. Immense quantities of lands belonging to the United States were sold to speculators, and paid for in moneys either directly or indirectly obtained from the pet banks. This money was paid to the receivers at the several land offices, and by the receivers deposited in the banks, when the same money was perhaps on the same day re-loaned to the land speculator, who again, with that very money, purchased other lands, when it again passed through the same process. To check, if not to put a period to this ruinous system, General Jackson, on the 11th day of July, 1836, issued his celebrated specie circular, by which he directed the receivers of money for the sale of the public lands not to receive anything in payment but gold and silver coin. This, together with the distribution of the surplus in the treasury, produced a revulsion tremendous in its consequences. A law or resolution was passed by Congress which nullified the specie circular, but General Jackson, that man of '*the iron will*,' refused to carry it into effect, on the alleged ground that it was indefinite and uncertain. The rage for the purchase of public land still continued, but the operation of the specie circular on the purchase of those lands produced a constant drain of gold and silver from the vaults of the banks. To add to the difficulties and embarrassments, the Bank of England, alarmed at the condition of the monetary affairs in America, refused to discount for the American bankers in London and Liverpool, and for the houses engaged in the American trade. The pressure began early in the year 1837, and by the first part of May, when a great amount of bills drawn by the New York merchants upon their correspondents, and on houses in which they believed they had credit in England, were returned protested, the distress became extreme. A delegation from the merchants in New York was sent to the President, (Mr. Van Buren) who requested him to rescind the specie circular, and to delay the collection of bonds given for duties. He complied with the last, but denied the first request. Immediately on the return of the delegation, all the banks in the city of New York, and within a day or two afterwards all the banks in the United States, suspended specie payments. At that moment they held in their coffers forty millions of dollars, which they had received in trust, and which belonged to the United States. By the condition of the charters of all the banks in the State of New York, a refusal to pay in specie their notes on demand was declared to be a forfeiture of their charters. In the present emergency they applied to the Legislature, then in session at Albany, praying the passage of a law authorizing them to suspend the payment of their notes for a limited time. The

R

Legislature granted their request, and on the 16th day of May enacted a law that 'every provision of law in force requiring or authorizing proceedings against any bank in this State, with a view to forfeit its charter or wind up its concerns, or which requires such bank to suspend its operations and proceedings in consequence of a refusal to pay its notes or evidences of debt in specie, is hereby suspended for one year.'"

The late Hon. Silas Wright, in a pamphlet styled "The Probable Continuance of the Suspension of Specie Payments by the Banks," held forth the following memorable arguments: "The incorporated banks have vast privileges, and still more important exemptions. Their privilege of issuing, by express authority of law, their paper promises to pay gold and silver on demand as currency, to take the place of gold and silver in the hands and pockets of the people, is nothing less than the delegation to them of one of the most delicate, important, and responsible prerogatives of the sovereignty of any civil government. Their exemption from liability to pay any description of their debts, beyond the mere amount of stock paid into the bank, is an invidious privilege to these artificial corporations over those extended to natural persons, the citizens, and free men of our country, which would startle every honest mind, not familiarized by custom and use, to the legislative preference for soulless paper existences, over the persons of God's creation, with hearts, and souls, and consciences, and at least some sense of moral obligation. The only real consideration to the community for this privilege of creating currency on the one hand, and exemption from liability for the most just debts on the other, is the single, simple, and most just obligation to pay on demand, *at the banking-house*, the gold and silver for their promissory currency, their bank notes, which are mere promises to pay gold and silver. The bank that issues notes which it cannot redeem in specie, while the obligation to pay specie imposed by its charter remains unannulled by legislation and unrevoked by the bank, practices a fraud upon the public, for which a natural person would be convicted of the crime of swindling, and have a cell assigned him in some one of the public prisons provided for the punishment of high crimes against the peace and safety of civil society. As we have receded from the days of the revolution, the sufferings of that period, and one of the most severe among them was a depreciated paper currency, have become dim in the recollection, and in just about that proportion we have increased our banks and our paper circulation. Now we have a revulsion entirely universal, and that immediately succeeding a period of prosperity such as no country upon the face of the earth ever before experienced, and without any national calamity of any character whatsoever preceding or accompanying it, with which it can be in any possible way connected. It has proceeded wholly from our trading, excessive speculations, and all kinds of extravagance consequent upon excessive banking, and the cheapening of credits in every department of business. All the banks have suspended specie payments, and we have an inconvertible currency depreciated, upon an average, full ten per cent. below the par value of money." The suspension of specie payments above described was 10th May, 1837. Another suspension of vastly increased proportions took place October 13, 1857, while agriculture, commerce, and manufactures were in a condition of unbounded prosperity. In addition to this, the mines of California had yielded over $600,000,000. On the 21st of November, 1860, the officers of the banks of the City of New York came to the conclusion that a committee of five persons be appointed to receive some of the best securities which the banks had to deposit; and thereupon the committee was to issue certificates to an amount not exceeding $5,000,000, which certificates were to be guaranteed by the banks jointly, and to be receivable at the Clearing House as gold. If this was not a virtual suspension of specie payments, it came so near to it as to have a decided tendency in that direction. It should be remembered that for a long time before this expedient, the banks had been bruiting their vast resources of gold. The *ruse* saved them, in the same manner as the Bank of England was saved from suspension in 1857, by issuing notes beyond the limitation of its charter. We have had suspensions of the banks at various times for the past fifty years, occurring about every ten years. In 1847–8 the banks were saved from suspension of cash payments by the timely occurrence of the Irish famine, which brought us gold and the right to draw exchange to the amount of $40,000,000. We have had the old United States Bank, which has been twice, most emphatically, put down by the suffrages of the people. We have had the New England system, which requires the capital stock to be paid in cash, but allows the cash to be abstracted and paper substituted, as soon as the cashier has made oath that a per centage of the capital stock has been paid in. We have had the safety-fund system of New York, which applied a small per centage of the profits of the banks towards constituting a fund for the redemption of the bills of any failed Bank under that act. A fair trial has demonstrated this system to be wholly unequal to the purposes of its institution; for, after amassing the gains of the fund for about ten years, the failures of two or three small banks in the northern part of the State completely absorbed the fund, and the billholders and depositors suffered loss. Lastly, as the crowning work, the *chef d'œuvre* of all inventions for making money out of debt, instead of gold, we have the New York general banking law, allowing the deposit of State stocks, and bonds, and mortgages, as a proper basis for the security of the redemption of currency in gold. This, too, has failed in 1857; partially, at least, in 1860; and most thoroughly in 1862. The United States bank and branches have not been equal to discharge the duties of a fiscal agent to the Government and people. The *pet banks* had a short run of it, and made but a wretched substitute for the old United States Bank. They owed the Government forty millions of dollars, and suspended cash payments; about thirty millions of these deposits were afterwards distributed among the States, and, in all probability, will never be restored to the Federal Treasury. The Pennsylvania United States Bank, under a State charter of $30,000,000, undertook to wind up the affairs of the old bank; and, in doing so, resolved itself into a factorage house for the purchase and sale of cotton, and of the State stocks of the new Western States. Its end is matter of history. The whole capital was sunk, and the billholders and depositors were great losers. The leading genius of that institution boasted, after the charter was secured from the Legislature of Pennsylvania, that he preferred it to a charter under the Federal Government. The poor man died demented.

Why is it that all these systems of banking have been failures in part, or in *toto?* Because they have attempted impossibilities. They have tried to make a currency of something which they called equal to gold, and based it upon credit, alias upon nothing, and sworn to the people that it was as good as gold. Now, what is the remedy for this awful disease that is dementing the minds and robbing the wealth of the people? Retrace your footsteps —go back to first principles; make the currency gold, and only gold; or paper, which represents gold in the hands of safe and responsible custodians. The paper minters have ruled for more than half a century; let the bullionists hold the reins for the next fifty years: they cannot make matters worse. The volume of currency in the nation is not of half the importance as the purity and standard of its sterling value. Degrade the value of gold by any alchemy of banking, and you make all business gambling. Fixity in the currency, so far as to really represent what it purports to, is as needful as fixity in the yard-stick, the half-bushel, the pound-weight, the gallon measure, the carpenter's rule, and the surveyor's chain: and, further, degrade the value of gold, and you banish it from the country; for gold flies from paper as honesty eschews gambling. The Hon. Silas Wright, in reviewing under the head of "the duties and responsibilities imposed upon the National Government by the suspension of specie payments by the State banks," makes these pertinent and forcible remarks:

"That the only currency known to the Constitution is a currency of intrinsic value, a metallic currency, a currency of coin according to the value placed upon it by Congress, is a fact too plain for contradiction or question. Congress derives no power from that instrument, to make, to establish, or to regulate the value of any other currency, nor is anything else recognized therein as *money.*

"Another duty imperative upon the Government, and much more interesting and important to the people, is that of a paternal guardianship over the rights and interests of the governed; and as one of the most vital among those rights and interests, the protection and preservation, by all the ways and means in its power, of the integrity, stability, and value of currency. That the power exists to require that the currency of the National Treasury shall be according to the value of the currency created and regulated by Congress under the express grant of power contained in the Constitution, no one, we trust, does or can doubt. It is the constant and continued and unvaried exercise of that power which we ask, and we do demand it. We know that it has been asked by some if there should be established for the Government a better currency than is allowed to the people. We answer, No! The thing is impossible. The currency of the Government is the currency of the people, as the Government itself is the Government of the people.

"If the Governments, State and National, require a sound currency for themselves, and provide for and secure it by their legislation, that same legislation will provide for and secure a sound currency for the people; the currency provided for, authorized, and sustained by law for the Governments will be the currency of the people; but when either or both Governments shall legislate for and permit, for their uses, an unsound and depreciated and inconvertible currency, the currency of the people must also be unsound, depreciated, and inconvertible.

"Among the responsibilities of the Federal Government, that of keeping safely the monies collected from the people so that they may be ready, at the calls of the public treasury, without subtraction or depreciation, stands prominent. At periods, when a proper relation exists between the revenues collected and the wants of the Government for expenditures, this responsibility may be discharged without difficulty or danger; but when over-trading in foreign merchandise, or over-speculation in the public lands, swells the sources of revenue greatly beyond the wants of the Government, it becomes one of great difficulty, delicacy, and hazard. The evils which destroy the equilibrium tend necessarily to impair the safety of the ordinary and natural depositories, the banks of the States, and offer temptations to unfaithfulness to individual guardians, should such be selected.

"Another responsibility resting upon the National Government is that of guarding and preserving, even beyond the reach of just suspicion at home or abroad, the credit of the United States as a body politic. This high trust can be but very imperfectly discharged, and cannot be discharged at all to the benefit of the people, for any length of time, with a disordered and depreciated currency sanctioned by its authority. In 1791 a National bank was resorted to as a means of extrication from the derangement of the currency and the great depression of public credit consequent upon the war of the Revolution. The charter expired on the 4th of March, 1811. In 1816 another charter for such an institution, to continue for the term of twenty years, was obtained from Congress. This second charter expired 4th March, 1836, and since that time the State banks have again been made the depositories of the public treasure, and the fiscal agents of the public treasury. A selected number of these institutions first received this high trust from executive order and regulation only, but a subsequent law of Congress sanctioned and adopted the system, and prescribed rules and limitations for it. It is important for us to notice but a single provision of this law, and that provision is, that no bank note shall be received in payment of dues to the Government, or paid out in discharge of debts due from the Government, which is not convertible into gold and silver coin at the will and pleasure of the holder. Under this law, with this provision incorporated in it, all the existing deposit banks accepted their high trust to the Government and people of the country, and received some forty millions of the public treasure; and yet, strange to tell, before a single twelvemonth had passed away, they all refuse to pay gold and silver for their notes. Nay, more, and further, and worse, they even refuse to pay to the Government anything but their own irredeemable notes, those notes which the law above mentioned prohibits the officers of the Government from either receiving or paying out, for the millions entrusted to their safe keeping. Still further, the drafts of the Treasurer of the United States, drawn upon a deposit bank for a mere trust fund, belonging to individual citizens, which fund was by the

Government imported from abroad in gold and silver, and in gold and silver placed in that bank for safe keeping, have been dishonored and returned without payment, because the holder of the drafts would not receive the irredeemable bills of that bank in satisfaction.

"These violations of law and contract by the deposit banks have compelled an extraordinary convocation of Congress, that measures may be adopted to relieve the Treasury from the embarrassments resting upon it from the provisions of the deposit law, and the failure of the banks to comply with their obligations.

"What ought Congress to do? is the great question. Can a National bank be resorted to, *even if it could remedy the evils we suffer?* Twice such an institution has been tried, and twice have the people pronounced their verdict that it shall not have existence within our confederacy; that its powers to produce expansions and contractions in the currency, and over tradings, speculations, panics, and pressures, are much superior to its powers to regulate, restrain, or sustain our circulating medium; that the political dangers and evils arising from it to the purity and stability of our free institutions, far outweigh any promise of benefits; that the Constitution of the United States has not conferred upon Congress any power to charter such an institution, and that no such charter shall emanate from the hands of their representatives. The voice in which this last verdict was so distinctly and clearly pronounced yet sounds in our ears, and warns us against repeating this doubly condemned experiment. Shall the State banks be further continued as public depositories and fiscal agents of the Treasury? Shall millions more be entrusted to these institutions, which refuse to respond for what they have received for safe keeping, except by their own irredeemable and faithless promises to pay? Shall Congress recede from the ground it has taken, that the debts of the nation shall be paid in a currency equivalent to specie, and convertible into specie at the will of the holder? Shall it legalize as currency, and establish as the circulating medium of the National Treasury the irredeemable notes of the State banks, and import gold and silver from other countries to be exchanged for such a *miserable representative of money?*

"We will not stop to argue a position which seems to be so plain, as that these banks have forfeited all further confidence from the Treasury, and cannot be relied upon as its fiscal agents.

"What, then, can Congress do? We answer, try the yet untried expedient. Produce a perfect and entire separation between the finances of the nation and all the banks of issue, *or discount*, however or by whatever authority existing; between the National Treasury and the artificial creations of legislation upon which we have hitherto unfortunately attempted to depend. We have tried the faith of these *soulless existences* in all their forms of being, and that faith has always failed us in the hour of utmost need. *Now* let us try the faith of natural persons, of moral, accountable agents, of freemen. Let Congress trust the safe-keeping of the public treasure with citizens, as such, and not as bank corporators—*with men responsible to itself*, and not to a moneyed institution. Let collections into the National Treasury be collections of *money*, or its equivalent, not of irredeemable paper; and when the Government owes a citizen, let him, for that debt, be able to obtain *money*, and not inconvertible bank notes. We are told, and no doubt truly, that the connection between the public Treasury and the banks has aided to produce the excesses we now so deeply deplore. *Let not the Treasury again contribute its agency to such severe inflictions upon the people.* When duties are to be paid to the Government, let them be paid in fact, not practically credited by a system of deposits in banks, which enables the merchant to withdraw with one hand what he places in the bank with the other. If lands are sold, let the money paid for them be retained by the Government to which it belongs, until its wants shall call for its use. Explode the mischievous doctrine now so generally promulgated, that the merchant, or the speculator, *has a right to the use of every dollar of money in the National Treasury*; and, when over-trading shall unduly increase the revenue from customs, or mad speculations swell the amounts received for sales of lands, let the accumulations of cash capital in the Treasury check these excesses, before their bitter fruits are realized, as now, in the destruction of credit, the derangement and depreciation of the currency, the depression of property, and the prostration of business generally."

These were the sentiments of that giant mind, Silas Wright, and are found in chapters VIII and IX of his Life, written by Mr. Hammond. Mr. Wright was chairman of the committee on finance, "and reported to the Senate a bill for establishing an Independent Treasury." Senator Benton added his testimony and influence to the reform. In speaking upon the bill, he says:

"The old confederation was often reduced low—often near empty-handed—but never saw itself stripped in an instant, as if by enchantment, of tens of millions, and heard the shout of triumph thundered over its head, and the notes of exultation sung over its supposed destruction! Yet, this is what we have seen—what we now see—from having surrendered to corporations our moneyed independence, and unwisely abandoned the precise advantage which led to the formation of this Federal Government. I do not go into the moral view of this question. It is too obvious, too impressive, too grave, to escape the observation of any one. Demoralization follows in the train of an inconvertible paper money. The whole community becomes exposed to a moral pestilence. Every individual becomes the victim of some imposition, and, in self-defence, imposes upon some one else. Thus, pecuniary, political, and *moral considerations* require the Government to retrace its steps, to return to first principles, and to restore its fiscal action to the safe and solid path of the Constitution. Reform is demanded. It is called for by every public and every private consideration. Now is the time to make it. The connection between bank and State is dissolved by operation of law, and by the delinquency of these institutions. They have forfeited the right to the deposits, and lost the privilege of paying the revenue in their notes, by ceasing to pay specie. Now is the time to act; this is the moment to restore the constitutional currency to the Federal Government; to restore the custody of the public moneys to national keepers; and to avoid, in time to come, the calamitous revulsions and perilous catastrophes of 1814, 1819, and 1837." (See Debates in Congress, vol. XIII, pages 389–390.)

Such were the pressures of the times which compelled the institution of the Independent Treasury by the Federal

Government. At that day it was regarded as sufficient if the Government took care of itself; and, no doubt, it was concluded by the friends of the Independent Treasury that if the connection between the banks and the Government were effectually severed—if their promises were no longer to be received in payment of duties, or the national revenue, such disability must achieve their downfall and ruin. But in this the friends of the measure had misapprehended the power which the immunity of making paper money confers upon banks. And although the Independent Treasury was a decided step in advance upon the matter of reform, still the experiment has demonstrated that, with more than 1,500 banks printing paper promises to pay dollars, these promises have ruled prices—have done the business of money—have made merchandise of our gold and banished it to foreign countries—have doubled our commercial debt—have doubled our war debt, over and above what it would have been under a gold currency; and hence have shown that, to give to the people and to the Government, either jointly or separately, the full advantages of the Independent Treasury, its provisions must be extended to the perfect reform of the national currency. It is but a small fraction of the good which the Treasury of the nation might be made to confer upon the people, to collect, keep, and pay out in coin the receipts of the revenue, so long as it is compelled to pay out this coin at the price of paper—so long as paper rules and makes laws for gold. Therefore, Government should be compelled to make the reform as efficient for the people as for itself; for if Government allows the debasement of the value of gold by the existence of illegitimate bills of credit, it neither renders its duties to itself or the people.

The action of a currency theoretically convertible into coin, while it is not really so, dollar for dollar, and under all circumstances, is precisely the same as the circulation of counterfeit coin which passes undetected. If the counterfeit coin passes, it makes prices for property and degrades gold. So of bank notes and credits, any beyond the point that the issuing bank holds specie to convert such notes and credits. And hence it is just as much the object and duty of Congress to regulate and purify these bank issues and credits, and to keep them within the exact limits of the coin which they possess for redemption, as it is to collect and disburse the gold of the revenue through the Treasury. And without such regulation by Congress of the *whole currency*, the Government cannot avoid paying out its gold at the price of paper, which is, of course, at a great depreciation on its exchangeable value ; or at what it would command in the marts of the Union if it were left to rule prices by the simple law of supply and demand. Hence, for self-protection even, nothing short of a thorough purification of the currency, *for the people as well as for the Government*, can save the Government from the immense loss of paying her gold on all undertakings and contracts at precisely the ruling of this trash called bank notes. She owes it to herself for self-protection : she owes it to the people, as the dispenser of that fostering aid which the Constitution invests in her, to call into exercise the industries of the Union at large. And, if the Government fails in this cardinal point of duty, the wealth of our country is left a prey to the avarice of foreign commerce.

The opinion of Daniel Webster upon the currency is pertinent, and I will quote from him in corroborating my position. He says :

"The power over the coinage is not the strongest, nor the broadest ground on which to place the duty of Congress. There is another power granted to Congress, which seems to me to apply to this case directly and irresistibly, and that is the commercial power. The Constitution declares that Congress shall have power to regulate commerce, not only with foreign nations, *but between the States*. This is a full and complete grant, and must include authority over everything which is part of commerce, or essential to commerce. And is not money essential to commerce? No man in his senses can deny that; and it is equally clear that whatever paper is put forth, with intent to circulate as currency, or to be used as money, immediately affects commerce. Bank notes, in a strict and technical sense, are not, indeed, money; but in a general sense, and often in a legal sense, they are money. They are substantially money, because they perform the functions of money. They are not like bills of exchange or common promissory notes, mere proofs or evidences of debt, but are treated as money in the general transactions of society. They pass under a legacy, or other form of gift, as money. And this character of bank notes was as well known and understood at the time of the adoption of the Constitution as it is now. The law, both of England and America, regarded them as money in the sense above expressed. If Congress, then, has power to regulate commerce, it must have a control over that money, whatever it may be, by which commerce is actually carried on. Whether that money be coin or paper, or however it has acquired the character of money or currency, if, in fact, it has become an actual agent or instrument in the performance of commercial transactions, it necessarily thereby becomes subject to the regulation and control of Congress. The regulation of money is not so much an inference from the commercial power conferred on Congress as it is a part of it. Money is one of the things without which, in modern times, we can form no practical idea of commerce. It is embraced, therefore, necessarily, in the terms of the Constitution.

"In reply to my arguments, on a former day, showing it to be the duty of the Government to regulate the currency, (which I can agree with the gentleman in calling the very life-blood of the political body) the honorable gentleman asserts that Government has no right to interfere with individuals. He therefore proposes individual banking, and maintains that credit is a man's private property; that Government has no more right to interfere with this than with any other kind of property; that Government has no right to put restrictions of any kind upon it. But this, which the gentleman asserts is not the right of Government, is the *very* and the *especial* object for which Government is instituted. Government *does* interfere and place restrictions, in a thousand ways, upon every kind of individual property; and it is done, and is necessarily done, by every Government, for the good of the whole community. Years ago, as well as now, we had private banking; everybody turned banker, everybody put out his notes for circulation, till it was at last found necessary to restrain this right, this *very right*, which the gentleman says the Government has not the right to restrain ; a right which, however, has more than once been proved to be, after all, nothing more than the right of practicing fraud and imposition upon the people.

"With respect to the TWO CURRENCIES—one of specie for the Government, and the other of depreciated paper for the people—the reasoning we have heard is this: 'Would you have Government take *bad money* for its dues? If the people are willing to take such a depreciated medium, ought the Government to take it?' This, Sir, is not our point of objection; we do not wish the Government to take *bad money* because the people are obliged to take it. What we complain of is, that the Administration does nothing, and proposes nothing, to make this *bad money* of the people *better*. We want an equality, that both Government and people may share the same fate, and use the same money, and that the Government may perform its duty of rendering the money, the currency of the people, sound and good.

"It is this equality which I desire; not that Government should take *bad money*, but that it should adopt such measures that there may be no bad money to take; that the people first, and then the Government, may have and receive good money. This can only be done by regulating the currency. The power of Congress, therefore, over the currency, its power to regulate *all currency*, metallic or paper, and its power and its *duty* to provide and maintain a sound and universal currency, belong to it as an indispensable and inseparable part of its general authority to regulate commerce." (See Works of Webster, vol. IV, pp. 338, 339, 363, 366, and 368.)

Here, then, we have most unequivocally the opinion of the great interpreter and defender of the Constitution, that the powers and duties of Congress are adapted to this very subject. Its neglect has cost California hundreds of millions of dollars, and the Union at large the whole of the gold which has been shipped to Europe in the last decade.

The only way to make this "equality" between the two currencies of gold and paper, which Mr. Webster urged so strongly, is to limit the issues of paper to the amount of gold coin pledged for its redemption. To do this, however, the Independent Treasury should be divided into two entirely distinct and separate departments; the department controlling the Customs not having anything to do with the department controlling the banks. The deposits of the respective branches should be under separate and independent custodians. This system, once fairly instituted and put into practical operation, would save the gold of our mines in the country, till the volume of currency was completely saturated with specie and gold bills. The Independent Treasury would then be of tenfold the advantage to the people which it is to the Government. And since it has done such wonders for the Government, why not extend its scope, and make it the means of thoroughly purifying the entire circulation of the nation? We have not the excuse for issuing a diluted currency which we had twenty years since. Our mines are amply equal to our most extended wants for circulation, and if we do not secure to ourselves the best currency on earth it will result from our own *lache* or dishonesty.

No. XV.

THE DUTY OF CALIFORNIA IN RELATION TO THE LEGAL TENDER ACT.

To maintain the public credit, it is indispensable that the undertakings of the State upon all matters of finance, shall be promptly and faithfully met, as they fall due from time to time. Economy, retrenchment, and reform, should be introduced wherever the same are practicable.

To keep the debt from increasing is as necessary for the good credit of the State, as the prompt payment of interest and the current expenses of the Government. The debt of California is measured by dollars; and real dollars are made of gold and silver. The staple of our State is gold, and our whole State policy should be to keep the exchangeable value of this gold, when measured by other wealth, as high as possible. The entire cash circulation of the State is less than four millions of dollars, while our mines yield that amount monthly. The constitutional rights of California to demand of the National Legislature that nothing be done to demonetize gold, or lessen its value, and to institute such national legislation as will render it impossible for States, or State institutions, to demonetize gold or lessen its value, are points of relation between the State and Federal Government which have never been discussed by any officer of the State, or member of either branch of Congress. The most vital interest of the State seems to have been ignored at home and at Washington. The yearly produce of gold in California may be safely assumed at fifty millions of dollars. And, since we export this amount of gold yearly, our imports will be more or less valuable, or the amount of goods which we can safely import will be greater or smaller, in proportion as the price of gold rules high or low in the Eastern markets. Money is not only a universal measure of value in all civilized countries, but a universal agent. Whoever possesses money can command, and is virtually the possessor of, any article of necessity or luxury of equal value to that money. Gold and silver being the only money which are recognized by the American Constitution, and the measure of all wealth and values, it follows that any act of a State Government, or of the Federal Government to debase gold, or to demonetize it, is a direct thrust at the vital interests of this State. If gold be reduced in value, it will take more of it to perform the same work. Such reduction would increase our State debt, increase our interest on the debt, without any increase of means to discharge such debt. Even the old States and the Federal Government, hope to return to cash payments upon their indebtedness. But, every one who examines the subject will see that the difficulties of such return to cash payments must increase in direct proportion as they assume debt, and in direct proportion as they depreciate gold. For the past thirteen years California has suffered in silence the infliction which a false currency, used at the East, has imposed upon her commerce. She has imported her goods from the old States, purchased and manufactured under a system of paper money, and invoiced to her under this system of false currency; and those invoices have been recognized as honest and legitimate dealings, and balanced dollar for dollar in gold. Her commerce is restricted to the old States by the American Custom-house. True, she can deal with other nations, but only by the payment of high rates of duties.

Since the year eighteen hundred and forty-eight, California has forwarded to the old States, and the world at large, the immense sum of eight hundred and fifty million dollars. Had the old States used a gold currency, the currency of the Constitution, one-half of her exports of gold would have paid for all the imports of the State, and left enough money in the State to build three Pacific railroads. Here is a useful theme for the contemplation of those who suppose that California is under obligations to the Federal Government. Had Congress regulated the currency of the Union upon the basis of gold, which it was the prerogative and duty of that body to do, in such case, one-half of the gold which California has sent forward would have paid for her imports. Inflated prices from paper money has, for the past thirteen years, (or, until the war broke out, which has demonstrated the difference between gold and paper) robbed gold of a large fraction of its value. It is contended by some that the Government owns the mines; and hence, that the losses on gold by the *laches* of the Federal Government to do its duty on the regulation of currency, so that paper issues and bank credits shall not lessen the value of gold, are not a subject matter which the State may press upon Congress, either for reclamation for the past, or reform for the future. The Government owns the mines, it is true; but its proprietorship is of the same nature as the owners of the treasure which was lost on the Central America several years since. It would cost the owners of the lost treasure ten dollars to recover one; hence the Courts would award the entire salvage and ownership to any individual or company who should recover the treasure. In like manner, if the Federal Government were to institute the business of mining in California upon its own account, it would cost the nation ten dollars for every dollar of treasure that it would develop and secure. The title of the gold mines is in the Government; but the title to the gold, extracted by the toil and money of the miners, is as truly the property of the miner as his coat, his boots, or his bread. It is his by the labor he has expended upon it; by the immense cost of flumes, water ditches, aqueducts, bridges, tunnels, drifts, shafts, steam engines, quartz mills, and all the needful appliances and appointments of the miner, expended by him and at his own risk. It is his by the tacit consent of the Federal Government, which has allowed the mines to be operated without charge, and the miners to make such laws to govern their operations as experience has demonstrated to be necessary. It is his also by the wisest policy which the Government could possibly have adopted: the policy of a strict non-interference with the mines; a policy which has developed them much faster, and secured a much greater annual yield of gold to the country than could have been attained in any other manner. The means of the people are the wealth of the Government; and while the people possess means, the Government can avail itself of those means by taxes, excises, or loans. Any restrictions by Congress upon the mines would lessen the yield of them, and thus lessen the money of the country; for all the yield of the mines goes from us to the East. Such restriction would also be a thrust at one of the vital interests of this State, and should be opposed by our delegation in Congress. The neglect of the Federal Government to do its duty, to excise and suppress the State bank circulation, has interfered most materially with the value of gold through the Union; and the miner has thus virtually paid an immense tax to the old banking system of the East, by loss in the exchangeable value of his gold. For, to the holder of gold it is a matter of little difference whether you take from him one-half the quantity he possesses, or reduce the value of what he possesses one-half. Such was the action of the bank currency upon the value of gold before the war commenced.

But, what right has California to dictate to thirty-two States the currency they shall use? Must thirty-two States bend their institutions and forms of business to one or two States on the Pacific Coast? To this it may be answered, they are not required to bend to one or two States; but, as a member of the Federal Union, California has a right to say, you must bend to the American Constitution, or resist it. If you resist it, you are acting to produce the same result, though in a different channel, as the most rabid Secessionist. The Union and Constitution must stand or fall together. California has the same right to ask protection of the Federal Government, in the matter of currency and the action of State bank issues and credits on the value of coin, as she has to demand protection from foreign foes or invasion of her territory by a public enemy.

At present, the war demonstrates the difference in value of gold and Eastern currency. In the City of New York there has been paid as high as one hundred and thirty-eight dollars of currency for one hundred dollars of gold coin.* And wide as is this difference between the real value of gold and paper, there is good reason to suppose that the maximum of difference has not yet been reached.

An eminent political economist makes the following remarks, which are peculiarly applicable to this State under the present condition of our fiscal relations to the Federal Government: "Let us suppose that the whole circulating money of some particular country amounted, at a particular time, to one million sterling, that sum being then sufficient for circulating the whole annual produce of their land and labor. Let us suppose, too, that some time thereafter, different banks and bankers issued promissory notes, payable to the bearer, to the extent of one million, reserving in their different coffers two hundred thousand pounds for answering occasional demands. There would remain, therefore, in circulation eight hundred thousand pounds in gold and silver, and a million of bank notes, or eighteen hundred thousand pounds of paper and money together. But the annual produce of the land and the labor of the country had before required only one million

* November, 1862.

to circulate and distribute it to its proper consumers, and that annual produce cannot be immediately augmented by those operations of banking.

"One million, therefore, will be sufficient to circulate it after them. The goods to be bought and sold being precisely the same as before, the same quantity of money will be sufficient for buying and selling them again. The channel of circulation, if I may be allowed such an expression, will remain precisely the same as before. One million we have supposed sufficient to fill that channel. Whatever, therefore, is poured into it beyond this sum cannot run in it, but must overflow. One million eight hundred thousand pounds are poured into it. Eight hundred thousand pounds, therefore, must overflow, that sum being over and above what can be employed in the circulation of the country. But though this sum cannot be employed at home, it is too valuable to be allowed to lie idle. It will, therefore, be sent abroad, in order to seek that profitable employment which it cannot find at home. But the paper cannot go abroad; because, at a distance from the banks which issue it, and from the country in which payment of it can be exacted by law, it will not be received in common payments. Gold and silver, therefore, to the amount of eight hundred thousand pounds, will be sent abroad, and the channel of home circulation will remain filled with a million of paper, instead of a million of those metals which filled it before." (Smith's Wealth of Nations, Book II, Chap. 2, p. 119.)

It results from this, that every dollar of paper circulation which California might sustain at the par of gold, would drive a gold dollar from circulation. Hence, a paper circulation can never be of the least use to this State.

If we suppose the currency of the country, before the issue of the Treasury notes, to be four hundred millions of dollars, of which one hundred and seventy-five millions were bills in circulation, and two hundred and twenty-five millions were inscribed credits in banks with all the power and virtue of currency, and that four hundred millions of dollars was all the currency that could possibly be floated at the par of gold; then, that after the country was thoroughly saturated with bank paper, the Government throws one hundred and fifty millions of legal tender notes on to the market, what would be the effect of such issue upon the bank currency and the Federal issues? The joint currency of the banks and Government would then be depressed precisely one hundred and fifty millions of dollars when measured by gold. In this case, gold would stand at a premium of twenty-seven and a half per cent. in currency. These figures are not pretended to be exact, but approximate, and sufficiently so to show the operation of any attempt to float paper at the par of gold, beyond a certain amount, even by the most stringent legislation. The attempt to issue legal tender notes by the Government, is a contest between it and the State banks for the circulation of the country. The Government entered upon the field under the disadvantage that the ground was pre-occupied. The country was thoroughly saturated with bank paper before the Secretary of the Treasury issued a dollar.

It was an impossibility that both currencies could keep afloat at the par of gold. Congress had the power to excise the issues of State banks to such an extent as would have prohibited their circulation. The banks, of course, would censure such a measure, but the people would incline to favor the Government circulation. One great error in the Treasury Note bill is, that it does not excise bank circulation, and bank credits also, beyond the average specie which the banks keep on hand. Beyond doubt, there is not an article in the Revenue Law which could be excised with such signal advantages to the nation as bank circulation and credits. For, putting the very best aspect upon it, all circulation of bank notes as money, beyond the amount of specie which the bank holds, and all bank credits beyond that amount, are a degradation of the national coin, a robbery of the honest gains of industry, and, in its practical operation on the body politic, precisely analogous to the action of alloying the legal coin with brass or copper. By such debasement prices advance most fearfully, the expenses of the war are multiplied, the Government paper is depreciated and more must be issued, while in the end, so far as Government issues are concerned, they must be paid by ourselves and coming generations in gold, or the whole evidences of debt will end in one general heap of individual ruin and national bankruptcy.

The unconstitutional system of State banking had been so long tolerated by the Federal Government that the banks felt as though they had the right and the power to dictate terms to the Secretary of the Treasury. At first he had to defer to them, until he could break their power by the action of measures of the Federal Government of similar unconstitutionality. But the existence of the old banking system compelled the Government to submit to all the extortions of it, and to pay all the paper prices it had instituted. And but for its existence, the currency of the old States to-day might as well have been five hundred millions in gold coin as in that amount of paper. No doubt the system will double the expenses of the war, and this is but one tribute which the people must pay to this engine of extortion and injustice—paper money. It is humiliating to contemplate the fact that our National Government has been compelled to make obeisance to the State banks, when they are entirely unconstitutional, and have wrought such untold evils upon both the body politic and the National Government. Into such straits has the system of State banking driven our country; and this, too, when Congress all the time had the prerogative to crush it at a blow.

The banks are now all under suspension, and will remain so indefinitely. If the Government needs the circulation, *and is justified in using it under the necessities of the war*, let the bank circulation be excised enough to amount to a prohibition.

If it were a time of peace, and specie payments restored, it would be the further duty of Congress to look to the deposit account and the inscribed credits in banks, and see that these exercise no pernicious influence on the value of coin.

The currency of California is one of intrinsic value. If the legal tender notes are such by the enactment of Congress, gold and silver coin are the legal tender by the Constitution of the United States. If the acts of Congress conflict with the Constitution, there can be no reasonable doubt as to which must be sustained before the courts of competent jurisdiction. The late Hon. Silas Wright, United States Senator, held the following opinion: "That the only currency known to the Constitution is a currency of intrinsic value, a metallic currency, a currency of coin, according to the value placed upon it by Congress, is a fact too plain for contradiction or question. Congress derives no power from that instrument, *to make, to establish, or to regulate the value of any other currency*, nor is anything else recognized therein as money." (Life of Silas Wright, page 161.)

The late Hon. Daniel Webster, United States Senator, holds the following clear and powerful opinion on the subject: "But if we understand by currency the legal money of the country, and that which constitutes a lawful tender for debts, and is the statute measure of value, then, undoubtedly, nothing is included but gold and silver. Most unquestionably there is no legal tender, and there can be no legal tender in this country, under the authority of this Government or any other, but gold and silver, either the coinage of our mints, or foreign coin, at rates regulated by Congress. This is a *constitutional principle*, perfectly plain, and of the very highest importance. The States are expressly prohibited from making anything but gold and silver a tender in payment of debts; and although no such express prohibition is applied to Congress, yet, as Congress has no power granted to it, in this respect, but to coin money, and regulate the value thereof, and of foreign coin, *it clearly has no power to substitute paper or anything else for coin*, as a tender in payment of debts and in discharge of contracts. Congress has exercised this power fully, and in both its branches. It has coined money, and still coins it; it has regulated the value of foreign coins, and still regulates their value. The legal tender, therefore, the constitutional standard of value, is established, and cannot be overthrown. To overthrow it would shake the whole system." (See the Works of Daniel Webster, vol. IV, page 271.) The same doctrine was held by the late Hon. Thomas H. Benton, and other men of distinguished talents in the Senate. These opinions are sound constitutional law, beyond all doubt; and the issue of Treasury notes can only be justified upon the ground of a war necessity. There is a class of men among us who think that, if Treasury notes were made our currency, gold would become merchandise, and go out of circulation, while the legal tender notes of the Government would pass at par for all chattels and estate. This, they suppose, would help the difficulty of compelling creditors to receive seventy-five cents on the dollar upon whatever might be due to them. Upon future operations prices of property must advance in the same ratio that the currency is at a discount. If the legal tender compels men to receive *indebtedness* in a depreciated currency, these parties will look to it that the tender shall not abstract their *property* from them except at its gold value. In this way the legal tender is a death blow to credits in the State.

If the Government pay out the legal tenders at par to contractors and office-holders, it would not help their case at all that our currency be changed from gold to treasury notes. For example, if under a gold currency five dollars in gold are equal to one barrel of flour, and six dollars in treasury notes are equal to the same, it does not help the case of the holder of treasury notes, that every one has to use them, and must pay six dollars of these notes for a barrel of flour. And, again, it does not injure the holder of treasury notes that the holder of gold can buy as much for five dollars in gold as the holder of notes can buy with six dollars in paper. The gold and the treasury notes are matters of distinct and separate valuation, as that of a horse and an ox. And it would be no more hardship to the owner of an ox that he could not sell his ox for a horse, and at the price of a horse, than it would be for the holder of a treasury note of five dollars to find fault because his note would not buy five dollars in gold. It would not help the case of a man who had lost a leg or an arm by accident that the whole community cut off an arm or a leg through sympathy, or by the compulsory action of some foolish legislation to maim the body politic in this manner. The most stringent legislation can never make values equal which are demonstrated by the laws of trade to be widely different. Fear may compel men to sacrifice their property and cancel debts, when they know that they are not receiving an equivalent. Evidently, however, any legislation which compels such sacrifice is tyrannical and unconstitutional. Government officers in California can do with Treasury notes as they do at the East, to wit: fund them in six per cent. bonds, the coupons to be paid in gold. This should not be counted a great hardship.

It results from these premises that it is useless and tyrannical to coerce a population of four hundred thousand to suffer an indescribable injury and injustice, on the subject of currency, because a few hundred office-holders and contractors are paid by the Government in this currency, especially as making this currency universal will not help their case in the smallest degree. It may, and often does, injure the holder of gold that the prices of property should be above a just gold value, when quoted in currency; but it never works any injustice to the holder of paper, because paper prices are always above gold prices. Therefore all the arguments by the champions of paper for a change of our currency are not only sophistry, but in reality absurd. In like manner it would not be of the least advantage to the Federal Government that California should change the currency from gold to paper; for in any case the Government will pay out the legal tenders at par on its undertakings.

The injury of the Eastern currency has been borne by California in silence, as it only bore upon the prices of such goods as she imported. But when it comes to destroy the validity of our domestic contracts, as does the legal tender notes, and this, too, without the slightest advantage to the Federal Government, we have just grounds to seek redress and reform of the grievance. The tender is thrust upon us, and every dishonest debtor, who intends to pay at all, avails himself of the legal tender protection, to pay his creditor in a currency most frightfully depreciated, and the extortionate gain inures to his own advantage. The channels of business are blocked; the loaning of money is stopped; for no capitalist will loan gold when he knows that the law justifies the debtor in paying his debt in a currency so inferior to gold. If the legal tender be forced upon us permanently, our State debt will increase with fearful rapidity. If our currency be changed from gold to paper, and paper so much depreciated, the advantage will neither inure to the benefit of our State, of the Federal Government, or the people generally. In such case our gold will become merchandise, and the Rothschilds, the Barings, the Hopes, and other giant capitalists of the old world will, through their agents, monopolize the whole. The change to us would work our most certain ruin. To preserve California from the immense vortex of bankruptcy which is threatening to deluge the old States of the Union, requires the most careful, yet the most bold and determined line of action in the premises. The golden standard of value must be adhered to by her, in spite of any and all opposition.

By some it may be thought that the law of Congress, making a legal tender of paper, must be of universal and equal action throughout the Union. That which is tender in New York must be tender in every State. Such is not the case in this instance. The only possible right the Government can have to issue any bills of credit, is derived incidentally, and very doubtfully, too, from the necessities of war. But the necessities of the war do not impose upon the Government the introduction into this State of a system of currency which will impair the validity of contracts, and destroy the most perfect currency on earth. This doubtful power of taking the property of our citizens by legal tenders at less than its value, should never be exercised by a Government, except at the call of the most stern necessity.

The Treasury Note Bill makes the issue under it legal tender for all claims and demands, public and private, "except for interest upon bonds of the Government, and duties on imports." Here, then, the bill excepts certain cases in which the notes are not legal tender. Now, if Congress has power to make a legal tender, and at the same time to except from its action certain duties due the Government, and interest due from the Government to the holder of bonds, then it may go a step further and enact that the States of California and Oregon shall be exempted and free from the legal tender clause of the bill. The reasons for this exemption are, that these States have commenced and continued a system of finance on the basis of gold for all their transactions, and that the change to paper will be, to them, unjust and tyrannical in its bearing, and useless to the Federal Government.

The legal tender is not onerous upon other States as upon California. Their currency has, for more than half a century, been a debased one—one subject to panics, revulsions, suspensions, failures, and all their attendant evils. The losses, resulting from such an unsound system of currency, are manifest in the fact that ninety-five per cent. of all the trading and manufacturing classes fail outright, or die insolvent. Still the system is continued to them by their own persistent action and choice. Their gains and their actual capital, as well as their lives and industry, are all a prey to the insatiable greed of banking institutions.

Gold enough has gone forward to relieve all their wants, and give them the soundest currency on earth : but they preferred the paper, and the paper has banished the gold.

If the war destroys the system of debt banking and organizing credits into currency, posterity may pass to its credit five hundred millions of dollars; provided the Federal Government will take the matter in hand and institute such legislation as will render it impossible for currency to exercise any pernicious influence on the value of gold. With what gold coin we now have in the United States, and California yielding fifty millions of gold yearly, and the fact demonstrated by experience that all of the wealth and industry of the nation, and a population of thirty-two millions may be moved, produced, and kept actively employed with a currency of six hundred millions of dollars, let us not jeopardize our commerce, our manufactures, our mineral wealth, our agriculture, and all our immense interests, by building them on any other basis than a gold currency, or paper representing gold, dollar for dollar. Let us not adopt in war any permanent system which will be destructive to our interests in time of peace. If the Federal Government legislates for the Union at large, and for the States of the Pacific in particular, she will institute no permanent enactment to demonetize gold, or lessen its normal value in the markets of the Union.

The preceding paper was published in November, 1862, a few days before the session of the Legislature. During the session the subject was considered with solicitous attention by the members, and the following resolutions were introduced, which were made the special order for the time appointed:

"WHEREAS, The ever loyal people of this State, upon forming their State Government, and being admitted into the Federal Union, found the then Territory of California to be a gold-bearing country, and, in view of that fact, adopted in their Constitution and in their polity and system a metallic currency, as a sole and only circulating medium, and ever since that time have pursued such system, to the exclusion of all banks of issue, and against a paper currency;

"AND WHEREAS, In consequence of said fact, and of other circumstances peculiar to this State, the law of Congress making United States Treasury Notes legal tender in payment of debts, works a hardship and public inconvenience to the citizens of California, far beyond that of any other State or people, and is not followed by any benefit or advantage to the Government of the United States. Therefore be it

"*Resolved*, By the Assembly of the State of California, the Senate concurring, that our Senators in Congress be instructed and our Representatives requested to urge these facts upon Congress, and to show to the general Government that said law operates to derange the finances of California, to create insecurity, alarm, and uneasiness, to assist unprincipled persons to defraud their creditors out of a portion of their just debts and dues, impairs the resources of the State, and materially weakens her power to aid our common country in this dark hour of her troubles without benefiting the good cause to any appreciable extent. And be it further

"*Resolved*, That our said Senators and Representatives in Congress be instructed and requested to use all loyal and honorable means to obtain the passage of an act of Congress exempting the State of California from the operations of said law.

"*Resolved*, That the Governor be requested to transmit copies of these resolutions to our Senators and Representatives in Congress."

The discussion of the subject in that Legislature, however, to their lasting honor be it remembered, loosed the Gordian knot; and, without any damage to the Federal Government, enacted a law which saved the State from bankruptcy and ruin. They wisely foresaw that any legislation by Congress would be too slow, and was quite too doubtful to depend upon for the relief of the pressing calls of the State. The Specific Contract Law was enacted, and stands to this day a proud monument of the wisdom of its makers, and is fully endorsed by every intelligent and honest citizen in the State. Time will increase its popularity, and demonstrate its wisdom and justice.

No. XVI.

PAPER CURRENCY.

TESTIMONY OF STATESMEN, FINANCIERS, ECONOMISTS, PHILOSOPHERS, AND PHILANTHROPISTS, UPON THE SUBJECT OF PAPER MONEY.

"In exact proportion as a nation alloys the precious metals, or pours paper money into the volume of the circulating medium, just in that proportion will everything in a country rise."—*George Washington.*

"Paper money will not benefit the farmer or mechanic. It will only benefit the debtor, as it will enable him to pay his debts with a shadow instead of a substance."—*George Washington.*

"A nation that can legislate a permanent value into a paper currency, will be a nation without a parallel on the globe."—*Swedenborg.*

"Banking in the United States is the most unrestrained and unsafe that there is in the world."—*Thos. H. Benton.*

"It is essential to every modification of the finances, that the benefits of an uniform national currency should be restored to the community."—*James Madison.*

"The American paper money system forms at present the most gigantic abuse by which an intelligent people ever permitted themselves to be disgraced and oppressed."—*J. R. McCulloch.*

"Paper money, by breaking up the measure of value, makes a lottery of all private property." — *Thomas Jefferson.*

"The emitting of paper money is wisely prohibited to the State Governments."—*Alexander Hamilton.*

"It is a tremendous power, that of increasing or diminishing the circulating medium of the country. It is a deep responsibility, and demands sound discretion and much wisdom in its regulation. Unfortunately there appears to be no unity of action, no controlling principle, in the management of this power."—*Nathan Appleton.*

"By a sort of under current, the power of Congress to regulate the money of the country has caved in, and upon its ruin have sprung up those institutions which now exercise the right of making money in and for the United States."—*J. C. Calhoun.*

"I consider the opinion entertained by some, that the bank ought to regulate its issues by the demand, as dangerous in the extreme."—*Francis Baring.*

"In every civilized country, supplying and regulating the circulating medium is a function of the sovereign prerogative."—*Tooke.*

"The exacting of security (other than the precious metals) from the issuers of paper would not obviate fluctuation in its amount and value, and could not therefore place the currency on a proper footing. All local issues of paper money should be suppressed."—*J. R. McCulloch.*

"I consider a mixed currency an unmixed evil."—*Amasa Walker.*

"I have been studying the currency question for forty years, and I die in the belief that all paper money is a swindle."—*Richard Page,* the "DANIEL HARDCASTLE" of "The Times."

Any element introduced into the currency which creates price without corresponding value, is subversive of every principle of sound economy, and must, if continued, bring destruction and ruin upon the country which resorts to such a desperate measure. That bank notes and inscriptions of credit in banks are each in an eminent degree such element in the currency, will be obvious to any one who will contemplate their nature. It is the attribute, the influence, and the effect of bank notes to create price without corresponding value. The same holds true of bank credits. This action upon prices, however, only rules in proportion as banks issue more notes for circulation, or give more inscriptions of credit than the actual amount of gold which they possess for the redemption of such notes and credits. If a bank note for one dollar represents a golden dollar on deposit, in such keeping that the gold dollar cannot be used for any other purpose but the redemption of that identical note, such issue of paper cannot depreciate the value of gold. However, no banks in the United States—California alone excepted—do their business on the righteous rules of scripture and the American Constitution. California bankers grant no credits unless the gold is deposited. They pay no checks but in gold and silver. Hence their business is done honestly and justly.

The issue of paper money in the State of California would result in one of the following positions, viz.: It would take from circulation a part of the gold which now forms the currency, and substitute for the same bank notes, making our currency a mixed currency, similar to the one they now have in the old States ; or it would not take from circulation any of the gold which now makes our currency, but be an addition to the present volume of currency exactly equal to the emission of such paper. In one or the other of these positions would result the experiment of issuing paper money in this State. We will examine each of these cases : First, would there be any advantage to the State in withdrawing from circulation one-half or two-thirds of our gold and substituting for it paper ? Manifestly not. The most radical paper-money champion does not contend that a paper dollar is worth more or is any better than a gold dollar. It is by increasing the volume of currency and making money plenty that the advocates of paper money hope to be benefited.

Again: suppose that the issuing of paper money did not drive any gold from circulation, but was an addition of so much to the currency as the banks might issue, how would such result tell on the business and prosperity of the State? It would double the volume of our currency at once; it would make high prices nominally, and increase bankruptcies tenfold. By increasing prices, it would take a much larger amount of money to carry on any kind of business than it now does under a gold currency. Everything we imported, used, and consumed, would be sold at such advanced price. But, while it stimulated high prices, it would by no means increase our means for paying for imports. Our gold alone would be shipped to pay for our imports, and thus the policy would be suicidal to California, for she could not pay for imports in her paper issue. In fact, for the insignificant consideration of circulating two or three millions of dollars in the State in paper money, (not so much as is dug out of the mines in a single month) we should be imposing upon ourselves the necessity of paying double prices for all that we consume, and thus virtually be parting with our gold for fifty cents on the dollar. Nor would it help at all at reducing the amount of interest which has to be paid for funds in the transaction of business. By vilifying the currency, which would be done by issuing paper money, you would make money plenty, but you would at the same time require a much greater amount to do the same business than is now required; and inasmuch as it would require more amount of currency to do the same business, there would be a necessity created to borrow more, and the more had to be borrowed, the more interest would have to be paid. Increasing the volume of currency would increase the aggregate indebtedness of the State immensely. For it is calculated by eminent political economists, that for every dollar of currency that is in circulation there will be ten dollars of indebtedness in the country. If the indebtedness is small in a country, the demand for money will be small, and the rates of interest will be low, especially on choice securities, for which capitalists will always be competing. On the contrary, if the indebtedness is large, the call for money will be immense, and the rates of interest will rule high so long as such indebtedness continues.

The rate of interest paid for money is not a correct measure of the value of money; for, while money is worth two per cent. monthly in California, and only three per cent. a year in Europe, it has been, and still is, flowing in a continual channel from the country of high rate to the countries of low rates of interest. The measure of value of money is shown by the quantity of the necessaries and luxuries of life which it will purchase, not the rate of interest which it will command. Hence, the great mass of our gold goes to Europe, for there it will buy more of the necessaries and luxuries of life. And there it will continue to flow so long as the old States use false money in place of real cash. Whenever gold is put up to the sterling value which it would bring at home if the American Constitution were rigidly regarded by the States, then the flow of bullion to Europe will immediately cease, until the normal value of currency in the country shall be filled with specie.

But, says one, the rates of interest in California are enormous. No business can pay the rates of California interest and flourish. This is true to a certain extent. But the rates of labor are as high as the rates of interest in California. And what establishes and confirms the rates of labor, is the price which a man can gain by his labor in the mines. So long as the mines will pay from two to five dollars per day for labor, so long other business must pay these prices, or it will be left undone. It is the rates of labor, as much as the rates of interest, that paralyzes our manufacturing interests. For either the one or the other is sufficient to make it impracticable to compete with the Eastern manufacturers. If our people were out of debt, the rates of interest would immediately come down to the lowest figure; probably to ten per cent. per annum. But so long as they are heavily in debt, the rates of interest will rule high.

Not so with the prices of labor. Labor will be high whether the people are in debt or out of debt, so long as the mines will pay high rates. There is another view in which I wish to examine this fancied relief of making paper money in order to make money plenty, and thus making the rates of interest low.

We are now doing business under a gold currency, and

this currency governs prices, except on such things as we import from the East. Upon our imports we pay paper prices, and we pay them in gold. For this there is no remedy but through the action of Congress. Now, if we double the amount of currency by adding paper to it, we shall double prices to what they now rule at. Hence, we shall have to pay double to carry on any business that we now pay for the same. And if interest ruled at two per cent. a month under a gold currency, and one per cent. under a paper currency, the interest account would be exactly balanced. People would have to borrow twice as much under the paper currency to do business, as they would require under the gold currency to do the same business. Hence you have saved nothing at all on interest account by the depreciation of the currency with paper money. And hence this talk about lessening interest by making paper money, is a complete fallacy. But what have you done by foisting this paper on the commonwealth? You have interfered with the validity of contracts. You have changed, or materially altered, the relation of debtor and creditor, for you enable the debtor to pay his contracts with a shadow instead of a substance.

You have made prices for everything without any corresponding value, and wherever you have increased prices by paper money above the mark they would have ruled at under a gold currency, you have introduced so much bankruptcy into the body politic. Now, if under a gold currency of two millions of dollars, which is not far from the actual currency of California, (the semi-monthly shipments of treasure of about two millions to the East, not being considered as any part of the currency of the State); if under this currency California does all her business at present, except the shipment of treasure semi-monthly, and her present population is four hundred thousand, and she is amply supplied with goods, wares, and merchandise of all descriptions, how are we going to help matters by instituting paper money? Can we sell any more goods than what the people need by increasing the prices of those goods, which would be the first effect of the introduction of paper money?

Suppose a country merchant buys goods in San Francisco under a gold currency to the amount of one thousand dollars, and that he has his note discounted in bank at three per cent. per month, for ninety days, to raise the money; then he pays for his goods one thousand dollars, and for interest ninety dollars—making one thousand and ninety dollars, which he must meet by sales of the goods. Again: suppose he buys the same goods under a paper currency, he would have to pay for the same goods fifteen hundred dollars, and for the bank loan of fifteen hundred dollars for ninety days—admitting that the rate of interest settled one-half by the introduction of paper money, at the rate of one and a half per cent. per month for the money—$67 50, or $1,567 50. Thus, under the paper currency, he would have to pay $477 50 higher for the same goods than he now pays. This difference, of course, must come out of the consumer. Hence the people, the dear people, and they alone, would be compelled to pay through the nose the grinding extortion which the consequences of paper money would inflict upon them. It is vastly better to have money at high rates of interest, and keep that money of sterling value, so that a little money will pay for much merchandise and property of any kind, than it is to have money debased by paper, copper, or brass, so that it takes a large amount of it to pay for few goods.

The difference at which prices of goods and property rule under a gold currency, or a paper one, is the index to the amount of bankruptcy which the people impose upon themselves by the using of a fiction in place of bullion. Hence, I make no hesitancy in saying that one-third to one-half of all the mass of indebtedness in the old States of the Union is hopelessly bankrupt. It may be transferred, change hands, kited, renewed, passed from one man to another; it may assume all the chameleon colors, forms, and shapes of credit which a fruitful imagination and a shrewd people may invent to save themselves from its disastrous consequences; but in bankruptcy it commenced and in bankruptcy it must end. Its nature can never be changed. Much of it will be shaken off on to the shoulders of men who have property, and they must bear the loss; and although it may not ruin such men, still their possessions will be reduced

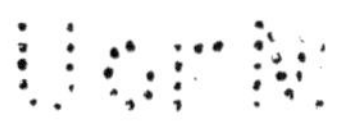

in precisely the amount which they have to sustain of this great load of bankruptcy which the American people are most unwisely and uselessly imposing upon themselves. Californians: this bankruptcy commenced in the currency. It is a leprous spot of deep dye on the old States. You are free from it. Yours is a pure and righteous currency, and long may it remain such. You need a paper currency just as much as your honest yeomanry need tares and darnels sown among their wheat. And while your quartz rock and river banks shall discount the precious oro to the stalwart arm of the miner who rives its fastnesses or digs its golden sands, let it never be said that California has rejected the substance and seized upon a shadow. Let California make no false step on this important subject of the currency. She stands almost alone among her sister States, a proud example of a sovereignty which has not yet bowed the knee to the idol of paper money. She is the treasure State of the Union, and under the shield of the American Constitution she has a right to demand of the Congress of the United States the suppression and extinction of every bank which issues paper money. This action on the part of Congress would double and treble the value of our gold. All our imports from the old States could be laid down in San Francisco for less than half that we now pay for them, leaving an annual surplus of gold in the State of over twenty millions of dollars for circulation. California wants no banks of paper issue, but she wants all such institutions suppressed in the old States. It is her right to ask this, and why should it be deemed absurd to ask our rights, which are guaranteed by the American Constitution? For the neglect of asking these rights firmly, during the past ten years, of the Federal Government, California has lost the immense sum of two hundred and fifty millions of dollars. And it is only by holding the old States strictly to the provisions of the Constitution on the subject of currency, that we can ever get from them the means to build the Pacific Railroad. The old States owe us the above amount, and it is ample to build the road twice over. How important, then, does it become that California should exact her rights of the Federal Government on the subject of currency.

March, 1860.

No. XVII.

BANK DEPOSITS AND INSCRIPTIONS OF CREDIT IN BANKS.

"The whole subject of bank deposits is beset with difficulties. The extent to which it has been already carried has deeply endangered the stability of the banking system, and we have seen that it is indispensable that it should be subjected to regulation."—*J. R. M'Culloch.*

The nature of bank deposits and inscriptions of credit in banks is not generally understood, and it is not the policy of the Eastern bankers to enlighten the public upon this important and extensive branch of their business.

Deposits in bank consist of gold and silver, certified and uncertified checks upon other banks, bank bills, certificates of deposit, and any species of paper which the bank recognizes as currency at sight. These are deposits proper. They are also inscriptions of credit in bank, as they pass to the credit of the dealer on the bank ledger, and are subject to his check. Another form of deposit, which is also an inscription of credit in bank, arises from notes discounted, the proceeds of which are passed to the credit of the dealer, and are subject to his check. Such inscriptions of credit are also called deposits, but it is entirely a misnomer to entitle them to any such distinction. Let us analyze their constituency, and see what they are made of. The merchant offers his note, at sixty or ninety days, at the bank for discount. The bank discounts the note—that is, computes the interest on the face of the note from the day it is offered until the day of its maturity, and deducts this from the amount of the note; the balance is called the proceeds of the note, and this balance passes to the credit of the one who offers the paper. Now, all the deposit which the bank receives is this note of the merchant, payable at a distant day. This deposit, as it is called and reported to the world in the periodical exhibits of the banks, is in fact only an undrawn loan. The New York banks, which I fully admit are the most powerful banks which ever existed in our own country on a wrong basis, are very guarded not to report the amount of their undrawn loans.

The undrawn loans are reported as deposits, and we have no data to reach their amount, except by careful comparison of a long series of their operations, and even then we are left to conjecture and doubt upon the subject. But from the best information I can draw of their actual condition, I am compelled to believe that of the line of the New York City banks reported as deposits, from thirty-five to fifty millions of dollars, and perhaps we might go as high as sixty millions, consists of the proceeds of notes discounted. Hence, that amount of their deposits, without stating it precisely, is entirely unworthy of the name. These deposits, as soon as the paper is discounted, become currency to all intents and purposes. They are subject to the dealer's check, and swell the volume of that element in the country which makes prices for all property, real and personal. They are, in fact, the grand fulcrum upon which all the large business operations of the commercial and mercantile interests of the country rest. To form a just idea of the relative proportion of the currency of the city of New York, we must bear in mind that while only eight millions of dollars are represented by bank notes, eighty millions of the currency are represented by deposits. In this view, they become an object of immense interest to the candid examiner for truth on the subject of currency. I know that a class of bankers, who are not willing that light should be poured into the minds of the people on the subject of currency, are unwilling that deposits should be regarded as currency. "Circulation," as described by an intelligent writer on banking, "is deposits inside out, while deposits are circulation outside in." Each form of circulation must be paid by the bank on demand, and the bank knows not when the payment of either may be demanded.

Bank deposits being currency to all intents and purposes, it becomes necessary that their quality should be of as high standard as bills in circulation; for it requires only the dealer's check to convert them into bank bills. From these premises, it follows that deposits in bank rule prices as much as bills in circulation. The circulation of bank bills in the old States has not advanced with the rapidity with which banking capital has been augmented by the alchemy of banking, in making State stocks a basis for the issue of paper. The reason of this is, that where one man kept a bank account in 1850, probably twenty men keep bank accounts in 1860. And every man who keeps a bank account leaves his spare cash on deposit, and checks for it as his business requires. Hence he does not keep bank bills in his safe, in any quantities. The circulation which the bank gets on its depositors' accounts is circulation outside in. In the country, where dealers live at a distance from the bank, they more commonly take the bills, and trust to the security of their own trunks and hiding places. In the city of New York, the currency is about eight millions of dollars in bank notes, and eighty millions of dollars on deposit, subject to check at sight.

It follows from these premises that if the deposit account of a bank is abused, or, in other words, if the credit which is given to a dealer in bank is not founded on gold or silver, that the bank, by extending such credit, is working the same injury on the body politic, in prices, as it would do by issuing its bills upon any other basis than bullion. This is the constant practice of all the banks in the old States, and the injury to the public through the medium of their deposit account is quite equal to the injury committed by their bills in circulation. Let us analyze their power and means of mischief. State stocks, bonds, and mortgages are organized into currency. Now, State stocks are only evidences of debt. Why should debt be made currency? If debt is a good basis for currency, sure we never need want for this article. There is no scarcity of debt in the market at all times. But so long as the real dollar is made of gold and silver, and you say a debt dollar is as good as a real one, it appears to my mind very much like the rich soup which the cook made by boiling the shadow of a piece of fat meat for half a day in water, and adding to it sawdust for thickening. It makes a negative idea—debt—perform the part of a positive substance—gold.

But this manufacturing of currency by the deposit account of the banks, is carried to a most alarming extent. Nothing has any check upon it but the Clearing House, which acts upon the city banks, and the banks and offices of redemption, which act upon the country banks. The Clearing House will check any bank which attempts to discount more than its proportion, but it will not prevent a general expansion on the part of all the banks in a uniform ratio to their capital.

Nothing limits the action of the banks in their course of mischief but their inability to do more without running themselves entirely into ruin. Through the deposit account of banks, every kind of *credit mobilier* and *credit foncier*, every *chose in action* and *chose at rest*, every species of property of real estate or personal, every kind of goods, wares, and merchandise, may be organized into currency.

The folly of banks thus tampering with the values of gold and silver results in general bankruptcy, which manifests itself in an overwhelming torrent about once in ten years, and a constant succession of failures, in the meantime, between these financial panics. Banks make currency, and currency makes prices. Deposits form a large part of this currency, and hence they should be under the control and guidance of the sovereignty. Deposits also possess, in an eminent degree, the power and quality of mobilization. Through the means of the telegraph they are transferred, or their power of action is transferred, from one extreme of the country to the others in a moment. Now, deposits would be shorn of none of their power or effect if they were limited to bullion, or paper strictly representing bullion. And if they possessed this quality, it would not be a necessary consequence, as it now is, that every man doing business of any kind must assume and pay a part of the general bankruptcy of the country. The banks in California deal in bullion, exchange, and discounting paper. All of these are honest, just, and necessary branches of the public weal. Their discounts are confined to their means of action, and they make no distress among the people by creating prices of property on false bases. Whenever a check is paid, the sum is honestly told out to the dealer in gold. Inasmuch as they pay only gold on checks, they will not credit a dealer for a deposit unless his deposit is strictly equal to gold. And I believe, firmly and truly, that very few of them put themselves into a position where two checks can be drawn at sight upon the same dollar. Notwithstanding all the assaults upon California bankers, on account of errors in times past, I believe that the present bankers do their business upon strictly honorable, just, and upright rules of action.

If the principles which California bankers act upon could be carried out in the old States, I know that they would be worth hundreds of millions of dollars to the American Union every year. I do not say that it is impossible for a California banker to abuse a deposit account. But I do say that if he does it for any considerable length of time, that a frightful retribution awaits him. And I further believe that the character which a banker possesses in California for integrity, wealth, and business talent, is a better guarantee to the depositor for the safe keeping and return of his money than could be gained by any legislative action which should transfer or divide responsibility from individuals or firms to banking associations, boards of directors, stockholders, presidents, or cashiers. Bad as some people think the system of bullion banks is, as now organized in California, I believe it the most honest system of banking in the world. And if our zealous champions for a change of our State Constitution, which is now one of the best constitutions of any State in the Union, shall include within its amendments the subject of banking, for the permanent good of the State, it would be far better that they should be sleeping than acting upon this matter.

The principles of banking at the East are founded on the fallacy that a bank is good so long as it remains in good credit, and so long as it redeems its bills. Now, it is not necessary to drive a bank to failure to prevent it from doing immense damage to the public. The mischief is done by making a currency which makes prices of every species of property, real or personal. Whenever the affairs of a bank are really winding up, and no substitute for it is resorted to in a community, the bankruptcy which this institution has induced and entailed on that community begins to be apparent to all. They see the impossibility of paying their debts on account of the contraction in the currency. The bank currency has driven the specie out of market; and prices of property fall, in many cases, even below what they would have ruled at under a gold currency.

The inauguration of the Eastern system of banking in California would commence with a sacrifice of the whole equitable indebtedness of the old States to this State, amounting to more than two hundred millions of dollars, which we want to reserve for the building of the Pacific Railroad, as before demonstrated. In the future, it would involve an annual loss of twenty millions of dollars on the shipments of treasure to the East. For, with what confidence could California assert her rights in Congress for reclamations of damages for the pàst, and guarantees of security for the future, that she should receive the full value of her gold, while her own Legislature had instituted the same system of iniquitous finance which the old States have adopted as heir-looms of their economy?

To me it is patent that our only redress of grievances is through the action of Congress, and if we cannot obtain our constitutional rights through this source, two essential bonds of union are wanting—the bond of interest and the bond of protection. For it is as much the duty of Congress to guard us from this ruthless sacking of our treasure by the old States, unconstitutionally, as from the attacks of foreign foes.

The adoption of the banking system of the old States by California would be selling her "birthright for a mess of pottage."

March 23, 1860.

No. XVIII.

PAPER MONEY TRIED BY THE DOCTRINE OF ETHICS.

Leviticus xix, 35, 36. "*Ye shall do no unrighteousness in judgment, in mete yard, in weight, or in measure. Just balances, just weights, a just ephah, and a just hin shall ye have: I am the* LORD *your* GOD."

Duteronomy xxv, 13, 14, 15, 16. "*Thou shalt not have in thy bag divers weights, a great and a small. Thou shalt not have in thy house divers measures, a great and a small. But thou shalt have a perfect and just weight, a perfect and just measure shalt thou have; that thy days may be lengthened in the land which the* LORD *thy* GOD *giveth thee. For all that do such things, and all that do unrighteously, are an abomination unto the* LORD *thy* GOD."

Micah vi, 10, 11. "*Are there yet the treasures of wickedness in the house of the wicked, and the scant measure that is abominable? Shall I count them pure with the wicked balances, and with the bag of deceitful weights? For the rich men thereof are full of violence, and the inhabitants thereof have spoken lies, and their tongue is deceitful in their mouth.*"

Proverbs xvi, 11. "*A just weight and balance are the Lord's; all the weights of the bag are His work.*"

Ezekiel xlv, 10. "*Ye shall have just balances, and a just ephah, and a just bath.*"

Proverbs xi, 1. "*A false balance is abomination to the Lord: but a just weight is his delight.*"

Proverbs xx, 10. "*Divers weights, and divers measures, both of them are alike abomination to the Lord.*"

The preceding expressive and momentous truths of Divine Revelation, (iterated and re-iterated by that faithful servant and lawgiver of God, the Prophet Moses, to his companions in the wilderness—the Children of Israel; and again embodied in the form of a proverb by the wisdom of Solomon, and still further impressed on the hearts of his people by the Prophet Micah) show, in the clearest light, the abhorrence with which the Divine mind views the sin of *unrighteousness in weights and measures.* It is a sin which is represented as utterly abominable in His sight. This sin, in its ordinary forms, is perfectly intelligible to the lowest order of understanding. I leave it to the eminent divines of the day to treat it under its proper phases. My purpose is to discuss, in this essay, a peculiar national form of evading, ignoring, transgressing, and trampling under foot these sacred injunctions of the Divine law, of rendering exact justice to all our brethren. This form relates to the national iniquity into which our people have fallen by the insidious and subtle agency of paper money and bank credits, which are so common in most of the States of the Union, and which are threatening the total ruin and overthrow of our system of free government.

The making of currency from anything but gold and silver, (or a substitute which represents these metals in some safe depository, with a responsible custodian, who can and will redeem such substitute on presentation in those metals) has a three-fold aspect.

First: A political view, which refers to national economy and prosperity of the country at large.

Secondly: A legal view, which involves the question of the right of an individual, a corporation, an association, or bank, to utter currency one dollar beyond their power of immediate redemption in gold; or at all to interfere with the rights of the sovereign, which the laws of nations make absolute on the subjects of coining money, the regulation of commerce, and by consequence the currency.

Thirdly: A moral view, which demands by what right an individual, a corporation, a bank, an association, or firm, may make currency from credit—may loan money when they have no money—may make the amount of currency virtually five, ten, or twenty times the volume of gold coin which they hold to redeem the same—may make prices for all property upon the basis that this inflated volume of currency, of their manufacture, is real cash—in fine, may lessen the exchangeable value of gold and rob its possessors, to make themselves or their constituents wealthy from the hard earnings of honest toil, and at the same time impoverish the country by driving its gold abroad? These are queries which look to the morality of modern banking, to its justice, equity, and right; and to this last view I will confine my present examination.

There are certain postulates which I shall ask of the reader, for I have not time to review what eminent theologians have so often and so clearly proven. If these postulates are not conceded, the argument will not be convincing to him who denies them. These are simply: that God exists—that he created this world and its inhabitants—that one of his attributes is justice—that his law is the standard of morality—that he has given to man a revelation of his will, to guide his actions with his fellow man, and that this revelation is the foundation of human justice. With the person who denies these postulates, who contends that gross injustice, practiced by one class of our population upon another, is right; that *divine law* should have no binding force; that might alone makes right—with such a perverter of reason and common sense, I shall hold no argument.

The sin of defrauding by weights and measures is nothing more nor less than a mean form of theft. It is so contemptible in practice that any trader who should be convicted of it would not only receive the just punishment for his dishonesty, but also be branded with such infamy that he would probably become a total outcast from all respectable society. Every man has a right to his own property; and every legitimate and honest vocation has its proper reward. Now, to every enlightened mind, the position must be intelligible that the sin of defrauding, cheating, and stealing, by false measures of value, is equal to, and identical with, the sin of stealing by false weights and measures of quantities. Its effect on the debtor and creditor are precisely the same. If you cheat a man one-half in measurement of quantity, or make him pay double value for what he receives, you inflict on him the same wrong, the same injury. And yet, marvelous as it may appear in an enlightened nation, this abomination of making the purchaser pay double prices for every article of consumption, is not only sanctioned by legislation, but is so inwrought and ingrafted in the whole transactions of society that men are compelled to use and practice it, willingly or otherwise, knowingly or in ignorance. The lever upon which all this system of financial iniquity is supported and built up, rests upon bank issues and bank credits. Gold and silver are the measures of value which have been ordained by the wisdom of God, and have been in use by the institutions of men, at least since the days of the general deluge. The patriarch Abraham used them as such, and all the civilized world have recognized their value. In the earliest records which we have in the Genesis the gold of Havilah is pronounced good. "And Abraham weighed to Ephron the silver, which he had named in the audience of the sons of Heth, four hundred shekels of silver, current money with the merchant." Genesis xxiii, 16.

That gold and silver were used as measures of value from the days of Adam to Noah, can only be known by inference. But this inference is strongly in favor of such theory. The Book of Job, which is supposed by many to have been written long before the general deluge, speaks thus of wisdom: "It cannot be gotten for gold, neither shall silver be weighed for the price thereof." "It cannot be valued with the gold of Ophir, with the precious onyx, or the sapphire." "The gold and the crystal cannot equal it; and the exchange of it shall not be for jewels of fine gold." (Job xxviii, 15, 17.) Here the patriarch Job seeks the most valuable gifts of earth to measure the worth of wisdom, and among these he numbers and reiterates gold and silver. For four thousand years gold and silver have been used by men to measure values, and to effect exchanges of property. If any one doubts that these are recognized standards of value, approved by the inspiration of the Bible, let him examine the texts referred to below, and he must be perfectly satisfied that they are measures of value instituted by higher authority than man. They are honest standards, and they are standards which are in the keeping of the Deity himself. Wherever the Bible would illustrate anything of eminent earthly value, gold and silver are used for such illustration almost universally.*

Deep in the caverns of the earth, in the secrets of the mountains, in the quartz rock, in the beds of the rivers, the cañons and the gorges, these treasures are deposited by the Creator in such quantities, and only such, as are needed for the uses of mankind. It requires the most laborious toil of the miner to penetrate the bowels of the earth and bring forth these treasures. Like everything else which is truly valuable, the getting of gold requires the most patient and enduring toil. Nothing truly valuable is gotten without great pains; and, in this respect, the getting of gold is no exception, but an apt illustration of the rule.

It has been objected to the value of gold and silver, that they are not valuable like other metals for their uses in the arts; that their value is conventional, by the tacit or enacted consent of civilized nations, to use them as measures of value, and the medium of exchanges. That, if a mountain of gold and silver, ten or twenty miles long, and half as wide, were to be found on the face of the earth, their value, as money, would be at once and for-

---

* Gen. ii, 12; xiii, 2; xx, 16; xxiii, 9, 13, 16; xxiv, 22, 35; xvii, 27; xxxiii, 19; xxxvii, 22; xlii, 25, 35; xliii, 12; xliv, 1, 2, 8; xlvii, 14, 15, 16, 18. Exodus xi, 2; xxi, 21, 30; xxv, 3; xxii, 17, 25. Leviticus xxii, 11; xxv, 51; xxvii, 3 to 8, 25. Numbers iii, 49; xvii, 16; xxii, 18; xxxi, 22. Deuteronomy viii, 13; xvii, 17; xiv, 25; xxi, 14; xxii, 18, 19. Joshua xxii, 8; xxiv, 32. Joshua vii, 21, 22, 24; vi, 19. Judges xvii, 4, 2. 2 Samuel viii, 11, 12; xxi, 4. 1 Kings xxi, 6, 15. 2 Kings v. 5, 23, 26; xviii, 16; xii, 4 to 16. 1 Chronicles xviii, 11; xxi, 25. 2 Chronicles xii, 9; viii, 18. Ezra i, 6 to 12. Nehemiah vii, 70, 71, 72. Esther iii, 9, 11; iv, 7. Job xxxvi, 19; xxii, 23, 24; xxiii, 10; xxvii, 16, 17; xxviii, 1, 6, 15; xlii, 11. Psalms xix, 10; cv, 37; lxxii, 15; xxi, 3; cxix, 72; lxviii, 30. Proverbs xx, 15; vii, 20; xvi, 16. Ecclesiastes ii, 8. Song of Solomon v, 14. Isaiah xlvi, 6; xii, 17; lii, 3. Jeremiah lii, 19; x, 9, 4; xxxii, 9, 10, 25. Lamentations iv, 1, 2. Ezekiel vii, 19; xvi, 13; xxii, 22, 25; xxviii, 4. Daniel ii, 32, 38; xi, 8, 33; v, 16. Hosea ii, 8; iii, 2. Joel iii, 5. Amos ii, 6. Micah iii, 10, 11. Nahum ii, 9. Habakkuk ii, 19. Zephaniah i, 11. Haggai ii, 8. Zachariah iv, 12; vi, 7; xi, 12, 13; xiii, 9. Malachi iii, 3. Matthew xvii, 27; xxviii, 13, 15; xxii, 19; xviii, 24. Mark xii, 41. Luke xv, 8; xix, 13 to 26; xx, 24. John vi, 7; xiii, 29. Acts iii, 6; xxiv, 26. James v, 3. Revelations xviii, 12, 16, 17; xxi, 18, *et passim.*

ever lost, by reason of such superabundance of quantity. This may be precisely so, and still I argue that such supposed contingency will not make any depreciation in the value of the precious metals. There happens to be an important "if" in the way, which renders the matter very secure. No such mountain has yet been found on the face of the globe, though it has been sought for thousands of years. No such mountain has been created by the Deity. No such mountain will ever be found, for the simple reason that God Almighty intended that His creature man should have and use gold and silver as measures of value, and hence He has never done anything to destroy that value. Whenever He chooses to destroy the value of gold and silver by its superabundance, we cannot find fault with the decrees of Heaven. "The silver is Mine, and the gold is Mine, saith the Lord of Hosts." Haggai ii, 8.

Still, it is very safe to trust our wealth in the hand of Him who gives us life, and breath, and takes them from us at His sovereign pleasure. Hence, if gold and silver are depreciated by a superabundance, no man on earth has any right to find fault with it. It is an act of Providence; the same as He takes from us houses, lands, friends, life, and every other blessing at His sovereign will. Having said thus much upon the determinate counsel and will of God Almighty in instituting and designing gold and silver as measures of value, and the medium of exchanges, I will now look at the abominations which have been entailed upon man by his attempt to tamper with these honest standards of value, and introduce substitutes instead of true measures. I use the word "abominations," because, if the reader will recur to the texts of Scripture first above recited, he will see that they are emphatically so styled by Divine Revelation. All false measures are an abomination in the sight of God; and paper money and bank credits, used any beyond an actual, equal amount of the precious metals on hand, in the bank which issues such paper, or gives such inscriptions of credit, are decidedly false measures of value. Their tendency is to work confusion, folly, mischief, disorganization, and wickedness. These agents stab in the dark. They are constantly changing the relations of debtor and creditor. By an enlargement or contraction of discounts and inscriptions of credit, these agents put up or thrust down prices of all property *ad libitum;* and if prices rise in market, this is but another form of expression for gold being depreciated; that is, it takes more gold to buy the same article.

Now, while it is perfectly right for Him who owns this earth and all it contains to vary the relative value of gold and silver to other property; while He can change at His will the relations of debtor and creditor; while He who owns us and all we possess can give us property and blessings at His sovereign pleasure, man has no right to exercise such sovereignty over his fellow man. He has no right to deal with him in any measures but those of equity, justice, and righteousness. Gold and silver are given to man as measures of value. He may barter property for other property; he may exchange a horse for a yoke of oxen, or a hundred bushels of wheat, or fifty sheep; he may make all kinds of property exchanges, and do no injustice. But he may not make this property, or property of any name, nature, or description, except gold and silver, and that only in amount, dollar for dollar, a basis for bank notes circulated, or inscriptions of credit in bank. If the banker exceeds this at all, then he is liable to the abomination of dealing with false measures of value. Then he becomes a robber of every man who owns gold and silver.

The bank bills go into market, or the inscription of credit in bank, to be checked for by the dealer, and gold and silver must take their place, side by side, and on a par with these issues and credits. In that way the volume of the currency of the United States is expanded from two hundred millions of dollars, its specie point, to an increase of two hundred millions more in bank bills, and two hundred and twenty-five millions in inscriptions of credit in bank to be checked for, making a currency of six hundred and twenty-five millions of dollars nominally, to measure the values of property, which, if reduced to the honest standards of the Bible and the American Constitution, would be only about two hundred millions of dollars.

If we throw a bucket of water into the harbor of San Francisco, it would make no sensible rise in the tides in the harbor of Boston; but, if a volume of water equal to the Pacific Ocean were thrown into the Atlantic, it would submerge the highest mountains on the American Continent. So, if one hundred American eagles were to be alloyed with brass one-half, and still to pass, and to remain as good currency for all time to come, and to be received and paid as sterling value, although such alloy would be so trifling as not sensibly to affect the value of gold in the aggregate, still it would have an infinitesimal effect. But if we alloy the whole circulation of the American gold currency two-thirds, with brass or zinc, is it not manifest how such alloy would tell on prices? The volume of the currency would be increased thereby so much, that whoever should be honest enough to balance real gold, ounce for ounce, against the alloyed coin, must be ruined in his circumstances, and bankrupt irretrievably and beyond remedy.

Precisely analogous to this action is the introduction of bank notes and bank credits into the currency, any further than the actual amount of specie which such banks possess, dollar for dollar. In other words, no bank should ever issue any more bills, or give any more inscriptions of credit on the ledger of such bank to be checked for, than the actual amount of specie funds on hand in such bank.

This would be squaring their business by the Bible rule of a just weight and measure, and the requirements of the American Constitution. The moment a bank or banker goes beyond this righteous rule of scripture, that moment he enters the toils of sin and Satan. Because, the moment he goes beyond this point, that moment he begins to issue a currency without specie basis, a currency depreciated, easily made, vilifying and lessening the value of gold and silver, cheapening money, compelling every man to pay higher prices for all that he consumes, and doing damage to the commonwealth beyond his power to repair, even if he could live on earth for ten thousand years to atone for his transgressions.

It is immaterial what is used as a substitute for real money, whether it be paper, leather, zinc, brass, iron, copper, lead, bank notes, or bank credits: all have the same effect upon sterling coin, so long as they pass current, and are received for real values. Their operation on the value of the precious metals is precisely the same as bogus or counterfeit coin. All these are produced much easier, much cheaper, with less toil and pains than the genuine dollar; and, of course, if they are used as substitutes, they rob the owner of gold and silver of a large fraction of their real values. They stimulate high prices of everything by misnomers, calling the "promises to pay" dollars the same as real dollars.

Individuals promise dollars because they think that bank notes will cancel and take up their notes or promises to pay in dollars. This is all that they think is necessary and right in the premises.

Banks promise dollars because they hold the promises of individuals to pay dollars. Thus the foundation of all the bankruptcies in the country is in the currency itself. Now if, for illustration, we assume that in the country there are only two hundred millions of dollars in gold and silver, and two hundred millions of dollars in bank notes in circulation, and two hundred millions of dollars of inscriptions of credit to dealers in bank, subject to their check at sight, we have for the currency of the country six hundred millions of dollars. But that portion of the currency made up of bank notes in circulation, and inscriptions of credit in bank subject to check at sight, is antagonistic to the genuine currency of gold and silver, and is wielding tremendous power to depress and vilify it. Nor is this influence wielded in vain; far from it. It is one of the most ingenious devices of Satan that was ever developed, thus to blind men to their true interests, and keep them all their lives grasping at shadows, while the bankruptcy in the currency swallows up their substance. And so long as our bankers, merchants, tradesmen, farmers, manufacturers, artisans, laborers, and every class of society, will adhere to this anti-biblical, anti-constitutional, wicked, poverty-stricken, nefarious and silly system, known and styled the American system of banks and banking, so long will the substance of our wealth and industry move onward to swell the coffers of the giant capitalists of the old world.

It is an element of human nature that men will remain content with any condition which they deem irreversible, while they revolt at injustice, extortion, and tyranny. The gift of gold to man is the boon of the Creator. The same power that sends forth the "early and latter rain," which causes the earth to produce her bounties to the toil of the husbandman, gives us this precious metal, for which all kind of wealth in civilized nations is seeking to be exchanged. This form of wealth—the gold of the country—is the immediate gift of the Creator. From this it follows that man must be reconciled to allow gold to depreciate if it be found in greater quantities than is needed for money and for use in the arts.

As a tender of value, nothing in existence has ever yet compared with it, for fixity and definite permanent worth, for cycles, for centuries, and for long ages of earth. The whole matter may then be summed up in a few words.—If gold falls by reason of its superabundance, no man has a right to find fault with the decrees of Heaven. But if gold falls by reason of disuse—by substituting paper for the metal which has no reference to it, and which does not represent it—then the voice of every patriot, statesman, economist, philanthropist, and honest man should be raised against the usurpation, the theft, the tyranny.

It is reasonable to suppose that the extensive increments of wealth which have been added to the world, during the past decade, in gold, have been given to man to allow him to achieve vast enterprises, and to act honestly; to sink the fiction paper, and to do his business upon an honest and firm basis; to banish gambling, and let a just equivalent, in the shape of money, measure his exchanges.

While banks are professedly paying specie for their issues, the action of a panic in the monetary system compels a redemption of their bills, and this redemption, for the time being, is an actual withdrawal of that amount from the currency of the country at the very moment it is needed most for public use. The banks dare not re-issue it, because they are bound to redeem in coin by their charters; and the issue of it has banished the coin from the country, while its circulation has stimulated credits generally in about the ratio of ten dollars for every dollar of such currency. There remains no alternative but to settle these credits in bankruptcy; and then the banks are ready to repeat this monstrous fraud on the public of making the prices of all commodities—of getting the people overwhelmingly in debt, upon the basis that their currency is sound and a just measure of values—to repeat the same game; but the people fail, and the endorsers of the paper must fail also, before it begins to affect the banks. For the sacrifice must come upon the bank debtors, and if the pressure be so severe that property will not bring one-third or one-half its ordinary appraisal, still it must be sold for cash, whether the debtors be thereby ruined or not.

The tendency of the issue of paper money, beyond an actual amount of gold on hand to meet such issue, is to drive the gold out of the country first; and, second, to bankrupt all who borrow at the bank, or who buy on credit. Now, if the banks loaned gold only, they would not have to redeem their money when the public needed it most, which they must do in the case of putting out their bills as money any further than they have the money to redeem them again. Thus, while a banker is able to loan gold to his customers, he is a very useful and very important member of society; but if he only loans his credit or his notes, he may be one of the most mischievous and disorganizing elements in the body politic. If his customers, by paying him all the profits they can make on their business, can merely live and support their families, and by rendering such tribute can make the banker opulent, why should the borrower not have the right to insist that the money loaned should be real cash, not a kind of money which must be redeemed by the banker himself in cash, and at a time which may ruin the dealers in bank beyond all hope of rescue. Well did the author of the declaration of American independence express his views of this evil in the following terse language: "Paper money, by breaking up the measure of value, makes a lottery of all private property." Hence it is to this wickedness of tampering with an honest currency, and measuring by false standards of value, that a large fraction of our trading community are compelled to bankruptcy as a necessary consequence. As well might you bind a millstone to one's neck and plunge him in the middle of the sea, and bid him breathe and live, as to compel a man to pay good dollars for his debts, while there are only two good dollars to twenty bad ones circulating in the currency. The whole mass of circulation which is afloat at any given time is absolutely necessary to be kept turning, in order that the debts which are made in the country under that volume of currency may be discharged. Hence, whenever banks contract, failures are as certain to follow as gravitation to act on a falling body. What an immense responsibility rests on these "paper currency" institutions! What a simple and unwise delegation of power, that the combined wisdom of our country should not, long since, have swept this abominable sin from our firesides!

The doctrine of many honest theorists on currency is that, if a bank be held strictly to specie redemption, it is amply sufficient for public protection; in other words, they may dilute the currency all they please, but if the public cannot corner them in it, if they redeem as fast as it is presented, this should be sufficient to satisfy the demands of the most exacting ultraist. With exultation and fancied triumph they will ask you: Is not a ten-dollar bill as good as a gold eagle, when you can command the eagle by presenting the bill at the bank? To this it may be replied, that if the bank holds eagles enough to redeem its circulation, then your bill may be very good; but if the bank only holds eagles enough to redeem one-tenth or one-twentieth of its circulation, your bill is of very doubtful value. The real value of the bill is mixed up with all the hazard which attaches to the chances of the bank being run upon and suspending cash payments. The doctrine is that as long as they redeem in cash they are all right, no matter what risks they are running, or what hazards they impose on the community. To make a comparison: what should we think of the casuist who should teach that men and women may live in a state of adultery, if they are thoroughly certain not to be detected in their intrigues?—that the crime is not in committing the transgression, but in being found out in their iniquity, and exposed to the scorn of the public. Such an abominable heresy in morality is exactly parallel with the one in currency, so strongly defended in these days—that banks should be allowed to issue all the currency they choose, provided they are held rigidly to specie redemption; and if you cannot catch them in their iniquitous practice, by presenting more than they can redeem, you, or the public at large, have no reason to complain. I maintain that this is as great a heresy in financial economy as the other is in ethics. The matter of detection is not necessary to fasten the moral guilt of the crime in either of the above cases. Each of these cases demand alike that men should cease to do evil. No reliance should be placed upon the chance that the evil act will never be exposed to society. And, to apply the argument to the issues of currency, these issues should never exceed the specie constantly kept on hand for their redemption. *This is the only touchstone by which to try bank issues.* The nominal redemption of banks and pretended specie payments, when they do not hold ten per cent. of their liabilities in coin, is all moonshine. Such issues work the evil in the country, whether you detect it or not. The currency of the country is like electricity: it permeates and governs the exchangeable values of all forms of wealth.

If merchants, and dealers in bank, insisted that bank loans should be made only in real cash, instead of bank notes and credits in bank, how different would the result be. A financial panic could never be known in the country. Now any considerable derangement in the commercial or mercantile world produces a money panic, and this comes on, too, at the very moment when the monetary power is most needed to sustain the country. Thus under our boasted American banking system, at the very time money is needed most, it is the most difficult, nay I might say impossible, to obtain it. The volume of currency which is necessary to be continued, to save the great interests of the nation from almost total destruction, is so much reduced that failures follow inevitably.

Every dollar of currency which the banks contract makes ten dollars of bankruptcy and insolvency in the community. So fatal is this system of making fictitious money, that its evils are only disclosed when panic and terror seize upon the minds of men, and they find that they have been lured into the error of promising to pay dollars for property which has been valued and measured by false standards ; and to meet these promises will more than absorb their whole possessions. It is the province and effect of paper money to create prices without corresponding values. Hence every one is more or less injured by it. From its insidious action no person can escape, if he lives where the abomination is tolerated. If a robber meets me on the public road, in open day, and takes from me one-half of my gold, he does me the same injury as the banker, who, by a dash of the pen in the bank parlor, deprives me of one-half the value of my money. There is, however, this difference, that if I happen to be armed, I may effectually resist the attack of the highwayman, and save my money ; but against the action of the bank president I have no recourse. His agency is like electricity, pervading all substances, and so subtile that locks, bars, and fastenings cannot exclude its influence. I may lock up my gold, and keep it under the closest custody; but so long as I am liable, through the action of bank alchemy, to lose half its value, I might as well lose half its quantity.

Another of the abominations of paper money is, that every one must receive it, and pay it, and use it as money, if he lives in a country where such a system of injustice is recognized by legislative enactments.

Wherever this monstrous fraud has gained the ascendency among the people, it becomes absolute, and crushes everything before it. No man can do business in a community, or in a country, unless he gives and takes such form of currency as others give and take in that community. No man can say in such a country, I will receive nothing but gold and silver, and I will pay nothing but gold and silver. Such form of self-proscription would ruin any man. If he adopted any such exclusive rule, no one would deal with him. Hence, right or wrong, the tyranny of paper money is completely absolute. If any man urged conscientious scruples on the subject, he would be ridiculed, or looked on as an ignorant zealot, seeking to reform society upon a point on which they are most determinately incorrigible.

But, notwithstanding all this perverseness on the subject, the fact is still patent, when tried by Revelation, that all substitutes for money which do not represent real cash in possession, are false measures of value, and are subject to the most decided condemnation, both by reason and a right interpretation of Scripture. The reader will understand me that, in excluding all substitutes for money, I do in no wise condemn any and all sorts of barter and exchanges of all kinds of goods, wares, and merchandise, to any extent which men may carry them. All such barter is honest, legitimate, and right; sanctioned by Divine and human law. But anything which deprives gold and silver of their value, or a large share of their value, except gold and silver themselves, works the same fraud and injury in the body politic which would be wrought by doing business with false weights and measures of quantities and capacities. From this the corollary is inevitable, that paper money in circulation, which does not represent legal coin, works the same injury to the public as counterfeit coin.

The whole volume of business which is wrought in any country, nation, or community, is subject to all the changes, chances, vicissitudes, and failures to which the currency of such nation is subject. Hence the absolute necessity of keeping the currency of a nation such that bankruptcy can never be introduced into it. And this can never be done except by making it gold and silver entirely. For real dollars are made of gold and silver only, with the legitimate alloy. But "promise to pay" dollars are made with the banker's pen and printing presses, and do, most essentially, lessen the value of real dollars, and are obnoxious to the sound logic of the American Constitution and the Christian's Bible. Does the Christian banker know that in issuing bank notes, or extending inscriptions of credit on the bank ledger, anything further than he has in actual possession—the hard dollars in gold or silver to meet the issue of such bank notes, or to take up the checks which may be drawn against such credit in bank—he is committing, in effect, the exact crime which the counterfeiter commits in making spurious coin? For the making of such coin, the counterfeiter is held to be a felon in the eyes of the law, and, on conviction, must serve out his time in the Penitentiary. This, under the United

States laws. But under the State laws, the counterfeiting of the State Bank issues is deemed a felony, and is liable to an equally severe penalty. Now, the effect of issuing and circulating counterfeit bills is the same upon the banks, provided such trash can get circulation, as the counterfeiting of the national coin has upon the sterling issues of the mint.

The evil of tampering with the currency is a grievance which interests every member of the body politic. To establish a pure currency, it must be made so efficiently. The moment any body of men have the privilege of making the medium of exchange for the country, by securing it on State stocks, mortgages, or any species or property security other than gold and silver, to them is delegated a power to commit infinite mischief. It will not do to convert any form of debt or property, save gold and silver, into currency; because, the moment this is done, gold and silver are shorn of a large fraction of their values. There is no way to keep their values as the Constitution contemplates, and as the Bible commands, but to exclude everything else except the precious metals, from being used as standards of value. All abominations of measuring by false standards must be cast aside, and the business of the whole country done by the righteous measures which a just and beneficent Providence has given to the American people—gold and silver. Whatever trade or exchange cannot be effected with these, in the nation, let it be done on the primitive and simple principle of barter, and bills of exchange from one part of the Union on another. Any affairs which cannot be done by these means, should be left undone till we augment enough of the national coin to transact them, without reducing the value of that coin by swelling the volume of currency with substitutes. Paper money, however, which is issued upon an actual deposit of gold coin in the hands of faithful custodians, or in the Treasury of the United States, and only issued dollar for dollar on such deposit, may be a great auxiliary to the business of the country.

We would not be among the number of those who "do evil that good may come;" who hold to the principle that the end justifies the means. Let us do right, when we know clearly what is such, and leave to a beneficent

Providence to show us that, if we persevere in the right, He will over-rule all things for our real, permanent good. But if we know the right, and persevere in the wrong, with the obstinate perversity that although we know our own acts are wrong to-day, yet we conceive good may come of our doing evil at some distant day, we are then "doing evil that good may come," and we are obnoxious to the fearful denunciation of the Apostle Paul, who says of such, that "their damnation is just." (See Rom. iii, 8.)

If to do justly, to act equitably, to measure honestly, to conform to the moral law given by God himself on Mount Sinai, to respect the Christian charge "to do to others as we would they should do to us," to live honestly with all men, to contend for righteousness and against extortion and iniquity—if these are acts of morality and Christian duty, then should the whole united phalanx of the Church militant on earth combine, to put down this nefarious abomination of false currency. With such opposition on the part of Christians, the leprosy which has so long tainted our people, and brought upon them such indescribable evils, would soon be banished from the body politic, and a healthful reform would be the happy result.

Whenever the people can understand that it is a Christian duty to oppose all issues of false currency, the days of this abomination will be numbered. The sin of idolatry, in the Scriptures of the Old Testament, is condemned in the most unmistakable language; while the New Testament discloses to us that *covetousness is idolatry*, and passes upon the sin in equal terms of severity. This sin, covetousness, is the parent of the abomination—false money, which brings it into being first, and then cherishes it with a parent's tenderness and regard.

An eminent ancient heathen moralist has left upon record a maxim which is often quoted by casuists, and which is worthy of deep reflection: "*Quem Deus vult perdere prius dementat.*" Upon this subject of currency it verily appears that the American people are demented. With gold and silver pouring in upon them in untold quantities, they insist upon continuing the old and nefarious system of bank notes and bank credits, and thus drive all the gold to Europe, where its real value is more justly appreciated. They are not even willing to commence a gradual system of reform, which contemplates ultimately a return to the honest standards of value recognized by the Bible and the American Constitution. Many of them really believe that a currency built upon State stocks is just as good as a currency built upon gold and silver. "Whom the gods would destroy they first make mad," was a Gentile maxim of fearful import; but the sentiment is iterated in language more terrible by the great apostle Paul, who speaks of men being* "left to believe a lie, that they might be damned." Every man who is so infatuated with paper money, as it is now established in the old States of the Union, and believes such currency as good as gold and silver, stands precisely under the awful denunciation of divine displeasure which the apostle has so forcibly unveiled in the text above quoted. Every man who does not believe such substitution as good as gold and silver, should, as a patriot, as a Christian, as a philanthropist, as a philosopher, as a statesman, and as an honest man, labor to effect a thorough reform through the country.

Let us glance, for a moment at the frightful catalogue of sins which are prompted by this abomination of tampering with the honest measures of value—silver and gold. It promotes and begets the following vices and sins to an immense extent: Dishonesty in trade, cheating, lying, deception, betrayal of trusts, embezzlement, false entries in mercantile and bank books, frauds, thefts, perjuries, forgeries, suicides, assassinations, murders, insanity, madness, destruction of families, gambling, betting, immoral associations; and as the vices are gregarious, and move together in gangs, it may be truly said that there is not a command in the moral law which God has ordained for men to keep, or a sin which he has commanded them to abstain from, but what receives direct nourishment and support from this ungodly abomination, which I am attempting to expose in its enormity to the American people. It is directly or indirectly the prompter and promoter of more than one-half of the sins and wickedness committed in the American Union. The

* 2 Thes. ii, 11 and 12.

Psalmist says in the 127th Psalm, "Except the Lord build the house, they labor in vain that build it." Now will God build up this nation when they found their measures in extortion and wickedness?—when He tells them to "have a just balance, a just weight, a just ephah, and let all their acts be built in righteousness." "The scant measure is abominable, and the bag of deceitful weights." "A perfect and just measure shalt thou have." "A just weight is his delight." Consider, then, that with God there is no difference whether a man cheats in false measures of quantity or in false measures of value. The sin is exactly identical, and its consequences will be equally disastrous to the presumptuous mortal who shall raise his feeble arm against the decrees of the Almighty, whether he cheats in measure or in value.

The volume of currency in a country is what makes prices, and any element introduced into the currency which makes prices without corresponding value, is continually compelling all consumers to pay value without receiving value, is compelling men to go in debt and promise to pay dollars where they do not receive equal value for such dollars; is working confusion and folly; is subverting the standards of value; is vilifying and cheapening gold and silver, and is consummating, as fast as possibly can be wrought by such agency, individual and national bankruptcy. In this connection it is relevant to state that the nature of money upon prices is like electricity. It permeates and saturates everything. Locks, bars, and bolts cannot exclude its influence and power. You may lock up your gold from the burglar, but you cannot hinder the action of bank notes and bank credits in taking from your gold a large fraction of its value.

From this it results that every kind of business in the United States, no matter how honest and praiseworthy, that even agriculture, manufactures, commerce, and all the most useful industrial pursuits of the population, are measurably brought into the scale of gambling. Our honest men are compelled, by the action of this abomination, this national plague spot, to assume risks in ordinary business equal to gambling operations, contrary to their own sound judgment and ardent wishes to act upon different principles.

The following truthful extract, from the pen of Matthew Hale Smith, is worthy to be treasured in the memory of all business men: "No passion is more ruinous than the 'haste to be rich.' It is condemned alike by revelation, reason, and the sound practical experience of life. It leads men into unsafe and ruinous speculation; it seduces them from fast-anchored property to the mirage that glitters. It allows the hands of industry to stand still on the dial-plate of life, while men grasp at shadows. It is this passion separates the business past from the business present by so wide a gulf. The modern merchant, with small capital, and that perhaps not his own, with his granite store, his mahogany desk, his country seat, fast horse, and rash speculations, scorns the example of his sire, who, at his desk of pine and green baize, sat sixteen mortal hours each day at his business, doing his own errands, and being his own clerk. With so wide a contrast, it is not strange that so many begin business where their sires left off, and leave off where the sires began."

The perversion of the currency is but an effect of avarice. What name should we give to a perverted currency, which by its action necessarily resolves the whole business of the country into a vast arena of gambling operations? Well does the Bible call the dealing with false weights and measures an abomination—an abomination abhorrent to God, and introduced by the wiles of the devil and the invention of his pliant tools, who hesitate not to practice these insidious acts of unrighteousness upon innocent and ignorant victims, who are daily and constantly driven to madness and ruin, as a necessary consequence.

The laws of God are irreversible, and a part of these laws are called the laws of nature. The Divine law most emphatically condemns this sin, and pronounces it an abomination. The laws of political economy condemn it, and hold it up to us as the precursor of inevitable ruin. The American Constitution is opposed to it, and this is the only bond which unites us as sovereign States. The Bible forbids it most emphatically in spirit, and if it had been a sin of early day, would have placed it in the category of "covetousness, which is idolatry." Such are some of the fruits of this sin. It might be enlarged upon almost indefinitely, but only the deep thinkers can follow the argument and see what ruin it is bringing upon us.

There is an ethical heresy in regard to amassing gold, against which I would record my testimony. Many suppose that to amass gold is a heinous sin, and to hoard it is completely abominable. That while it is perfectly right and honorable to add house to house, and land to land—in fine, to secure every other form of wealth in any quantities which heart could wish, or industry could achieve—to amass gold is called the essence of avarice, and the heinous sin of the miser. No such distinction as this exists in the moral law; and if any sin attaches to amassing wealth of any kind, it is no more sinful to amass gold than other forms of capital. The reader will note, that I am not discussing the question, whether it be lawful for a Christian to amass great wealth in any shape? I simply aver that it is no more immoral, no more inconsistent with Christian character, to amass gold than any other form of wealth. If a man possess half a million of dollars in various kinds of good property, surely he should not be deemed unwise, a bad citizen, or an enemy to his race, if he chose that the excess of his estate, over this sum, should be kept locked up in gold, and producing him no interest at all. So long as he gives an equivalent for his gold, he gets it honestly; and if he loses the interest upon it by hoarding during his life, he will leave to the next generation a form of wealth which is perennial; and will also render the country an essential service by saving the coin, which Americans seem determined shall only be possessed by foreign capitalists.

How far the Christian is justified in amassing any form of wealth, is a matter for him to decide in his own conscience. It would seem that the laudable use which he purposes to make of it, is the only excuse which he can have for any uncommon exertions to acquire it. A competence is requisite for the comfort and happiness of all men: but great wealth is a snare to its possessor. It may do him and his family vastly greater injury than though he had been content with reasonable possessions. Again, the world only contains a given amount of wealth : if it falls into the hands of comparatively few, the multitudes must groan in poverty. These considerations are for the professed Christian only; for with the world at large they would pass as unreasonable, illogical, and impracticable.

"The earth is the Lord's, and the fullness thereof." Of course, He has a right to impose any condition upon the possessor of it which His will may dictate. And, beyond controversy, the lines are rigidly imposed upon the Christian. "He that hath two coats let him give to him who has none." "Go and sell what thou hast and give to the poor, and come and follow me, and thou shalt have treasure in heaven." If these commands interdict the possession of mammon by the Christian, they forbid every form of it alike ; and the professed disciple who adds acre to acre, house to house, land to land, is Pharisaical, if he thinks himself any more righteous than his brother, who adds to his increments of gain in the form of gold and silver.

Most fitting and proper is it that the clarion notes of reform of the currency should be sounded from the Pacific Coast. That from the State which furnishes the Union with the means of deliverance from the thraldom of debt and false currency, should come forth the demonstration, that it is for the highest interest of the whole people of the Union to use the wealth which a beneficent Creator has given them in ample quantities to do the business of the States, and to reject and cast from them, as beneath the dignity, intelligence, and honesty of a people of such high privilege, the machinations of designing men, and vampires who devour their real substance. But if the people of the old States will not hear to the voice of reason, to the call of truth, to the dictates of wisdom, and to the still higher claims of justice and the commands of God, if they will perversely cling to "the flesh-pots of Egypt," if they have "sold themselves to work evil in the sight of the Lord," when too late it may be said to them, as of an ancient unfaithful servant, "Ephraim is joined to his idols, let him alone."

The American people of the old States are diseased with the leprosy of paper money, and, loathsome as is the complaint, there are not wanting empirics who would inoculate California with the same disgusting malady. These States are unwilling to use the remedies which a beneficent Creator has put into their hands, and which, if freely and rightly used, would be a sovereign remedy for the disease which is literally consuming them. But, as the unfaithful and covetous servant Gehazi, who knew his master's will and still acted in opposition to it, was visited by the awful denunciation of the prophet, "the leprosy of Naaman shall cleave unto thee and unto thy seed forever," so, if California shall enter into this same abomination of the old States, without even a semblance of excuse for so doing, she will be more guilty than any other State in the Confederation, for she will sin not only against light and knowledge, but wantonly, and without any necessity or temptation for so doing. Yet if California can be the instrument, in the hand of a merciful Providence, of bringing our brethren of the old States to search into and thoroughly reform this national plague, she will perform for them a service even more valuable than her treasure can confer, for she will institute a reform most salutary to their morals—a return to true Christian principles, to the standard of justice and righteousness.

The preceding essay was written shortly after the failure of the banks in 1857. This failure came on in a time of peace and unexampled prosperity, with our garners loaded with the bountiful crops of years of abundance, our manufacturers doing a most extended business, our commerce whitening the seas and oceans of earth with its spreading canvas, and withal, after California mines had yielded nearly five hundred millions of dollars. With such a vast aggregation of individual and national wealth, the banks all suspended cash payments as soon as the ball was set in motion. The impetus which first disclosed the rottenness of the system was, the failure of the Ohio Life and Trust Company for about two and a half millions, and the wreck of the Central America, bearing one and a half millions in gold, upon which the speculators of Wall street were depending to fulfill their contracts and turn their corners. Money immediately rose from four per cent. per year to four per cent. a month, and was hardly to be obtained upon any terms. Every system of banking, which had existed in the United States before 1857, had been demonstrated to be a practical failure. But this failure demonstrated the boasted New York free banking system to be no exception. It has been estimated that the contraction of the currency, by the banks in the country, during the panic of 1857, created bankruptcies to the extent of 500,000,000 of dollars. This ruin and devastation came upon the people almost as suddenly as the terrors of an earthquake. It proved most conclusively that, after such immense receipts of gold from California, if the system of the banks had been a sound one, they would never have suspended cash payments at so comparatively insignificant cause as above mentioned.

The National banks are instituted upon the same foundation as the New York free banking law, their issues being secured upon Federal stocks instead of State. The principle is exactly the same—monetizing debt, and demonetizing gold. So long as their issues are made upon such a basis, they will be liable to the identical charges which have been preferred against that system. No system of currency which promotes gambling, or which measures by false standards, should receive the least toleration or support at the hands of a people who profess morality and wisdom.

"Because sentence against an evil work is not executed speedily, therefore the heart of the sons of men is fully set in them to do evil." (Ecclesiastes viii, 11.) It is probable that there is no public evil, of an extended nature, which is more signally rebuked and condemned by the preceding words of revelation, than this sin of vitiating the constitutional currency of the land, by substituting one of greatly inferior value. The action of the substitute is slow and subtle, but it permeates every form of business and industry. It being so generally diffused, so wide-spread through all the ramifications of business, its evils are not visible; and yet, it is pre-eminently "*an evil work*" of most incalculable magnitude. Sentence is not, for these reasons, speedily executed upon it; and, therefore, the hearts of men, making gain out of this iniquity, are fully set in them to do, and to continue to do, this immense evil to the products of honest industry. The profits on the circulation of a common medium of exchange, which is below what it purports to be worth, is a direct spoliation upon the community which tolerates it, and is virtually a tax upon them many times over the amount of such circulation. And because the State banks have availed themselves of this form of plunder with great success, therefore, the Congress has seen fit to inaugurate the same form of iniquity, and screen it by national legislation.

We are trying the National bank issues now by the standard of morality laid down in the Scriptures of truth. These are abundant and iterated. To quote them all is not needed, but in Deuteronomy the Divine law is express. (See ch. xxv, 13–17.) "Thou shalt not have in thy bag divers weights, a great and a small. Thou shalt not have in thy house divers measures, a great and a small. But thou shalt have a perfect and just weight, a perfect and just measure shalt thou have; that thy days may be lengthened in the land which the Lord thy God giveth thee. For all that do such things, and all that do unrighteously, are an abomination unto the Lord thy God." And if measures of quantities are so exactly defined in the Scriptures, are not measures of values to be guarded with equal or greater exactness? In the Legal Tender Acts of Congress, and in the act establishing the national currency, the National Legislature has trampled under foot the Divine law, which positively forbids having divers measures. It is mockery to pretend that we trust in Him, and stamp it on the coin, while our laws are framed in such unrighteousness that we are not permitted to use this coin at its just value, because of a substitute, legitimated by the Acts of Congress, of far inferior value. "Except the Lord build the house, they labor in vain that build it." (Psalm 127.) We may rest assured that He will not build the house, if it is founded on injustice; for He can never ignore one of His own attributes.

The Congress has enacted that the promise of a dollar shall be as good and the equivalent of a metallic dollar.

And is this not having in the bag divers weights, a great and a small?—the gold dollar worth one hundred cents, and the promise worth half or two-thirds as much. Congress would seem to show its devotion to right and principle by impressing on the mint coins that "IN GOD WE TRUST." A proper and worthy motto for a Christian people; but if we would really prove that we trust in Him, we must obey His laws; and, above all, the National Legislature should not enact laws in direct conflict with the Divine laws. "They that plough iniquity and sow wickedness reap the same." (Job iv, 8.) "For they have sown the wind, and they shall reap the whirlwind." (Hosea viii, 7.) "Be not deceived; God is not mocked: for whatsoever a man soweth that shall he also reap." (Gal. vi, 7.) It seems like mockery and gross irreverence for Congress to attempt to propitiate the outrageous act of making all the United States use false measures of value, in instituting the legal tenders, by stamping on its coin "IN GOD WE TRUST." The proof of such trust would be more visible and more satisfactory by doing away with all unrighteousness in our national currency and legal tender bills—not holding in the bag double weights, a great and a small; but adjusting everything by the gold standard. When will the nation act upon the principles of righteousness?

No. XIX.

ENLARGEMENT OF THE POWERS, USES, AND BENEFITS OF THE INDEPENDENT TREASURY.

"The issue of currency and its regulation is an attribute of sovereignty, and everywhere is exercised by the sovereign power, except in the United States. Here, also, it was intended to be an attribute of sovereignty, and was placed in the hands of Congress, *and limited to the issue of gold and silver, and the regulation of its value.*"—*Thomas H. Benton.*

"Our present Government was formed by hard-money men, who had seen and felt the disastrous and *demoralizing* effect of paper money, and were anxious to save their posterity from such calamities as they had suffered. They did their part to save us. Shall we be false to ourselves and to them?"—*Thomas H. Benton.*

"Deposits and circulation are essentially the same thing; they are convertible into each other at the pleasure of the possessor."—*Nathan Appleton.*

"Circulation is deposits inside out, while deposits are circulation outside in."—*A. B. Johnson.*

"We ought to include deposits with circulation, as the bank check goes as far as the bank note in making purchases and payments."—*William M. Gouge.*

"The whole subject of bank deposits is beset with difficulties. The extent to which it has already been carried has deeply endangered the stability of the banking system, and we have seen that it is *indispensable* that it should be *subjected to regulation.*"—*J. R. McCulloch.*

"The effect of an alteration in the value of the article selected as the standard of value, is evidently to impair its utility in that respect. Fixity is the first essential in a standard measure; any alteration in the measuring instrument is clearly a source of confusion."—*London Economist.*

"So far as the currency of a country is alloyed; so long as anything inferior to bullion is allowed to ride as a dead weight on bullion's back, it is of little consequence whether such dead weight be composed of lead or copper, paper or leather; nor so far as a country's *home trade* is concerned, does it matter whether the substitute for bullion circulates in distinct pieces, or is incorporated into the gold and silver coin at the mint. As things are now managed, American trade and industry are made to *buy paper* of the banks at the price of gold, and to sell gold to foreigners at the price of paper. It should be borne in mind, however, that so far as paper money is *a clear and only title to gold or silver in the keeping of a good custodian*, it is *not* false money, and in no way weakens the purchasing power of gold and silver coins. It is only when banks sell money that they do not own, or agree to deliver money that they have not received, that they falsify the measure of value, or derange trade, or impoverish industry."—*John H. Hunt.*

In a former paper on the subject of bank deposits and inscriptions of credit in bank, it was my purpose to show that deposits were virtually currency. As they hold this high relation to the values of all property, both real and personal, indeed, as they may be said to make the prices of property in the country quite as much as bank circulation, no institution under a State charter should be allowed to grant such inscriptions of credit unless the national coin, or paper absolutely equal to the national coin, was deposited to meet such credit. Bank deposits are the currency which pays all large debts, while bank notes are the currency which pays all small debts. They are equally currency. Now, as Mr. McCulloch well remarks, "it is indispensable they should be subjected to regulation." Even if the American Constitution did not expressly give to Congress "the power to coin money and fix the value thereof," it would belong to them under the law of nations, which makes it an attribute of the sovereignty to regulate the currency. Hence Congress has full right to protect the Union from the wanton waste of treasure which has been brought upon the people of the United States by the action of State banks. A thorough protection in this regard will involve a surveillance and regulation of the deposit account of banks, as much as of their bills in circulation.

The great aim of the public in watching banks has been to keep them in a position to convert their circulation of bank notes at sight, while the deposit account has scarcely been thought of. Such watchfulness does not strike at the root of the evil. The panic of 1857 demonstrated that the deposit account—the internal circulation of the banks in their own vaults—was what they most dreaded; and this, too, with good reason. The heaviest bank in Wall street, with a capital of nine millions, issues no notes at all. Several others of the New York city banks, with capitals of one and a half and two millions of dollars, do not circulate over one hundred thousand dollars of bills. Their whole profits are inside circulation—that is, their deposit account. These all suspended together in October, 1857. "Why did the banks which issued next to nothing in comparison with their capital, suspend?" Because their depositors checked on them for funds on deposit. Or, more properly, because their depositors checked on them for funds at their credit on the ledgers, for which credits the banks had no real funds on hand but discounted paper, due at a distant day. That is, the banks had promised to deliver money without receiving money. Hence they had promised an impossibility. By so doing, they had to suspend specie payment. Still that is precisely the business they are now doing. No salutary lesson has been taught them by their imprudence.

They are pursuing the same old beaten track again, and in due time they will be brought up with a whirlwind more furious than the blast of 1857. But in the mean time they are doing the country great mischief. California suffers immensely by them. She has in time past paid double prices on all she has imported from the old States; for a false currency has made prices without corresponding value on all her imports from the old States, and she has lost thereby two hundred and fifty millions of dollars. She is continuing to lose at the rate of twenty millions of dollars per annum by the action of this unjust and illegal system of the old States. Nor does the sacking of California of her treasure in this unjust manner inure to the benefit of the old States; for England and Europe take it from the old States as fast as we send it forward to them. No tariff can stop it but the edict of the people, who should at once rise in their majesty, and resolve that gold and silver shall measure the values of property in future in the United States, and *not* bank notes and bank credits. Let us glance at the balance sheet of the nation for the last ten years. In 1850 Americans owed to foreigners $168,000,000; in 1860 they owed $450,000,000. This is all chargeable to the making of a bankrupt currency; that is, a currency which makes prices for everything on a false basis; a currency which is said to be good so long as it is not called for, but when called for in earnest proves to be nothing but the device of the genius of speculation and mischief; a currency which gets every one in debt by its easy system of multiplication, and suddenly contracts and leaves the suffering victim to get out the easiest way he can, or die in the attempt; a system which reflects both upon the honesty and intelligence of the American people. The Americans work, toil, and labor with marked diligence; they exhaust their lives in industrial pursuits, and wear themselves out to get wealth; but they grasp at the shadow and miss the substance; they "sow to the wind and reap the whirlwind"; they are all at work for the giant capitalists of Europe. The banks are an organized system of agents or factors, professing to pay the people money for their labor, but in fact are only the instruments through which foreigners abstract from us the mass of the wealth of the country. The banks are careful to get names worth three or four dollars for every dollar of fiction they discount, so that when loss comes they will be protected. The losses fall on the manufacturing, agricultural, trading, and industrial portion of the community. The banks are the capillary vessels by which the gains of the whole community are taken up in small increments and disbursed from a smaller to a larger institution of finance, till at length they fall into the great maelstrom of foreign shipments, and are almost a total loss to the country.

If the crowned heads and potentates of Europe had held a Convention, to devise the most efficient measures to despoil the United States of the mass of their wealth, they could not have adopted a more perfect system to achieve their purpose than our own *régime* of finance and banks. The champions of paper and credit money say other nations have the same system, and why may we not continue it? To this I reply that paper money, like a metallic currency, may be debased in any given ratio to the sterling coin. The sterling coin might be alloyed with base metals one-half, two-thirds, three-quarters, or any other fractional amount. So paper money might be bad ten, twenty, fifty, or ninety per cent., in proportion as any bank issues such paper beyond its specie means of redemption. The difference between the paper money of Europe and the United States is, that the former is decidedly bad, and the latter is extremely bad—both are bad; and if I were called upon to express the comparative degree of debasement relatively between the two systems, I would say that the dollar in silver or gold, being represented by its par of 100, most of the currencies in Europe would stand at about 75, while that of the United States would not stand higher than 50. Here is difference enough in the currencies to send all of our money to Europe; and there it goes, and will continue to go, so long as we cling to this foolish system of doing business with a debased currency.

To remedy these evils the American people need the action of Congress upon the currency. This is the opinion of our soundest economists, but none of them have shown the precise action which is needed in the premises. After much thought and study upon the subject I have drawn up a bill, which, if it can be passed and become the law of the land, will gradually place us upon a sound and solid basis. It will protect American industry better than a thousand tariffs. It will save, after it comes fully into operation, thirty-three millions of dollars a year to the Federal Government, and ten millions of dollars a year to the State Governments. It will bring our imports and exports annually on to an equality, and will leave to the country the whole yield of the gold mines of California, to redeem the people from the bankruptcy which they have voluntarily assumed, or which they have consented that the banks should impose upon them. It will make the Independent Treasury of ten times the use to the people which it has ever been to the Government, and will multiply its uses to the Government many fold. To California the passage of the bill is not second in importance to the Pacific Railroad. These will be the advantages of the bill. That a bill, contemplating such vast interests, should be drawn perfectly at first, would be uncommon: yet it contains the salient points, and many of the details, of a bill for the enacting of which by Congress the whole American people are suffering. I submit the bill to my countrymen, and have done my duty in the premises.

AN ACT to enlarge the powers and the usefulness of the Independent Treasury of the United States; to create one more officer in the Federal Cabinet; to assume the control of all banks of issue and deposit in the United States and in the Territories and Districts of the United States; to provide for the gradual suppression of the circulation of all bank bills and bank notes which are not founded on a specie basis; to raise the quality of deposits in banks gradually to the specie standard; and for the restoration of the currency to the standard value of gold and silver contemplated by the Constitution of the United States.

Be it enacted by the Senate and House of Representatives of the United States of America in Congress assembled.

SEC. 1. That on and after the first Monday of January, A. D. 1861, the Independent Treasury of the United States shall be divided into two separate and distinct departments.

SEC. 2. *And be it further enacted,* That these Departments shall be known and designated as the Department of Revenue and the Department of Finance.

SEC. 3. *And be it further enacted*, That the Department of Revenue shall embrace the Independent Treasury as heretofore organized; and the Department of Finance shall embrace the organization, powers, functions, duties, and offices as hereinafter provided by this Act.

SEC. 4. *And be it, etc.*, That there shall be one more Cabinet officer appointed, under the title of Controller of Finance, and his salary shall be the same as the salary of the Secretary of the Treasury.

SEC. 5. *And be it, etc.*, That the Department of Revenue of the Independent Treasury shall be under the control of the Secretary of the Treasury, and the Department of Finance shall be under the control of the Controller of Finance.

SEC. 6. *And be it, etc.*, That the two departments of the Treasury shall be kept entirely separate and distinct from each other.

SEC. 7. *And be it, etc.*, That the Department of Finance shall have one principal office in the city of Washington, D. C., one branch office in the city of New York, one branch in the city of New Orleans, one branch in the city of Boston, one branch in the city of St. Louis, and one branch in the city of San Francisco; also as many more branches in the United States as Congress in its wisdom may from time to time hereafter appoint.

SEC. 8. *And be it, etc.*, That each office and branch office shall have one vice controller, who shall be at the head of the affairs of the office where he is appointed, and as many clerks, tellers, book-keepers and assistants as the duties of the office shall require.

SEC. 9. *And be it, etc.*, That each office shall have one legal counselor, with a yearly salary of three thousand five hundred dollars.

SEC. 10. *And be it, etc.*, That the salary of each of the five controllers shall be three-quarters of the salary of the Controller of Finance, except the vice controller of the branch of the city of New York, which shall be the same as the controller.

SEC. 11. *And be it, etc.*, That the salaries of the cashiers, clerks, tellers, bookkeepers, and other assistants, shall be fixed by the controller or vice controller of the office where such vice controller is principal, and shall be graduated as nearly as possible to what is paid for similar services in banks and offices of discount.

SEC. 12. *And be it, etc.*, That the controller shall appoint the cashier, clerks, tellers, bookkeepers, and other officers necessary in the principal office at Washington, subject to the approval of the President and other officers of the Cabinet, and shall fix their salaries. He shall also take good and sufficient bonds for the faithful and honest discharge of the trusts and duties of their office. He shall also take good and sufficient bonds of all the vice controllers of the various branches, and all of these bonds shall be subject to the approval and acceptance of the President of the United States and all the Cabinet officers. The vice controller shall, at first, be appointed by the President of the United States, by and with the advice and consent of the whole Cabinet; afterwards, as vacancies in the office of vice controller shall ensue, from death, resignation, or any other cause, the offices shall be filled by appointment of the President of the United States, by and with the consent of the Senate. Any vacancy occurring during the recess of Congress may be filled by appointment of the President of the United States, subject to approval of the Senate when next in session.

SEC. 13. *And be it, etc.*, That the Controller of Finance shall be appointed by the President of the United States for the first year, and afterwards by the President of the United States, by and with the consent of the Senate.

SEC. 14. *And be it, etc.*, That the department of Finance shall issue certificates of deposit for American gold coin which may be deposited in sums not less than one hundred dollars; and any sums above one hundred dollars which can be divided by the number ten without a remainder, always rejecting cents, or any fraction of a dollar.

SEC. 15. *And be it, etc.*, That the certificates of deposit shall run to the depositor (by name) or bearer, and shall pass without any endorsement except that of the person to whom issued, and he shall endorse the same without recourse.

SEC. 16. *And be it, etc.*, That the Treasury shall not be responsible for any loss occurring to any person or persons by reason of any certificate of deposit being paid to any one that does not own the same.

SEC. 17. *And be it, etc.*, That whenever notice is given to the office or any branch, of any certificate of deposit being lost or stolen, the payment of such certificate shall be stopped, to aid the real owner in the recovery of his money; but if such certificate has been paid by the department, or branch, before such notice has been served, then there shall be no recourse on the Treasury—the loss must fall on the owner.

SEC. 18. *And be it, etc.*, That certificates of deposit shall never be issued in duplicate by the department; but in cases where the loss is proven beyond a doubt, such certificates may be paid after the lapse of one year from the time of loss, if the owner gives satisfactory bonds to the department that the lost certificate or certificates shall never be demanded of the department, and shall hold the Government harmless for all costs and damages by reason of such payment.

SEC. 19. *And be it, etc.*, That all certificates of deposit shall be presented for payment within six years from the time of their issue, or they shall be barred from payment by limitation.*

SEC. 20. *And be it, etc.*, That the office at Washington may draw exchanges on any of the branches created under this act, at the current rate of exchange between the places, or at such rates as the Controller of Finance shall establish; also, the branches may draw exchange on the office at Washington, and on each other, at such rates as the Controller shall establish; such exchange to be paid for only in American gold, and at the time the bill is drawn.

SEC. 21. *And be it, etc.*, That no duplicate bill, or second of exchange, shall be drawn in less than three months after the date of the original bill, nor shall it then be

---

* The first United States bank was chartered in 1791, and its charter expired 4th March, 1811. The second United States bank was chartered in 1816, and its charter expired 4th March, 1836. The business of the last institution was closed by the Bank of the United States, a corporation chartered by the Legislature of Pennsylvania. In closing the affairs of the second bank, the charter of which expired in 1836, bank notes issued by the old bank of 1791 were presented for payment. It is needless to add, they were a total loss to the holders. For this reason I inserted in the bill section nineteen, which might appear to many as supererogatory.

drawn unless there is satisfactory evidence that the original bill has been lost.

Sec. 22. *And be it, etc.,* That bills of exchange shall be drawn to the person applying for them or bearer, and they shall be indorsed by the person to whom they are payable, without recourse. Bills of exchange shall be drawn at sight, or at one day's sight. No bills shall be drawn for less than one hundred dollars, and any sum above one hundred dollars which can be divided by the number ten without a remainder, rejecting all fractions of a dollar.

Sec. 23. *And be it, etc.,* That bills of exchange shall be presented for payment within six years from the date of their issue, or they shall be barred by limitation.

Sec. 24. *And be it, etc.,* That all bills of exchange and deposit certificates shall be filled from proper printed forms, bound in separate books, with a wide margin or stubble. The margin shall be kept in the book, and upon the margin shall be registered the date of the bill or certificate of deposit, the amount of the same, the number of the bill or certificate, and the name of the person to whom the bill or certificate was issued, and upon what branch the bill was drawn. The books of stubble shall be carefully preserved, and as fast as the certificates of deposit and bills of exchange are returned to the office or branch which issues them, they shall be canceled by cutting a cross through the paper and stamping them with printer's ink, PAID. Also, by erasing the signatures with a pen and black ink. They shall then be pasted on to the stubble in the book from which they were originally issued. The forms of the blanks shall be with the most ingenious devices of engraving and checks, to prevent counterfeits. Bills of exchange and deposit certificates shall never be re-issued; they shall be charged over to the branch which issues them, and sent back as fast as practicable and safe.

Sec. 25. *And be it, etc.,* That the books of the department and branches shall be kept in double entry form, and balance sheets shall be rendered to the Department at Washington once a month.

Sec. 26. *And be it, etc.,* That the Controller of the Department of Washington shall make a statement semi-annually, on the first Tuesday in January and the first

Tuesday in July, each year, which statement shall be printed in one of the newspapers of the city of Washington, and one of the papers in the city of New York. This statement shall show the amount of gold on deposit in the office and each of its branches; the amount of gold which belongs to individual depositors, and the amount which belongs to banks and banking institutions; the amount of bills of exchange and deposit certificates which have been issued by the department and each of its branches; the amount of bills of exchange and deposit certificates which have been redeemed and canceled; and shall show the balance outstanding and due from the department or any of its branches; the amount of premiums on bills of exchange, incidental expense account, and any other items necessary, proper, and correct to report, to make a lucid, plain and intelligible balance sheet, showing to the public its exact standing. And, also, the statement for the first Tuesday in January of each year shall be submitted to a committee of the Senate for rigid examination and approval. The said committee to consist of three of its members, who shall have access to any and all the books and papers of the department, and may examine any officer of the department under oath as to any facts relevant to the report of the real situation of the department. The said committee shall be appointed by the President of the Senate.

SEC. 27. *And be it, etc.*, That the Department of Finance, of the Independent Treasury of the United States, shall be vested with further powers, functions, duties, and prerogatives, with the view of restoring the currency of the United States, its territories, and districts, to the pure standard of value contemplated by the constitution of the United States, and to protect the owners of gold from loss by State banks.

SEC. 28. *And be it, etc.*, That every bank in any State of the United States, in the Territories, and in the District of Columbia, which issues bills of credit or bank bills, or that receives on deposit and pays such bills, shall comply with the terms of this act, or its business operations shall be immediately enjoined by the United States District Court in the district where such bank is located, and its affairs shall go into an immediate process of liquidation.

SEC. 29. *And be it, etc.*, That on or before the first Monday of January, 1861, and yearly, and every year afterwards to and including the first Monday of January, 1870, and on the first Monday of each month of January of every year intervening between said years 1861 and 1870, every bank in the United States, in the District of Columbia, and in any territory of the United States which issues bills of credit, or bank notes, or which receives bank notes or bills of credit on deposit, shall deposit yearly, on the first Monday of January of every year, commencing on the first Monday of January, 1861, ten per cent. of its capital stock in American gold coin, in the department of finance of the Independent Treasury of the United States, or one of its branches, and shall continue said deposits yearly thereafter of ten per cent. per annum, till their whole capital stock shall be converted into gold.

SEC. 30. *And be it, etc.*, That on depositing the said yearly installment of ten per centum per annum of their capital stock with the department of finance, or either of its branches in the United States, the department or branch with which such deposit is made shall issue to the bank engraved stamps, in sums of not less than ten dollars, in the usual form, size, and shape of bank notes now in circulation in the State of New York; and sums above ten dollars shall be for twenty dollars, fifty dollars, one hundred dollars, five hundred dollars, one thousand dollars. No stamps shall be issued but for sums that can be divided by ten without a remainder. These stamps shall be issued to the depositing bank for exactly the amount of gold which such bank deposits; and the gold shall be kept in the department of finance, or one of its branches with which it is deposited, for the redemption of these stamps, and for no other purpose. Across the face of the stamps shall be plainly impressed or printed the words "Secured by deposit of gold in the Treasury of the U. S." The stamp shall be numbered, registered, and countersigned by the vice controller, cashier, or by two of the tellers of the department, or of the branch which issues the same.

SEC. 31. *And be it, etc.*, That the department shall number all its issues of stamps, from number one and upwards, so that the number which any stamp bears shall show the exact number issued or prepared for issue; and these stamps shall all be registered, and a record truly kept of the same; also, the bank to which such stamps have been issued. Each branch shall also commence its numbering of stamps with the number one, and comply with the above conditions of this section, so that the numbering of the stamps issued shall agree with the actual number which has been emitted by the department or by the branches. The dies for these stamps shall be gotten up and engraved by the most skillful artists, to prevent counterfeiting. They shall be impressed or printed on fine paper, prepared expressly for the purpose, and every sheet of the paper shall have a water mark and colored lines passing through it. The number of sheets of paper shall be carefully counted by two of the tellers or officers of the department or branch, and handed to the printer, and the number of sheets returned by the printer shall be counted with the same care, to see that the whole of the paper is returned to the department or branch. The dies, plates, chemicals, ink, paper, and all the matter connected with the making of the stamps, shall be under the immediate keeping and control of the department or the branch for which they are made. One of the tellers or clerks may be commissioned to watch the dies and plates every moment they are out of the office for impressions.

SEC. 32. *And be it, etc.*, That these stamps may be used, by the bank to which they are issued, as money, and will be redeemed at sight, when presented, in gold, at the department, or at the branch which issues them—meaning that the department shall redeem the stamps which it issues, and that each of the branches shall redeem the stamps issued by such branch whenever the same are presented for payment. And on the last week of every alternate month, commencing to reckon from the 1st of January, 1861—that is, to begin on the last week in the month of February, 1861—the cashier of the department, and the cashiers of all the branches, shall give notice to the banks that have opened accounts with them of the amount of stamps which they have redeemed; and the banks which receive such notice shall have four weeks longer to return the gold into the department or branch which gives them such notice. And on depositing the gold again, the department or branch shall return to such bank the stamps taken up, for re-issue.

This will allow a circulation of about ninety days on the stamps, at which time they must be taken from the department or branch by a new deposit of gold. Any bank failing to make the new deposit, and not taking up the stamps at the end of thirty days after the date of the notice by the department or branch, shall forfeit and pay interest to the department or branch at the rate of six per cent. per annum upon the amount of stamps reported due for the space of thirty days longer; and if at the end of said thirty days they are still defaulters, it shall be the duty of the controller or vice controller to enjoin their further business in banking, and coerce such banks into liquidation. Notices of the amount of stamps redeemed will be sent to the banks about every sixty days.

SEC. 33. *And be it, etc.*, That no bank shall keep an account with or receive the notes of a bank which has become a defaulting bank, and is reported such by the Department of Finance of the United States. This section is not advisory, but imperative on all banks which may keep an account with the department or its branches.

SEC. 34. *And be it, etc.*, That the Department of Finance shall be liable for the safe keeping and return of all gold deposited to the owners thereof; also for the redemption in gold of all stamps, certificates of deposit, and bills of exchange issued by the department; also, for any defalcation, embezzlement, or theft, of any funds in their keeping by the officers of the department or branches, or any burglary or robbery committed by thieves or robbers, and also for any losses by fire, lightning, or any accident.

SEC. 35. *And be it, etc.*, That in the year 1861, commencing the first Tuesday of January, ten per cent. shall be paid in gold or Treasury stamps on all checks, drafts, bills of exchange, and every form of paper paid at any bank in the United States, or in the District of Columbia, or in any territory of the United States; the balance may be paid in currency, if the creditor elects. In the year 1862 twenty per cent. shall be paid in gold and silver on all such paper or Treasury stamps, and so on increasing yearly ten per cent. more on all bank payments, in gold or Treasury stamps, till in the year 1871, and ever afterwards, all payments of every name and description made at the banks shall be in gold or silver, or in Treasury stamps. *Provided, nevertheless*, that no person dealing with any bank is obliged by this act to receive anything but gold and silver for the whole amount of dealing between such person and the bank; but the banks are compelled and required to pay on all checks and demands of every kind, in the respective years above named, the per centage in gold or silver or stamped paper of the department as above stated. Nothing contained in this act shall be so construed as to compel any person to receive at any time anything but gold and silver in tender for debts.

SEC. 36. *And be it, etc.*, That on and after the 1st day of January, 1861, all notes, bills of exchange, drafts, or any species of debentures or evidences of debt, which shall be discounted in bank, or upon which a loan shall made by any bank, shall be paid to the owner or person who offers such paper, in the following manner: not less than ten per cent. in gold or silver, or in the stamped paper of the Department of Finance, the balance in currency. On and after the 1st day of January, 1862, on all such paper above described, twenty per cent. shall be paid in gold and silver or the stamped paper of the Department of Finance; on and after the 1st day of January, 1863, thirty per cent. shall be paid in gold or silver on all such paper, or in the above stamped paper; on and after the first day of January, 1864, forty per cent. shall be paid on all such paper in gold or silver, or in stamped paper of the Department of Finance; on and after the 1st day of January, 1865, fifty per cent. in gold and silver, or in stamped paper of the Department of Finance; and so on, increasing the payments in specie annually ten per cent. more on all discounted paper of every description, and in the year 1871 the banks shall pay gold and silver, and nothing else, except stamped notes of the Department of Finance, on all loans and discounts made by them of every name, nature and description; and from that time forward all paper money based on any other foundation than gold and silver, shall be confiscated, and become the property of the Federal Government.

SEC. 37. *And be it, etc.*, That all paper discounted in bank, and all loans made by banks to dealers or customers, shall be paid off at the time the discount is made or the loan effected. And the proceeds of discounted paper or loans shall not be passed to the credit of the dealer or customer, and reported as deposits. And further, that no bank shall discount or loan at once more than the amount of its paid-up capital and two-thirds the average line of its deposits.

SEC. 38. *And be it, etc.*, That all deposits in bank, from and after the 1st day of January, 1861, shall be, for the first ensuing year from that date, at the rate of at least ten per cent. of such deposit, in gold and silver or Treasury stamps, as provided by this act; the balance may be in currency. For the second year from that date, twenty per cent. in gold and silver or Treasury stamps, as above, and so on, increasing the per centage of gold and silver or Treasury stamps, at the rate of ten per cent. higher every year, till in the year 1871 all deposits in bank shall be in gold and silver or Treasury stamps, or paper upon which the payment is secured in gold at sight. All notes paid into bank shall be paid in the same ratio of specie or stamps in the above years.

SEC. 39. *And be it, etc.*, That it shall be the duty of United States marshals, collectors of customs, postmasters, and navy agents to report to the Vice-Controller of Finance, if they know any bank doing business in opposition to the provisions of sections 35, 36, and 37 of this act. And if the infringement of the act is continued after due notice, the Controller or Vice-Controller shall close their accounts with the department, and the offending bank shall go into liquidation.

SEC. 40. *And be it, etc.*, That the department and each of its branches shall do its business in a good, thorough, fire-proof building, of convenient size and shape, adapted to the uses for which it is to be occupied; which building shall be so constructed as to have a capacious fire-proof and strong vault of stone, brick, and iron, and with at least three massive iron doors, with powerful locks, bolts, and fastenings, and a capacity inside sufficient to hold twenty or thirty large-size iron safes, which are to be fire-proof. Every night the Controller or Vice-Controller shall hold the key of one of the above doors, the cashier shall hold a key of one of the doors, and the head clerk or first teller shall hold one of the keys.

SEC. 41. *And be it, etc.*, That for each bank that keeps an account with the department or either of its branches, shall be prepared a moderate-sized drawer, locker, chest, or trunk, with the name of the bank painted on the same; and whenever such bank makes a deposit of gold in the department or either of its branches, such gold shall remain on deposit in the special drawer, locker, chest, or trunk in such bank; and whenever the department or either of its branches shall redeem any of the registered stamps which have been issued to such bank, the gold for such redemption shall be taken out of such drawer, locker, chest, or trunk, and the registered stamps so redeemed shall be deposited in the same drawer, locker, or chest which is appropriated to such bank; and no other papers, bills, or gold, except such as relate to such bank, shall be kept in such drawer, locker, or trunk. And such drawer, locker, or trunk shall be well secured with a strong lock, and shall be so arranged that it can and shall be locked up in some one of the iron safes during the night, on holidays, and all days on which the department or branches shall not do business. The amount of gold on hand in such drawer, locker, chest, or trunk, or the amount of gold and registered stamps redeemed and on hand in such drawer, locker, chest, or trunk shall always equal the amount of gold originally deposited by such bank as part of its capital stock, and shall agree exactly with the balance indicated as due to such bank by the ledger of the department or branch.

SEC. 42. *And be it, etc.*, That the cashiers, tellers, clerks, and bookkeepers shall all be thorough, competent, business men, well versed in the science of bookkeeping by double entry, and thoroughly prepared to take each other's places in cases of necessity to do so for any cause.

SEC. 43. *And be it, etc.*, That the controller or vice-controller may, in his discretion, order a rotation of services among the officers of the department or branch, at the several desks; but that the additions and extensions upon the books of every officer in the department or any of its branches shall be thoroughly examined, checked, and proved, by some other officer, teller, or clerk, and if any erasures, alteration of figures, or interlineations or blots are made on the books, the officer who makes such erasure or alteration shall satisfy the cashier of the reason why such has been made. Every officer's or teller's work in the department or branch shall be reviewed and proved by some other officer, and any mistake that is found shall be immediately reported to the controller, vice-controller, or cashier.

SEC. 44. *And be it, etc.*, That the Senate of the United States shall appoint one of its members, who is skilled in finance, and the House of Representatives shall appoint one of its members, also skilled in finance, and the President of the United States shall appoint a citizen of the United States, of undoubted powers and capacities, and of thorough competency to act, and that the three shall form a Committee of Finance, to last for four years after such appointment; and the duty of this committee shall be to visit the Department of Finance and each of its branches once a year during the recess of Congress, and to make a thorough examination of all the books of the department and branches, to ascertain the actual amount of gold on hand in the department and each branch, the amount of registered stamps redeemed and in the lockers or trunks of the banks with which the department does business, the amount of loans, the nature of the security, the amount of deposit certificates issued, and the amount redeemed and canceled, and the amount of exchange issued by the department and each of its branches, the security of the safes, vaults, and depositories from fire or burglars, the opinion of the controller and vice-controllers upon the action of this statute on the public weal and the prosperity of the Confederation, and to report these matters, and any others they may deem proper, to both Houses of Congress at its next session, after such inspection and examination have taken place.

SEC. 45. *And be it, etc.*, That the "Committee of Finance" shall each receive five dollars per day while they are actually employed in the duties of their office, and while traveling, and also mileage at the rate of ten cents per mile on the actual travel they make in the Government service. This service to be paid out of the Department of Finance at Washington, and the Controller of Finance to apportion it among the office and branches as he shall deem right and just.

SEC. 46. *And be it, etc.*, That, whereas it is desirable that the Department of Finance of the Independent Treasury of the United States should be self-sustaining: to that end and for that purpose, the following powers and privileges are granted to the department and each of its branches: to issue certificates of deposit for American gold in sums, which may be deposited with the department or either of its branches, of one hundred dollars, and any sum above one hundred dollars which can be divided by the number ten without a remainder, which deposit certificates shall bear interest at the rate of three per cent. per annum if deposited for one year, two and a half per cent. per annum if deposited for six months, two per cent. per annum if deposited for three months, and one per cent. per annum if deposited for two months. The deposit certificates in all cases to show on the face of them when they are due.

SEC. 47. *And be it, etc.*, That no deposit certificate shall draw any interest for a less time than sixty days, unless it be in time of great money pressure or panic, and in such case the controller or vice-controllers may allow, in his or their discretion, interest on deposit certificates for thirty or sixty days, at as high a rate as twelve per cent. per annum.

SEC. 48. *And be it, etc.*, That no deposit certificate shall draw interest unless the certificate reads for interest, nor shall it draw interest after its maturity if it is not presented at the time it is due.

SEC. 49. *And be it, etc.*, That the issues of deposit certificates shall be carefully registered, and the time of their maturity noted, so that in making loans the department and branches shall know their exact means and liability.

SEC. 50. *And be it, etc.*, That the Controller of Finance shall report to Congress if he shall find any deficiency in this act which could be amended for the promotion of the objects set forth in the title of this act.

SEC. 51. *And be it, etc.*, That there shall be trusty and efficient men hired to watch in the rooms of each of the departments and branches, convenient to the doors of the safe, who shall be armed effectually with revolvers and other arms, to guard the vaults and safes from burglary during the night season.

SEC. 52. *And be it, etc.*, That the proper board to decide on making loans which shall be applied for, shall be, in the department at Washington, the Controller of Finance, the cashier of the department, and the attorney of the department. In each of the branches the Board of Discount shall be the vice-controller, the cashier, and the attorney of each branch. To obtain a loan on discount, the vote of the Board of Discount must be unanimous, and all the sessions of the Board of Discount shall be duly recorded, with their acts, in a proper book to be kept for that purpose.

SEC. 53. *And be it, etc.*, That all loans made by the department or branches shall be secured by mortgage on good real estate, the title to which shall be perfect ; and in making loans, no estate shall be considered security for more than one-third its assessed value for taxation. And if a part of such valuation be for improvements in buildings, such part shall be further secured by insurance in some good fire insurance company, and the policy made over to the United States. Also, the Board of Finance may require that loans shall be further secured by one, two, or more good names or firms on the paper. Securities upon well-cultivated farms, and real estate which pays a constant rental, will always be preferred.

SEC. 54. *And be it, etc.*, That all expenses of examining titles, drawing deeds or mortgages, recording, canceling mortgages on record, and notary fees, shall be paid by the applicant for the loan, and shall go for the benefit of the department, the same being a part of the duty of the attorney, whose fees for such services are considered fully paid by his yearly salary.

SEC. 55. *And be it, etc.*, That all mortgages, notes, and securities given to the department, or either of its branches, shall run and be made payable to the United

States of America, at the Department of Finance of the Independent Treasury of the United States, in the City of Washington, if the transaction is made with the department, or at the branch of the Independent Treasury where such transaction was made.

SEC. 56. *And be it, etc.*, That the rates of interest which may be charged on loans, until an act is passed by Congress regulating the rate of interest for the whole Union, shall be such rate as is legal in any State where such loan is made; and that a condition in any mortgage binding the party who gives such mortgage to pay all the expenses of foreclosing the mortgage, and of the sale of the property, shall be held legal.

SEC. 57. *And be it, etc.*, That there shall be in the department and each of its branches the following business desks, conveniently arranged with clerks, tellers, and bookkeepers enough to transact the business, namely: one desk at which the gold deposits of the banks are received, and the registered stamps returned for such gold to the depositing bank; one desk where the registered stamps are redeemed in gold on presentation; one desk where certificates of deposit are issued for gold deposited, either on demand or at a future period; one desk where bills of exchange are drawn; and on each of these desks shall be kept a waste book and journal, which shall show exactly the business which is transacted at that desk during each day of business. There shall also be one or more desks for the ledgers for posting from the journals. One of these ledgers shall be lettered and marked on the back Bank ledger. Upon this ledger shall be posted all the transactions with banks in regard to the issue to them of registered stamps, and all the gold received from them on deposit as part of their capital stock; and the cash account with the banks shall be entirely separate from the cash account on the general ledger. There shall also be a ledger, above mentioned, marked on the back General Ledger, on which shall be posted the accounts of all the journals, except the bank journal above described.

SEC. 58. *And be it, etc.*, That there shall be a fund called the banking fund, which shall be kept separate from all other funds, consisting of gold deposited with the department or branches for the redemption of registered stamps by the banks of the country and cities, which shall also be kept, as heretofore provided, in the locker, drawer, or trunk assigned to each bank which owns the deposit.

SEC. 59. *And be it, etc.*, That there shall be a general fund, which shall be made up of gold received for the issue of deposit certificates on interest and deposit certificates not on interest, the sale of bills of exchange, the payment of mortgage notes, the interest on loans, the premium on exchange, and any profits which may inure to the department or any branch.

SEC. 60. *And be it, etc.*, That the ledger balances shall always show the amount of cash on hand, and the exact standing of the department and branches, with the assets and liabilities.

SEC. 61. *And be it, etc.*, That in keeping the accounts of the department and branches, the issue of registered stamps shall be regarded and treated as cash. When stamps are registered, numbered, and countersigned by the department or any of its branches, ready for delivery to the bank or banks for circulation, the journal entry will be, Cash Dr. to registered stamps for the amount so countersigned, (naming the numbers) from such a number to such a number, inclusive. When stamps are delivered to any bank for circulation, the journal entry will be, Bank Dr. to cash for the amount of registered stamps so delivered to them. When gold is received from any bank on deposit as part of its capital, the journal entry will be Cash Dr. to the bank which makes the deposit for so much gold deposited this day. When gold is received for a deposit certificate, the journal entry will be, Cash Dr. to deposit certificates for amount received, naming the person to whom the certificate was issued for the same. Upon the general ledger shall be kept a cash account, incidental expense account, profit and loss account, exchange account, and accounts with the department and each of its branches; also, in time, a stock account. The stock account shall be made of the net balances of profit of the department and of each of its branches, each branch to retain its own profits to do business upon, and the net profits of each branch to be carried yearly to the credit side of stock account, till they amount to the sum of three millions of dollars in each branch; and in the same way of the department at Washington. After the stock account reaches the sum of three millions of dollars in the department, and three millions of dollars in each of the branches, the net profits of the department and each of the branches shall be paid once a year, on the first week in January, into the Department of Revenue of the Independent Treasury of the United States.

SEC. 62. *And be it, etc.*, That the Department of Revenue holding the bonds of merchants and others for duties, knowing that such bonds will be paid at maturity, and wishing to anticipate the funds on such bonds for the use of the Department of Revenue—such bonds, if the controller or vice-controller should think proper, may be discounted by the Department of Finance, or any of its branches, at the usual rate of discount where such transaction may be made; and, on the other hand, if the Department of Finance should be short of funds, and the Department of Revenue possessed funds which it was sure would not be needed for a certain time, the Department of Finance might borrow such funds of the Department of Revenue upon some of its bonds or mortgages, or any good assets. *And furthermore*, the Department of Finance and its branches, when in funds, may discount the paper of first-class business houses and individuals which have been discounted by banks, under the guarantee and indorsement of such bank or banks, but not without such indorsement or guarantee. In all loans and discounts, the Department of Finance and branches must have a careful regard to the time that the deposit certificates fall due, and no discounts or loans shall be made to interfere with the prompt payment of such certificates at maturity.

SEC. 63. *And be it, etc.*, That of every and any officer of the department, or any of its branches, it is made the duty to report to the controller or vice-controller, if he knows of any failure in duty, any transgression of any section of this act, or any act or agency of any person in the employment of the department or any of its branches, whereby loss could possibly result to the Government from such act or neglect of duty, and to report the same immediately to the controller or vice-controller, or be liable for such neglect to immediate discharge from his office.

SEC. 64. *And be it, etc.*, That for embezzlement, fraud, misapplication of the funds of the department, or either of its branches, forgery, willful alteration of entries in any book or books of account, to cover or conceal fraud, the abstraction of any paper or papers from the department, or any of its branches, the appropriation, purloining, or removal of any registered stamps, deposit certificates, bills of exchange, the fraudulent issue or re-issue of any such, the abstraction of any coin, or any other fraud upon the department, or any of its branches, shall, on conviction of the offender, be punishable by imprisonment in the State Prison for not less than three years, nor more than sixty years; the time between these terms to be fixed by the Court according to the nature and heinousness of the crime. The President of the United States shall have no power to pardon a convict upon any of the above charges unless full restitution and payment have been made to the Government of all losses by reason of the crime of which the prisoner had been convicted.

SEC. 65. *And be it, etc.*, That in order to carry this Act into effect, the Secretary of the Treasury may solicit bids for a loan of not more than two millions of dollars, payable in the city of New York in manner following, that is to say, five hundred thousand dollars on the first of August, 1860; five hundred thousand dollars on the first of January, 1861; five hundred thousand dollars on the first of July, 1862; the balance, if needed, on the first of January, 1863—at a rate of interest not exceeding five per cent. per annum, and payable on the first day of January, 1865, in the city of New York. The interest to be payable yearly in the city of New York, as above. With these funds, to prepare and make ready suitable buildings, with vaults, safes, fixtures, and appurtenances—also, proper books of account, dies, plates, engravings, paper, stationery, fixtures and appointments, suitable for carrying out the designs and purposes of this Act in all its bearings.

SEC. 66. *And be it, etc.*, That no officer of the department or either of its branches shall be a zealous politician of any party whatever, nor shall any favors in discounts or loans be made to any person, firm, bank, association, or corporation, to promote political views; nor shall any funds be used to favor any election of any candidate to office. The violation of any of the above provisions shall be deemed good cause for the immediate discharge from office of any one connected with the department or either of its branches.

SEC. 67. *And be it, etc.*, That appointments of the controller and vice-controller shall last for six years, or until a successor or successors are appointed; that appointments for cashiers shall last for four years; that appointments of other officers will remain entirely with the controller or vice controllers; no political sentiment shall ever have any weight in the appointment to office or removal from office of any officer of the department or branches.

SEC. 68. *And be it, etc.*, That this Act shall go into operation on the 1st day of July, A.D. 1860.

Published in the San Francisco Times, Steamer Edition, April 20, 1860.

The principal features of the preceding Bill may be thus recapitulated:

First: The addition of another Cabinet officer, to be styled the Controller of Finance, whose duties are set forth at length in the bill; and the division of the Treasury into two separate and distinct departments. This provision of the bill is largely supplemented in the National Bank Act of 1864, in section one, which establishes a bureau of the currency, and a chief officer of the bureau, denominated the Controller of the Currency.

Secondly: The coercive and imperative legislation of Congress, using their power to control the currency of the Union, and imposing upon the State banks the necessity of converting ten per cent. annually of their bills, in circulation into gold coin of the United States, and depositing that coin in the Treasury and its branches, and, in lieu of the coin, taking from the Department of Finance bills of an equal amount to the gold deposited, withdrawing an equal amount of their old circulation, and substituting the new bills, based on coin in the Treasury.

The bill applies solely to the old State banks, which were the only monetary institutions of the country then in existence. It might easily be changed, to have reference to the National banks. However, I have proposed a simpler and more efficient mode of reaching their case. (See page 127.) The object of each of these means is to stop the circulation of all bank notes not fully secured by gold in the Treasury.

Thirdly: The next object of the bill is, to raise the quality of the deposits in banks gradually to the specie standard. The introduction of the element of credit into the currency is entirely different in its effect on all manner of business operations, to introducing it into any other of its usual chameleon forms in the body politic. The currency should always be hard cash, or paper which represents the coin in the hands of a safe custodian.

Congress has power to "repel invasions." Now, one definition which Webster gives to the word "invasion" is "an attack on the rights of another." Then, if the issuing of "bills of credit" by the banks in the East is an attack on the rights of California, Congress has power by the Constitution to repel such invasion. Again, Congress has power "to coin money and regulate the value thereof." By the emission of bills of credit by the banks, the power of Congress to regulate the value of money is entirely neutralized or nullified. Again, Congress has power by the Constitution "to make all laws which shall be necessary and proper for carrying into execution the foregoing powers, and all other powers vested by this Constitution in the Government of the United States, or in any department or officer thereof." Hence, all banks which issue paper money exist only by the sufferance of Congress. And if their existence is only by sufferance, their whole internal policy may, properly, be made subject to the laws of the Federal Government. There is still another clause in the Constitution which makes the Federal Government absolute upon the subject of paper money in all the States, and which ought to regulate not only the issue of bills, but the entire subject of bank credits. No State can "make *anything* but gold and silver coin a tender in payment of debts." If States cannot do this in their sovereign right, they cannot give to banking institutions the right to do it. Hence Congress has absolute right to prohibit the issue of "bills of credit" by banks, and also the right to determine upon the quality of the deposits in banks, and to say that if banks receive paper on deposit as money, which is not based upon gold, they shall not be allowed to re-issue such paper as currency, thereby invading the rights of honest men, lessening the value of gold by their spurious issues, and working unbounded mischief in all legitimate business of the country.

At the first view of this subject, it would seem to be an invasion of the rights of persons, to say that Congress has the power to limit banks in their issues of credit. But, upon careful examination it will be found that such is not the case; for every man in the community must so exercise his own rights as not to infringe the rights of others. If the issuing of bank credits (which make currency, and currency makes prices) does rob gold of a part of its exchangeable value, then the principle upon which Eastern banks are gotten up and conducted, is a principle diametrically opposite to the interest of all owners of gold. Upon a careful examination of the subject, it will be found that Congress has a right to the absolute control of the whole matter of currency.

The opinion of Daniel Webster I will quote in corroboration of my position. He says: "In reply to my arguments on a former day, showing it to be the duty of the Government to regulate the currency, (which I can agree with the gentleman in calling the very life-blood of the political body) the honorable gentleman asserts that Government has no right to interfere with individuals. He, therefore, proposes individual banking, and maintains that credit is a man's private property; that Government has no more right to interfere with this than with any other kind of property; that Government has no right to put restrictions of any kind upon it. But this, which the gentleman asserts is not the right of Government, is the *very* and *especial* object for which Government is instituted. Government *does* interfere and place restrictions, in a thousand ways, upon every kind of individual property; and it is done, and is necessarily done by every government, for the good of the whole community. Years ago, as well as now, we had private banking; everybody turned banker, everybody put out his notes for circulation, till it was at last found necessary to restrain this right, this *very right*, which the gentleman says the Government has not the right to restrain; a right which, however, has more than once been proved, after all, nothing more than the right of practicing fraud and imposition upon the people." (See Works of Webster, Vol. iv, p. 363.)

Adam Smith, in Book II, chapter 2, p. 133, Wealth of Nations, writes thus: "To restrain private people, it may be said, from receiving in payment the promissory notes of a banker for any sum, whether great or small, when they themselves are willing to receive them; or, to restrain a banker from issuing such notes, when all his neighbors are willing to accept them, is a manifest violation of that natural liberty which it is the proper business of law not to infringe, but to support. Such regulations may, no doubt, be considered as in some respects a violation of natural liberty. But those exertions of the natural liberty of a few individuals which might endanger the security of the whole society, are, and ought to be, restrained by the laws of all governments—of the most free as well as of the most despotical. The obligation of building party-walls, in order to prevent the communication of fire, is a violation of natural liberty, exactly of the same kind with the regulations of the banking trade which are here proposed."

The sovereignty of the nation possessing absolute control of the currency, it follows that the deposits in banks, which are a large part of the virtual currency, are subject to the control of Congress. But the National banks, being creations of Congress, are subject to any terms which the Federal laws may require. Hence, it is very easy for Congress to regulate them as the interests of the nation may demand.

Fourthly: The bill contemplates and provides for large dealing in domestic exchange. The condition of the country has materially changed since the bill was prepared; but, although I may differ with some on this subject, I consider that the salutary action of the Treasury upon domestic exchanges might be made one of undoubted benefit, both to the people and Government. The Treasury is destined for the next century, so surely as our Government shall continue, to be the depository of immense amounts of coin and paper which represents coin. The national revenue will be of vast amount, and will require immense transfers.

We have recently established a line of steamers from San Francisco to Japan and China. When the Pacific Railroad is finished, it will almost revolutionize the American trade with China. Even before the completion of this work we may anticipate great changes in that respect. The high price teas, which are injured by long sea voyages, with the most careful preparations, will come to San Francisco, and reach New York *via* Panama.

During the year 1866 the Treasury shipments of gold coin from San Francisco to New York amounted to the sum of twelve millions of dollars. Upon all this treasure the Government were compelled to pay freight and charges, and to take the ocean risk, as it is not their custom to insure. The freight and insurance upon this treasure (and the insurance must be counted, even if the Government assume it) was worth $300,000. We will now see how this may be saved to the nation, and the people served at the same time. Suppose that a firm in New York, in the China trade, wishes to place $200,000 in Hongkong for the purchase of teas and China goods. He steps into the Treasury office in New York, and purchases exchange on the treasury in San Francisco. His money is then half way to China without any cost, and the Government's money is in New York without costing a dollar. The New York merchant forwards his exchange to his factor in San Francisco, and he ships the funds to China in silver or gold, as his orders may instruct. The Government can furnish large amounts of such exchange, at rates far below what private or corporate banks could draw. But, while it could furnish such exchange and at the same time help the people and the Treasury, if it should attempt to impose onerous terms on the public, it could never advance rates beyond what sound banks and bankers would be willing to do the same business: consequently it would have no motive to become extortionate in its charges.

Fifthly: The bill further contemplates Government banking, but thoroughly and solely upon a gold basis. Hence the action of such measures upon the commonwealth would be entirely different to the action of the old United States Bank, or any other system which ever existed in the country. The vast amounts of gold that will be in the Treasury, for an indefinite future, might be made very useful to the Government and people, in the way of direct loans to solvent banks and individuals upon undoubted securities which they had discounted, bearing the indorsement of such banks and bankers, and further secured, if necessary, upon the Government bonds: which will be a large source of valid security that the people may easily pledge for loans. This will be immeasurably better than the scheme of selling gold, because such sales are only for shipment abroad and speculators' purposes. But loans of gold, repayable in gold again, would be driving the miserable trash, now called money, from existence, and restoring the constitutional currency. Most especially and timely could such Government aid be extended to the banks and people, while the crops of autumn were moving forward to market. An extra hundred millions thrown into the market from the 1st of September to the 1st of January each year, would be a most efficient aid in distributing the agricultural products of the country, and also of silencing the hue and cry that the currency must be elastic, and of course subject to be falsified by issues which do not represent it.

Government loaning may be conducted uprightly, as well as coining for the nation; and if so conducted, it would be one of the most salutary auxiliaries to general industry and business operations that has ever been instituted. Further—it would be one of the easiest and most popular forms of taxation that could be devised. Loans might be made upon pledges of the Government stocks, the borrowers hypothecating double the amount of stocks to the amount of coin they receive.

But, if we are to have a Treasury bank, it should be founded and conducted thoroughly upon a gold basis. Not upon such a basis as the old United States Bank; not upon such a basis as any of the old State bank systems; and above all, not upon such a fatuous and unjust basis as galvanizing paper issues with value by making them legal tender through the acts of Congress. This last is the worst form of paper issues that was ever devised by an intelligent and honest people.

Gold, if left to assume its normal relative value to other wealth, is one of the most conservative elements of national prosperity in existence. It is self-regulating, and at the same time it rules all industrial interests upon a sound and honest basis. It banishes gambling from the marts of trade and commerce, and gives employment and just reward to industry and the gains of labor. It begets in a wonderful manner various kinds of employment, and makes new channels for advancement and progress. Contrary to a false currency, when it institutes new avenues of business, instead of making them fitful and capricious, they are permanent, and the gains are reliable. Hence, the same amount of currency, however strongly guaranteed by State stocks, bonds, and mortgages, can never be as good as gold, for gold is intrinsic value and needs no redemption.

The United States possess the means to saturate themselves with a currency of gold if they will be true to the teachings of science, and abandon the follies of monetizing paper and debts. They possess these means within their own domains, and can command them without the return of one dollar in specie for their vast commerce with other nations. But if they persist in vilifying gold by the use of paper and the fiction of bank credits, they will continue to be the servants of foreign capitalists—to dig, coin, and transport our treasures of gold and silver to those nations of the civilized world which can more justly appreciate their value.

If an act similar to the one I have given could have been the law of the land in 1848, it would have saved the failures and suspensions in 1857, the virtual suspensions in November, 1860,* and the grand final close of specie payments in the State banks on the 31st December, 1861, never to be resumed again. Such an act would have secured a currency based upon gold, dollar

---

* See Hunt's Merchants' Magazine, January Number, 1861, pp. 76 and 77.

for dollar, and would have enabled the Government to carry on the war, keeping the prices of commodities at the gold measure of value, thereby saving to the nation one-half of the public debt, also the immense amount of interest which must be paid before that unnecessary portion of the debt is canceled, and the unavoidable expenses of collecting such amounts from the people—in all, not less than two billions of dollars. This would have been the saving to the nation. The saving to the people would have been greater even than to the Government.

After such exhaustive experience as the country has now had, with the lights of science shining forth on all sides, with the history of the world before them, with the uniform failures which have attended all systems of paper money whenever tried by severe commercial crises, with the knowledge that our mines of the precious metals are amply sufficient to supply the utmost demands of our population for a sound currency, with the fact demonstrated that by using substitutes for coin which do not represent it we do essentially lessen its home value and send it to other nations—with all of this experience and demonstration before us, shall we continue to pursue the same beaten track, the same financial system which, in the past eighteen years, has sacked us of more than one billion of dollars in coin and bullion, and given it to other nations without any just equivalent?

Whether in the future we are to have the National banks, or a Treasury bank, or both of these simultaneously, the duty of Congress is to see that neither the Treasury bank nor the National banks shall be allowed to circulate any form of paper currency, further than such currency is fully represented by gold or silver coin in the Treasury. In this connection it is relevant to state that the preceding bill contemplates nothing but gold coin as a proper basis for circulation. Silver is only a lawful tender up to five dollars. Obviously, however, it is an immeasurably better basis for the issue of currency than Government debt, State debt, or any form of property. The Government is so involved in debt that it would be expedient for the next thirty or fifty years to allow the silver coin of the mints to be used as a basis for the issue of currency. The bills, however, which may be secured by deposit of silver coin, should promise that specific kind of coin, as the bills secured by deposit of gold coin should promise the same. The gold bills and silver bills would then rank in value exactly as gold and silver ruled in the marts of commerce and trade.

Gold would be the standard, but citizens should have the right to make their contracts payable in either currency, and the laws should protect and enforce such contracts in good faith. There will always be a difference in the relative value of gold and silver, and no doubt gold is by far the most proper standard. Such being the case, there will be a slight variation in the value of the gold and silver dollar; and for these reasons it is better to let the course of trade adjust that difference, which it will do with mathematical accuracy, if left free from any obnoxious legislation. Silver, being so incomparably better basis to issue currency upon than Government debt, or any form of property, our people should have the right to use this basis, at least while the national debt remains with such gigantic proportions—leaving the gold dollar to be the legal tender, and the silver dollar to take its rank by it, as trade and commerce shall rule.

the nonce that it is $50,000 per mile, which is certainly extravagant for the level portions of the road. This would require for one thousand miles of the road, $50,000,000. If we allow for the mountain passes an equal amount, we have a round $100,000,000 as the cost of the road. The rolling stock, cars, locomotives, station houses, appointments, and other incidental requisites might amount to $20,000,000 more. I have no doubt that every one of these estimates is largely over-rated. That, however, is not the great point which we are to look at. The moment the road is built, the United States will be worth $500,000,000 more than before, and this wealth will be only the beginning of its aggrandizement to the nation.*

The Government is in duty bound to build the road *as a war measure*, for the protection of the Pacific States. The difference between giving lands and giving bonds, is too insignificant to count upon; although the lands will,

---

* The following extract is taken from an article in De Bow's Review, Vol. II, No. 6, p. 612, entitled "Railroad History and Results." The entire article is well worth a careful reading. "In Georgia, lands which were in the market in 1846 at from ten to fifty cents per acre, commanded, in 1849, when the Chattanooga Railroad was in operation, from ten to twenty dollars. On the Mobile and Ohio Railroad, lands without a purchaser for thirty years, advanced at once to three dollars, and in many cases eight dollars per acre. The estimate on the pine lands was an increase from 500 to 5,000 per cent. In Ohio, the taxable property was in amount $136,000,000, when there were only eighty-nine miles of railroad, and $840,000,000 when three thousand miles of railroad had been constructed. In Illinois, the rise was from $72,000,000 when twenty-two miles existed, to $402,000,000 with two thousand five hundred and ninety-eight miles. In Indiana, an increase of thirty miles to one thousand eight hundred and sixty-two miles, increased the value of property from $119,000,000 to $317,000,000. Maryland, by building sixty-five miles, increased the property valuation to $116,000,000; Georgia, six hundred and nine miles railroad, $248,000,000 property; one thousand three hundred and seventy miles, $600,000,000 property.

TENNESSEE.

	Miles R. R.	Valuation Property.
1848	18	$129,501,074
1852	68	186,621,610
1854	300	219,061,047
1856	500	260,319,611
1858	773	377,208,671

no doubt, from sales, if applied to a sinking fund, pay the bonds long before fifty years.

Another view of the subject: We have just passed through a cruel war; and the amount of debt for that war is $2,600,000,000, besides what we have paid in taxes and excises, say $1,000,000,000 more, making the cost of the war, at least, $3,600,000,000. I will not pretend to say what amount it will cost to pay off this debt and interest; but it is very safe to estimate that it will cost FOUR BILLIONS OF DOLLARS to bind the Union together, North and South. Would it be an unjust or an unreasonable expenditure for the Federal Government to give two hundred millions of dollars to bind the Union together, East and West?—this, too, when every dollar expended would make her two dollars richer?—this, too, when the measure is needed as a means of national defense quite as much as the army or the navy?

Let it be observed, that this immense sum has been expended in the work of war and destruction, to unite the North and South. Would it be unwise to expend in the works of peace so small an amount comparatively as is needed to complete this great continental thoroughfare, and bind the East and West together in bonds of friendship, interest, peace, prosperity, and national defense?

In a former article, on page 147, I have shown that the tariff has heretofore taken from the value of our staple—gold—more than $419,000,000; that, counting this fine which we pay to the Government for trading with foreigners, we are now paying $28,289,589 yearly to them. Even four years' receipts of this last amount would be ample to build the Pacific Railroad, and equip it most thoroughly in all its appointments. It is entirely impossible for the Federal Government to reimburse the State for the vast amount of bullion that has been absolutely despoiled from her by the illegal action of Eastern banks, their issues depreciating our gold far below its constitutional value, (which would be its normal value if such paper had not circulated) and which it seems to be the policy of the Federal Government to continue under the system of the National banks. These losses of California have resulted from the neglect of the Federal Government to keep the value of currency up to the gold standard.

There is a point upon which I would wish to disabuse my countrymen. It is very common to impute all the expenses of the Pacific Coast to California, and say these are far in excess of what she returns to the Federal Government. California is a member of the American Union of States. The States are united for mutual defense from foreign aggression. To complete this defense, an army and navy is requisite. Now, if it be necessary to build ironclads, war steamers, arsenals, military stations, forts, etc., etc., in California, these are all for *National defense*, as much as though they were built in Maine or New York. They are not justly chargeable to California. We often hear it said, the Government is doing this and that for California, when the real truth is that it is all *national.* And when we come to the truth of the matter, all the Federal Government can do for the State is to give it protection. If we have lost $419,000,000 in time past, and are losing more than $28,000,000 yearly now, we certainly are entitled to something to show for it.

The Pacific Railroad is more necessary, *as a measure of national defense to the Pacific Coast*, than all of the navy of the United States. With it, the Government could transport any needed army into the State in two weeks; and with it the State would fill up so rapidly with population, that it would soon become perfectly self-reliant.

I am not in favor of enlarging the public debt, unless the circumstances of the case fully justify it; but if we have imposed on ourselves such a vast debt to bind the country together North and South, and California must, as the treasure State of the Union, stand in the gap to pay the interest upon that debt, in gold coin; and if the tariff takes one-third the value of our gold for uses in foreign markets, and forty to fifty per cent. from its value for uses in our home markets, by reason of advancing the prices on home-made commodities which compete with foreign goods: then, I maintain, that after the Federal Government has built the Pacific Railroad, she has only commenced to pay the debt she owes to California. It is through the neglect of the Federal Government to do its duty in the matter of keeping all the currency of the United States equal in value to gold coin, that California has suffered such immense losses upon her treasure. (See Hunt's Merchants' Magazine, Vol. XLIII, p. 705.)

If the gift of lands will advance the work faster than bonds, the Government should give them. On the other hand, if bonds will advance the work more rapidly than the gift of lands, the Government should not hesitate to advance the bonds. No expense should be spared by the Government to press the work forward at the most rapid rate possible. The crowning excellence of the scheme is, that it will advance the value of the public lands, of the mineral lands, and of the whole domain west of the Rocky Mountains, ten times the cost of the enterprise. It will fill California and the Pacific States with a teeming population, and develop the resources of the country beyond any and all other means which have heretofore been put forth.

The Federal Government should also aid all of the railroads in California with potential and efficient endowments. The interests of the two Governments are most inseparably united. The Federal Government needs our gold to an immense amount; and through the legal tender of Congress and the American tariff she has had this gold at fearful rates of discount upon its just value. To return the favor to us, and to return it, too, in a manner which will be worth to the Union at large from two to ten dollars for every dollar expended, let the Federal Government foster and *aid all of the railroad enterprises which have been commenced in the State of California.* In doing this she will return but a small amount of the taxation which is unequally imposed upon us under present laws, and in a measure enable us to submit to such fearful sacrifice upon our treasure as we seem to be doomed to bear for the support of the Union.

The causes which retard the progress of the State are not to be attributed to the currency. It is not because California has the soundest currency on earth that her growth is slow. It is not because she uses a form of currency, which is produced annually $50,000,000 in excess of her needs, for money, and ships this treasure to pay for other forms of wealth. It is not because her dollar is worth one hundred cents at all times, that she seems to move so slow, and yet so sure. We must look has suffered such immense losses upon her treasure. (See Hunt's Merchants' Magazine, Vol. XLIII, p. 705.)

If the gift of lands will advance the work faster than bonds, the Government should give them. On the other hand, if bonds will advance the work more rapidly than the gift of lands, the Government should not hesitate to advance the bonds. No expense should be spared by the Government to press the work forward at the most rapid rate possible. The crowning excellence of the scheme is, that it will advance the value of the public lands, of the mineral lands, and of the whole domain west of the Rocky Mountains, ten times the cost of the enterprise. It will fill California and the Pacific States with a teeming population, and develop the resources of the country beyond any and all other means which have heretofore been put forth.

The Federal Government should also aid all of the railroads in California with potential and efficient endowments. The interests of the two Governments are most inseparably united. The Federal Government needs our gold to an immense amount; and through the legal tender of Congress and the American tariff she has had this gold at fearful rates of discount upon its just value. To return the favor to us, and to return it, too, in a manner which will be worth to the Union at large from two to ten dollars for every dollar expended, let the Federal Government foster and *aid all of the railroad enterprises which have been commenced in the State of California.* In doing this she will return but a small amount of the taxation which is unequally imposed upon us under present laws, and in a measure enable us to submit to such fearful sacrifice upon our treasure as we seem to be doomed to bear for the support of the Union.

The causes which retard the progress of the State are not to be attributed to the currency. It is not because California has the soundest currency on earth that her growth is slow. It is not because she uses a form of currency, which is produced annually $50,000,000 in excess of her needs, for money, and ships this treasure to pay for other forms of wealth. It is not because her dollar is worth one hundred cents at all times, that she seems to move so slow, and yet so sure. We must look for the cause of slow progress—if such be a true charge against a State which was admitted into the Union in 1850, and whose commercial metropolis has a population larger than either New York, Boston, or Philadelphia possessed after they had been settled for two centuries. The first cause which has retarded the growth of California is her isolated position and great distance from the large populations of the world, together with the expense, delay, fatigue, and risk of reaching her glebe. Secondly: the want of a correct knowledge of her resources to sustain a large population. Thirdly: the want of a certain market for her agricultural products, and of reasonable freight charges upon these, when sent to the markets of the world. These have conspired to lessen the products of the State materially.

But whatever position the products of agriculture, wool-growing, and manufacturing are to assume in the future, it is beyond controversy that during the past eighteen years mining has been the chief business of the industry of the State. It is also fully demonstrated, by the most undoubted statistics, that the returns of the mines have been immense. Furthermore, it is demonstrable that through the action of the old State bank systems from 1848 to 1862, and the action of the various tariffs supporting and sustaining their form of currency far in excess of the normal specie volume of the country, *and yet at the nominal par of gold*, California has lost upon her treasure a large fraction of its intrinsic value. Still further: from 1862 to 1867, at this writing, the banks at the East have all been under suspension of cash payments; gold has been most thoroughly demonetized in the United States, except for paying duties on imports and interest on the public debt. The effect of thus demonetizing gold, by the Government, has acted with momentous results upon the prosperity of the State.

We have the authority of the honorable Secretary of the Treasury for stating, that the prices of most articles were higher when gold stood at forty-seven per cent. than they were when it was one hundred and eighty-five. (See pp. 165, 166.) Such being the case, and it is proven by the highest financial officer of the nation, California has been counting dollars worth one hundred cents against dollars worth about thirty-three cents. This is the infliction which demonetizing gold by Congress has imposed upon the prosperity of the State. On the whole, then, computing the losses under the old State bank systems, and the different tariffs, the Legal Tender Acts, the Morrill tariff, and the National banks, it is an estimate entirely within bounds to conclude that California has, from all these causes, lost fully one-half the aggregate product of her mines since the year 1848. This would be, in round numbers, say $450,000,000. If we add interest to it for only half the time, or nine years, at six per cent., we have $243,000,000 for interest, making in all the vast sum of $693,000,000 loss on the treasure of California and interest. These figures ought to satisfy any reasonable mind of the cause of the slow progress of a population of less than half a million, which has paid and lost such an amount in the brief period of eighteen years.*

I have long been fully sensible of the great disadvantages under which we have been laboring, in counting dollars worth one hundred cents against dollars worth only half as much, and calling them equivalents. To compute the exact losses by such an infliction upon the State, would be impossible. It is enough, for my purpose, to show that they have been immense—so much so that to express them numerically requires hundreds of millions of dollars to measure the direct and positive losses.

I do not suppose that it will ever be possible to prevail upon Congress to make direct restitution to California for the unjust spoliations which have been made upon her treasure by the old State banks, or more recently by the National banks. But I have hoped that if Congress could see the immensity of the losses in times past to the State, and could further see that in aiding

---

* When gold stands at only thirty per cent. above currency, and, by reason of its being demonetized, prices of commodities rule at one hundred per cent. above the mark they would stand at if gold were the only currency in use, it will be seen with what telling effect such an abnormal state of things acts upon the real value of the national coin for domestic uses as money. For uses abroad, we have demonstrated its losses by reason of the tariff. (See pp. 143, 144, 165, 167.)

the Pacific Railroad to the amount of one hundred millions of dollars, and of further aiding the local railroads in California one hundred millions more, such aid, though comparatively small to the actual losses which have resulted to the State from the neglect of Congress to keep the currency of the country up to the par of gold, would be a most essential service to the entire Pacific Coast; and while it would help us so signally to recuperate from former losses, would at the same time be adding to our means for national defense, and increase the national wealth in population, in extended territory, in ability to meet taxation, in the vast advance of the national domain, in the development of our mines, our agriculture, our commerce, and, in fact, of our national opulence and aggrandizement of every form and description. Under these considerations, our delegation in Congress should ask, with confidence, of the Government efficient aid for the Pacific Railroad and for the other roads in California, to the amount of two hundred millions of dollars; and the excellence of the scheme is, that, while this is only an act of justice to California, and a small portion of her former losses on the currency, the gift, if rightly expended, will be worth manifold the amount to the nation, as a lasting bond of interest and continual prosperity. These are the only reclamations which we can get for the past; but for the future, we should demand that for domestic uses no national or State legislation shall be enacted which shall lessen the normal value of the constitutional currency of the United States.

APPENDIX.

(A.)

A SCHEME FOR A LAND BANK IN ENGLAND.

The historian, T. B. Macaulay, gives the following account of a project to establish a Land Bank in England, in 1695, which is a lucid exemplification of the absurdity of trying to perform impossibilities by the issue of currency:

"Pre-eminently conspicuous among the political mountebanks, whose busy faces were seen every day in the lobby of the House of Commons, were John Briscoe and Hugh Chamberlayne, two projectors worthy to have been members of that academy which Gulliver found at Lagado. These men affirmed that the one cure for every distemper of the State was a land bank. A land bank would work for England miracles such as had never been wrought for Israel, miracles exceeding the heaps of quails and the daily shower of manna. There would be no taxes; and yet the exchequer would be full to overflowing. There would be no poor rates, for there would be no poor. The income of every land-owner would be doubled. The profits of every merchant would be increased. In short, the island would, to use Briscoe's words, be the paradise of the world. The only losers would be the moneyed men, those worst enemies of the nation, who had done more injury to the gentry and yeomanry than an invading army from France would have had the heart to do.*

---

* A proposal by Dr. Hugh Chamberlayne, in Essex street, for a bank of secure current credit to be founded upon land, in order to the general good of landed men, to the great increase of the value of land, and the no less benefit of trade and commerce, 1695; pro-

"These blessed effects the land bank was to produce simply by issuing enormous quantities of notes on landed security. The doctrine of the projectors was, that every person who had real property ought to have, besides that property, paper money to the full value of that property. Thus, if his estate was worth two thousand pounds, he ought to have his estate and two thousand pounds in paper money.* Both Briscoe and Chamberlayne treated with the greatest contempt the notion that there could be an over-issue of paper as long as there was for every ten-pound note a piece of land in the country worth ten pounds. Nobody, they said, would accuse a goldsmith of over-issuing, so long as his vaults contained guineas and crowns to the full value of all the notes which bore his signature. Indeed, no goldsmith had in his vaults guineas and crowns to the full value of all his paper. And was not a square mile of rich land in Taunton Dean at least as well entitled to be called wealth as a bag of gold or silver? The projectors could not deny that many people had a prejudice in favor of the precious metals, and that therefore, if the land bank were bound to cash its notes, it would very soon stop payment. This difficulty they got over by proposing that the notes should be inconvertible, and that everybody should be forced to take them.

---

posals for the supplying their majesties with money on easy terms, exempting the nobility, gentry, etc., from taxes, enlarging their yearly estates, and enriching all the subjects of the kingdom by a national land bank; by John Briscoe. "*O fortunatus nimium bona si sua norint Anglicanos.*" Third edition, 1696. Briscoe seems to have been as much versed in Latin literature as in political economy.

* In confirmation of what is said in the text, I extract a single paragraph from Briscoe's proposals. "Admit a gentleman hath barely £100 per annum estate to live on, and hath a wife and four children to provide for. This person, supposing no taxes were upon his estates, must be a great husband to be able to keep his charge, but cannot think of laying up anything to place out his children in the world; but according to this proposed method he may give his children £500 apiece, and have £90 per annum left for himself and his wife to live upon, the which he may also leave to such of his children as he pleases after his and his wife's decease. For first having settled his estate of £100 per annum, as in pro-

"The speculations of Chamberlayne on the subject of the currency may possibly find admirers even in our own time. But to his other errors he added an error which began and ended with him. He was fool enough to take it for granted, in all his reasonings, that the value of an estate varied directly as the duration. He maintained that if the annual income derived from a manor were a thousand pounds, a grant of that manor for twenty years must be worth twenty thousand pounds, and a grant for a hundred years worth a hundred thousand pounds. If, therefore, the lord of such a manor would pledge it for a hundred years to the land bank, the land bank might, on that security, instantly issue notes for a hundred thousand pounds. On this subject Chamberlayne was proof to ridicule, to argument, even to arithmetical demonstration. He was reminded that the fee simple of land would not sell for more than twenty years' purchase. To say, therefore, that a term of a hundred years was worth five times as much as a term of twenty years, was to say that a term of a hundred years was worth five times the fee simple; in other words, that a hundred was five times the infinity. Those who reasoned thus were refuted by being told that they were usurers; and it should seem that a large number of country gentlemen thought the refutation complete.

"In December, 1693, Chamberlayne laid his plan, in all its naked absurdity, before the Commons, and petitioned to be heard. He confidently undertook to raise eight thousand pounds on every freehold estate of a hundred and fifty pounds a year, which should be brought, as he expressed it, into his land bank, and this without dispossessing the freeholder.* All the squires in the House must

---

posals 1, 3, he may have bills of credit for £2,000 for his own proper use, for 10s. per cent. per annum, as in proposal 22, which is but £10 per annum for the £2,000, which being deducted out of his estate of £100 per annum, there remains £90 per annum clear to himself." It ought to be observed that this nonsense reached a third edition.

* Commons' Journals, Dec. 7, 1693. I am afraid that I may be suspected of exaggerating the absurdity of this scheme. I therefore transcribe the most important part of the petition: "In consideration of the freeholders bringing their lands into this bank, for a

have known that the fee simple of such an estate would hardly fetch three thousand pounds in the market. That less than the fee simple of such an estate could, by any device be made to produce eight thousand pounds, would, it might have been thought, have seemed incredible to the most illiterate fox-hunter that could be found on the benches. Distress, however, and animosity, had made the landed gentlemen credulous. They insisted on referring Chamberlayne's plan to a committee; and the Committee reported that the plan was practicable, and would tend to the benefit of the nation. But by this time the united force of demonstration and derision had begun to produce an effect even on the most ignorant rustics in the House. The report lay unnoticed on the table; and the country was saved from a calamity, compared with which the defeat of Landen and the loss of the Smyrna fleet would have been blessings."

The instituting of banks for the issue of currency with security founded upon land, is not more preposterous than making such security based upon national bonds. The idea of Chamberlayne, as to the value of land, was wild as a lunatic. But that there is a vast amount of real estate in the country which could be converted into cash as favorably as national or State bonds, there can be no doubt. Such estate, if as easily convertible as the bonds, would be just as good security for issues. Why, then, is not good real estate as proper security for issues as the bonds? For my own part, I have no doubt of it. But the truth is, neither the bonds nor the real estate are any proper security for the issues. If real estate be good security for issues, we might issue

---

fund of current credit, to be established by act of Parliament, it is now proposed that, for every £150 per annum, secured for one hundred and fifty years, for but one hundred yearly payments of £100 per annum, free from all manner of taxes and deductions whatsoever, every such freeholder shall receive £4,000 in the said current credit, and shall have £2,000 more put into the fishery stock for his proper benefit; and there may be further £2,000 reserved at the Parliament's disposal towards carrying on this present war. * * * The freeholder is never to quit the possession of his said estate unless the yearly rent happens to be in the arrear."

almost indefinitely. If Government bonds are good security, we might also issue billions of dollars, provided the limitation in the Bank Act were removed. But if it be good to issue $300,000,000 of currency upon national bonds, why not good to issue four times that amount? Evidently because such issue would so thoroughly sink the value of money as to make it almost useless. The truth is, that no basis is good, proper, economical, or wise, (especially for a gold-producing country) for the issue of currency, but the coin itself which such issue promises. All other foundations are attempts to perform impossibilities, and must end in failures and bankruptcies. If banks, instituted upon other foundations than cash, can do business and make money, their gains must result entirely from the losses upon other branches of business, in communities which tolerate such exactions. (Page 23.)

The one-twenty-fifth of the value of the entire wealth of a nation is an ample supply and proportion to hold in money. But whatever the requirement is, that should be kept in real cash; and it would be so kept, and, in gold-producing countries, would soon be acquired and accurately adjusted to the wants of the people, were it not expelled by issues of paper currency.

The yield of the mines of the country is not less than $75,000,000 annually. In four years this yield would, if properly applied, displace the whole circulation of the National banks; but by tolerating this circulation, and legalizing it, we lose outright the whole product of our gold and silver mines. Surely Dr. Chamberlayne's scheme would do well to keep company with that of the National Banks. (See pp. 162, 163, 168, 169.)

THE POSSIBILITY OF A METALLIC CURRENCY.

Professor J. L. Tellkampf, LL.D. of the University of Breslau, in Prussia, writes thus: "We are not to infer, because the precious metals have hitherto formed so small a share of the whole circulating medium of some countries, that therefore specie would be entirely inadequate for the purpose. Were all engagements now pending canceled or discharged, and had not the habits of some people become adjusted through a long course of years to an expanded currency,—in other words, were all the operations of business about to commence anew, and were gold and silver to form our only medium of exchange, it is evident that prices would at once adjust themselves to the quantity of coin. The price of an article, which is but another name for its value estimated in the current medium of exchange, may as well be expressed by *one* as *five*. If *one* dollar of an unmixed specie currency will command as many necessaries and luxuries as could have been commanded by *five* dollars of a mixed medium, it is evident that in itself it is just as useful. It is incorrect, therefore, to say, as is often done, that there is not enough metallic money on earth to measure and exchange the values which are employed in trade. The only effect of employing such a medium exclusively would be to advance its value greatly, and thus enable a given amount of it to effect a much greater number of exchanges." (See page 33.)

(B.)

AMERICAN BANKING.

"In all other matters except banking, the American people learn wisdom by experience. But the repetition, every ten or fifteen years, of a period of great commercial and monetary distress, like that from which we are now emerging, the direct consequences of the over-issues of paper currency—*all issues are over-issues*—has, as yet, no effect to teach them that "paper money" is no real or substantial element in the nation's prosperity. They either will not or cannot see that credit is not wealth; that the excessive use of credit has the same effect upon a nation in the aggregate that it has upon the individual. They will not see that bank paper gives rise to wild speculation, great over-trading, enormous importations, mountains of foreign indebtedness, and last, to widespread and unavoidable bankruptcy. They will not believe that bank notes are no more money than notes of hand signed by John Doe or Richard Roe ; that the multiplication of these notes adds not a dollar to the weal of the country, though every man should have a hatful of the pictured promises to pay. We do not expect that every man in the country will be a political economist, well read up in the workings of the modern machinery by which capital controls labor ; but it is not too much to hope that the time may soon come in which all men, who can read, see or hear, will understand and believe the following plain statement : Banking is a system under which the borrower gives his note, with security and interest, for the lender's note without security and interest ! When this fact is universally comprehended in this country, banking—we mean the issuing of "paper money"—will take its place alongside of astrology and divination, among the lumber of the past; and men will wonder that their predecessors bore, for so many years, with a system so totally useless and radically absurd. Then the country will enter upon a career of prosperity from which nothing except some convulsion of nature can cause it to diverge. In the meantime the masses will be content to bear the alternate excitements and depressions of the times ; to be rich one decade and poor the next, with the hope of being rich again during the third ; and what is worse, they must endure the mortifying reflection—although conscious of the truth—that if the foreign debts of the country—those contracted long ago, and those of a more recent date—all the result of excessive bank issues—were paid, the United States would be stripped of the last dollar. Not a dime would be left."—*From the Philadelphia Daily Ledger.*

(B.)

RETURNS OF THE NATIONAL BANKS.

October 26, 1866.

RESOURCES.

Loans and discounts	$601,238,808
Overdrafts	2,008,695
Real estate, furniture and fixtures	17,122,117
Expense account	5,298,375
Premiums	2,490,891
Remittances and other cash items	103,676,649
Due from national banks	107,597,858
Due from other banks and bankers	12,136,549
United States bonds deposited to secure circulation	331,703,200
Other U. S. bonds and securities	94,954,150
Bills of other banks	17,437,699
Specie	8,170,835
Other lawful money	205,770,641
Other stocks, bonds, and mortgages	15,887,490
Aggregate	$1,525,493,960

LIABILITIES.

Capital stock paid in	$415,278,969
Surplus fund	53,359,277
National bank notes in circulation	280,129,558
State bank notes in circulation	9,819,719
Individual deposits	563,510,570
United States deposits	30,420,819
Deposits of U. S. disbursing officers	2,979,955
Due to national banks	110,531,957
Due to other banks and bankers	26,879,804
Profits	32,583,328
Aggregate	$1,525,493,960

If we analyze this return, we have results as follows :

Owed by the banks—Circulation	$289,949,277
" " Balance due banks	17,677,354
" " Deposits	593,931,389
Total due on demand	$901,558,020

In the event of a return to specie payments, this must be paid in specie, and the banks have only $8,170,835. But they hold—

Paper money	$305,000,000	
United States bonds	436,657,350	
Loans and discounts	601,238,808	
		$1,342,896,158

Now, in view of these official returns of the condition of the National banks, and the fact that a return to specie payments may, even with all the calls for currency, drive them into hopeless bankruptcy, what friend of California could wish to see the same system of currency adopted upon the Pacific Coast, while we are exporting the best currency on earth in scores of millions annually? (See pp. 35–38.)

(C.)

EXTRACT FROM ELLIOT'S DEBATES IN THE FEDERAL CONVENTION, UPON THE SUBJECT OF EMITTING BILLS OF CREDIT BY THE UNITED STATES.

"Mr. Gouverneur Morris moved to strike out 'and emit bills on the credit of the United States.' If the United States had credit, such bills would be unnecessary; if they had not, unjust and useless.

"Mr. Butler seconds the motion.

"Mr. Madison. Will it not be sufficient to prohibit the making of them a *tender?* This will remove the temptation to emit them with unjust views; and promissory notes, in that shape, may in some emergencies be best.

"Mr. Gouverneur Morris. Striking out the words will leave room still for notes of a *responsible* minister, which will do all the good without the mischief. The moneyed interest will oppose the plan of government, if paper emissions be not prohibited.

"Mr. Gorham was for striking out without inserting

any prohibition. If the words stand, they may suggest and lead to the measure.

"Mr. MASON had doubts on the subject. Congress, he thought, would not have the power, unless it were expressed. Though he had a moral hatred to paper money, yet, as he could not foresee all emergencies, he was unwilling to tie the hands of the Legislature. He observed that the late war could not have been carried on, had such a prohibition existed.

"Mr. GORHAM. The power, as far as it will be necessary or safe, is involved in that of borrowing.

"Mr. MERCER was a friend to paper money, though, in the present state and temper of America, he should neither propose nor approve of such a measure. He was, consequently, opposed to a prohibition of it altogether. It will stamp suspicion on the Government to deny it discretion on this point. It was impolitic, also, to excite the opposition of all those who were friends to paper money. The people of property would be sure to be on the side of the plan, and it was impolitic to purchase their further attachment with the loss of the opposite class of citizens.

Mr. ELLSWORTH thought this was a favorable moment to shut and bar the door against paper money. The mischiefs of the various experiments which had been made were now fresh in the public mind, and had excited the disgust of all the respectable part of America. By withholding the power from the new government, more friends of influence would be gained to it than by almost anything else. Paper money can in no case be necessary. Give the Government credit, and other resources will offer. The power may do harm, never good.

"Mr. RANDOLPH, notwithstanding his antipathy to paper money, could not agree to strike out the words, as he could not foresee all the occasions that might arise.

"Mr. WILSON. It will have a most salutary influence on the credit of the United States, to remove the possibility of paper money. This expedient can never succeed whilst its mischiefs are remembered; and, as long as it can be resorted to, it will be a bar to other resources.

"Mr. BUTLER remarked, that paper was a legal tender in no country in Europe. He was urgent for disarming the Government of such a power.

"Mr. MASON was still averse to tying the hands of the Legislature *altogether*. If there was no example in Europe, as just remarked, it might be observed, on the other side, that there was none in which the Government was restrained on this head.

"Mr. READ thought the words, if not struck out, would be as alarming as the mark of the beast in Revelation.

"Mr. LANGDON had rather reject the whole plan than retain the three words, 'and emit bills.'

"On the motion for striking out—New Hampshire, Massachusetts, Connecticut, Pennsylvania, Delaware, Virginia,* North Carolina, South Carolina, Georgia, ay, nine; New Jersey, Maryland, no, two." (See Vol. V, Supplement, pp. 434-435.)

Here we have the authority of James Madison, one of the members of the Convention for framing the Constitution, giving the vote of the Convention, upon the subject of allowing Congress to issue bills of credit; and the same was stricken out by a vote of nine to two. (See pages 64-70.)

(D.)

LEGAL TENDER NOTES. — HAS CONGRESS THE POWER TO MAKE NOTES A LEGAL TENDER?

OPINION OF JUDGE SHARSWOOD, OF PENNSYLVANIA.

If any point may be considered as well settled, it is, that the Constitution of the United States is a special grant or delegation of limited powers to the Federal Government. "It has been truly said," observes C. J.

* This vote in the affirmative by Virginia was occasioned by the acquiescence of Mr. Madison, who became satisfied that striking out the words would not disable the Government from the use of public notes, as far as they could be safe and proper; and would only cut off the pretext for a *paper currency*, and particularly for making the bills *a tender*, either for public or private debts.

Marshall, in the United States *vs.* Fisher (2 Cranch, 212) "that under a Constitution conferring specific powers, the power contended for must be granted or it cannot be exercised." The same thing has been affirmed by Mr. Justice Story, in Martin *vs.* Hunter's Lessee (1 Wheat. 326). "The Government of the United States can claim no powers which are not granted to it by the Constitution, and the powers actually granted must be such as are expressly given, or given by necessary implication." And not to multiply citations—on so clear a principle—again by C. J. Marshall, in McCullough *vs.* the State of Maryland (4 Wheat. 405): "This Government is acknowledged by all to be one of enumerated powers. The principle that it can exercise only the powers granted to it would seem too apparent to have required to be enforced by all those arguments which its enlightened friends, while it was depending before the people, found it necessary to urge. *That principle is now universally admitted.*"

It follows that to sustain the constitutionality of an act of Congress—to determine that it is a law—an authority for it must be affirmatively shown. That authority must exist in the Constitution in express words, or the act must appear to be necessary and proper for carrying into execution some power or powers vested in Congress, in the Government of the United States, or in some department or officer thereof.

By this rule we are now to decide whether that clause of the act of Congress, approved February 25, 1862, entitled "An act to authorize the issue of United States notes, and for the redemption or funding thereof, and for funding the floating debt of the United States," which provides that the notes issued in pursuance of that act "shall be lawful money, and a legal tender in payment of all debts, public or private"—is or is not a law of the land.

The counsel of the defendant—recognizing that on him rested the burden of maintaining the affirmative of this issue—claimed that the provision referred to was an exercise of authority vested in Congress under one or other of the following clauses of the enumeration in Section 8 of Article 1:

Paragraph 2. To borrow money on the credit of the United States.

Paragraph 3. To regulate commerce with foreign nations, and among the several States, and with the Indian tribes.

Paragraph 5. To coin money, regulate the value thereof, and of foreign coin, and fix the standard of weights and measures.

Paragraph 18. To make all laws which shall be necessary and proper for carrying into execution the foregoing powers, and all other powers vested by the Constitution in the Government of the United States, or in any department or officer thereof.

I propose to examine these clauses, with such other parts of the Constitution as have been supposed in the course of the argument to illustrate them. I feel some degree of confidence, not only from the well-known ability, learning, and research of the counsel for the defendant, but from my own investigations, that if the act of Congress in question cannot be sustained on either of these clauses, it cannot be sustained at all.

I will begin with the last paragraph of the enumeration, because its proper construction has an important bearing on the others. Par. 18: "To make all laws which shall be necessary and proper for carrying into execution the foregoing powers." I will not here revert to political and controverted grounds, nor to the arguments by which in the *Federalist*, No. 44, and elsewhere, the objections of the enemies of the Constitution to the sweeping words of this clause were met and answered by "its enlightened friends." I mean to take exclusively as my guide the principles judicially settled by the Supreme Court of the United States in the leading case of McCullough *vs.* the State of Maryland (4 Wheat. 316). The rule established in that case is well expressed by the reporter in the syllabus. If the end be legitimate, and within the scope of the Constitution, all the means which are appropriate, which are plainly adapted to that end, and which are not prohibited, may constitutionally be employed to carry it into effect. Let us recur, however, to the very words of the opinion as delivered by C. J. Marshall. "We think the sound construction of the Constitution must allow to the National Legislature that discretion, with respect to the means by which the powers it confers are to be carried into execution, which will enable that body to perform the high duties assigned to it in the manner most beneficial to the people. Let the end be legitimate, let it be within the scope of the Constitution, and all means which are appropriate, which are plainly adapted to that end, and which are not prohibited, but consist with the letter and spirit of the Constitution, are constitutional." (P. 421.)

This is certainly a very large charter to the discretion of Congress, yet as a rule for judicial cases, I am willing to accept it. It is apparent, however, from the very terms in which the principle is enunciated, that this discretion is not without limits.

It is not Congress which is to be the final judge as to whether a measure is necessary and proper for carrying into effect any of the delegated powers. Were it so, the enumeration would have been a vain and delusive mockery, and the fundamental principle that the Federal Government is one merely of limited authority, an unmeaning formula of words.

The limits plainly set in this language are these: 1. The end must be legitimate, and within the scope of the Constitution. 2. The means must be appropriate and adapted to the end. 3. The means must not themselves be prohibited, but consist with the letter and spirit of the Constitution.

There is, however, another limitation upon the discretion of Congress in the choice of necessary and proper means. It is clearly stated in McCullough *vs.* the State of Maryland, and indeed the principle of it may be considered to have ruled that case. I quote again the very words of the opinion:

"The power of creating a corporation, though appertaining to sovereignty, is not, like the powers of making war or levying taxes, or of regulating commerce, a great substantive and independent power, *which cannot be implied* as incidental to other powers, or used as a means of executing them." (4 Wheat. 411.)

I understand the Supreme Court in this language to lay down the simple and reasonable—I might perhaps say the self-evident—proposition, that no one enumerated power can be incidental to another enumerated power. Three cases are stated as examples of substantive powers, but clearly only as examples. We have no right to say that any one of the express powers is more substantive and independent than another. Their very expression authoritatively stamps their character. If, therefore, a power is delegated, but in terms which import a limitation or qualification, it cannot be exercised as incidental to some other power, disregarding the limitation or qualification annexed to the express grant. Indeed, such limitation or qualification may be considered as a prohibition against the exercise of that power in any other way, and therefore within the limit which the Supreme Court places upon the discretion of Congress in the enunciation of the general principle, viz: that Congress cannot employ a measure, however necessary and proper it may be, for carrying into effect some express power, if that measure has been prohibited.

I pass now to the consideration of those grants from which, by the aid of the last paragraph of the enumeration, it is contended that Congress have authority to issue what this act calls "United States notes," and to make them a legal tender in payment of all debts, public and private.

1. "To regulate commerce with foreign nations, and among the several States, and with the Indian tribes." Art 1, sect. 8, par. 3.

It must be admitted that standards of value and of weights and measures, are means very appropriate and adapted to the regulation of commerce. But then we have in this enumeration a clause which expressly grants and defines the authority to create such standards. If it directs of what they shall consist, Congress cannot make another kind as incidental to the regulation of commerce.

With equal plausibility might it be pretended that, for the regulation of commerce, Congress could lay duties, imposts, and excises, and pass bankrupt laws. Such measures might be very appropriate and adapted to that end. Yet surely it will not be maintained that assuming these powers as incidental, Congress could disregard the rule of uniformity, which limits and qualifies the express delegation of them. This qualification is, in fact, a prohibition of any duties, imports, or excises, which shall not be uniform throughout the United States—of any laws on the subject of bankruptcies which shall not, in like manner, be uniform throughout the United States. (Art. 1, sect. 8, par. 4.) These cases present a perfect illustration of the soundness of the limit to the discretion of Congress, prescribed by the Supreme Court, that a substantive power shall not be exercised as incidental. I do not, however, consider them as any more perfect than the very case before us. If the power to create a standard of value and medium of exchange is expressly delegated, but confined by its terms, as we will presently see, that is to coins—foreign or domestic—it is a prohibition of any other kind of money. Congress cannot, under the pretext of regulating commerce, infringe the prohibition thus laid on them.

2. "To borrow money on the credit of the United States." (Art. 1, sect. 8, par. 2.)

It has been argued that under this clause Congress may issue these "United States notes," because they are only acknowledgments of debt in a negotiable form, and in order to give them greater credit, make them a legal tender. That there may be constitutionally issued to the public creditor certificates of the amount due, transferable by assignment—or bonds or notes payable to bearer, which can pass from hand to hand by mere delivery—I do not deny. These are all securities, and Congress is vested expressly with power "to provide for the punishment of counterfeiting the securities and current coin of the United States." (Art. 1, sect. 8, par. 6.) This language is accurate. Securities *ex vi termini* are something different from money. This view is strengthened when we find the coin described in the same paragraph as *current coin.*

These United States notes are not securities for money which may be issued under the authority to borrow, but they are "bills of credit"—things distinct and different from securities. That there is such a distinction may be clearly shown by the judgments of the highest tribunal, which gives the law on these subjects to all other courts.

According to that tribunal, bills of credit are not certificates of loan—not Treasury bonds or notes—not acknowledgments of indebtedness, all of which are mere securities—but bills invested with the functions of money—just such bills as the United States notes issued in pursuance of the act of Congress in question. In Craig *vs.* the State of Missouri, (4 Peters, 431) C. J. Marshall, in delivering the opinion of the Court, says: "In its enlarged and perhaps literal sense the term 'bill of credit' may comprehend any instrument by which a State engages to pay money at a future day: thus including a certificate given for money borrowed. But the language of the Constitution itself, and the mischief to be prevented, which we know from the history of our country, equally limit the interpretation of the term. The word 'emit' is never employed in describing those contracts by which a State binds itself to pay money at a future day for services actually received or for money borrowed for present use; nor are instruments executed for such purposes in common language denominated 'bills of credit.' To 'emit bills of credit' conveys to the mind the idea of issuing *paper intended to circulate through the community for its ordinary purposes as money*, which paper is redeemable at a future day. This is the sense in which the terms have always been understood." The definition here given was subsequently reconsidered, and sustained in Briscoe *vs.* the Bank of Kentucky (2 Peters, 257).

According to this clear and authoritative exposition, what distinguishes bills of credit from such securities as are issued to the public creditor is, that the former are, and the latter are not, intended to circulate as money. These United States notes, then, are not acknowledgments of debt, nor "securities of the United States," but "bills of credit"—in other words, "money." Indeed, this act of Congress of February 25, 1862, intends to leave no doubt on that point, for it expressly declares that they shall be "lawful money." In conformity, then, to the principle, as settled by the Supreme Court in McCullough *vs.* the State of Maryland, we must turn to the money clause to ascertain whether Congress had authority to make them "lawful money." That body cannot, as incidental to the power to borrow, create any kind of money which will not stand the test of the express power, which is granted on that subject.

If any doubt remains as to whether the right to emit bills of credit—to make paper money—can be exercised as incidental to the borrowing power, it ought, as it appears to me, to be entirely dissipated by the proceedings of the Federal Convention when this clause was before them. I freely submit that the opinions expressed in that body are not conclusive upon the interpretation of the Constitution. That instrument is to be construed like all others—by its four corners. But surely as C. J. Marshall relied "on the history of our country" in limiting the meaning of the words "bills of credit," we may resort for light to the opinions and votes of the men who framed the Constitution in deciding whether in the words "to borrow money" was intended to be included "to emit bills of credit," for that is the precise question we have here to consider.

By the ninth of the old articles of confederation, section 5, it was declared that "the United States in Congress assembled shall have authority to borrow money or emit bills on the credit of the United States. "In the plan of the Constitution, as reported to the Convention by the Committee of Detail, of which Mr. Rutledge was chairman, this clause was copied: "to borrow money and emit bills on the credit of the United States." On the 17th of August, 1787, in convention, Mr. Gouverneur Morris, of Pennsylvania, moved to strike out the words "and emit bills." There was a debate on this motion, which is reported by Mr. Madison. It was argued by some—and Mr. Madison himself among the number—that the words had better remain, with a provision prohibiting them from being made a legal tender. Mr. James Wilson, of Pennsylvania, afterwards one of the Justices of the Supreme Court of the United States, appointed by President Washington, contended that it would have a most salutary influence on the credit of the United States "to remove the *possibility of paper money*." Other members who spoke, concurred with him in this view. The motion was carried, and the words stricken out by a vote of nine States to two. Mr. Madison has added in a foot-note, that the vote by Virginia in the affirmative was occasioned by his acquiescence, because he became satisfied that striking out the words would not disable the Government from the use of public notes, so far as they could be safe and proper, and would only cut off *the pretext of a paper currency*, and particularly for making the bills *a tender either for public or private debts.* (5 Elliot's Debates, 434, 435.) I do not know how these proceedings may strike other minds, but they have convinced me that the Federal Convention understood by "bills of credit," not securities—certificates of loan or indebtedness—Treasury notes—or Exchequer bills—but just what Chief Justice Marshall afterwards defined them to be, "paper money," and meant to deny to Congress the power to make such money.

Luther Martin, in his address to the Maryland Legislature in justification of his course in retiring from the Federal Convention, has also given a brief sketch of this interesting debate, which corresponds in the main with that of Mr. Madison. He declares in the most emphatic manner that "a majority of the Convention, being willing to risk any political evil rather than admit the idea of a *paper emission in any possible case*, refused to trust this authority to the Government." (Secret Proceedings of the Federal Convention, p. 57.) He afterwards informs the Legislature, as indicative of the temper of the body, from which he had withdrawn, that as the Constitution "was reported by the Committee of Detail, the States were only prohibited from emitting them (bills of credit) *without the consent of Congress*; but the Convention were so smitten *with the paper money dread* that they insisted that the prohibition should be absolute." "It was my opinion, sir," he proceeds to say, "that the States ought not to be totally deprived of the right to emit bills of credit; and that as we had not given an authority to the general Government for that purpose, it was the more necessary to retain it in the States."

The members of the Federal Convention truly represented the views and feelings of the people of the States by whom they had been chosen. No one acquainted with the history of the Revolution can be surprised at the extreme jealousy entertained of investing either the Federal or State Governments, or even both, by joint action, with any discretion on this subject. It is plain that the men who framed the Constitution—the men who ratified it in the State Conventions—the great mass of their constituents—meant nothing less than to exclude forever *in any possible case*—(Mr. Martin)—*the possibility of paper money* (Mr. Wilson). The public faith again and again solemnly pledged for the redemption of the Continental bills of credit had been shamefully violated. The tender laws of the States, enacted at the urgent solicitation of Congress for the purpose of sustaining their credit, had utterly failed. The amount of private wrong thereby inflicted on individuals and families was incalculable. Congress in a circular address in 1779—after promising solemnly that the amount of the bills should on no account exceed $200,000,000—indignantly repelled the idea that there could be any violation of the public faith, or that there did not exist ample funds to redeem them. The emission, however, very soon after swelled to $379,000,000, and having ceased to circulate, quietly died in the hands of its possessors. (3 Story on the Const., 223–224.) No financiering was found so easy, so attractive, and at the same time so delusive and destructive, as that of resorting to paper money. "Who," said a member of the Revolutionary Congress in debate, "will consent to load his constituents with taxes, when we can send to our printer and get a wagon-load of money, and pay for the whole with a quire of paper?" (Breck's History of Continental Money, p. 13.) Well said Mr. Read, of Delaware, in the Federal Convention, that such a power would stamp the Constitution with "the mark of the beast in Revelations;" and Mr. Langdon, of New Hampshire, only expressed the feelings of the entire country when he declared that he would rather reject the whole plan than retain the three words "and emit bills." It requires but a slight knowledge of the times to conclude that if these three words had been retained, or had it been imagined that, though stricken out, as by comparing the new with the old system everybody could see that they were, they still lurked in the instrument as incidental to some other power, the Federal Constitution would never have been ratified by nine States. In the discussions and publications which followed on the promulgation of the plan, before proceeding to vote on it in the State Conventions, as well as in the debates of those bodies so far as they have been preserved and handed down to us, though every hole and corner of the instrument was ransacked to find objections, I am not aware that it was ever suggested that it might possibly contain so odious and unpopular a power. The voice of the instrument itself appeared sufficiently marked and unmistakable.

3. I now come to consider the remaining clause, which has been relied on as the source of authority to pass the act in question. "To coin money, regulate the value thereof, and of foreign coin, and fix the standard of weights and measures." (Art. 1, sect. 8, par. 5.) It is evident, not merely from the words, but from their juxtaposition with the clause for fixing a standard of weights and measures, that the Constitution intends that the money of the United States shall be not merely a medium of exchange, but *a standard of value.* Uniformity and stability were the ends in view, and for this reason those powers were vested exclusively in the Federal Government. Here, and here alone, and not as a mere incident to something else, are we to look for whatever authority Congress possesses over the subject of money. These words seem to me to sanction only coins or metallic money. In the *Federalist*, No. 42, this is taken for granted: "All that need be remarked on the power to coin money, regulate the value thereof, and of foreign coin, is that by providing for this last case the Constitution has supplied a material omission in the articles of confederation. The authority of the existing Congress is restrained to the regulation of coin *struck* by their own authority, or that of the respective States. It must be seen at once that the *proposed uniformity in the value of the current coin* might be destroyed by subjecting that of foreign coin to the different regulations of the different States." Judge Story thought so, for he says: "The power to coin money is one of the ordinary prerogatives of sovereignty, and is almost universally exercised, in order to preserve a proper circulation of *good coin of a known value* in the home market." (3 Story on the Const., 17.) But the Supreme Court of the United

States have not left this to inference, but have distinctly declared the same opinion in the United States *vs.* Marigold, (9 Howard, 560) in which an act of Congress, punishing the offense of importing spurious coin, was held to be constitutional, on the ground that the provisions of the act appertained, to use the very words of the opinion, "to the execution of an important trust invested by the Constitution, and to the obligation to fulfill that trust on the part of the Government, namely: the trust and the duty of creating and maintaining a *uniform and pure metallic standard of value* throughout the Union. The power of coining money and of regulating its value was delegated to Congress by the Constitution for the very purpose, as assigned by the framers of that instrument, of creating and preserving the uniformity and purity of such *a standard of value.*"

The word *coin* is one of well-settled meaning. The primary sense of the *noun*, according to Dr. Webster, is "the die used for stamping money;" and the undisputed signification of the *verb*, according to most, if not all, the lexicographers, is "to stamp metal, and convert it into coin." In Wharton's Law Lexicon (*ad verbum*) it is said: "Strictly speaking, coin differs from money as the species differs from the genus. Money is any matter, whether metal, paper, beads, shells, etc., which has currency as a medium in commerce. *Coin is a particular species, always made of metal, and struck according to a certain process called coining.*" It was urged at the bar—I do not know whether seriously or not—that printing is stamping, and these notes might therefore literally be said to be coined. No such use of the word in any author has been shown. We may say figuratively *to coin a story*, meaning to invent one, but never *to coin the book* in which it is printed. The story is a fiction—the coinage of the brain—the book a reality. Surely, however, no one will contend, in earnest, that if a sufficient number of clerks had been employed, and these notes had all been written with the hand, they would have been unconstitutional, but that printing them makes them valid. To state the case thus, is to reduce the argument to an absurdity.

It may seem like laboring unnecessarily to substantiate

a very plain proposition, but I will hazard some further illustrations.

The notes in question draw a plain distinction on their face between themselves and coins. They promise to pay *dollars*. What is a *dollar?* To a similar question—what is a pound?—Sir Robert Peel answered: "A pound is a definite quantity of gold, with a mark upon it to determine its weight and fineness." Many pages have been written to controvert this definition, and to prove that a pound is a mere abstraction—something like a mathematical point, without length, breadth, or thickness. But common sense, I think, vindicates Sir Robert Peel. A standard measure must be some actual length or capacity—a standard weight, some actual weight. How else can other weights and measures be compared with it? This is the object of a standard. So a standard of value must be some actual value. I would say, drawing the definition from the statute book—I know not where else to look for it—a dollar is a silver coin, weighing four hundred and twelve and one-half grains, or a gold coin, weighing twenty-five and four-fifths grains, of nine-tenths pure to one-tenth alloy of each metal. These notes, then, promise to pay coins. To say that they are themselves coins is to make the promise and performance identical.

As they do not state on their face when they are to be paid, in law, if issued by an individual or a corporation, they would be payable on demand. Whitlock *vs.* Underwood (3 B. and C. 187). Story on Notes, par. 29. Payable in what? In themselves, if they are coins or dollars. They are promises to pay on demand, payable in promises to pay on demand. A promise to pay may represent coin, and circulate as such. It is properly designated as *currency*, and is one of many modes by which the use of an expensive standard may be spared by the substitution, as a medium of exchange, of public or private credit. It is safe and convenient, as well as economical, as long as it truly represents the standard by being immediately convertible into coin. But in its very nature it is not coin. Its value, or power of purchasing other commodities, depends as well upon the confidence of the community in the ability and intention of the issuers to redeem it as upon the amount issued. Coin, on the other hand, possesses present, actual, intrinsic value. If you obliterate from the pound weight the public mark, which attests its conformity to the standard, it still weighs the same as before. So you may erase the image from the coin, yet its value remains. Blot out, however, the superscription from these pieces of paper, and nothing remains—they are worthless. The stamp on the coin is really nothing but a certificate of the weight and fineness of that piece of metal. Government guarantees nothing but this—makes no contract to deliver corn, wool, or leather in exchange for it. The power of regulating its value can only extend to declaring that in law a certain number of one coin shall be deemed the equivalent of another of a different denomination, in contracts and other transactions. In the market, unequal values cannot be made equal by law. Congress has no power to enact how many bushels of wheat an eagle shall exchange for; and if it had, and should make the experiment, the act, like all attempts by Government to change the laws of value, which are natural laws, would be futile.

The legislation of Congress upon this subject recognizes the difference between these United States notes and coin, and that they are not of equal value.

The act before us (Feb. 25, 1862) requires duties on imports and the interest of the public debt to be paid in coin, and provides that the notes "shall be received *the same as coin at their par value*, in payment for any loans that may hereafter be sold or negotiated by the Secretary of the Treasury." So by the act of March 17, 1862, the Secretary of the Treasury is authorized to purchase coin with them at such rates and upon such terms as he may deem most advantageous to the public interest. And the act of March 3, 1863, prohibits the loan of *currency* or money on the security of gold or silver coins, exceeding in amount the *par value of the coin* pledged or deposited as security. By the first of these acts coin is treated as the standard; by the last, paper. The one speaks of the *par value of the notes*, the other, the *par value of the coins.*

If the word *coin* has any more general or figurative

sense in the phrase *to coin money* than that I have assigned to it, it must be held to have the same in other parts of the article. In foreign coin will be included foreign paper money, and Congress may regulate its value, and make it a legal tender. They may thus treat notes of the Bank of England and France, Austrian and Russian Government money—but not State bank notes. Congress has no power of regulating the value of any money except foreign coins and money coined by its own authority. If to coin money mean to stamp paper, then the clause which forbids the States "to emit bills of credit" was unnecessary; the prohibition "to coin money" included it. The terms of that very prohibition show that in the minds of the makers of the Constitution 'to coin money" and "to emit bills of credit" were two entirely distinct and different things. In short, in whatever point of view it is regarded, it seems to me that the position that this clause authorizes or permits any other but metallic money is untenable.

The restrictions on the States illustrate and confirm the opinion which I have expressed upon the proper construction of the paragraph before us. "No State shall coin money, emit bills of credit, make anything but gold and silver coin a tender in payment of debts, or pass any law impairing the obligation of contracts." (Art. 1, sect. 10.) The whole power over contracts resided in the States before the ratification of the Federal Constitution. This section admits it and leaves it there, subject only to two restrictions—both having the same end in view—the inviolability of contracts. Inasmuch as the States cannot coin, and the Federal Government alone can, and inasmuch as the States cannot make anything but gold and silver a tender in payment of debts, it follows that gold or silver coins, foreign or domestic, as regulated by Congress, constitute the only lawful money. This was evidently Mr. Webster's opinion in that able speech on the Specie Circular, which was cited at the bar, and in which he declared "*that gold and silver*, at rates fixed by Congress, constitute the legal standard of value in this country; and that neither Congress nor any State has authority to establish any other standard, or to displace this." And still more emphatically: "Most *un-*

questionably there is, and there can be no legal tender in this country, under the authority of this Government, or any other, but gold and silver. *This is a constitutional principle, perfectly plain, and of the very highest importance.* The States are expressly prohibited from making anything but gold and silver a tender in payment of debts; and although no such express prohibition is applied to Congress, yet as Congress has no power granted to it but to coin money and regulate the value thereof, *it clearly has no power to substitute paper or anything else for coin as a tender.* The constitutional tender is the thing to be preserved, and it ought to be preserved *sacredly, under all circumstances.*" (4 Webster's Works, 271, 280.) I must confess that upon a question of this magnitude—amid the conflict of opinion by which I am surrounded—my mind has rested with confidence and satisfaction upon this clear and decided conclusion of a great intellect. Mr. Webster's fame rests mainly on his eminence as a constitutional lawyer. The Constitution had been the study of his life—the subject of most of his professional and political efforts. He belonged to no school of strict construction, but on all occasions was found earnestly contending for the broadest charter to the Federal Government. The opinions he expressed in his seat in the Senate of the United States, under the sanction of his official oath, are entitled to be received as deliberate and well considered.

With Mr. Webster, I regard these provisions of the Constitution, upon the subjects of contracts and tenders, as "of the very highest importance," and "to be preserved sacredly under all circumstances." They rest upon sanctions which ought to be considered as of the most inviolable solemnity, at all times and in all emergencies. The true strength of a government—the best foundation on which can rest the confidence and affection of its people—is the security which it guarantees to property. This depends, in this country, upon those constitutional provisions which absolutely protect, under the Ægis of the Courts of Justice, alike the daily earnings of the poor, and the accumulated savings of the rich man, not only from fraud and violence, but from the Government itself, except in the form of open and equal taxation.

It has been strongly urged upon us that Congress has the power of debasing the coin, either in weight or fineness, without changing the denomination or legal value. What, it has been asked, is the difference between that and issuing paper money, even though that paper should be, at the time, depreciated below the value of coin? I answer that because Congress may possibly accomplish a certain end by constitutional means, it does not follow that the same object can be attained by means which are not constitutional. Though, by the process of debasing the metallic standard, Congress may perhaps reduce all debts, public and private, fifty per cent., it does not follow that they can enact directly that the man who owes one hundred dollars to another shall be quit upon the tender of fifty. We apply no such principle to other cases. Because under a power a man may dispose of an estate by will, we do not hold that he can do the same in any other way than that directed or prescribed.

But considering it merely as an argument of the intention of the framers of the Constitution, it appears to me equally inconclusive. There are very important differences between debasing the coin and issuing paper money, though their practical results may in some respects be similar. It may well have been intended to leave to Congress discretion as to the one, but to deny to either branch of the Government—State or Federal—any discretion as to the other.

1. The debasing of the coin as a financial measure, for the purpose of discharging the public debt, would be an open, gross, and palpable breach of faith, scarcely possible in the present age of the world. Changes, however, for the mere purpose of regulating the value of the currency, may be occasionally necessary. "Arbitrary Governments," says Albert Gallatin, "have, at various times, in order to defraud their creditors, debased the coin, whilst they preserved its denomination, and thus subverted the standard of value, by which the payment of public and private debts and the performance of contracts ought to have been regulated. This flagrant mode of violating public faith has been long proscribed by public opinion. Governments have, in modern times, substituted for the same purpose issues of paper money,

gradually increasing in amount, and decreasing in value. It was to guard against these evils that the provisions in the Constitution on that subject were introduced." (Considerations on the Currency, p. 72.)

It is true that the coin has been debased in our own times and country, but never with a view to defraud either public or private creditors. When the coinage of the United States was first regulated, 1792, a double standard, both of gold and silver, was adopted, and the proportion of these two metals fixed at one to fifteen, which was then about their true relation in the market. But though the relation between gold and silver is certainly more steady than that between any two other commodities, at least within short periods of time, yet it is not immutable. Accordingly, about the year 1821, a change was observed to have occurred. An ounce of gold, instead of being worth only fifteen ounces of silver, was really exchangeable for about sixteen ounces. Of course, no one would pay a debt with sixteen ounces of silver, when he could do so with fifteen. The consequence was that the gold coins disappeared entirely from circulation, in obedience to the invariable law that the metal legally undervalued is always expelled. Silver became practically the only standard. The act of June 25, 1834, commonly called the Gold Bill, undertook to restore the true relation. To do this, either the gold coin must be debased or the silver enhanced. The latter course would have been fraught with more injustice and mischief than the former; though the true policy may have been to let things alone, or to have established as the only legal what had practically become the actual standard. Yet many pure and eminent statesmen were then, and still are, wedded to a different policy. Subsequently, by the act of January 18, 1837, the weight and standard of the coin of both metals were slightly changed, with no design but to maintain, if possible, a currency of both gold and silver. Silver, however, being now undervalued, was banished from circulation, as gold had been before. By the act of February 21, 1853, a much more considerable reduction was made in the weight of silver coins less than the dollar, but evidently only for the purpose of supplying a subsidiary currency for small payments: for by the same act it was provided that the silver coins issued in conformity thereto should be legal tenders in payment of debts for all sums not exceeding five dollars. I have no doubt that all this tampering with the coin was unwise and unjust. Whatever may be the advantages of a double standard, they are too dearly purchased by the frequently recurring necessity for these changes. But I do not see that there was, in any of these instances, a criminal breach of public faith, or an intention to interfere with private contracts. In 1834 the public debt had been then recently liquidated in full, and at the period of none of these measures was anything to be gained by the Government from them, but rather the reverse.

2. There is another important difference between the two measures of debasing the coin, and of issuing paper money. When an act is passed debasing the coin, all the mischief is done. On the day following the prices of all markets adjust themselves to the new standard. Commodities, real or personal, lands or chattels, are of exactly the same exchangeable value as before, the only difference being that their value is expressed in different figures. An ounce of gold will still buy the same number of bushels of wheat, whether it is coined into twenty pieces called dollars, or forty pieces. True, debtors are richer at the expense of their creditors. But that gross injustice also is finished. Every man, creditor or debtor, capitalist or laborer, knows exactly where he stands. Not so with paper money. As to all existing contracts, the same and even worse injustice is done, if the paper depreciates, than when the coin is debased. All equality is at an end. To-day a man pays at one discount, to-morrow he receives at another. *There is, in truth, no standard of value whatever.* The paper money varies like the mercury in the barometer, acted on by the superincumbent column of air, swayed to and fro by the tides of the atmosphere—now high, now low—now rarefied, now condensed. Thus, as confidence rises or falls, but more certainly as issues are increased or contracted, the value of every man's property, and the real price of his labor, what he can procure for it of the necessaries and comforts of life, fluctuates from day to day. This was

just what the men of the Revolution, who met in the Federal Convention, who assembled in the State Conventions and ratified the Constitution, had not merely heard with their ears, but seen with their own eyes, touched and handled with their own hands, and felt in their own pockets. They had not the advantage of reading the same history repeated in a more rapid and aggravated form, in the paper money of revolutionary France. But they needed it not. They had quite enough, in their own experience, to make them determine to deal an effectual death-blow at paper money.

On the whole, then, I am of opinion that the provision of the act of Congress of February 25, 1862, declaring the notes issued in pursuance of that act to be lawful money and a legal tender, is unconstitutional.

If the preceding logical, perspicuous and constitutional argument is not enough to convince the most skeptical of the illegality of the Legal Tender Acts, recently passed by Congress; and if such examiners would seek for further proof, they may find, in the Merchants' Magazine, Vol. L, No. 1, pp. 64–76, the opinion and argument of Judge Denio, of New York, which is completely exhaustive of the subject, and is a document which should be studied by every one who has any remaining doubts upon the question. His arguments are completely unanswerable.

(D.)

LEGAL TENDERS UNCONSTITUTIONAL.

"In a case relative to ground rent, lately decided by Judge Alexander, of the Court of Maryland, the validity of the Act of Congress making greenbacks a legal tender in payment of debts, was involved. The Judge has filed the opinion that Congress has no power to declare these notes legal tenders. The decisions in a number of cases assimilating in principle to the one before the Court, are referred to as sustaining the view presented by him. In those cases it was conceded that there was no authority vested in Congress for the purpose above stated, though it was deemed a matter of policy that the enactment should be sustained. The complainant took an appeal from the ruling of the Court, and all the points thus controverted will have to be determined by the Court of Appeals of Maryland, whose decision on them will be looked for with anxiety. In case the decision is sustained by the Court of Appeals, the question will be taken to the United States Supreme Court, for final arbitrament."

(D.)

LEGAL TENDERS DECLARED UNCONSTITUTIONAL IN KENTUCKY.

The Court of Appeals of the State of Kentucky has rendered a decision, declaring the Legal Tender Act of Congress to be unconstitutional. Judge Robinson gave the opinion of the Court, declaring as follows:

"Whenever a jurist inquires whether a statute is consistent with the State constitution, he looks into that constitution, not for a grant, but only for some limitation of the power inherent in the people's legislative organ so far as not forbidden by their organic law.

"But, as Congress derives its power from grants by the people of pre-existing State sovereignties, an enlightened inquirer into the constitutionality of any of its acts looks only to a delegation of power by the Federal Constitution; for that Constitution expressly declares that all power not delegated by it is reserved to the States, or to the people. In this class of cases, therefore, he who asserts the power holds the affirmative; and, unless he maintains it, the controverted act should not be enforced as law by the judiciary. On the contrary, the party affirming that a legislative act of a State is prohibited by the State Constitution, must prove it; and unless the proof be clear, the contested act must be admitted to be law. The distinctive difference between the two classes of cases is, that in the former, the power must be shown to have been delegated; but, in the latter, it must appear to have been prohibited.

"And in this case, therefore, the power to pass the Tender Act must satisfactorily appear to have been delegated before the judiciary should recognize and enforce it."

(D.)

ILLUSTRATION OF LEGAL TENDER.

"As favorable a view as we can take of the Legal Tender Act is, that it enacts in substance as follows:

"*Whenever any debt is discharged within the United States, the creditor shall forfeit to the debtor such per centage of the debt as is equal to the depreciation of legal tender notes since the debt was contracted.* This is in fact the sum and substance of the enactment. It made every promissory note, every bank bill, every dollar of bank stock, every bond of every State and railroad corporation, and indeed, every promise to pay money, *a real unavoidable bet*, which the creditor wins when gold goes down, and the debtor when gold goes up. This, in fact, is the result of every system of irredeemable legal tender paper, and must continue to be while human nature remains as it is. * * * To the lover of justice, the discussion of such a subject of spoliation, from a merely utilitarian point of view, must be repulsive in the extreme. No man who believes that honesty is the best policy; no man who believes in the moral government of the universe; no man who believes that the laws of nature always act to preserve the good and destroy the evil, will ask for any other judgment on the system than that which will be pronounced by his own conscience. But it will be instructive to trace all this injustice to its economic effects, present and future, if only to show how we are punished for transgressing a moral law.

"It is plain that while gold has been rising from par to a premium of 130 per cent., the creditor class of the community, represented by the owners of bank stock, depositors in savings banks, holders of bonds and mortgages, and the frugal poor who have loaned their savings, have, on the whole, been subjected to heavy and unjust losses; while the debtor class, represented by those who live beyond their income or do business on borrowed capital, have made heavy and illegitimate profits. Owing to the different functions of the two classes in social economy, their gains and losses are productive of effects which virtually concern the best interests of society, and are therefore well worthy the serious consideration of the philosopher and statesman. The debtor class, having been from time to time relieved of a per centage of their equitable liability, have found less difficulty than usual in meeting their obligations. Hence there have been fewer failures than common, as well as larger profits, and unusual business prosperity. For the country is naturally considered prosperous when there are few failures and large profits."—*Newcomb.*

(D.)

A FURTHER ILLUSTRATION.

"Three years ago two hundred mechanics each put one hundred dollars into a savings bank. The savings bank loaned this $20,000 to a ship-builder, who employed it in building a ship. He sends the ship to England and sells her for $22,000 in gold, making a legitimate profit of ten per cent. By every principle of justice $20,000 of the money belongs to the savings bank. But now the legal tender clause comes in and declares the builder relieved from the debt in payment of twenty thousand paper dollars. He therefore buys the paper with perhaps $8,000 in gold, pays them to the bank, and keeps the additional $12,000 [in gold] for his own private use."—*Newcomb.* (See page 74.)

(E.)

THE SUPREME FOLLY OF PREFERRING PAPER TO GOLD CURRENCY IN CALIFORNIA.

In the present inflated condition of the currency of the United States, it becomes a question of much importance to California—a gold-bearing State of the Union—to know what fraction of the value of gold results from the fact that this metal is money by constitutional provision, and what would be its value if demonetized, and thrown upon the world as merchandise. The value of money is in a direct ratio to demand, and in an inverse ratio to the supply. If the supply be ample, the price rules low; if it be limited, the value increases. By making a legal tender of paper, the domestic call for gold is greatly reduced, and it is driven to foreign countries for a market. But if all civilized countries rejected gold as money, its value as merchandise would not be one-fourth of its present value as money. Again: if all civilized countries made gold their only money, rejecting all forms of paper issue as such, its value in the markets of the world—and by its value I mean its exchangeable power for other forms of wealth—would be greatly advanced.

If then, three-fourths of the value of gold results from the fact that it is money, what should be the wise policy of a gold-bearing State like California? Certainly to continue to support her staple, and keep it in use as money and for money; not to deprive herself of three-fourths of its value by insisting that it shall only be merchandise, and that our money shall be nothing but credit and promises. Our mines yield more gold in six months than the whole circulation of the State. Would it not be suicidal to reduce the value of gold by shadows and substitutes?—And above all, by legislative enactments, to coerce it from circulation as our medium of exchange and measure of value?

When the State of Maine shall legislate that white pine boards shall no longer be used for covering the roofs of buildings there, but that all her roofing material shall be tules imported from California; when Massachusetts shall enact that water power shall no longer be used in that State to propel the machinery of her manufactures, but that all her power of manufacturing shall be slaves imported from the Southern States; when New York shall make a law that in future commerce shall not be carried on by means of ships and ocean steamers, but that all commerce of the State shall be done in balloons, which shall navigate the air, and move with inconceivable velocity; when Indiana and Illinois shall legislate that bread shall no longer be made of wheat flour, but a substitute for it shall be rye flour and potatoes; when Ohio shall enact that hams, bacon, and mess pork shall no more be eaten there, but a substitute shall be found in importing cod-fish from Newfoundland; when Pennsylvania shall legislate that coal shall no longer be used there as fuel, but that wood shall be brought from the forests of Canada; when Missouri shall make a law that railroad iron shall no more be made from the iron ore of her mountains; when Louisiana shall decree that the sugar from the cane shall no longer be used there, but that beet-sugar shall be imported from France; when Alabama shall enact that goods manufactured from cotton shall no longer be used in that State, but that all her articles of clothing shall be made of gunny-bags and sackcloth; and when all the other States of the Union shall enact laws equally sottish and equally destructive of their vital interests—then, and not till then, let California cap the climax of folly, and ordain that gold coin of the mints of the United States shall no longer be money here—shall no longer measure values in our State, but that we will import from the East paper promises redeemable twenty years hence, or long after we shall have any earthly cares to annoy us, and we will swear that these are the best measures of value that were ever instituted; and as we look on the devastation and wide-spread ruin which such legislation has induced, like Nero who danced and fiddled while Rome was in ruins, we will shout pæans of joy, and, IO TRIUMPHE! SIC ITUR AD ASTRA!! (See pp. 75 to 81.)

February 6, 1864.

(E.)

THE MASSACHUSETTS ANTI-SPECIE DECISION—THE OPINION OF THE COURT IN FULL.

(From the Boston *Traveller* of 20th January, 1864.)

The Supreme Court of this State have recently decided in the case of Wood *vs.* Bullens, argued last September, that the plaintiff in action upon a promissory note payable on demand in specie, can only recover judgment for the amount of the face of the note and interest thereon, although he offers to prove that at the time when payment of the note was demanded, specie was worth a premium above par. The note on which the action was brought was as follows:

"Chicopee, December 31, 1861.

"$500.—For value received I promise to pay Joseph E. Wood or order five hundred dollars on demand, with interest—the above payable in specie.

"A. BULLENS."

The opinion of the Court was prepared by Judge Chapman, and was as follows:

"This action is brought upon a promissory note for $500, payable on demand, and interest, with the additional words, 'The above payable in specie.' The plaintiff proved that he had demanded payment of the note in specie, and offered to prove that on the day he made the demand specie was worth a certain premium above par. He contends that he is entitled to recover judgment for the amount of such premium in addition to the sum of $500 and interest. This position assumes that specie is to be regarded as an article of merchandise, and not as money. For if we regard it as money, it is itself the standard of value, and the statement that a dollar can be above or below par is absurd. It is, in effect, a statement that a dollar can be worth more or less than a dollar. Dealers in money may for their own convenience, and especially in respect to foreign trade, treat money as merchandise, and speak of gold and silver as being above or below par. But when a gold or silver dollar is spoken of in this manner, it is with reference to something else as a standard of par value. Thus it sometimes happened that the market value of these two metals has changed, and that a dollar in silver has been worth more in market than a dollar in gold. Yet the Courts have been compelled by law to treat them as money, and to reg rd a dollar of one metal as equal to a dollar of the other. Equality may be wholly or partially restored by debasing one species of coin or improving that of the other. It is one of the attributes of sovereignty to do this; and when it is done, courts of law must conform to the change, and regard that as a dollar which Congress declares to be so. A judgment in a suit upon a note must be rendered for a certain sum in money, expressed in dollars and cents. Execution must issue for this sum, with costs, and the amount is to be collected. If we were to add to the amount of the note and interest a further sum—for example, one hundred dollars as a premium on specie—the execution would still be collectable in money. If the officer could seize a sufficient amount of gold or silver to pay the execution and costs, he would pay to the plaintiff the specie, and thus the plaintiff would obtain more than the amount of his debt. If the defendant's goods should be sold at auction on execution, and the purchasers should pay in specie, the same result would follow. If land should be set off on execution, its value may be so changed by the condition of the currency as to affect the interests of the parties materially. It may be that the judgment will remain unsatisfied till gold, as merchandise, shall sink below par. This would again affect the interests of the parties and the value of the judgment. The weekly fluctuations of the gold market are constantly operating in the same way. But these are matters which are beyond the reach of courts of law. They involve values, and sometimes equities, which no judicial tribunal can adjust or regulate. All that courts can do is to treat as money that which the statutes of the United States legally enacted declare to be money. *If it were in our power to render a specific judgment, designating the species of currency in which it should be paid, we might avoid some of the existing difficulties, but we have no such authority.*"

Here we have a case in Massachusetts, where the ruling of the Court would have been made payable in specie, according to the promise of the signer of the note, if there had been a statute of the State allowing the Court to render a specific judgment, designating the currency in which it should be paid. Certainly nothing could be more pertinent, or show the utility of the Specific Contract Law of California more clearly, than this ruling of Judge Chapman. Every State in the Union needs a law which will enable courts and sheriffs to enforce the payment of contracts in gold coin, when the parties to such contracts stipulate such form of payment. (Pages 75 to 81.)

A RECENT DECISION.

The following case came before the United States Court, Judge Smalley:

"Lawrence Gladstone et al. *agt.* William Chamberlain et al. The defendants chartered the British vessel John of Gaunt from plaintiffs, to bring a cargo from the island of Ceylon to the United States, and in the contract agreed to pay plaintiffs $29,000 cash, in consideration thereof. On the delivery of the cargo, the defendants paid the above amount to plaintiffs in legal tender notes, and contended that that was a discharge of their obligations. Plaintiffs consider that only so much paid on account, and contended that the word cash in the contract meant specie —gold or silver.

The question in relation to this point was, from the evidence, left to the jury to decide, which they did by bringing in a verdict for plaintiffs for $18,066—that being the difference in value between gold and greenbacks at the time of the delivery of the cargo, with interest added to date.

This verdict was strictly in accordance with the ruling of the Judge."

"PUNISHING TRADE FOR THE SINS OF PAPER."

"The truth is, this 'protective system' bore so unequally on different branches of industry, and on different sections of country, as to give some a license to extract tribute from others, and to excite dishonest hopes and wishes in nearly all. Government having once opened the flood-gates of favoritism, each workman and each class was too weak to stem the torrent, and naturally strove to win as much and lose as little as possible. The hatter aimed to get the highest possible duty on imported hats; the shoemaker on imported shoes; the owners of cloth factories, on imported cloths: and so on, through all the trades which foreign competition could affect. Some were more successful, and some less; some got five per cent. 'protection,' some twenty, some thirty, some fifty, with a juggle of false valuation that might raise it above one hundred in practice; but all who got or tried to get any favoritism at all, became as truly implicated in the crime as those who got most, and as truly belonged with the opponents of free trade and natural justice. Hence the long endurance of the system, notwithstanding its impolicy and wickedness.

Great pecuniary losses resulted from the fallacious hopes thus raised — hopes which led thousands to embark in 'protected' branches of industry that they did not understand, trusting to a congressional abrogation of God's laws of trade for their customers and profits—yet all pecuniary losses have been as nothing compared with the injury done to our national dignity and our political morals. The Protective System was a second dagger planted in the heart of democratic government, paper money being the first. It transformed our Government from an upholder and obeyer of God's justice into a framer and enforcer of antagonistic laws; from a protector of man's personal rights into their violator and betrayer; from a public watchman into a public abettor of trespass and extortion. It created a new order of nobility, in fact if not in form; for it privileged men to make free with other men's rights and earnings. It degraded the laborer, by segregating him from the world-wide

Republic of Industry—a republic where merit or the best workman governs by divine right—and compelling him, on local grounds, to spend his substance with those who could *not* serve him cheapest and best. By stripping him of his just rights over *his own purse*, the fruits of his own toil, it robbed him of his manhood and made him a Slave—a Government Chattel—who must buy and sell, not according to his own will, but the will of a master. I say this, not in the language of passion, but in scientific exactness; for, certainly, so far as a man holds his personal rights subject to the power of another—so far as he is deprived of any *just* liberty, whether by an individual or by Government—so far is he a slave, if not in title, yet in truth. Nor is the injury or the degradation any the less, because it is inflicted by the victim's government instead of open enemies. Government can no more make or unmake the personal rights of its citizens than a farmer's watch-dog can make or unmake his title to his sheep. All that governments or majorities can rightfully do, in regard to any man's natural rights and liberties, is to guard them faithfully and strike down every invader. The fact that I and my fellow-citizens have clubbed together and employ a common guard to stand sentry over our rights and liberties, gives me no claim to any right that is theirs, and gives them no destroying power over any right that is mine. They have no more right to rob me of my money, or of my right to spend it with whom I please, because I live under the same government that they do, than I have to shoot them because they live under the same government that I do.

If we consider the Protective System in its other aspect, that of a system of taxation for the support of Government, it is, if possible, worse still. It apportions the burdens of Government without the slightest regard to equity, stripping some men and sections of perhaps a fourth of all their toil, while giving bounties or pensions to others, whose lives are no more virtuous, and whose industry is no more useful. Under the tariff of 1828, two men, A and B, might each take his year's produce to the old world and sell it for the same amount—say $1,100. If A brought home the proceeds of his crop in lace and jewelry, he would be taxed on his return seven and a half per cent. on $1,100=$82 50. If B brought home his crop in the form of one thousand yards of woolens, at one dollar and ten cents per yard, Government would tax him at forty-five per cent. on an *assumed value of* $2,500=$1,125, or $1,042 50 more than A. Less than one-thirteenth of A's crop would go for taxes; Government would eat up the whole of B's!

Another wrong of the Protective System is, that it throws the whole burden of federal taxation upon one kind of property, or the producers thereof, while practically exempting all others. It throws the whole burden upon those producers *who sell their work in the world's market, or abroad;* leaving those who produce nothing for, and carry nothing to, that market, tax free. Worst of all, (and this is the secret of its *protective power)* it enables this latter class to levy taxes or tribute upon the former, for their own private pleasure and emolument; for, to prohibit those who sell their crops in the world's market from buying their supplies there, is to force them to buy in the *protected* market, and to put them in the power of those who *sell* or keep stands in it.

* * * * * * * *

To understand distinctly where the weight of the tariff falls, and whence the profits it conveys to pet interests are taken, (for every weight must bear on something, and all money-profits must be parted with by somebody before they can be pocketed by anybody) we must ponder these cardinal truths of financial science, viz :—That all schemes for making either persons or nations rich without work, or out of proportion to the wealth they may actually produce, are utter fallacies, or else schemes of spoliation. That, as it is impossible for darkness to cover all the earth at once, so long as the sun shall shine in the heavens, neither can any financial imposition darken all nations at once so long as Truth shall reign. That genuine labor-products, such as gold, wheat, cotton, and things whose value depends on true human needs instead of mesmeric and governmental illusions, will always have a world-wide currency; while conventional wealth and might can only be kept up by being kept within the charmed circle or mesmeric sphere of their imagination-forcing creators. That there must always be a world's market, or center of trade for all nations, where things without intrinsic value are but losing ventures, and whither only things of true use can be profitably sent: such world's market being not so much a geographical center as a *region of commercial sanity*, wherein no man can be a merchant any further than he respects verities, and takes things for exactly what they are. That the true financial health and strength of a country are known by the ability of its producers to sell their works in the world's market readily and profitably; which they can do in proportion to the lightness of their taxes, impositions and extortions, and the extent of their industry and skill. That as the farmer gains in purse, not by the grain he eats, but what he sells, so the only persons (save miners of the precious metals) who add aught to the moneyed wealth of a nation, are those who send and sell their labor-products abroad; and a Government that obstructs such sales by taxing its citizens, or confiscating portions of their goods as they return from foreign markets with their purchases, not only commits a sin, but a fatal blunder also. That cotton, and all products readily convertible into specie in the world's market, or that answer the purposes of cash therein, are virtual specie to that extent ; and every injury done to specie by the issuing of paper, is equally an injury to such cash-products, or, rather, to their producers and owners. That in proportion as the wealth-producers of a country are compelled, either by law or custom, to give real wealth for paper wealth, real work or service for sham work or service, the cost of production among them is increased, and their ability to compete with other nations is diminished. That the real object and operation of a protective tariff are, to force a home market for such citizens as are thus shut out of the world's market at the expense of such other citizens as, owing to peculiar advantages of soil or climate, or to superior skill in certain kinds of work, are *not* shut out of the world's market. Thus, a protective tariff is a bludgeon to prevent people from making good bargains abroad and bringing wealth into their own country, by way of driving them into bad bargains at home. It would never have been thought of but for the disturbing influence of paper money. It is as powerless as a land-tax to *create* wealth, though it *can* be used to force existing wealth out of its natural channel, and to wrest it from its owners. It can sometimes help a starving operative out of work to knock down and strip some less starved fellow-citizen as he travels along trade's highway; but it never put a cent in any starveling's purse, without first taking it from some one having a better right to it than the taker."

* * * * * * * *

"Such have been the fruits of the 'Protective System'—of our forty years' struggle to escape God's vengeance against paper money—nor are they any the less bitter because that system's advocates fancy, or have persuaded themselves, that they are actuated by patriotism instead of covetousness." (Book of Finance and Politics, pp. 120–131.)

The preceding truthful and forcible representation of the action of the tariff ascribes, and no doubt justly, the origin of the system to the disturbing influence of paper money. But, while California must submit to the damaging operation of this national legislation upon all her imports from the markets of the world, she is called upon to bear a grievance, if possible, more intolerable, viz: that her gold is shorn of half its value in the domestic markets of the country, because our people will not use it as money—will insist upon making merchandise of it, and substitute promises to pay it, while the promisers have not the coin to redeem their issues.

The Eastern people are clamorous for higher customs. They seem to be regardless of the action of high duties upon other States, if they can become wealthy from the losses which such confiscations impose upon other sections of the country. It is time that the intelligent and honest portion of their population should cease to attempt to control the affairs of the nation upon unjust, unequal, or inequitable principles.

They need no higher duties than what are now imposed; and, if they would follow the teachings of science, they could become wealthy under a scale of customs far below what is now enacted. What they need is a sound currency—a currency worth one hundred cents on the dollar, in gold coin. With such a currency, they could build factories, make their machinery, purchase their raw materials, pay for their labor, and turn out the finished articles at about one-half the present prices ; and, in this manner, could compete with foreign manufacturers altogether more surely, more permanently, and more efficiently, than through an unnatural, forced, and violent support, by unjustly compelling the owners of gold to trade in domestic markets, which are so greatly above those of foreign countries, and protecting this unequal form of taxation by Federal law. We must make our currency as good as that of foreign nations, or give up manufacturing; or support manufactures by direct spoliation from other forms of national wealth.

If the Eastern people would dismiss their inveterate attachment to false money, and use gold and silver, their trade with California would be greatly enlarged. The truth is, that, notwithstanding the enormously high tariff under which we are struggling, such is the baneful action of paper money in the old States, that California can still pay the duties on imports and do better than to pay the advanced prices which currency makes on domestic manufactures. The only remedy for this element of national disorganization is a gold currency, or its absolute equivalent. While the burdens of the nation are unequally imposed, we cannot expect to advance in prosperity, harmony, opulence, and peace. It seems to be almost supererogatory to pursue the argument.

A recent work of great merit has been published in Boston, written by the Hon. Amasa Walker, an author of the highest standing as a political economist, from which I will make some extracts. In treating on the effects of a mixed currency, he says :

A mixed currency discourages domestic manufactures, disturbs the proper relation of exports and imports, and puts the balance of trade against the people employing the greater proportion of credit.

These effects will be recognized as injurious by all classes of persons ; but those who are so solicitous for the positive encouragement of domestic manufactures, and for the restraint of imports, as to favor the enactment of prohibitory or protective laws imposing duties on the foreign article, will, of course, most fully appreciate and deeply feel this tendency of a mixed currency.

The course of this will be best observed in an illustration from the manufacture of a specific article :

" Suppose that a certain kind of broadcloth can be afforded by the foreign manufacturer, delivered at New York, for two dollars per yard: the same article might be made in this country, but would *cost* two dollars a yard, without any profit whatever. Of course, then, we cannot afford to make the article. The Government, in order to encourage its production here, lays a duty upon the imported article of fifty cents per yard; but at the same time establishes banks which manufacture a mixed currency, and double the natural amount of money. The American manufacturer now proceeds to erect his mills; but wages and materials have so advanced in price, by the expansion of the currency, that it costs him twenty-five to fifty per cent. more than it otherwise would have done. He builds machinery; but this also costs him proportionably high. He proceeds to purchase raw materials, and employ labor in manufacturing; but all are advanced in price for the same reason. His own expenses for living are also greater; and should he be obliged to hire money, that will generally be found to have advanced in price, or rate of interest. Under these circumstances, he cannot make the cloth so as to afford a profit; and it will not be surprising if he should clamor for more protection. But it may be said that the same causes that have advanced the expenses of living, and consequently of labor, will equally have advanced the price of broadcloth. Not so. The price of the broadcloth will be determined by the rate at which it can be afforded by the foreign manufacturer; and if he can pay the duty of fifty cents per yard, and yet obtain a fair profit, he will send all the market demands.

"There is another view of the matter. Suppose we would export our plain cottons, for example, to India. We there meet the English article, made under a currency more valuable than our own, which can consequently be afforded for less; since, with the *same* amount of the money of India, (*i. e.*, value money) the English manufacturer can pay for much more labor in England than the American manufacturer can in America. It is true that the *rate of wages* is lower in England than in this country; but *in addition to this* England has the very great advantage of a currency nearer the cnrrency of international exchange, which is always strictly *value money*. In such a state of things, not all the tariffs that ever were or ever will be imposed can adequately protect our manufactures. So far as they have arisen or flourished, it has been in spite of these disadvantages."*

During the continuance of the compromise tariff, established in 1832, and which terminated in 1842, the currency varied from $11 82 to $17 61 per capita, equal to an expansion of more than fifty per cent.; while during the same period prices fluctuated to a greater extent. The variation in prices was larger even than the per centage of protective duties.

So the tariff of 1842, which began to take effect in 1843, when the currency was $6 18 per capita, was more than counterbalanced by the expansion of the currency to $9 94 in 1846. But the manufac-

---

* Walker on Money and Mixed Currency, p. 39.

turer suffered as much from the periodical contractions as from the expansions that preceded them; for while by the latter, the duties were rendered nugatory, all business men met great losses from the failures and the general derangement and stagnation which the former produced. No tariff of reasonable extent, such as the people of the whole nation would endure, can ever place the domestic manufacturer in a position of security and of reliable profit, while competing with such an immense advance in prices as must certainly accompany an expansion of the currency. Nor can it fail to be true that the normal industrial development of any country, in which such a currency exists, must to a very great degree be interrupted or distorted. All ordinary business calculations are overturned. An element of hazard is introduced fatal to the shrewdest schemes.

The terrific struggles through which American manufacturers have passed, ever since the establishment of the first tariff in 1816, have been caused, not by foreign competition solely or mostly, but by a false and delusive domestic currency. Fully as we are opposed to the policy of protective duties, we are still more opposed to that system of currency which neutralizes them, and renders the legitimate success of home manufactures impossible, even after so great sacrifices to introduce them. (The Science of Wealth, pp. 190–193.)

See Nos. VIII and IX, pp. 142, 150.

INDEX.

	PAGES.
Achievement of Congress in regard to Currency—bringing it under the governance of the National instead of the State Legislatures	25
Amendment of the National Bank Act needed; withdrawing the Bonds as Security for Issues, and depositing Gold Coin	26
Amount of Coin needed, in 1860, to make the entire Currency of Metals, $377,500,000	29–31
Acts of Congress which conflict with the Supreme Law are Illegal	39
Admission of California into the Union with a Hard Money Constitution, estops Congress from forcing on her any form of Paper Currency	60
A great Objection to making National Bonds the basis for the Issue of Currency	109
Authority of Congress over the Currency	117–118
A Wrong System of Currency gives our Gold to Foreigners in dead Loss to the Nation	120
Acts of Congress have a most blighting Effect upon the Value of Coin	150
As to which should be allowed the Permanent Circulation of the Country—the Legal Tenders or the National Bank Currency	181
Action of Legal Tender on California	191
Borrowing Money on the Credit of the United States, is a Power delegated to Congress	48–49
Borrowing and Lending imply Volition—Free Agency	54
Bills of Credit defined by Chief Justice Marshall	114–115
Banks of California are based, entirely, on Gold Coin	130–131
"Balance of Trade," by C. H. Carroll, Esq	159–164
Banks should no longer make Profits from Circulation	172
Banks—their System Exists by the Sufferance of the People	172
Banks should not be the Custodians of the Coin for the Redemption of their Issues: the Coin should be held by the Federal Treasury	178–179
Bankers who Loan Real Money are among our most useful Citizens; but those who Loan Credit instead, are working Mischief and Disorganization	245

PAGES.

Bank Deposits.................................... 263–264
Bill to Enlarge the Scope and Usefulness of the Independent Treasury.................................. 266–285
Brief Recapitulation of the Salient Provisions of the Bill. All Banks of Issue exist by the Sufferance of Congress. The Credits of Banks may be controlled by Federal Law, if the Public Weal requires it, as well as their Outward Circulation. Opinion of Daniel Webster on the Right of Congress to restrain Banking. Adam Smith on the Right of Government to restrain Natural Liberty (pp. 285, 286, 287, 288). A similar Bill, if it had been the Law of the Land in 1848, would have saved to the Union, in eighteen years, two billions of dollars..................... 291–292

Civil War demonstrated the impotence of State Banks... 24
also demonstrated the need of Stronger Monetary Institutions.............................. 25
Currency of the Country—should never be any form of Credit.................................... 26
Congress should not tolerate any Currency which sacks the Nation of Gold........................... 26
Currency of the Country in 1860...................... 30
Currency—The Difference to California between Coin and the National Banks 37
Constitution of the United States—the Authority of California for using Gold Currency ....
Comparison of the Values of United States and British Gold Coin.................................. 42
Congress had no Authority to enact a New System for Raising Funds, where the Constitution had already provided one.................................. 48–56
Creditor should not be compelled by law to give the debtor a large fraction of his claim, for the benefit of the Nation, without Restitution by the Government... 53
Conflicting Provisions of the Legal Tender Act with the Constitution................................ 56
Currency should not be based on anything but Coin, dollar for dollar........................ 87
Congress *cannot regulate the Value of Coin unless it rules the Value of Currency*, and makes Currency equivalent to coin............................... 85, 86, 117
Congress, the Supreme Court of the United States, and Courts of the several States, must recognize the difference in Value between the Coin of the Mints and the Inconvertible Promises to Pay that Coin...... 97–98
Circulation of the United Kingdom.................. 100–101
Currency—whenever it represents Coin, dollar for dollar, the issues of Paper will be essentially lessened.... 177
Congress has the same Right to *Expel* California from the Union as to *Compel* her to use Paper Money... .. 104
Comparative Prices of National Stocks................ 121

PAGES.

Currency cannot be Pure unless Equivalent to the Standard.. 133
Currency may be Inflated in an equal per centage to the Tariff, without any check from imports........... 168
California Banks are Models of Banking for the World... 233-234
Causes which have, most efficiently, retarded the Progress of California..............................298, 299, 300

" Dollar "—the Legal Tender Act destroys its quality as a Standard...................................... 43
" Dollar "—it has ranged from 95 down to 35, and from 35 up to 70 cents on the dollar; the Statutes at Large maintaining the absolute equivalent of the two Currencies for payments between Citizens 43-44
Demonetizing Gold Coin in the markets of the United States, for all purposes except Paying Duties and Interest upon the Public Debt, is a direct thrust at its Value at home............................. 156
Damages which it inflicts on California................. 167-168
Difference between Lending Real Money and a Substitute. 177
Demonstration that a Paper Currency could not help California.. 211-212
Debt is no proper basis for the issue of Currency........ 231-232
Deposit Account of Banks—how it may be abused...... 232
Defrauding by False Measures of Value as dishonorable as Cheating by False Measures of Quantity.......... 237
Domestic Exchange—might be drawn by the Treasury with great mutual advantage to the Government and People..................................... 288 289
Decision in the United States District Court, New York, on Greenbacks................................ 338

Extracts from Elliot's Debates in the Federal Convention 310
Extracts from Walker's " Science of Wealth," a work of high merit, on the action of the Tariff and Currency upon Domestic Manufactures 343-345
Extortion of the Legal Tender Acts.................. 44-45
Equal Taxation is designed by the Supreme Law 142
Establishing a Currency, by the Government, which is not immediately Convertible, is Revolutionary in its tendency, and thoroughly Demoralizing.......... 180
Expenses of Working the Mines...................... 210
Every man is compelled to use such Currency as the Community where he resides tolerates........... 248

Failures in Currency make failures in General Business in a Ten-fold Proportion....................... 27
Fixity and Exactness requisite in all Standards—preeminently so in Standards of Value............. 40-41

PAGES.

Failure of the Legal Tender Act to keep Treasury Notes at the Par of Gold, an Effect of the Laws of Trade, not the Operation of Speculators or Brokers 45
Forced Loans by the Government 54
Framers of the Constitution purposely and decidedly Rejected the Power of Issuing "Bills of Credit" by Congress 64, 310
Failures of 1857 .... 123, 257-8

Government Bonds not a Proper Basis for the Issue of Currency 305, 306, 26
Gold Coin should never be Cheapened by Issues of Paper 89
General Banking Law of New York a Failure in 1857. 140
Gold Act of June, 1864 156
Government Circulation—The Gains from it are but an insignificant Consideration, compared with the Damage to the Nation in Advanced Prices 180
Government Power and Influence Reduced the Value of a single Shipment of $1,200,000 from California about $250,000 (foot-note) 187
Gold taken from the Mines belongs of right to the miner. 189
Gold, its Value, and the Constitutional Rights of the Pacific States, should be Efficiently Represented in Congress 191
Government Losses, by Paying Gold at Prices made by Paper 203
Government should make the Reform as Efficient for the People as for itself 203
Gold and Silver were intended for Mankind as Money ... 238
Gold and Silver are recognized Standards, and given in needful quantities only 239
Gold and Silver, if depreciated by superabundance, no one may complain of it 240
Government Banking—if ever instituted—should be thoroughly upon a Gold Basis: the easiest and most popular form of Taxation that could be devised ... 290-291

How the Government could raise Money Constitutionally 66
How the Legal Tender Act subverts Justice and the Constitution 70, 71, 73
High Rates of Interest do not so thoroughly Demoralize a People as a vitiated Currency 119
How to Resume Specie Payments 124-130, 137-138
How Banks of Issue force Coin from Circulation 171
How to Appropriate the Sinking Fund 187-188
How the Pet Banks used the Government in 1837 193-194
How the Legislature of California loosed the Gordian Knot 221
How to Try Paper Money 247, 252, 253-254

PAGES.
Increase of Currency augments Demand for it........ 20
Impossible Conditions should never be introduced into the Currency 21, 92
Implied Powers cannot be exercised by Congress where Express Powers are given for same purpose 48
Issues of Currency should be governed with as much Absolutism and Precision as the Issues of Coin...... 112
If Paper Money is a National necessity it is the bounden Duty of Congress to keep it equivalent to Coin ... 134
Issue of Currency an Attribute of the Sovereignty...... 142
If the state of the Union be such that California must lose so immensely on her Gold, she should be compensated by some Equivalent....................... 157–158
Imports during the year 1857; estimated loss to the country upon those imports, in gold value, equal to $72,000,000.............................168, 169, 170
Independent Treasury—its Uses and Advantages should extend to the People as well as the Government .. 203
Inflating Currency saves no Interest to a Country....... 223–227

Justice one of the Columns upon which our National Government is founded, p. 39. The Legal Tender Act subverts Justice 53

Kent, Chancellor, on the right and duty of Courts...... 56
King James' Legal Tender 58

Legal Tender Act Examined.......................... 39
Laws of the Mints relating to the purity of Coins...... 40
Losses direct by Inflating Currency...................45, 46, 47
Losses by Inflation have doubled the cost of the war.. 47
Legal Tender, practically illustrated.............49, 51, 333, 334
Legal Tender Act, if Constitutional, would quadruple the National Debt, pp. 51, 52; ergo, not adapted to the purposes for which it was enacted.
Legal Tender Act contributes to enrich thousands by impoverishing millions........................ 68
Legislation of Congress against Gold has been Vindictive 105
Legal Tender—National Banks demanding of Congress that their issues be made a complete Tender.... 111
Legal Tenders will not be Funded so long as the Banks and People can make them Tenders in Fact....... 136
Losses on Currency, how settled and balanced.......... 154–155
Losses to the Body Politic by the Currency............ 206
Legal Tender Act allows States to make Treasury Notes a tender, whilst the Constitution forbids them to make *anything* but Gold and Silver Coin such tender... 71
Legal Tender Notes—Has Congress the Power to make Notes a Legal Tender? Opinion and irrefragable argument of the Honorable JUDGE SHARSWOOD, of

PAGES.

Pennsylvania, demonstrating that the Legal Tender Acts of Congress are unconstitutional, pp. 312–331. Opinion of JUDGE ALEXANDER, of Maryland, that Congress has no power to declare these notes legal tender, pp. 331–332.—Opinion of JUDGE ROBINSON, of the Court of Appeals of the State of Kentucky, declaring the Legal Tender Acts unconstitutional, pp. 332–333.—Illustration of Legal Tender, quoted from S. Newcombe.......................... 333–334

Land as Security for Issuing Paper Money, p. 302. An early Project to establish a Land Bank in England. The Scheme described by Lord Macaulay. The wonderful Effects to result from this Innovation, p. 303.—Every Person who had Real Property ought to have, besides that Property, Paper Money to the full value of that Property. The speculations of Briscoe and Chamberlayne on the subject of Currency. The tenacity of these champions to their demented project, p. 304. — Government Stocks compared with Land security as a Basis for issues. Neither of these a proper basis for Currency.

Money should Possess Value to exchange for Value, p. 15.—Monetizing Gold gives it a large fraction of its Value.................................... 21

Manifests of Gold shipments from San Francisco to March, 1866.............................. 31

Mint Laws of Congress are in Accord with the Constitution and Justice. Same Laws in Conflict with the Legal Tender Acts, p. 54.—Both cannot be Constitutional 55

Massachusetts Anti-Specie Decision, showing the necessity for a similar law to the California Specific Contract Act, in every State of the Union......... 336–337

National Banks—their Charter may be amended 26

National Bank System in California would work interminable Mischief 38

National Legislation, in conflict with justice and morality, is opposed to the permanent welfare of any People 59

National Banks, not organized on a proper basis to save the Wealth of the Country..................... 120

National Banks—*How to Resume Specie Payments*....... 124–130

National Banks clamoring to make their issues legal tender 133

National Credit is largely dependent upon the annual Yield of the Mines........................... 190

No Advantage to the Federal Government to change the Currency of California......................... 217–218

Nature and quality of Bank Deposits................... 229

Newcombe, Simon, on the Legal Tender Act........... 333–334

National Bank System, ethics of...................... 258–259

PAGES.

One Treasury Note is Legal Tender for another of the same tenor. This virtually bars redemption in coin.. 44

Only Regulation which can keep Currency at the Par of Gold.. 178

Possibility of making the basis of the Currency Gold Coin, dollar for dollar........................ 27–29

Paper Money lessens the purchasing power of Gold.... 35

Principle of the Specific Contract Law recognized....... 81–82

Protection of Coin includes standard weight and fineness, and the suppression of all Currency Circulation which does not represent the Coin........... 86–87

Power of Congress over the Currency................. 117

Paper Money might discharge all its functions equally well and represent coin on deposit, dollar for dollar 134–135

Prices of Goods in Foreign Markets.................. 144–145

Profits of the Mines greatly over-estimated at the East—takes a Mine to work a Mine.................... 190

Pacific Railroad—The Pressing Claims upon the Government for its speedy completion. Estimate of its Cost. Is required as a Measure of National Defense. FOUR BILLIONS of dollars have been paid and incurred to bind the Union together, North and South. Would $200,000,000 be an Unreasonable amount to expend in binding the Union, East and West? pp. 294, 295, 296.—More necessary and efficient, as a measure of National Defense to the Pacific Coast, than the entire American Navy, pp. 296, 297.—The claims of California on the Federal Government for direct aid are immeasurably greater than those of any other State in the Union, pp. 298, 299.—These are for Losses on her Treasure in the past eighteen years, $693,000,000. In addition, the work should be accomplished for National Defense. Still further, when done, will make the Union at large worth many fold the entire cost of the enterprise.........................299 300 301

Possibility of a Metallic Currency. Opinion of the great Political Economist, Dr. Tellkampf, of the University of Breslau, in Prussia....... 306–307

"*Punishing Trade for the Sins of Paper.*" The Protective System described, Financial Science, etc., etc., from the Honest Man's Book of Finance and Politics.. 339–342

Quotations from Scripture, proving the Abomination of all False Measures............................ 235

Quotations, proving that Gold and Silver are recognized by the Scriptures as Measures of Value.......... 239

PAGES.

Rapidity of Circulation cannot compensate for deficiency of supply.................. 16
Reduction of the Public Debt 69
Regulation of the Currency the right and duty of Congress.. 85
Resumption of Specie Payments—how to Resume....... 124–130
Responsibility of the Federal Treasury................ 139
Restrictions upon the Mines by the Government will lessen their product 210
Returns of the National Banks, October, 1866: liabilities, $901,558,020; specie on hand, $8,170,835......... 309–310

Say, J. B. on the adaptation of the precious metals for Money. 16
Substitution of Currency for Money, demonetizes real coin by expelling it from the country (p. 18). Dr. Adam Smith's Rule for Circulation................... 18
State Bank Issues—have been upon a wrong basis....... 25
State Banks have no more right to issue Bills of Credit than to coin Gold—the Supreme Law forbids both 25
Sacrifices consequent upon the Use of Paper Money..... 27
States cannot Coin Money—of course, must use the Coin of the Mints, since nothing else is legal tender 57
Specific Contract Law of California—Extracts from the law 76
" is not Unconstitutional in Coercing Gold Payments......................... 76–77
" All the Mint Laws corroborate the Act.. 78–79
" is an Act to bring in force one of the cardinal points of the Supreme Law............. 80–81
Solvency of the Currency should never be at the Hazards of general business............................ 93–94
Specific Contract Law of California, or one similar in scope, should be passed by Congress for the benefit of all Citizens of the United States.................... 104–105
Specie Payments—how to resume.................... 124–130
Specie in the Banks—New York, Boston, Chicago...... 132–133
Secretary McCulloch on Prices....................... 165–166
Sales of Gold—should not be made to buoy Currency. How to use the excess of Gold in the Treasury. The difference in value between Gold and Currency should be universally admitted and acted upon...183, 184, 185, 186
Silver Coin of the Mints—incomparably better basis for the issue of Currency than Government or State Stocks, or any form of wealth, except Gold coin... 292–293

Treasury Notes, by enactment of Congress, being legal tender, such law does not keep them at the par of Gold 65
The Independent Treasury Bill.... 107
The National Losses under the old State Bank systems.. 108
The fundamental principle of Issue of the national banks, upon a wrong basis 112

PAGES.

Tribute which the People must pay to the State Bank Systems....... 123–124
Tariff of the United States—acts with crushing influence upon the prosperity of California....... 143
" " is estimated to yield from 50 to 75 per cent....... 143
" " *takes one-third from the Value of Gold for uses in the markets of the world*....... 144–149
" " its action upon different interests....... 145
" " everything should bear its just proportion of the nation's burden (p. 146). "A house divided against itself cannot stand." Each of the great sources of national wealth have equal claims on the fostering care of the Government (p. 146). Immense losses which the Tariff has imposed upon California (p. 147). Loss for the year 1866 $28,289,589, including Internal Revenue....... 147
The Tariff bolsters a vitiated Currency in direct proportion to the amount imposed....... 152–153
The Interests of the Union at large, and of the Pacific States specially, concurrent and identical in the matter of Metallic Currency....... 164
The Interests of the Union and the Pacific States should not be sacrificed to favor Banking Monopolies....... 167
The Statutes at Large should not aid injustice by coercing equalities in Currencies which are not equivalents. 188
The various Systems of Banking that have been tried in the United States....... 196

United States—need not depend upon Commerce for Gold Coin....... 30
Uniformity and Equality in Taxation and Imposts the design of the Constitution. The Legal Tender Act is in direct conflict, *in this respect*, with the Supreme Law....... 52–53
Unlimited Liability of Stockholders—no proper basis for the issue of Currency....... 91–92
Undrawn Loans—proceeds of notes discounted should not be considered Deposits....... 230
Unwise Legislation for California....... 335–336

Values would be adjusted to Coin with great exactness, if not interfered with by Paper Currency....... 22
Value of Gold should not be reduced by substitutes....... 35–36
Values adjust Currencies....... 37
Value of the Pound Sterling in American Gold coin....... 42
Value of Coin cannot be kept up while the Power to issue Bills of Credit runs riot....... 133
Valuable Opinions on Currency, etc., etc....... 221–222

PAGES.

Why all Systems of Banking, hitherto inaugurated in the Old States, have been partial or thorough failures 197
Wright, Silas, upon the Constitutional Currency........ 197
" " on the Duty of the Government......... 197–201
Without regulating the whole Currency, and keeping it equivalent to Coin, Government must pay Gold at paper prices, even when banks are nominally paying specie.................................... 204
Webster, Daniel, the Expounder and Defender of the Constitution, on Legal Tender....................... 215

Yield of the Pacific Mines—has been enough, in ten years, to saturate the country with a Metallic Currency... 32
Yield of the Mines to January, 1866, $1,109,500,000 (eighteen years)................................ 32

A SEARCHING ANALYSIS

OF THE

ACTION OF PAPER MONEY UPON THE TRADE AND PROSPERITY OF THE UNITED STATES.

The close relation existing between the yearly national gains of commerce and the exact value of money, which is the common medium of exchanges, renders it a matter of great importance, that this medium should be exactly what it purports, and of the precise value which it exchanges for in the commodities of the world. A double standard of value, bearing the same name and widely different in worth, if not an impossibility in practice, is a constant source of mischief and interminable losses.

The national gains of commerce are greatly lessened by instituting a kind of currency which bears the same name as the national coin, while such form of currency is essentially of less value than the coin itself. If a dollar means a coin impressed in our mints, of standard weight and fineness in gold or silver, then, to pervert its meaning by the intervention of law is to throw away a large fraction of the profits of our commerce with other nations, not to speak of the injury we impose upon ourselves by such fatuity. Individuals engaged in business relations with foreigners will look to their own interest, and see that their profits shall not be wasted by the fallacy of a false currency; but the nation at large will lose from its commerce directly as the money of the country

FF

is diluted beyond what it purports as its sterling value. In calling a dollar one hundred cents, and again seventy-five cents, we open the door for foreigners to despoil us; and our Statutes at Large actually legalize the outrage.

The United States is a nation of such extensive power and commerce that it cannot afford to be wrong in a matter of such vital importance as results from the use of a deceptive or inflated currency.

The ingenuity of man has been tasked for the past half century to produce a kind of money which shall fulfill all of the functions of gold and silver coin, and still be wanting in the essential attribute of such coin—intrinsic value.

Bills of credit, commonly called bank notes, have been the substitute for real money; and the fallacy in the public mind in regard to this kind of money is, that, while banks redeem in specie, such money is not only harmless but very useful. No matter how much such form of currency circulates in excess of the normal specie volume, so long as banks are paying specie it is deemed harmless. The checks upon issues of bills of credit while banks are nominally under specie payments result from their mutual action upon each other. The issue of a bank may be *pro rata* to its paid-up capital. Each bank may issue the proportion of circulation which its capital bears to the aggregate circulation of all the banks. While it confines its circulation to this limit it will not be drawn upon for specie to adjust balances; but will collect the relative amount of circulation to its liabilities as fast as other banks collect its issues. If its bills are in good credit—receivable at other banks in good standing—the citizen is not expected to intermeddle in their affairs, or raise any question of their solvency or mode of business. To do this is deemed not only an act of inexcusable impertinence but a positive proof of hostility. But these monopolies, which are allowed by Congress to issue "bills of credit" not representing specie, if they are not to be tried by the judgment of public opinion, are doubtless responsible to the body which gives them a corporate existence.

The old State bank systems have nearly passed away, and an opportunity is afforded to the national legislature to build up the monetary interests of the nation upon the basis of the precious metals, which our mines will yield in ample supplies for all the needs of the nation in currency.

The lesson of the recent disastrous civil war through which the country has passed, should not be forgotten, or left without producing important financial fruits for coming generations. Beyond all controversy the existence of the old State bank systems banished nearly one billion of dollars of the precious metals taken out of our mines, between the years 1848 and 1860. Beyond controversy, if two-thirds or even one-half of the gold taken from our mines in the past nineteen years could have been in the country in the year 1861, when the war commenced, the contest could have been carried through for less than half it cost under a false system of a paper legal tender. Half the national debt then is directly chargeable to the imperfect and false system of currency which had been built up and entailed upon us by the State banks before the extensive and vast mining wealth of the Pacific Coast became the territory of the United States.

On the accession of this immense field of national prosperity no legislation was adopted by State or federal government to change the old monetary system, but credit money became more rampant than ever, and gold was used almost exclusively as merchandise. Indeed it is questionable whether at this time, (1867) after the mines have yielded $1,200,000,000 in gold and silver, there remains more than $50,000,000 of coin in excess of the coin in the country in the year 1848.

If we say there are at this time one hundred million dollars in the Federal Treasury; ten million dollars in the National banks; twenty-five million dollars in the Pacific States; and five million dollars in the hands of the people, we shall have as the sum of all the coin and bullion in the country, at this date, one hundred and forty millions of dollars.

Now, how much coined money did we have in the year 1848? The State banks held forty-eight millions. If we allow as much more for the amount in the Federal Treasury and in the hands of the people, we shall have ninety-six millions as the coin of the country in the year 1848.

We have received from immigrants since 1848, at a moderate reckoning, not less than twenty millions, and from commerce in the same time, not less than sixty millions. If these estimates are near the truth, then, the coin in the country in 1848, the returns from commerce, and the amounts brought in by immigrants during the same period, would make the sum of one hundred and seventy-six millions of dollars, which is thirty-six millions more than we now possess. And since we do not possess at this time so much as we held and have imported since 1848, it follows that an amount of bullion greater than the whole product of our mines has gone from us during the past nineteen years. In this manner our systems of State and Federal banking have despoiled us of the whole product of our bullion, which is not less than $1,200,000,000.

To save the gold of the country, we need a radical change in our monetary system. After having lost so immensely upon our gold products during the past nineteen years; after having entailed upon ourselves a national debt, during the war, at least twice as large as it need have been if our money were a reality in place of a credit; if it had been gold instead of the promise of gold, which all know was not convertible; after such lamentable errors in our fiscal management—errors which must cost the toil and tribute of generations to come—we might now have the discretion to learn from such disastrous policy in the past, and follow the lights of science and truth for our future guides. We want a national policy, to be well and thoroughly understood, that the United States are able to have an entire currency of gold coin, or paper representing gold dollar for dollar. Our losses have been so immense in the past by reason of an erroneous fiscal policy, the system of gold coin or paper which represents it should be inaugurated as the national policy, as fast as our mines will furnish the means to achieve the reform. We are not at all prepared for war without this reform of the currency. Such a fiscal reform is as necessary as the army and navy; and further: we shall lose the entire yield of our bullion from the mines until we inaugurate this reform.

The interest of banks is to make money, and swell their dividends to shareholders. Like other business, they have a right to pursue it so far as it does not militate against good morals, truth, justice, equity and the permanent weal of the nation. But if their mode of business is materially detrimental to citizens and to the body politic, it should be reformed by the compulsory interference of national legislation.

The profits of banks should result from the loan of their actual capital, from the allowance of a low rate of interest for deposits, which are the normal gains of the industries of the people, and loaning these deposits at a higher rate of interest than they pay for them, adapting their loans in the time of maturing, to the time when their deposits should become due; and in this way knowing their precise power of giving aid to the wants of business. Another source of revenue to banks should be from domestic and foreign exchanges. These are the legitimate sources of gain to banks; but every dollar made by circulation which usurps the place and function of money, which is not a representative of an actual metallic dollar, is a theft from the value of coin, and an element of loss and bankruptcy acting in a tenfold proportion to the amount of such fictitious circulation. We need such reform in our monetary system as would bring all of our banks more upon the principle of Savings' institutions, while they would have power to render all needed facilities to commerce and trade, and still every dollar of their circulation represent real, metallic dollars.

Hitherto the vast wealth of the United States has sufficed to sustain the country in spite of a most depraved and vitiated currency. The old State banks, by suspending specie payments every decade or oftener, and by the immense amount of losses which their form of money imposed upon the gains of industry in all its branches, were enabled to make money for their shareholders, and to decree for the people how valuable the medium of exchange in common use among them, should remain. The terms which they imposed were these,—to dilute the currency as far as possible and yet sustain what they called specie payments. Having obtained this power and ascendency over the people, it is natural to suppose that they would hold on to it with unyielding tenacity. Until the year 1848 the champions of paper money contended that it was entirely impossible to move the industries and distribute the products of the country with a currency of gold and silver. Whether they were right or wrong in this position, it is useless at present to argue. The time has passed, and the error cannot at this period be amended.

In the year 1848, the treaty between our government and Mexico was ratified. This treaty conveyed to the United States the territory of Alta California, and a part of New Mexico. A new era was then opened to the industry and commerce of the nation. And how did the wisdom of the people provide for this vast accession of wealth, which was so suddenly poured in upon them? Did they avail themselves of the great privilege which was so amply placed before them, to destroy the miserable, poverty-stricken system of paper money, and allow the national coins to do the business? Far from it. The old State banks continued in power, and maintained that a reserve of five, ten or fifteen per cent. in specie, against their immediate liabilities, was an ample fund to keep idle—as they considered their reserve idle capital. And what has been the result? In 1857 there was a general suspension of specie payments through the country, notwithstanding the immense amount of gold that had gone forward from California. Still the banks were dominant, and were enabled to dictate their own terms not only to the people but to the States; and after the war commenced, the federal government itself was found supplicating favors of these powerless institutions. And what was the consequence of all this want of wisdom to regulate the currency of the country according to the teaching of sound financial science? Simply this:—these banks, by the continuation of their system of making credit money—promises to pay dollars which they did not possess—and the State laws upholding and defending them in such nefarious and mischievous practices, did most effectually drive the gold from the country to other nations, to build up their commerce and manufactures and to break down our own in a corresponding degree. The result of banishing the gold from the country, by the action of the State bank systems, compelled the people to use the only remaining form of currency that existed among them, which was the issues of the State banks.

When the rebellion broke out, in 1861, the country had been sacked, in a great measure, of all the gold product of California. The first effect of this upon the monetary affairs of the government was to humiliate the nation, to the extent of asking favors of the very institutions which had worked all this mischief in the body politic. The action of this system of banking upon promises to pay dollars which the issuing banks do not possess, and maintaining that such promises are as good as the coin of the mints, is an effectual mode of driving the gold from the country. If the Congress of the United States had put forth its power, and exercised its bounden duty to protect the monetary interests of the country at the time of the transfer of California to the United States, and had then taken the matter of the issue of currency by the State banks in hand, and enacted that these banks should yearly and every year convert ten per cent. of their capital stock into gold coin, and deposit the coin in the Treasury of the United States, and take from the Treasury gold bills for circulation only to an equal amount of such deposit—had such law been passed by Congress in 1848, the whole circulation of bills in the country would have been based upon gold coin in the Treasury; the failures of 1857 would have been avoided; and what is of vastly more consequence, the war would have been passed through with a national debt of not more than one-half its present magnitude.

The Congress has power to fix the exact weight and fineness of the various coins which the mint laws have instituted. Some suppose that its power ceases here; but if such were the case, it would be most thoroughly inadequate to protect the weal of the nation. Fortunately its power is not so limited, in the matter of insuring to the people the purity of the national coin and *of fixing its value.* Sec. VIII, paragraph 6, of the Constitution, gives to Congress authority "to provide for the punishment of counterfeiting the securities and current coin of the United States." Without this provision, what would the simple right to fix the weight and fineness of the coins of the mints amount to? If the mint coins could be counterfeited by substituting ingeniously devised coins, consisting largely of base metals, which were such perfect imitations of the genuine coin that none but adepts could detect them, and there were no law to punish such fraud upon the people, is it not manifest how such counterfeit coin would injure the value of the genuine coin of the mints? Congress has express power granted to provide for the punishment of counterfeiting the coin of the United States. It also has power "to coin money, regulate the value thereof, and of foreign coin:" par. 6, Const.

From this delegation to Congress of the right to coin money and fix its value comes, *incidentally but* undoubtedly, the right to control the issue of all forms of currency to circulate as a common medium of exchange; because, without regulating such currency, Congress has no means of fixing the relative value of coin to property, and no means of fixing the value of real money—the mint coins.

The delegation, by the Constitution, to Congress, "to provide for the punishment of counterfeiting the national coin, and the power to coin money and regulate, or rule, the value thereof," gives to Congress absolute control of the money of the country; and further, it gives Congress absolute control of *all* forms of money which do virtually and positively act in any manner to vary or lessen the value of the gold coin of the mints. By consequence, it gives Congress power and sovereign control over all paper money issued in the United States, so far as this, that Congress may and is in duty bound to regulate or rule such issue of paper money, as that it cannot in any way impinge or lessen the value, or exchangeable power of coin for commodities and wealth in general.

If Congress establishes a currency worth less than gold or silver coin, it acts without authority; for it has no power delegated to make any other currency but the coins of the mints. It results, that its power to govern currency is purely incidental, and can only be exercised to coerce currency to be really of the identical value of gold coin dollar for dollar, and not to drag down the value of coin to that of currency by tyrannous and unjust legislation. If a paper currency is assumed to be a national necessity, Congress has power to insist that it shall be the equivalent of the gold coins of our mints, dollar for dollar. If it is not a national necessity, Congress has no power or duty in the premises but to suppress its circulation entirely—this, on the ground that it lessens the value of gold coin. But while Congress has the right delegated to fix the value of coin, (and it has the right incidentally to govern the currency, because it cannot protect the value of coin without this) it has no right to institute, legislate or provide *any currency which shall be of inferior value to the mint coins.* Were it otherwise, Congress might, by instituting false standards of value, and enacting that such should be legal tenders, impose upon the people a form of tyranny which would despoil them as effectually as a hostile army could do by invading and destroying their substance. It is this incidental power, resulting from the necessity of keeping up the value of coin, that gives Congress *the right* to suppress the issues of State banks. Yet, with all these powers and charges for the good and permanent weal of the body politic, how does Congress exercise such important trusts and Constitutional behests? It has, in addition to all of the legal tender notes in circulation, chartered and issued bills of credit to the National banks to the amount of $300,000,000. Its legal tender notes are held to be such upon all demands except for duties. The legal tenders amount to about $417,000,000. In addition to this, the National banks have the power of making currency through the action of the deposit account, and deposits are virtually currency to all intents and purposes. These deposits are more than $600,000,000.

We have demonstrated that the old State bank system banished the gold from the country, and doubled the expenses of the war. Let us now examine the effects of paper money upon commerce and trade at home.

The old State banks had a circulation in the year 1857

of $214,778,822, and held deposits amounting to $230,351,352. The result was, that they were compelled to suspend specie payments, after the enormous yield of the mines of California for eight years. During the year 1858 they reduced their circulation and deposits about one hundred and four millions.

Again the policy of expansion was renewed, and, in 1860, their circulation and deposits amounted to $460,904,606. In April, 1861, the civil war commenced, and in December of the same year, every bank in the United States east of the Sierra Nevadas had ceased to pay specie. During the war, Congress assumed its constitutional right to deal with the currency of the country, and in its dealings brought the State banks under the National bank law. While it is possible that Congress did the best that could be done, during the war, to annihilate the State banks, and bring the governance of the currency under the national authority, it is now more than six years since the war was commenced, and well nigh three years since peace was established; yet, under the National banking system, we seem to be further than ever from specie payments. These banks were never subject to specie payments. Of course their success, or failure, as useful institutions to the country, is matter upon which men differ.

Nothing is clearer, however, than this: that institutions which possess a monopoly of printing promises to pay dollars, and are protected by the laws of Congress in such promises, so far as this—that they may redeem these promises with the promises of other banks to pay dollars, or with the legal-tender issues of the Government itself, which are openly and notoriously inconvertible; so long as Government will tolerate such injustice and folly, the banks may make large dividends, while the people are constantly being impoverished by the circulation of such a medium of exchange. While the stockholders in these institutions are making money so rapidly, they will use all their efforts and arguments to continue this impoverishing system, and stave off specie payments. It is only necessary that the people should know the real nature of money, and with what irresistible force any interference with the National standards of value reacts upon all of their interests—industrial, commercial, manufacturing, mining, agricultural, mechanical, and, I may add, social and moral—to consign all forms of money, which are not exactly what they purport to be, to utter destruction and annihilation.

The annual yield of bullion from all the mines in the United States and Territories will be about $80,000,000. It is manifest, then, that if we have now in the country $140,000,000 in coin, and can hold on to the yield of our mines for only four years, we shall have a currency in coin equal to $460,000,000.

And why can we not retain the yield of our mines? Why has the total yield of our mines for the past nineteen years gone from us, and why does it continue to go from us? Because we make a substitute for coin, in the form of Government promises and National bank promises; and because our Statutes at Large make the Government promises legal tender upon all debts, and the National bank promises a tender upon debts due the Government. Evidently, then, so long as the Statutes at Large give sanction to such forms of money, our real money—gold coin—will go to other parts of the commercial world where its intrinsic value is duly recognized. It is worth the attempt to try to portray some of the fearful consequences to the nation, of substituting bills of credit for our coin, and thus driving the coin from the country.

The coin of the country differs from all other forms of national wealth in this regard, that it is of a perennial nature—that, while other kinds of wealth are consumed by their uses, coin may be used millions of times, passing from one to another, and still not lose any appreciable amount of its weight or value. We need, then, only to fill up the avenues of circulation with coin; and if the laws and usages of our people do not banish this coin, we shall have a currency of value which would last for centuries. The action of bills of credit, commonly called bank notes or bank bills, is insidious and destructive to the weal of the nation. To the body politic this action makes all the difference between doing our business upon real cash or credit; and all experience proves that every form of industry can be moved more efficiently with real money than credit. Furthermore: credit can be extended far enough for the permanent weal of the country, without allowing it any place in our money, or medium of exchange. Yet, while our laws tolerate such an invasion of private right, and the Statutes at Large recognize such an unjust principle as the making of irredeemable paper a legal tender on all debts between citizens, it is important to demonstrate the bearing of such measures upon the prosperity of the country.

We have shown that banks can do business under reputed specie payments, and keep their issues nominally at the par of coin ; and yet their issues may be far in excess of the coin which would circulate if no such bills were issued. That, in order to create this inflation, it is only necessary for them to issue in a *pro rata* amount to their respective capitals.

Suppose the normal amount of currency needed in the country to move all its industries be placed at $300,000,000,* and that the banks have increased it 50 per cent., making the volume of currency equal to $450,000,000 ; what is the effect of this inflation upon the body politic ?

Its direct effect is to raise the prices of all commodities fifty per cent. Having produced this effect upon prices, it becomes the needed volume of currency, and this need protects the banks in its issue, and they may issue safely fifty per cent. beyond the normal specie volume of the country, always provided that their issues are not extended beyond their just ratio to their capital—or that they may issue beyond the specie volume, in the same ratio as other institutions issue, without clashing with each other and without drawing on each other, except in insignificant sums, to adjust balances. The reader will understand that I am now traversing the effect upon the nation of allowing banks nominally under specie payments, to issue bills beyond their specie on hand.

The United States is a commercial nation, and we must adjust our balances not only at home but also abroad.

---

* All economists admit that the relative value of gold to other forms of wealth might be three or four times as much as it now is, and serve the offices of money as well as at its present ruling.

If we assume that the imports of the country are $365,000,000 yearly, and the interest of the public debt held in foreign countries is $30,000,000 yearly, we have an annual balance to settle abroad, equal to $395,000,000, upon a gold basis.

Our exports we will suppose to be approximately thus:

In cotton, tobacco and Southern products......	$225,000,000
In breadstuffs and Northern manufactures.......	100,000,000
In gold coin and bullion........................	70,000,000
Total..................................	$395,000,000

Again; if we assume that one hundred and forty millions of our imports are made and sold for foreign account—sold by the agents and factors of foreign countries residing among our citizens—sold for such form of currency as is the common medium of exchange among us—and this currency nominally at the par of gold, but really and in fact inflated beyond the gold volume or normal amount of money at least fifty per cent., what will be the effect of such inflation on the balance of the trade?

Its first effect will be to increase prices fifty per cent. beyond the point they would rule at under a gold currency, thus enabling foreign factors to sell their goods that much higher in our markets than they could do under a currency of intrinsic value. The currency being collected after the goods are sold, if the banks are under specie payments, can be turned into coin at par. In this manner, upon the $140,000,000 imported and sold on foreign account, the people will pay 50 per cent., or $70,000,000 more in gold equivalent than they would do if the currency were kept not nominally but really and beyond question at the par of gold.

The volume of currency in the country not only governs but makes the prices at which commodities are exchanged. Supply and demand undoubtedly may vary these prices when one is in a normal and the other in an abnormal condition. If flour is very scarce and currency very plenty, flour will rule high in the market; and *vice versa*. But if both flour and currency are in a normal condition—the supply and demand about equal—then the volume of currency in circulation will fix the price of the article. If the currency be inflated fifty per cent., flour will be sold at fifty per cent. higher than it would be under a specie currency. This rule will be universal in its application to all forms of commodities and manufactures, and it is under a normal condition of these that it must be tried. It results from these premises that all inflation of currency is a direct gain to the foreign countries with which we have commerce, and direct loss to ourselves.

If the above estimate, that $140,000,000 of the yearly imports of the country are made and sold on foreign account, is correct, then, we pay $70,000,000 yearly on our imports to foreigners, to support a system of currency among us which inevitably entails this annual loss. This seventy millions is a total loss to us, and it must be counted as the equivalent of gold coin in some form of our exports.

But how does the country sustain such an exhaustive drain upon its resources? The annual gross products of the United States are estimated at $6,858,000,000 in currency, or in gold value, at about $4,800,000,000. The probability is, that nine-tenths of this vast amount is consumed yearly among us, leaving only one-tenth, or $480,000,000, to be added to our increased wealth yearly —and even this is reduced nearly one-half by taxation. This would leave the gain of the country about $240,000,000 yearly, out of which we must deduct $70,000,000 yearly for our direct loss and foreigners' direct gain, by reason of our using an inflated currency. This loss is sustained entirely unnecessarily, by reason of our rejecting the teachings of science and acting upon a headstrong will in maintaining that the promise of a dollar is the just equivalent of the dollar, whether the dollar be in possession to redeem the promise or not. It inures to the gain of the banks, but to the poverty and bankruptcy of the people at large. Before we had made a national debt of such colossal magnitude, such were the immense resources of the country, we could lose $70,000,000 yearly (about the annual product of our mines in gold and silver) and scarcely miss it. This is proven by the fact that all of our gold and silver—the yield of our mines since 1848—amounting to $1,200,000,000 has gone from us. We had in the country, in 1848, in coin, about $96,-

000,000. We have, in 1867, about $140,000,000—but we have received from commerce and by immigration, enough to make the stock of 1848 far beyond our present possession of coin; thereby proving, that an amount as great or greater than the entire yield of our mines for the past nineteen years has been sent to foreign countries.

With the paralyzing influence of our public debt hanging over us, we need to stop every great and unnecessary public loss of our wealth—we need to make all of our dollars worth a hundred cents each, and suppress this wholesale sacking of our treasure, which results from dealing through unjust measures of value. Let us look at the effects of this iniquitous system, which takes from us seventy millions annually, upon our future progress and prosperity.

The average duration of human life is placed by physiologists at thirty-three years. If we reckon thirty-three years as a generation, what will be the difference to the people who are born in 1867, when they reach the year 1900, whether the country loses $70,000,000 yearly, by reason of a system of false currency, or saves that amount by a system of currency which is truthful and just? It is easy to see that the loss of principal in thirty-three years would be $2,310,000,000. If we compound the interest, we shall find that it amounts to the further sum of $4,895,414,488; and principal and interest added will make the vast sum of $7,205,414,488 as the loss to the country by the foreign drain, resulting from having an inflated currency. The domestic losses we shall consider hereafter.

Some may argue that, in estimating the losses to the country by using an inflated currency, it is not right to compound the interest, because money at compound interest is so overwhelming that it would bankrupt the world. So long, however, as our National debt does virtually call for compound interest, by making the interest payable semi-annually, so long is money worth compound interest to the Government; and so long as capital in its most available and concentrated form—gold and silver coin—is worth six per cent. interest, to use in the multiplied forms of business in the country, so long is it proper, in estimating the damages resulting to us by a system which virtually sacks us of the entire product of our bullion, to add compound interest to the same, for the very simple reason that the nation is virtually paying compound interest; and that the gains of industry amount to compound interest as fast as they are saved to be put to new uses.

It follows from these premises, that the losses to the nation by using an inflated currency, will be, in the next thirty-three years, more than seven billions of dollars ($7,000,000,000); and this loss to us will be a direct gain of an equal amount to other countries. This loss, however, vast as it is to contemplate, only shows our foreign waste. Our domestic losses, by using a false and inflated currency, are manifold those of our foreign; yet this difference exists between them, that in one case the value leaves the country and inures to foreigners; while in the other it is an endless round of losses and bankruptcies which is preying upon the industries and gains of the people, robbing one class of citizens to enrich another: and although the wealthy may increase their possessions under the system, still, as it is founded in most thorough dishonesty, even these must pay the tribute which it exacts of all, by instituting false measures of value for all commodities.

If it were possible to approximate to anything like accuracy in computing the vast amount of losses from inflated currency, in producing and distributing about four billions of products annually among our population, we might show the waste to the people in using false measures of value. The truth is, that the products of the country are so immense, that a loss of a heavy per centage upon them is not apparent to our citizens. It should be remembered, however, that "a small leak will sink a large ship" if it is continued and neglected.

The domestic losses fall upon the country, and what one loses another gains. But all are finally wound up in real losses, or balanced off in bankruptcies. The amount of losses which are paid from the gains of industry are probably ten times as great as those that are settled in bankruptcy. Hence the losses of the country cannot be estimated by the amount of indebtedness of those who avail themselves of the insolvent Acts of the States, or the general bankrupt law of Congress. The effect of using a false standard of value as a true one tells upon the business and expenses of every member of society, from the highest to the most humble. Such a subversion of justice may not ruin the wealthy; but if it ruins the middle classes, and makes paupers and beggars of the rest, it will ruin the prosperity of the country; and when that is gone, the wealthy must feel it as well as the most abject. Besides, the production and distribution of wealth under false standards of value, must demoralize any people, and make a vicious state of society. When sifted down to its essential elements, it is nothing more nor less than a toleration, by the laws and Government, of direct dishonesty and swindling.

We have traced the disastrous consequences which result to the nation from the use of bills of credit, or bank notes, which are issued upon credit, and which are reputed to be equal to the coin of the mints; and we have demonstrated that such bills may be issued in this country largely in excess of the coin which would circulate if such issues were prohibited by law; and this, too, while the issuing banks were reputed to be under specie payments, and their bills were passing at the par of gold. We have shown that the effect of such issues was not only to degrade the value of gold in the country, but that it has sent the entire yield of our mines for the last nineteen years to foreign countries; and that there is not in the country at this time as much coin as has been brought by immigrants and commerce in nineteen years in addition to what was in the country in 1848. It is, therefore, clear that every system of banking which has been in the country before the year 1861 has been radically wrong, and has worked untold evils for the nation at large. That under the various State bank systems which have existed heretofore, the gross product of our mines for nineteen years has been wasted and squandered, amounting to $1,200,000,000; and this fatal policy in our financial administration—allowing the dollar worth far less than one hundred cents to usurp the place of the real dollar, has sacked our country of coin, and more than doubled the expenses of the civil war.

The war, however, inaugurated a new system of currency, now known as the National Bank System, under the auspices and legislation of our National Congress. Is the new system any way superior to those we have had before? The old State bank systems have been thoroughly efficient in banishing all the gold which our mines have produced since 1848. What will be the action of the National bank system? It possesses two important points which are wisely introduced in the bill, and may produce good results. The system is under the governance of our National Legislature instead of a multiplicity of State Legislatures. It is also subject to amendment and repeal of any or all of its provisions. Congress has the power to make it a useful system of finance. Will it have the wisdom and honesty to put this power into efficient action?

In creating the National Banks, Congress has adopted the old fallacy of the State bank systems—that the redemption of bills secured by the pledge of stocks is as good basis for the issue of currency as the mint coins. This is the grand error of the National Banking Law, and it cannot be too soon amended; for the truth is, the nation can have no permanent prosperity on a grand scale till such reform be instituted. Any kind of money which is not replete with the very identical form of wealth which the coin of the mint contains—gold and silver of the standard mint fineness—does not possess the functions of money, and cannot be adapted to the uses and purposes of a standard in the exchange of values. When we measure our values by dollars, we have reference to, or should have reference to, the coins of the mints. The prices should be made by the relative amount of gold coin in circulation in the country to the amount of commodities to be exchanged. If paper be used for convenience, it should represent gold on deposit to its full amount. The principle of issue, then, is the overshadowing one which must be guarded by national legislation. Any system of banking which allows the issue of bills of credit which do not represent the coin on actual deposit will be a curse to the country. But why may not the redemption of bank notes be secured upon any form of wealth other than coin, as well as upon the coin itself? For this reason: The moment you begin to issue bills upon other securities than coin, to circulate as money, you begin to impinge the value of coin.

Several years ago the grain dealers in Chicago were in the habit of issuing warehouse receipts for wheat taken on deposit. These certificates were often pledged by the holders as collateral security for money borrowed of capitalists. In time, these warehouse receipts became so plentiful that they were seriously reducing the prices of wheat in the market, from the fact that they represented a much larger amount of grain than the warehouses contained. The evil continued to increase, and to annoy the farmers, until a law was enacted in the legislature making it a misdemeanor to issue these receipts in any greater amounts than the actual quantity of grain received on deposit.

Precisely analogous to this action is the circulating of bank notes for a greater amount than the bank holds or has pledged the coin in the National Treasury for the redemption of such issues. These notes may become so plenty, and yet be reputed equal to gold, that they must degrade the value of coin. The coin will exchange for much less amount of commodities than it would if such issues were prohibited by law.

The objections to the attempt to secure circulating bills upon other forms of wealth than coin are manifold.

First: Such securities drive our gold to foreign countries, and give them the very essence of our vitality, to build up their own interests and to cripple ours in the same degree. So long as we hold to the financial heresy that the promise of a dollar is as good as a real dollar, even though the real dollar be not in possession to redeem such promise, and allow such promises to circulate among us as the common medium of exchange, so long will the entire product of our mines, in bullion, be at the service of foreign capitalists.

For illustration: Suppose that one man possesses ten thousand bushels of wheat; another, ten thousand bushels of corn; another, ten thousand bushels of salt; another, one thousand oxen; another, ten thousand sheep; another, ten thousand yards of cloth; another a valuable farm; another, a fine ship, etc., etc. Now these are good and valuable possessions. There is nothing of an imaginary or fanciful nature to them. How are we to ascertain their value? I answer; their value is measured by the relative demand for them to the amount of currency, or medium of exchange which measures values, in circulation. If this medium of exchange be confined to the gold coin of the mints, evidently the prices of these forms of wealth will rule much lower than if the markets of the country are glutted with a form of currency which is reputed equal to coin, and passes as such, but is really and in fact far below the value of coin.

But suppose every citizen who possesses one thousand bushels of wheat shall be allowed to issue bills of credit to the amount of one thousand dollars, to circulate as money, these bills promising upon their face *to pay dollars*, (which are not wheat but coined money) because wheat is worth one dollar per bushel, how long would wheat be worth one dollar in coin? Now, if the trade of the country would be facilitated by the farmer's giving his note for one thousand bushels of wheat, rye, corn, barley, *or any wealth which he possessed*, I would not care how much such notes circulated. The utterance of such notes would not injure the value of gold coin. But the moment notes were given by the farmer or banker upon the strength of this grain, or any form of wealth other than coin, to take the functions of money—to circulate as a medium of exchange—that moment the issues would begin to organize property into money, that is, local money, and to rob real money of its intrinsic value by bringing it down to the level of this fiction—the promise to deliver it by those who do not possess it.

If money secured upon valuable property, other than coin, is as good as gold coin, there never need be any scarcity of money. But the truth is, that every attempt to make such form of money equal to coin is impossible; and such attempt, so far as it seems to succeed, is nothing but a robbery from the value of coin. The only honest way to convert good property into money is, to sell it for coin, and put the coin in our purses. If all the wealth of the country may be converted into coin by issuing promises to pay the coin, what would be the value of coin?

If we must have a medium of exchange by organizing wheat, corn, cattle, horses, sheep, houses, farms, ships, merchandise, or any other real or personal property, or *chose in action*, into local money, through the action of printing presses, and by the process of printing promises to pay such an amount of *real dollars* as the said property held may be deemed worth—and then circulating these promises as money, and claiming for them the exact equivalent of their face value in gold coin of the mints—if such organization of currency shall be deemed necessary by the wisdom of our people, let us insist that these circulating notes, instead of being promises to pay in dollars, shall be promises to pay in kind—exactly what they represent. Thus: if notes represent wheat, let them read for so many bushels of this grain; not for dollars. If notes represent sheep, let them read for sheep; if they represent wool, let them read for so many pounds of wool. Make these notes payable in bushels, pounds, yards, or whatever form of meter is used to indicate the amount of the particular kind of commodity which the note calls for. Such notes, if they could get any circulation at all, would have their affinities with circulating property—they would not belong to money; nor would our people class them as such if they were payable in the particular form of property which they truly represented. These various kinds of property dollars (if I may use such a misnomer for illustration) are more closely allied to the constituent element of the deposit account in Eastern banks; and thus monetizing them, through the deposit account, puts them strictly on the par with bills in circulation and is the foundation of the chaotic action which is so often making itself apparent in all the business relations of society, and is further the most efficient agent in driving our gold from us.

But if the deposit account of banks is a representation of the circulating property of the country, and by founding our business upon these, instead of the bullion of our mines, it is certain to make for us a form of currency which shall inflate all prices to such an extent as, if continued, to lead to certain ruin, *how much more certainly shall we attain this ruin by basing our currency upon the national debt!*

Having shown that our very best forms of wealth, other than coin itself, are entirely out of place as currency—do not possess the functions needed in a standard of value—could not be circulated as money if the notes which represented this wealth promised the identical goods instead of promising dollars—if a circulating medium based upon these real resources would be not only inefficient, but so difficult to manage as to develop at once its infeasible nature, how much more certainly must losses and ruin follow in the country which bases its currency upon debt? Debt is the negative of wealth; gold is real money, and the positive and most concentrated form of wealth. If the positive form of wealth be indispensable in money, by what financial charlatanry can our people be so far duped as to suppose that debt money is as good as gold money? Debt is not as good basis for the issuance of currency as even good available property; and we have shown that this is entirely out of place when pledged for the redemption of circulating notes. The principle of organizing debt into currency is not only illogical, it is fatuous—absurd, unworthy of an enlightened or honest nation, for it conflicts alike with good sense and probity.

Is it not enough that the credit system is extended by notes and mortgages, by commercial and mercantile credits, by book accounts and the thousand forms of delayed payments which enter into the customs of our people, without instituting and upholding by law the demoralizing and disorganizing principle of introducing credit into our currency; nay, more, of piling credit currency upon the country to a greater amount by far than it ever knew under the old State bank systems?

The national statistics show that the circulation of all the banks in the United States, on the first of January, 1860, was $207,102,477, and their deposits were $253,802,129, making a currency of bills and deposits equal to $460, 904,606. The issues of the National banks are a trifle under the full limit allowed by the charter, or about $299,000,000; while their deposits are about $600,000,000, making a currency of bills and deposits of about $899,000,000. It should be noted that this currency is almost entirely used and circulated in the Northern and

Middle States—the South having but an insignificant fraction of it. It should also be observed that the balance of circulation and deposits of the old State banks which have not yet closed business, being about $25,000,000, is proper to be added to the $899,000,000. It is apparent from this, that two-thirds of the States have, at this time, more currency *from the banks*, *national and State*, than double the amount which was circulating in all of the States before the war. It is further apparent that, in addition to all this immense amount of currency furnished by the banks—more than double the amount in circulation in all of the States in 1860, the country is staggering under the legal tender issues of Government—about $420,000,000 more; making a bloated currency of approximately $1,300,000,000, which is certainly $900,000,000 more than a healthful state of business would require.

The old State bank systems, which buoyed a currency of only $460,904,606 in all the United States in 1860, were amply sufficient in their chaotic operations to drive the gold of our mines to other countries. This fact was fully proven by the failures and bankruptcies of the year 1857, and was sent home to us with a vengeance by the teachings of the last war. The reserves of specie in the banks in 1857 were less in proportion to their immediate liabilities than they were in 1848. If the system was right, where were the $500,000,000 of gold which California sent them? I answer: In the coffers of foreign capitalists, where our fatuous and silly system of substituting promises to pay coin, secured upon State stocks, and circulating these promises as money, had banished our coin. If the system of uttering such form of money was right, why did the banks fail, or, as they modestly term it, suspend? It is plain that there was bankruptcy enough in the currency to swallow up all the yield of our gold mines down to the year 1860, and to leave the country to wage the most expensive war that was ever fought, with empty coffers, and the people themselves relying upon credit for their money. But how will the National banks compare with the State banks in relation to their specie reserves? The State banks owed, in 1860, for deposits and circulation,

$460,904,606. They held in specie, $83,594,537, about eighteen per cent. The National banks owe for deposit and circulation about $899,000,000; they hold in specie about $9,000,000, say one per cent. upon their immediate liabilities. When I call to mind the fact that our mines have yielded $1,200,000,000 in bullion since 1848—that the Bank of England held in coin and bullion, on the 30th of August last, the sum of $114,926,790, and that the Bank of France, doing business in a country which has no gold mines to fall back upon—left entirely to the resources of trade, commerce and manufactures—this bank reports a bullion reserve of $185,104,213; when I see these reports and contrast them with the reports of the combined National banks of America—a country of immense wealth in gold and silver mines—reporting only $10,284,000 in specie, the comparison is so contemptible that it is almost a national disgrace to institute it.

My countrymen: can you not see where your gold has gone, and where it is still going? Can you not see what sacks you of your treasure? It is the unjust, nefarious, and absurd system of banking which is fastened upon you. Can you not see that other commercial nations get the real money—gold and silver—while for yourselves remains nothing but the shadow—the promise to pay dollars which is irredeemable? This too in face of the fact that our land is pre-eminently a gold-producing portion of earth's surface! Are our people ignorant, incompetent or dishonest? One or more of these reflections will apply to them. We lost all of our gold product under the old State bank systems—it becomes an important query, whether the national bank system will save it for us? Why do we need a vitiated or inflated currency? Some will answer: Our public debt is so large that we cannot pay the interest and current expenses of government without we pay in a depreciated currency. If this be true it is only repudiation in disguise. We pretend to be paying in good money and upon honest principles; but in fact, we are paying by the forced operation of legalizing a dollar worth seventy cents or less, and making it a tender for the dollar worth one hundred cents.

Our debt bearing coin interest was, Oct. 1st, 1867..$1,745,161,418
" " " currency interest.............. . 461,074,680
" " bearing no interest....................... 424,118,907

It is manifest that an inflated currency cannot aid us in paying the coin interest, for that must be paid in coin. Hitherto it has been raised exclusively from the customs, which are payable in gold coin. About two-thirds of the debt bears interest in coin, even now; and this will be increasing. About one-sixth of the debt bears interest in currency, and one-sixth more bears no interest. Will any sane man argue that it is expedient to keep the whole business of the country in a state of chaos, for the difference between paying interest in gold or currency, upon four hundred and sixty-one millions? The interest upon $461,000,000 would be $27,660,000 yearly, payable in specie. If paid in currency, it would be about seventy cents on the dollar, or $19,362,000 gold. The latter sum deducted from the former, leaves only $8,298,000 annual saving as the difference between paying our interest in coin or currency. Are our whole national industries to suffer for fifteen years to save such a sum by keeping the currency worth less than coin?

But when these sapient economists see the absurdity of working such immense injury to save such a small amount of interest, they cling to the position that the currency must be kept cheapened, in order to pay off the principal of the debt in currency. They say the debt was contracted in currency, and currency ought to pay it. The national honor is no consideration with such disorganizers. It is needless to argue what has been so vigorously and clearly set forth already by others, as to the expediency of keeping the public faith untarnished and above suspicion. If we can show that it will be easier for the nation to pay the whole debt in gold equivalent, and save the honor of the country beyond all question, such a view of the subject should command close attention by our legislators. It does not require a lengthy argument to establish this position. The way to do it is to stop paying the debt. Pay the interest with scrupulous fidelity; and fund the debt as fast as possible, in long bonds. This might be done in 5-90's and 5-180's; then the government could, whenever it had a few millions of spare funds on hand, advertise for the surrender of these bonds, by the holders, at the lowest rates. The lowest bidders would of course get the funds. One reason why it is much better to pay 100 cents on the dollar and save the honor of the nation, is, because it will be much easier to pay par on the debt in the distant future than it is to pay 70 cents on the dollar at this time. Congress has authorized the Secretary of the Treasury to reduce the debt at the rate of four millions per month. In the present financial distress of the country this is quite as rapidly as the debt ought to be reduced. Probably two millions per month for the next ten years, would be better for the permanent weal of the nation. In fact, we cannot hope for much reduction until the Southern States are restored in their normal position, and their products added to our annual exports. All attempts at reducing the debt, with the action of only two-thirds of the States, must be done by such grinding exaction as to paralyze the energy and efforts of the people.

In the course of twenty years we shall have a population between fifty-five and sixty millions ; and it is plain that a debt which would crush us, if we attempted to pay it, could be easily managed by the increased power which time and our vast resources will bring to the nation. The policy of the United States then, manifestly, is not to pay the debt any faster than it can be done with entire ease to the people, without exhausting their vital resources or burdening them with excessive exactions. The interest of the debt, however, should be paid with scrupulous promptness.

It has been urged that the bonds should be retired, with issues of legal tenders, as fast as the terms of the same allow the government to pay them ; and that such payment would be entirely honorable, just, and without any tinge of repudiation. This question is only one more of the chameleon forms which the people must pass through, so long as the Legal Tender Acts disgrace our Statutes at Large. It is another phase of these Acts which shows their enormity and injustice. If the legal tender notes are good money—the equivalents of gold coin—there is no repudiation in paying debts with them, whether the debts be against the government or individuals. In fact, *if the Legal Tender Acts are Constitutional*, there is no repudiation in paying government debts with currency any more than individual debts. The bonds were sold largely for currency when it was worth not more than sixty cents on the dollar—why may they not be redeemed honorably when the currency is worth seventy cents on the dollar, with a dollar of currency to one dollar of bonds?

The people lost immensely by the Legal Tender Acts, for creditors were obliged to surrender their demands to debtors on the tender, in a currency worth a little more than half the one for which they contracted; and the laws upheld this iniquitous extortion under the penalty of a forfeiture of the debt, if the creditor did not accept the tender. Such was the tyranny of the law. Its utility or expediency would not be held for a moment by sound jurists; for the Supreme Law ordains that "private property shall not be taken for public use without just compensation." Now, if the Government shall make up to creditors all the losses resulting from the unjust spoliations of their claims against debtors, by reason of the legal tender laws, then these laws would be the greatest drawbacks to the nation that could have been instituted; for they would quadruple the national debt. But the Government do not pretend to be under any obligation to citizens for their private losses by reason of the Legal Tender Acts. These were forced loans, they say, but loans which are never payable to the real sufferer.

The Constitution makes it obligatory upon Congress to fix the value of coined money. The laws do this when they specify how much silver and gold the Mint coins shall contain. The whole matter, then, is resolved thus: If the establishing of the Mints by Congress and making fixed laws to bind their operations be constitutional, then is the making of any kind of money a tender of less value than the Mint coin, unconstitutional. Either the gold dollar must be the standard, or the paper greenback. One or the other is plainly unconstitutional.

And whichever is the standard, it is honorable and just to use in payment of all demands, governmental or individual. My opinion is, that the Legal Tender Acts are subversive of justice, right, equity, honorable dealing, and every principle which should guide national or individual probity. That, without regard to what the Government has received for her issue of bonds, we must pay them in specie, or its just equivalent. That we shall justly incur the scorn of repudiation if we attempt to pay bonds which read for dollars in any currency worth less than the coin of our mints. And yet all these conclusions would be exactly reversed if the Treasury notes were in reality a good legal tender.

Every one who firmly believes in the constitutionality of the Legal Tender Acts, must, to be consistent, believe that it is perfectly honorable for the Government to pay any debt in such currency, save such as they are bound to pay in coin by stipulation. Hence, we must either say the Legal Tender Acts *are unconstitutional*, and the debt must be paid in coin equivalent; or the Legal Tender Acts *are constitutional*, and the debt may be paid entirely in greenbacks, as fast as the terms of the bonds will admit of their being retired. The sooner we return to the irrefragable laws of value, and admit that the legal tender laws are flatly against the Constitution, and against the best interests of the country, the sooner shall we be in the way of justice, morality, and prosperity.

Suppose the Government should retire $400,000,000 of its bonds by the issue of that amount of legal tender notes, what would be the effect upon the country at large? Precisely the same as resulted from the law making such notes a legal tender. Such a further inflation of the currency would put the quotations of gold up to about 300—that is, one dollar in gold would buy three dollars in greenbacks; but the greenbacks being legal tender, all creditors would have to submit to a loss of a large fraction of their debt, to enable Government to pay bonds in legal tenders. Thus, the further issue of legal tenders would be a virtual direct tax upon creditors for the benefit of debtors. The excuse for the issue is, that it is "lawful money," and may be issued honorably and fairly by the Government. To this I reply, it cannot be done with honor, nor can it be done with justice, unless Congress at the same time provides that all losses of creditors by such legislation shall be refunded from the Treasury.

If it were of any use to cite the Supreme Law upon this point, I would adduce the clause of the Constitution which ordains that "private property shall not be taken for public use without just compensation." If, then, Congress acts honorably, justly, and constitutionally, it must appropriate funds from the Treasury to make up losses to individuals which must result from a further issue of greenbacks to take up the bonds. It is also manifest that the confusion and losses to individuals by such issue would be greatly beyond any gain to the Government; and would be a most unequal mode of taxation.

But, after all, the question is open—How and when will the Government take up the greenbacks?

Shall we make them the money of the country, and leave all our interests in a languishing condition for a century, or how shall we retire them? They will read for dollars—the promises of the Government to pay dollars—will the nation redeem them in dollars, or virtually repudiate them? The truth is, it is inexpedient and very bad economy to issue any more of such currency, for any reason whatever; but more especially is it madness to issue such currency to pay the national debt. Beyond all controversy, it will be easier for the country to pay one hundred cents on the dollar fifty years hence, than it would be to pay even fifty cents on the dollar at this time. However, even after taking up the bonds by issuing legal tenders, the legal tenders would read for dollars, and must be paid in full or retired by partial or total repudiation. In this view of it there would be no gain, but an immense loss to the country, by any such attempt at financial charlatanry. It is not a matter for investigation at this lapse of time, what value has been received upon the bonds; they must be paid in dollars or equivalents, or we must submit to the scorn and contempt of repudiation. Other nations of the world are content with paying their interest, leaving the principal to take care of itself. We might follow their example for ten or fifteen years, or at least be satisfied with a reduction of four millions per month—the amount which Congress has authorized the Secretary of the Treasury to retire. Further than this we ought not to undertake before the nation has recuperated, for at least twice or three times the duration which was required to make the indebtedness. And if the experiment shows that four millions per month reduction is oppressive, let two millions monthly suffice.

Our present rate of taxation amounts to about $267,000,000 from internal revenue, and $173,000,000 from customs. The former is paid in currency, the latter in gold coin. Estimating gold at 140; this would make our revenue in currency equal to $509,200,000, and in gold coin $363,905,000. If the Union were thoroughly reconstructed such taxation would be most unreasonable and insupportable. The whole debt is less than $2,500,000,000, including funded and unfunded. If the legal tenders and all other government debentures were funded, our interest would be less than $150,000,000; and certainly, $125,000,000 ought to be the utmost extent of the expenses of administering the government in time of peace. Former administrations, which have been so lavishly berated by the dominant party for extravagant expenditures, never exceeded $87,000,000 in a year; and this amount was never reached but once, in time of peace, by any administration.

If we allow for interest upon the public debt $150,000,000, and for the entire expenses of government $125,000,000, we shall require $275,000,000 annually to administer the government and pay the interest, upon a gold basis. Inasmuch as we are collecting $363,905,000 in gold equivalent from the people, it results that our taxes and imports might be reduced $88,905,000 yearly, and still allow of a yearly expenditure of $125,000,000; which would be $38,000,000 larger than was ever used under any former administration in time of peace, and in a single year. It results from these premises, that we are collecting yearly in gold equivalents $88,905,000 more than is necessary to administer the government and pay our interest, and more than is consistent with true economy to impose upon the people. Suppose, then, that we do not pay a dollar of our debt for twenty years, but pay the interest promptly in gold, and bring the administration of all our internal fiscal relations upon a gold basis, and allow for the expenses of the government $125,000,000 yearly for the next twenty years; what would be our means of payment in twenty years?

We should save in taxes yearly $88,905,000; we should save in interest account, nineteen years' interest upon it, eighteen years, do., etc., etc., etc. Our saving would then be stated thus: $88.905,000 × 20 = $1,778,100,000 of principal, and $1,013,217,000 of interest—the interest not being compounded—making in the aggregate $2,791,317,000; which is nearly $300,000,000 more than the present amount of the public debt. If we compound the interest upon this saving—and no doubt the action of collecting this annual tax from the people operates in effect in that manner—we shall find it amounts to a sum of immense magnitude; without stating it in numerals it will be comprehended more readily to say, that it will equal one-third of the value of the United States. This is truly a cogent argument for delay in paying the debt.

If the business of the country were brought on to a gold basis, it would be far easier to pay taxes than it is while every material interest is in vacillation and confusion. It is better to make the gold coin of our mines and mints the money of the country, thereby fostering every form of national industry in the most efficient manner, than to drive this money of intrinsic value from us by substituting paper promises to pay it which are notoriously false and irredeemable. If we build up our industries we can pay our interest, our current expenses, and ultimately extinguish the debt. But if we break down our industries by false currency, we shall at last fail in payment of both interest and principal; and there is no way on earth more certain to produce this disaster, than to send our gold coin abroad and adhere to the stupid opinion that money made by organizing debt into currency (I care not whether that debt be represented by national bonds, State debentures, or any form of contract which allows of delay and forbearance of payment) is equal to the coin in possession. The term "repudiation" is obnoxious to American ears. It is well that such jealousy should guard the national honor. When, however, we would guard this honor, let us do it intelligently and efficiently; not in a spread-eagle manner, which allows in fact the very essence of the evil which we deprecate.

The truth is that the Government and people of the United States have been under partial repudiation ever since the legal tender Acts of Congress were passed, making treasury notes a tender in payment of debts. Debts have not been paid in gold equivalents, except in the States of California and Oregon, since these laws have been spread on our Statutes at Large. And further: we may make all the pompous diction we please about national honor and probity—the nation will be under virtual repudiation as long as Congress tolerates a currency worth less to the dollar than gold coin. The legislation of Congress, to make greenbacks at the par of gold by investing them with the quality of legal tender, has been powerless to produce this effect. By enacting that greenbacks shall be a legal tender on all debts, however, there is not a doubt but Congress has greatly lessened the demand for gold in the United States. This lessened demand is not a healthful action upon the business interests or prosperity of the country. Hence we see that, while prices of all commodities have advanced greatly, these prices have been graded and scaled by the existing currency, and gold has not advanced *pari passu* with these. It is a result of momentous damage to the nation that our gold does not advance in price at the same rate that commodities rise. This result acts with immense force against us, and gives our most concentrated form of capital—gold coin and bullion—to other nations at a large fraction below its intrinsic value.*

We have shown that the action of the old State banks upon the currency was sufficiently disastrous to our monetary interests to drive the whole products of our mines, for the past nineteen years, from the country. That the United States does not possess near as much coin at

* When I speak of gold advancing in price, I use the expression in the incongruous manner which most of our people adopt. Such misapplication of language comes from the unreasonable laws of Congress making paper legal tender, and consequently gold coin merchandise.

this time as it had in 1848, plus the amount received from immigrants and general commerce. That the issue of bills by the State banks was only, in 1860, $207,102,477. That these banks were nominally under specie payments, and held to the doctrine that their issues were as good as gold coin. Now if the disastrous action of uttering $207,000,000 of paper in connection with the extended currency made through the deposit account of the banks has been equal to work such immense mischief as to drive from us $1,200,000,000 in bullion in so few years, what reform is necessary to save our gold in the future?

The governance of the currency has passed into the hands of the national legislature. This ought to be a long stride towards its perfection. Evidently it could never approximate to anything like perfection, when banking institutions were made and governed by all our State Legislatures.

The grand feature of national legislation upon banks should be directed to the issuing of bills. No bank should be allowed to circulate more bills than the gold coin which it should deposit in the national treasury. Tried by this rule, will the national banks, as at present instituted, be of any permanent use to the country? If the element of securing their issues upon Government bonds is to be a permanent principle of their action—if they have such a strong hold on the avarice of stockholders, the indebtedness of the public at large, and the frailty of members of the national legislature as to enable them to keep off any amendment to this provision—then they will be among the most unmitigated evils which have found patrons upon American soil. The old bank of the United States was a merciful and useful institution in comparison with these. If the monetary system of the State banks was so grossly faulty, that even under specie payments they have sacked the country of its gold since the acquisition of California, what have we to hope from the national banks as our fiscal agents? The State banks had a circulation of $207,000,000, and deposits of about $254,000,000, equal to a currency of $461,000,000. The National banks have a currency of $300,000,000, and deposits of more than $600,000,000, making a currency of $900,000,000 in deposits and circulation.

So long, then, as the National bank charters remain as at present; so long as "greenbacks" are legal tender for the redemption of National bank notes, so long will specie payments be delayed, and so long will these institutions have the power, virtually, to sink to the nation, in dead loss, a yearly sum of not less than $100,000,000. Their power of mischief, at present, transcends by far any power which the old State banks ever had, and the power of the latter was sufficient to sack the country of its entire bullion product. "Greenbacks" should not be a tender, or receivable in redemption of National bank notes, for another day. It is an imposition which is permitted by law, but the banks should no longer have this shield to protect their avarice.

We have shown that the yearly losses resulting to the country with an import of $365,000,000, of which $140,000,000 was assumed to be made on foreign account—sold here for the benefit of foreigners by their factors and agents among us, would and has sacked the country of about $70,000,000 yearly in bullion and gold value, allowing and enabling these agents of foreigners to sell their goods at prices ruling at least fifty per cent. higher than could have been obtained if our prices had not been made under an inflated currency.

Now let us see the continued action of this foreign trade among us, under a currency which is acknowledged to be thirty cents on the dollar less valuable than coin. Instead of being able to sell at fifty per cent. higher than would be done under the State bank system, the foreigner will sell at one hundred per cent. more under the National bank system. This fact is based upon the admitted theory that, under ordinary supply and demand, prices will rise or fall with the volume of currency. If the volume of currency be doubled in relation to the commodities for sale, the prices of those goods will also be doubled, when measured by the currency. Now suppose that $140,000,000 of our imports are owned by foreigners and sold here for their benefit—sold, of course, for such currency as is the common medium of exchange; and, after being converted into such currency, it seeks the next most favorable form of exchange for remittance to Europe ; under the old State bank system I have estimated the losses at fifty per cent.; but under the National bank system it would be nearer one hundred per cent. For, when gold is only forty per cent. above National bank notes, the prices of all goods are from one hundred to one hundred and fifty per cent. above the prices which would rule if our currency were kept down to the specie basis. The National bank currency is, under these circumstances, converted into gold at rates far exceeding its real value, and the profits of all this foolish legislation, making paper a legal tender beyond its value, is just so much gold taken from Americans and put into the pockets of Europeans—absolutely without value. The extra prices which the excessive issue of currency allows foreigners to make on the sale of their goods in American markets, in connection with the stupid and nefarious Legal Tender Acts, which demonetize gold for all purposes except payment of duties, degrades the value of gold, and actually gives it to foreigners at from forty to fifty cents on the dollar less than its intrinsic value, and less than we should receive for it if our currency were kept strictly equal to gold coin.

Gold does not stand with us at its relative value to commodities, by a vast difference. It is impossible for an economist to say exactly what this difference is ; but beyond all doubt it is far below its value. The present quotations are about 140 currency for 100 gold. Now I venture to say that 200 currency for 100 gold is nearer the real, honest difference of the two currencies. We cannot try this by the standards of truth and justice, because these nefarious Acts stand upon our Statutes at Large, making greenbacks a tender upon all debts, public and private, except in payment of duties. The only way this could be tried experimentally and honestly, would be upon the supposition that gold, the constitutional currency, were restored to its honest position as money, and that no paper, either governmental or of National banks, were in circulation unless it represented coined gold. I say unhesitatingly, that our inflated currency, tried by this rule, would stand at least 200 currency to 100 gold, and quite probably 250 to 100. If these figures are anything like correct, we are losing one-half or more the value of our gold, and we are giving it out and out to foreigners without value. It is balanced in advanced prices on goods which foreigners sell in the country, the currency allowing them to realize these prices, and the laws of Congress enabling them to convert a currency which is worth less than fifty cents on the dollar, intrinsically, into gold at seventy cents on the dollar.

The nation has such vast resources that, were it free from debt, it might suffer immense losses, and still be advancing in general wealth. This, however, is not the case; and so large an annual waste as $100,000,000 in gold equivalent, should be stopped as soon as possible. It is further plain that it will be totally impossible to stop this national waste, so long as the Statutes at Large and the courts uphold laws which virtually degrade the value of gold one-half. The whole power of Congress, the whole force of our judiciary, the whole power and influence of the National banks, besides divers other influences of vast magnitude, are acting to continue the nefarious operation of destroying the just national standards of value and substituting others which are not equivalents.

It is needless to say that this entire action is in the way of disorganization and national as well as individual bankruptcy. We are now at peace with all the world. Why should we persist in calling anything a dollar which all acknowledge is not worth a real dollar? Above all, why should the proscription of gold as money be longer sustained by our National Legislature? Why should gold be any longer a contraband article? Some will say gold is not a contraband article, any one has the right to receive it and pay it. This is not what is needed at present. We want a national law that shall apply in every State of the Union, which authorizes citizens to make contracts payable in gold coin of the mints, and protecting such contracts against all of the legal tender laws, not only allowing such contracts, but sustaining them by the judgment of the Courts, and making it obligatory upon Courts to render judgment upon such contracts payable in gold coin. In fact, virtually re-enacting in substance the Specific Contract Law of California, for the benefit of the Union at large. Such an Act need have no reference to past contracts. But where is the harm in enacting it for the future, and placing under the ægis of law the currency which the Constitution prescribes as the only "legal tender in payment of debts"? Citizens would then begin to make contracts payable in gold coin. Gold would begin to be the money of the people, and in proportion as it became money it would remain with us, to build our permanent interests and to found order and justice in the land.

So long, however, as the National banks have the ruling of funds—so long as they can redeem their issues in the irredeemable notes of Government—in fine, so long as the laws of the country allow the common medium of exchange to be of any less real value in gold than it purports to be, and so long as the laws of the country will not uphold and support the collection of gold coin between citizens when they contract for such coin, so long will all our prosperity be hopeless, and our wealth be moving to foreign countries as fast as commerce may transport it.

If foreigners can sell their goods among us at the high price which our inflated currency makes and collect the National bank currency, then turn that currency into gold at 140 currency for 100 gold, while the honest difference in the currencies is 200 or 250 currency to 100 gold, is it not patent how they get our gold for nothing?

In estimating the imports which are made and sold in the country for foreign account at one hundred and forty millions yearly, it is placing such imports at a very low figure. We may willfully close our eyes to the fact that the ruling of gold in relation to the value of commodities does not represent its true value, but the losses of our policy are bound to be entailed upon us, in defiance of our obstinate perverseness and forced legislation to forfend such consequences. All the nefarious gold bills which the venom of tyranny and demented legislation may enact will only work the more certain consummation of our ruin. If we reject the cardinal principle of justice and the teaching of science, we shall dash on blindly to our own destruction.

There is only one way to reckon, with any approximation to accuracy, as to what is the proper and just value of gold in relation to other forms of wealth, and this is to be inferred by considering how prices would rule in gold coin if there were no legal tender notes or National bank notes in circulation. Is it supposable that, under such circumstances, the prices of commodities would be at anything like the present rates?

Whatever this difference in prices would be is loss to us, and upon goods imported and sold among us by foreigners, is direct gain to them. If foreign agents sell us one hundred and forty millions yearly, and their profits are first enlarged by our vitiated currency, then further magnified by being able to convert such currency into coin at 140 to 100, when the real difference should be about 200 or 250 currency for 100 coin, is it not patent how they are consuming the vitality of the nation? This result is an inevitable consequence of governmental interference in tampering with the standards of value, passing the recent Legal Tender Acts, which now disgrace our Statutes at Large, in connection with inaugurating a system of banking which organizes federal debt into national currency. In this manner the United States laws, by degrading gold below its sterling value, are crushing its own citizens and building up foreigners.

We have counted the damage which a yearly loss of seventy millions in gold, or its equivalent in other forms of wealth, would entail upon the country in the space of one generation, or thirty-three years. This, with interest compounded, amounts to more than seven billions (7,000,000,000) of dollars. But I warn my countrymen that seventy millions in gold values will not meet the yearly losses to the country, if they continue the system of allowing the National banks to issue currency upon Government bonds—in this manner monetizing debt, making something to pass as equal to gold which is not its equivalent by a large per centage upon its face value. The factors of other countries will multiply among us in direct proportion as our laws give them the means of abstracting wealth without a just value in exchange. No policy can be more ruinous to our prosperity than for the Government to enact laws which bring gold below its just value in comparison to commodities, while the prices of commodities are far above their proper ruling when measured by coin. It is virtually giving the sinews of the country to other nations, and it is a boon to them for which we get nothing in return.

It results from these premises that the country will be more opulent by at least seven billions of dollars in the next thirty-three years (A.D. 1900) by using a gold currency than by rejecting it and substituting a medium of exchange based upon the public debt.

It is allowed by all logical reasoners upon the subject that the issue of currency upon the basis of the public debt must be limited in amount to keep up its value, and that this issue should not exceed the normal volume of currency required in the country. This admission on the part of the friends of paper issues, is positive proof of its inexpediency and want of adaptation for the uses of money. There is no limit to the amount of gold and silver which may be coined by the mints. Why should not the amount of coin be limited as well as the amount of paper money, if they are equally valuable? Obviously for this reason: that when coin is in excess of the national requirements it flows to the markets of the world and finds its level. Paper issues have no such outlet, *because they are not intrinsic value*, but remain at home and aid in driving the gold from us by lessening the domestic demand. Now if it be well to issue $300,000,000 currency on the public debt, why not $900,000,000? Simply because we achieve nothing by it, but to advance prices very greatly, *and not to advance gold by any means in the same proportion.*

It is a statistical fact that our mines are amply equal to the most extended requirements of the nation for currency, if we would institute some efficient mode to save their products in the country. It is, then, a matter of choice with the American people whether they will have gold currency and ultimate opulence, or rag currency and certain destitution to the mass of the population.

The issues of the National banks are about one hundred million dollars in excess of the highest issues of the State banks; while their deposits are about fifty millions more than double the amount which the deposits of the

State institutions ever reached. Of course, then, they are efficient agents which can and will do double the mischief which was wrought by the State banks.

It has been proposed that the Government, as fast as it receives the National bank notes for revenue, shall retain this circulation, and issue legal tenders in place thereof. As fast as these notes are received by the Government, they would be redeemed by the issue of government legal tenders. The bonds held as security for the redemption of the notes could then be canceled, and relieve the Government of an annual gold payment of $18,000,000. To this proposition it is objected by those in interest that the Government is bound in honor to allow the National banks to do business for twenty years, upon the basis of pledging government bonds for the security of the circulation which they issue. No such "honorable" restrictions are put upon the action of Congress in the premises. On the contrary, they may amend or repeal the National bank law *ad libitum*. The National banking law would be a thorough imposition of tyranny upon the people if, when science and experience demonstrated that its provisions caused a yearly loss to the country of one hundred millions of dollars, Congress had no power to amend or repeal it, but was bound in honor to allow it to remain in force for twenty years.

As to the right of the Government to amend or repeal the law, there cannot be a shadow of doubt. As to the expediency of issuing three hundred millions more of Treasury notes, it is matter for careful deliberation. If they are to be issued to take the place of the National bank notes, with the full purpose that they shall be retired by funding them as fast as possible in long bonds—say, 5-90's, then the scheme may be the most practical and feasible one to get rid of this national evil.

If, however, these banks should desire to issue gold bills, (and I think about one-third of them would find it convenient to do so) they should have the privilege of receiving gold notes from the Treasury of the United States, to be countersigned by the officers of the Treasury, to any amount which they deposited gold coin of the mints in the Treasury for their redemption.

The whole matter of regulating the currency would

then be most efficiently in the hands of Congress, and the resumption of specie payments would be exactly when the Government should determine it.

There is one safeguard which should be indispensably practiced in all public securities, such as the National bonds, Treasury notes, bank notes, etc., etc.; the signatures should be with pen and ink, and should be the autograph of the parties signing. The art of photography may become so perfect, that there will be no security in any form of debentures. Even now, experts and adepts differ as to the genuine and counterfeit notes of the Government, and the counterfeits have been redeemed by the Treasury department or its branches. Signatures with pen and ink are vastly preferable to engraved names, to prevent counterfeits.

The suggestion that any bank should issue gold notes is deemed by some preposterous: for, they reason, why should banks issue gold notes rather than the gold coin, if they are compelled to deposit the coin to secure the notes? Why not bank on the gold coin at once, *à la California?* An excellent way, indeed! if the people of the East could only be induced to save the gold of our mines, and try the experiment. Gold bills would circulate only for convenience: all profits of circulation beyond actual capital would be at an end. But in large cities like New York, immense sums pass daily through the banks and clearing houses. The large city banks would circulate gold notes just as fast as they found it for their interest; the balance of their transactions would be in coin, and through their deposit accounts. If the banks of New York found that they could save expenses—that their business could be done with one-half the tellers, accountants, and attachés, and with less liability to errors by putting a large fraction of their capital in gold notes, they would, no doubt, avail themselves of the economy. Half-a-million of dollars in gold notes, of one hundred dollars each, could be counted by an expert in two hours; but to count it in gold would be a much more difficult matter. Therefore, gold notes would be substituted for coin just so far as economy should dictate, and no further. In depriving the National banks of their circulation resting on the public debt, I think they should be allowed to circulate gold notes to any amount they choose to deposit the coin in the Treasury to secure these notes. The expense of this issue, if paper issues are a national necessity, should fall largely upon the Government, for it is as much its duty to keep paper circulation up to the value of gold as it is to keep gold up to its right value by the strictest regulation of the mints, in regard to the purity and weight of the coin.

It would not be safe to allow banks to issue bills upon a simple provision in their charters that they should always hold as much specie as they had notes in circulation. The temptation to issue would be too strong for human frailty; and the moment they began to inflate the medium of exchange, by issues beyond their specie, that moment the insidious operation of false money would commence its action upon the Commonwealth, in the shape of robbery through high prices of commodities. Hence it is as impolitic and unjust to allow banks to prepare their own issues of paper without any supervision of the Government, as it would be to allow them to coin dollars of zinc or brass, because they might be under a legal requirement to redeem these spurious issues in the genuine coins of the mints.

The currency of the United States, in the form of legal tender notes, National bank notes, and deposits in the banks with the power of currency, is about $1,300,000,000. This currency is mostly in circulation among what have been called the loyal States—the ten States which have been doomed as military districts having but a small fraction of it. The entire currency of the country before the war was less than one-half this amount. That it was then largely expanded beyond the normal specie volume, there can be no reasonable doubt. Even then its expansion was sufficient to drive our gold from us, and leave the banks to a modest form of failure, *termed suspension*, after receiving most lavish products of bullion for ten years from the mines of California. If this be really so—if our currency was far too much expanded in 1857, with only $600,000,000—what must be the blighting influence upon the country to enlarge this volume of currency more than double? Nothing but ultimate bankruptcy and destruction of all our material interests, private and national, so long as we allow such volume of currency.

The problem is before the country, to reduce the currency more than one-half its present volume, as rapidly as possible, without inducing a general bankruptcy. The question which agitates the public is, whether the National bank currency shall be withdrawn first, or the legal tenders. The scheme upon which the National bank notes are issued, being wrong in theory, and in perpetual collision with the rights of the mining States and Territories, and the permanent interest of the nation in general, in making debt the basis of its circulation instead of coin, thereby vilifying and degrading the value of our coin and exalting the value of such issues far above their just standpoint in the markets of the United States; and further, the allowance of any such issues by the National banks being a usurpation of power by Congress which is not delegated by the Constitution, it follows that all circulation of the National banks, (except such as they choose to utter under a deposit of gold coin in the Federal Treasury to cover such bills in amount dollar for dollar, and which will require an amendment of the National bank bill to provide for) should be withdrawn as rapidly as possible. It can be done by a further issue of greenbacks to take their place as fast as they are collected for revenue. This will use them up faster than by any other process. Taxing them out of existence might do, but it is too slow a process while the country is being paralyzed so thoroughly by their effects.

When the Treasury has issued $300,000,000 more of greenbacks, and taken up $300,000,000 of National bank notes, the way will then be clear for wise action. The Government will then be ready to take the first steps towards raising the value of the currency.

This new issue of greenbacks should be in bills which can be easily distinguished from each other, and in four separate and distinct series. The first series might be dated July 1, 1868, and be issued in the amount of $75,000,000, and not to be a tender for longer than six months, but to be fundable in U. S. bonds of 5-90's, payable principal and interest in gold coin; the interest to be made at a reasonable rate. The second series to be dated July 10, 1868, to be issued in the amount of $75,000,000, and not to be a tender for longer than one year from their date, then to be funded as above. The third series to be dated July 20, 1868, to be issued for $75,000,000, not to be a tender longer than eighteen months, but to be fundable as above. The fourth and last series to be dated July 30, 1868, to be issued for $75,000,000, not to be a tender after two years, and to be then fundable as above.

In this manner $300,000,000 of Government circulating notes would be issued to retire the National bank issues. It would not be necessary to galvanize these with vitality any further than the National bank notes are now made tenders by the law of Congress which creates them. We should then fund $75,000,000 of this circulation, January 1, 1869; $75,000,000 July 1, 1869; $75,000,000 January 1, 1870; and $75,000,000 July 1, 1870. It is certain that we ought to reduce our circulating notes as rapidly as this scheme contemplates.

There are multitudes who are ready to inquire, What is the gain in funding circulating notes? We are retiring a species of paper which bears no interest, and putting out one which must pay interest. I answer: The weal of the nation requires the change in the most imperative manner. It is the difference of feeding a man upon bread and water and exacting from him laborious toil, or feeding him upon the fat of the land and requiring him to render a similar service. If we paralyze all the industries of the country by a false and vitiated currency, the people are not competent to support the Government with the vigor they might do if the currency were so sound as to sustain all their sources of wealth.

Suppose that by funding three hundred millions of the excessive paper money which is afloat among us we increase the national interest $18,000,000 yearly, and at the same time increase .the productive capacity of the Union at large thirty per cent., the people could then pay this interest upon the funded debt and save to themselves ten times the amount in surplus product; whereas by keeping the volume of the currency so inflated it would act directly to crush them, and to prevent them from putting forth any efficient or profitable system of industry. Thus, if the people are well fed, they can work wonders; but if they are oppressed by unwise or unjust currency, their powers of endurance and action are at once felled to the ground. Surely, then, it is better that the Government shall fund the circulating notes, so far as they are in excess of the normal specie volume, and increase the interest debt, and at the same time multiply the power of the people tenfold to pay this interest in taxes, than to allow this excessive volume of currency to circulate and prostrate all of our energies and vital resources.

This scheme if carried out would reduce the circulating notes $300,000,000 by July, 1870. This, however, should not satisfy our people. We ought to continue to withdraw the circulation of paper at the rate of forty millions a year after July, 1870, which will be about one-half the yield of our mines in bullion, and allow this withdrawal to fill up with coin. The financial policy of the United States should aim at a perfect system of currency—a system which shall allow of no notes to circulate as a common medium of exchange, unless they represent coin in the Treasury of the nation. If we require a currency of $600,000,000, all we need to amass it is, to have a thorough and efficient national Statute to save our bullion. Our mines are abundantly equal to this—nay, more, they are equal to it if we required double this amount. But we do not require this—for it is a fact, admitted by our most learned writers, that gold might bear four times its present value to commodities and discharge the functions of money as well as at the present ruling. Without this legislation, it is as certain that our gold will leave us as that natural causes produce their consequent results. Why have we mined $1,200,000,000 in gold on the Pacific coast, and possess not as much coin as we had in 1848 plus our receipts from other sources? It is not the want of means to institute a correct and perfect system of currency—for our mines are equal to this; but it is the want of salutary laws to save the gold of our mines in the country. We shall always be poverty-stricken and short of money while we allow ourselves to be the prey of foreign nations through the action of a vitiated and debased currency. Thousands will raise their voices to the skies and insist that a paper currency is just as valuable as a gold one. The bullionists deny this *positively;* but even if it were true, where is the use of making such currency? If it is equally valuable, it must be *intrinsically valuable;* not a parasite which leans upon something else to sustain itself. If it is equally valuable, where is the use in emitting it? Why not emit the genuine coin? If it is equally valuable, there can be nothing saved by emitting it. If it is only *reputed* equally valuable as coin, or if the tyranny of law makes it so, while in fact it is far inferior in value, then its action can be none other than mischievous in the extreme. Nothing but undoubted equivalents of coin should ever be allowed to pass as the common medium of exchange.

The condition of the United States in regard to their fiscal relations to the rest of the world, is so different to that of the nations of Europe towards each other, that we can scarcely institute correct comparisons, which will bear mutually alike between them. The nations of Europe are divided by rivers, mountains, geographical lines, etc., but are all contiguous. The United States are separated from them by an ocean three thousand miles in width. Hence, it would be impossible for one of the nations of Europe to vitiate its currency to a great extent and sustain specie payments, in comparison with the currencies of other countries immediately contiguous to it. This rule does not hold good in the United States. Their currency may be, and has been, far below the currencies of Europe; the distance from that continent, the want of exact information in relation to business matters, and above all, the overshadowing blight of an enormous tariff in connection with the imperative call for currency at home—a call which is first made by a vitiated currency being issued, then perpetuated by its necessity after inflating the prices of all forms of property—these causes, influences and agencies all combined, have enabled banks to issue largely in excess of the specie volume, or normal amount of currency needed; and yet, the course of trade does not check this fallacy, or bring banks to retribution for such disorganizing action, except through sweeping and general bankruptcy which passes largely over the country about once in five years, and with the power of the typhoon's blast about once in each decade. Nor is the whole yield of California's mines sufficient to avert these financial crises, so long as our people will cling to the folly of a vitiated paper currency. We had immense failures in 1857, we should have these repeated in 1867 with ten-fold increase if the whole country east of the Rocky Mountains were not already under suspension and virtual bankruptcy; being enabled to conceal this, and stave off its consequences, only by perpetuating this system of calling two-thirds, or half of a dollar, the equivalent of a whole dollar, and balancing imports by sacrificing government' bonds.

The product of the mines of the United States has not been used to build up and perpetuate a sterling currency, but to keep the currency as rotten as possible and not be discovered. The organizing of State or federal debt into our medium of exchange, is a direct utterance of this vitiated currency—subversion alike of the value of the true currency and our best national interest. We hear the National bank notes lauded as being a uniform currency. Of what avail is uniformity of printing and external appearance of the bills, while they are all under—not suspension of specie payments, for they never pretended to pay specie, but really disguised bankruptcy—calling seventy cents equal to one hundred cents?

Uniformity of currency amounts to nothing if it be not the equivalent of the coin which it promises. The quality of uniformity desirable in currency is honest equivalent. The dollar in Maine and Georgia, in New York and California, in every city, village, hamlet and town through the length and breadth of our country, should mean in law, in business and in equity, a strict measure representing equivalents. This kind of uniformity—value—can never be attained while the dollar represents anything else in law and in business than the mint coins.

The National bank notes, then, should be withdrawn from circulation as rapidly as they come into the Treasury for internal revenue, and not re-issued, but canceled, and effectually destroyed.

There is a matter which I have never heard alluded to in regard to these banks that is most outrageous upon all who wish to deal upon honest principles and with dollars of the mint coinage. These banks are allowed to do business upon such principles as demoralize the whole affairs of a nation—making immense profits—declaring huge dividends, and carrying large amounts to the credit of their profit and loss account after such dividends—*allowed by law to do all this and still remain under non-specie payments.* Such monopoly in a free government is utterly unpardonable. Not a dollar should be divided among shareholders till the banks recognize and act upon the principle that "a dollar" means one hundred cents, and is represented as a standard by our gold coin of the mints. To allow banks to issue currency and make huge dividends while they are under non-specie payments—which is rather a solecism and might perhaps be more properly termed virtual or partial bankruptcy—to allow them to do this is giving them legal protection, first, in ruining the people, afterwards covering themselves behind the shield of the law in continuing their work of destruction.

The most prompt and efficient reform which can be instituted in regard to the National bank issues, will be to hold on to their bills as fast as they come into the Treasury and its depositories—cancel them, and allow the banks to issue nothing but gold notes, secured by deposit of gold in the Treasury in equal amount to such issue; the Treasury notes which it may be necessary to issue to take their place to be funded as rapidly as consistent with the fiscal relations of the country. But, if it is impossible to get Congress to consent to this measure so much needed for the prosperity of the country—perhaps it would not be too much to say, so much needed to save the country from repudiation and national bankruptcy—if Congress will not consent to the immediate withdrawal of the National bank circulation by substituting Treasury notes, there are other ways of reaching the evil and correcting it.

The profits of the National banks are about forty million dollars yearly in currency. Their capital is in federal bonds. Suppose, then, it is made obligatory upon them to convert all of their profits into gold coin, and, under the direction of the Secretary of the Treasury, sixty millions of the bonds which are held for security of the circulation ; this would be converting forty millions of profits and sixty millions of bonds into gold coin yearly. The forty millions of profits in currency might bring $28,000,000 in coin ; and the sixty millions in bonds might bring $47,000,000 in coin. This would amount to $75,000,000 a year in coin. For this, the banks might receive from the Treasury gold bills to the amount of $75,000,000, *on the surrender of* $75,000,000 *of the circulation now secured on bonds*, to the Treasury. The circulation would then be growing sound at the rate of $75,000,000 per year, for it would be changing from a debt basis to one of gold, at that rate. In four years, then, the whole issue would be changed from debt basis to a gold basis, dollar for dollar.

The present value of currency is about 71 to 72 cents on the dollar. The thaler of the Northern States of Germany is worth 71.7-10 cents. Hence the German thaler represents at present very nearly the value of our currency dollar. The National banks would lose nothing by converting their thalers into the coin of our mints ; because, after they had made the conversion, the real value of their money would be equal. I say the real value would be equal, for I am now reasoning upon the assumed premise that the currency dollar is worth a German thaler. This is not my own opinion, by much allowance. I do not believe that gold stands at anything near its value when measured by currency. This difference would be altogether in favor of the banks making the conversion. For this reason, if the banks could change their currency profits into gold, calling currency equal to thalers when it was only equal to *half-dollars*, they would gain largely by the operation. But it is certainly right to allow them to convert their profits, and their bonds, into coin, in the best manner which the markets of the country and the world will allow. During the conversion into real dollars, the banks would hold one kind of dollar, worth one hundred cents ; another kind of dollar worth only a thaler, or seventy-two cents.

To digress from the argument, for the purpose of making an important point in the interest of California : it is assumed above that the banks should have the right to sell their bonds in the markets of the world, and bring their proceeds to this country. Suppose they sell for gold coin, should they have the privilege of bringing this coin to the United States, free from duty? Protection is the order of the day, and why should not California's staple—gold --be protected as well as New England manufactures and Pennsylvania iron? Everything which increases the purchasing power of gold is a direct aid and stimulus to the mining interest. If gold becomes so depressed by making paper legal tenders—National bank notes "lawful money," and enacting tariffs which prohibit its uses abroad, except at such enormous rates of customs upon the commodities purchased, when these reach our custom-houses, why should not gold be protected by a duty upon all imports of the article? If it is desirable by the Government that the gold of our mountains should be extracted from the fastnesses of the quartz rocks, and coined into money, why should not this branch of national industry be protected by a duty on all imports of gold of forty or fifty per cent., or even as high duty as upon other articles of import? My own sentiments are for free-trade as far as possible, but if *protection* is to be the order of the day, let us all have our share of it. Put the duty on imports of gold as high as upon merchandise.*

In my scheme for converting the National bank currency into money, worth the exact value of the Mint coins, I have proposed that it be done at the rate of about $75,000,000 per year. This would throw upon the banks two kinds of dollars—the currency dollar and the gold dollar. Of course, it would be indispensable that they should keep accounts in currency and gold, while they were in the transit from the depreciated dollar to the genuine coin. This could all be done—with some difficulty, perhaps, in many cases, but not so much, after it was thoroughly organized, as might be imagined. "Where

* If the coal and iron of the mines of Pennsylvania are protected by a heavy tariff, why should not the gold and silver of the mines of California receive the same protection? But let it be observed, that, while the mines of coal and iron are largely protected, the mines of gold and silver receive no protection, but their products are subject to tax on the assays of the metals. What models of uniformity, equality, and consistency are our tariff laws!

there is a will there is a way;" and it can never cost men too much to do right. Discounts could be made in gold or currency, and kept as distinct as dollars and thalers. The protection of law would then be necessary to *compel* the individuals or banks which contracted to pay in gold, to make good their undertakings. The banks would then be changing their basis from bonds to gold coin, at the rate of twenty-five per cent. per year upon their capital stock. I have no doubt the withdrawal of the National bank currency from circulation and substituting the greenbacks, would be the easiest way to get rid of our debt currency; but the greenbacks should also be withdrawn *by funding*, with as little delay as possible. The axiom, that all paper money which does not represent the gold coin of an equal amount in possession, is blighting to the true interest of the country, cannot be too strongly impressed upon the minds of the people. It is the people who have the ruling of this matter through their delegations in Congress; hence it is of the greatest importance that the people understand the subject, and exact wise legislation from their representatives. As it regards the two currencies—the greenbacks and the National bank issues—one or the other should be withdrawn from circulation immediately; and both should be withdrawn as soon as possible.

But whichever Congress shall see fit to have withdrawn first, or whatever delays may be in the way of a thorough reform of the currency, there is a matter of justice to the Pacific States which has been withheld for nearly three years, or since the close of the war at least, that should be immediately granted by Federal legislation. I refer to the proscription of gold and silver coin. The Constitution makes these legal tender. The laws of Congress make Treasury notes legal tender. But the citizen who contracts for gold coin cannot collect it in any State but California and Oregon; because the law will not discriminate between money which is "lawful money," whether the dollar be worth seventy cents or one hundred cents. Hence, if the creditor gives value and contracts for gold dollars, the debtor may pay in "promise dollars"—legal tenders, as they are called.

Congress should enact immediately that none of the

Legal Tender Acts, passed from 1861 to 1865, should have any effect upon contracts made by citizens or corporations, after the first of January, 1868, where such contracts were made payable by stipulation in the gold or silver coin of the United States Mints, but that all courts in the United States and territories thereof should give judgments upon such contracts payable in such kind of currency as the parties contracting had agreed upon, and upon such judgments executions should issue collectable in such form of currency as the original contract between the parties had specified. This is only a simple act of justice to the Pacific Coast. Why should our staple—gold—be longer driven from the American markets by the action of the legal tender laws? Why should it be shorn of a large fraction of its value, to force that value down to greenbacks, in time of peace? As the law stands, we may contract in any State for gold coin; the wisdom of our representatives will not hang us for this; but when the time of payment comes, the debtor can pay in a currency worth from one-quarter to one-third less than what the contract stipulates; and further, if he tenders the greenbacks, and the creditor does not accept the tender, *the whole debt is forfeited.* In the name of justice, equity, and right, is such tyrannical legislation needed at this day to support the Legal Tender Acts? When is gold to be money again by law, as well as by the Constitution? The Constitution has to bend to Acts of Congress. When will Congress recognize the Constitution and Justice? When will the Constitution of the United States be "preserved, protected, and defended" by the members of the federal legislature?

There are many well disposed citizens who are inclined to censure the Secretary for holding so large an amount of gold in the Treasury. They think it might be used so as to save a large amount of interest. These advisers take but a narrow view of the matter. It is necessary for a merchant with large liabilities to keep a heavy deposit account, to protect his credit. Now, one hundred millions in coin is not too large a balance for the National Treasury to contain when the public debt is twenty-five times that amount. The loss resulting in managing the debt with a depleted treasury, in changing one form of securities for another, might be manifold greater with empty coffers than with a full amount of bullion. The price of our bonds abroad is ruled largely by the known amount of gold in the Treasury. The keeping of such amount in coin helps the sale of the bonds and national credit far beyond the loss of interest. Still further: To talk of a loss of interest in keeping one hundred millions in coin, while we have four hundred millions in greenbacks in circulation, is an absurdity. If we circulate four times as much currency as we hold gold in the Treasury, then surely we cannot be said to be losing in interest account.

But suppose the Secretary were to sell the gold for greenbacks, it would not bring anything like its real relative value to this form of currency. Consequently it would be purchased by foreigners among us seeking exchange to send to Europe for goods which they have sold in our markets at currency rates, or it would be purchased by bill-drawers and dealers in foreign exchange, who would make large profits upon it. There will be times, while we are coming down to specie prices, when it may seem that there is not a wide difference between the value of gold and currency, and still such appearances be entirely fallacious.

Gold is money in the United States only for the payment of duties. It is true that the Government uses it for payment of interest, but it first collects it from the people for duties. Hence gold is only money among the people for the payment of duties. This is an exceedingly restricted use for the application of *real money* in the vast domain of the United States. But money—local money, currency, bank notes, and legal tenders—that form of money which is the cheapest to obtain and which will at the same time discharge debts—is in immense demand. Large dealers who are holding very heavy stocks of merchandise, and are owing money, these, upon a falling market for goods, are hoping a return of high prices, and as they see plainly that without such rise of prices they are bankrupt beyond a remedy, will use every exertion to raise money to tide themselves over what they hope may be only a temporary fall in prices. This makes a demand almost unlimited for currency, while for gold there is no demand except for duties. And further: While there is such a strain in the fiscal matters of the country to buoy up war prices and hold on to goods, importations will largely cease, and the demand for gold, even for duties, will be greatly lessened. Under these circumstances, for the Secretary to sell gold would be for the Government to part with it at a large fraction less than its real value, and would help none but gold speculators and foreign bill drawers. That it would leave the country as fast as it left the vaults of the Treasury, is matter of certainty. Hence it is the true policy of the Government to fortify itself, to keep all the coin in its vaults possible, at least so long as it circulates such an immense amount of greenbacks, and let gamblers and speculators look out for themselves.

If gold is demonetized by law for all purposes except the payment of duties, it is as plain as the meridian sun in his splendor that its relative value to currency is reckoned and affected only upon so much as is needed for such duties.

When the banks are coerced into specie payments and the legal tenders are withdrawn, the value of gold will then be known by the increased amount of commodities which the dollar will purchase. But even after they resume payment gold will not take its just relative value to merchandise and wealth in general if the laws allow the public debt to be organized into currency by banks issuing bills of credit guaranteed by the pledge of the evidences of this debt.

The national debt is distinct and separate from the currency, and should ever remain so. Any attempt by Congress to blend these together can produce nothing but chaos, ruin, and bankruptcy. The debt may be under the par of gold for a long time, or it may be above the par of gold, according to the rate of interest which it bears, and according to the esteem in which it is held by capitalists in the money markets of the world. The consolidated debt of the United Kingdom is below par, even at this distant day. So the debt of the United States may be below par for an indefinite period. But this is not the least reason why the currency of the country should be below the gold par. And it is matter of certainty that so long as we tolerate a legal tender dollar worth less than our gold dollar, so long will foreigners get our gold for a small fraction of its just value.

Since the immense national debt of our country has been contracted, it furnishes a form of remittance which is easy to make, but which may mislead us entirely as to the true balance of trade between us and other nations. If we sell foreigners our debt at seventy-five cents on the dollar, taking it in merchandise, we shall be getting in debt to them at a rapid rate, while we appear to be paying as we go on. Individual indebtedness will be discharged by substituting national; but the nation will be in debt one dollar for every seventy-five cents which we may thus import.

The National bank circulation would be far better than greenbacks if it represented coin instead of public debt. It results that the National bank circulation not representing coin should be retired immediately, and never again issued upon any other basis than gold, dollar for dollar; for it is plain that so long as we must have paper currency—if it represent nothing but debt—the country has a right to the profits of such circulation rather than favored monopolies. And yet the greenback circulation is immensely disastrous to our prosperity. Hence the problem for Congress and the wisdom of economists to solve is, how to bring all currency which is a common medium of exchange up to the par of our gold coin. But the scheme of keeping the currency below gold coin, for the sake of paying the public debt in a depreciated paper, would be attended with such great losses that it might be virtually paying the debt many times over. The Government should make no excessive demands upon the people to pay the debt; but the interest should be paid at any needed sacrifice. It is not the custom of nations to pay funded debt, and our Government may be content to follow the common rule for twenty-five years. Long before this we ought to have all our currencies at the par of gold, and the country will have so far recuperated that it may begin to reduce the debt with ease, and at a rate of marked progress. The country cannot be justly amenable to the charge of repudiation so long as it pays its interest promptly, even though it postpone payment of the debt for a century. We may reasonably expect that our population will be double its present amount during this century, and such increase will render the debt less onerous in a corresponding degree.

If our interest is paid promptly, we shall have no trouble in issuing new bonds to retire old ones; for, if the holders are unwilling to make the exchange, new bonds can be sold to raise funds for payment of those which are about maturing. It is manifest, then, that the grand secret of managing the debt is to keep the interest paid up, to the satisfaction of the holders of the bonds. The principal should be reduced only so rapidly as may be quite easy, and for the good of the commonwealth.

The people, then, should understand, that the public debt is a separate matter entirely from the currency—that they ought not to be blended together in any manner—and above all, that the debt ought not to be organized into currency by pledging it as security for the issue of National bank bills.

While this matter of a currency of intrinsic value is of such vital importance to the nation at large, it is equally important to the Pacific States and all our bullion producing territories west of the Rocky Mountains. The following is from the *Alta California:*

"We have received from the Bureau of Statistics at Washington the following official table, giving the shipments of domestic commodities from New York to San Francisco, via the Isthmus, for the fiscal year to June 30, 1867. It is of great interest, since it is the first time the values of goods by that route have been definitely stated:

"Statement of the Shipments of Domestic Commodities from New York to San Francisco, via the Isthmus of Panama, for the fiscal year ended June 30, 1867."

The statement contains a specification of 130 kinds of commodities, shipped via Panama to San Francisco, valued $34,276,421.

The same authority gives the following:

"Statement of the shipments of Foreign Commodities from New York to San Francisco, via the Isthmus of Panama, for the fiscal year ended June 30, 1867.

Commodities.	*Quantity.*	*Value.*
Cotton, manufactures of................	......	$ 49,850
Fancy articles...........................	......	4,326,500
Silk, manufactures of....................	......	4,467,800
Spices—		
Cloves...........................lbs.	11,150	1,000
Pepper, black and white...........lbs.	7,870	800
Tobacco, unmanufactured....	......	600
Wines in casks....................galls.	9,870	3,684
Wines in bottles...................doz.	100	1,900
Dress goods...........................	......	65,151
Total..................................		$8,917,285

Those values are given in currency, and the aggregate of the Domestic commodities, in gold equivalents, equals $24,480,152. The gold value of the Foreign goods is equal to $6,368,781. This amount is embraced in the figures which we recently published of the imports of foreign goods into this port. The two items of importations then combine as follows, with an approximate statement of the goods received by sail from the East:

Eastern goods, by steam............................	$24,480,152
Foreign goods......................................	14,856,188
Eastern, per sail, estimate..........................	14,363,109
	$53,584,449
Freights....	7,356,507
Total	$60,940,956

This is an approximation of the amount of goods purchased in a year for this coast at invoice prices, and which is covered by the exports of produce and treasure. The value of Cotton manufactures imported is about $8,200,000 foreign and domestic, and some $5,000,000 worth of clothing."

Of the preceding described imports, California received by steam, via Panama, of domestic goods...$24,480,152
And by sailing vessels, via Cape Horn...... 14,363,109

Domestic goods, via Panama & Cape Horn.$38,843,261
Foreign goods, via Panama & Cape Horn..$14,856,188

In round numbers, our imports were of domestic goods, about thirty-nine millions, and of foreign goods, about fifteen millions, for the year ending June 30, 1867. The freights were $7,356,507.

On the domestic imports above cited, California had to pay at least fifteen millions in gold value, more than she would have done if the Eastern States had used a gold currency. And upon the foreign imports the duties were not less than six millions in gold coin. The prices of the domestic goods were advanced upon California by reason of the tariff rates on foreign goods; because foreign goods could not begin to compete with the home-made till the duty was paid. Thus it becomes a statistical fact that, for the fiscal year ending June 30, 1867, California lost to sustain the diluted currency now in use at the East, on her purchases of domestic goods, fifteen millions of dollars, and she paid for duties on foreign goods, six millions. This makes an aggregate of twenty-one millions of dollars, which represents the loss to California, by the joint action of an inflated currency in the old States and the enormous tariff upon foreign goods in a single year. If we add to this five millions and a half, collected for internal revenue, we shall have the amount which California pays yearly to support the government, and to support the system of currency which is destroying the people at the East, as well as breaking down the value of coin and sending it from the country. The tax which California pays virtually to sustain the government by reason of the tariff, and to support the system of diluted and dishonest currency universally recognized in the old States, amounts to twenty-six and a half million dollars yearly in gold coin. Truly, this is no small burden to impose upon a population of 400,000. Such are the bitter fruits which California is reaping by reason of the joint action of the tariff and a vitiated form of currency in circulation in all the States east of the Rocky Mountains.

The policy of inflation, or at least of keeping the volume of currency at its present abnormal and gigantic proportions, is considered by many an absolute national necessity. In proof of their position, they say that gold falls as soon as the prospect of the currency remaining constant at its present volume, seems to be reasonably probable. To this position I would further add, that the difference between gold and currency would be still less apparent if currency were received for duties. Gold would then be thoroughly demonetized in all the States east of the Rocky Mountains. After it ceased to be money, there would be but little call for it in the country. Its disuse as money would reduce its value greatly, and drive it to the arts and to foreign countries as merchandise. Such a thrust at the value of gold, however, would have no tendency to reduce the prices of commodities when measured by currency. On the contrary, let it be well understood that inflation—or even that the present volume of currency is to be continued indefinitely—is to be the permanent policy of the government, and prices will not only keep up, but actually advance—and gold will be gradually declining, unless its value shall be sustained for remittances as exchange, and to pay duties on imports.

The truth is, there can be no return to specie payments while the volume of the currency is so inflated. We may force down the value of gold, and give it to other nations by demonetizing it; but in doing this we shall not bring the value of paper up to gold; for the banks could not sustain cash payments any longer than it would take to count the money in their vaults. Their bills and deposits would be demanded in specie at once; not from any ill will—but because the gold would be worth more to foreigners than we were holding it at, by forcing gold down to currency, while currency was so distended. Other nations, who have their factors among us selling merchandise, rejoice at our fatuous policy of forcing down the value of gold by making paper legal tenders. They are making themselves rich out of our stupid economy. Any national policy which depresses gold without reducing general prices in a corresponding degree, will be ruinous to the country.

The present feature of our financial *savans* seems to be, to try to keep the currency at its present enormous inflation and to render gold comparatively valueless by *its disuse as money*; then to shout: "Gold is rapidly declining, it will soon be worth no more than currency—do you not see this end is being reached without any reduction of the volume?" Aye, I see it; and I see further that foreigners are getting our gold quite as fast as our mines yield it; and I see they are also getting our bonds a great deal faster than is desirable for the welfare of coming generations; and that we shall be compelled to be their tributaries, in interest account, for an indefinite length of time. All this is very plain; and it is equally plain that our silly policy of organizing debt into currency, and enacting in our national legislature that paper money shall be a legal tender, are producing in the most efficient manner these national losses; that by fatuous legislation, in making paper legal tender, we have unnecessarily and unwisely, but most certainly and efficiently, brought upon the nation immense loss and useless debt; that we cheat ourselves with a fatal fallacy when we suppose that gold—demonetized as it is by law—can or does bring its just and relative value to currency, or to commodities in general. This fallacy is not only sinking our gold, but it is sinking our general wealth at an enormous rate, and stuffing our purses and vaults with debt currency and legal tenders, which can never take their proper ruling to coin so long as the Government and banks are under suspension of cash payments —or so long as such paper is legal tender or partial tender; and so long as such form of money commands our gold coin at a large fraction less than its intrinsic value. The longer we pursue this course, the greater amount of losses and bankruptcies must be entailed upon the country at large.

With all the teachings of science and experience; with the fact demonstrated by the history of the nation that we have lost the whole product of our bullion since 1848; with the further proof that the war debt is quite double what it would be if we had saved our gold coin and sunk the fiction debt currency; with the experience that the National bank system is no improvement upon the old State bank systems as an efficient agent to save the gold in the country; with the truth plain that our people are ground by excessive taxes, and our material interests declining on all sides; with all these demonstrations before us, we ought to abandon, and forever, the fallacy of making debt the basis of our medium of exchange; making our money, in fact, out of the public debt instead of making it from the bullion of our mines.

While we possess so treacherous an element of remittance to balance our foreign trade as the national debt, which individuals may part with at two-thirds or three-quarters of its face value because they have purchased it at such sacrifice to the nation, the country will be going in debt to other nations at a fearful rate, and still we may not see through this mirage anything but apparent prosperity. When foreigners get the whole of our debt at about seventy-five cents on the dollar—paying us for it in merchandise, coming generations will open their eyes and say, why did not our forefathers use gold coin for money, and avert from us this wide-spread ruin?

Suppose, for example, that we import $365,000,000 yearly, and export the same amount in our own products, in manufactures and in Government bonds, exclusive of any gold shipments whatever. Our exports and bonds then would seem to balance the imports. The losses on the bonds we are not at present considering. We should then seem to be saving to ourselves the whole product of our bullion. But this conclusion is qualified by a very important consideration. Of the above $365,000,000 of imports we assume that $140,000,000 are imported by foreign agencies established in our country, and sold to us by these foreign agents—sold for our form of currency, and at such prices as that currency shall institute.

Then if we assume that the normal specie volume of the country would be $300,000,000, if all paper circulation were prohibited, but that this volume has been enlarged fifty per cent. or to $450,000,000 by the utterance of such paper, and made the prices of all commodities upon the basis that the enlarged volume of currency is the true one, it follows that the enlarged volume of currency could be sustained unless commerce prevented it. In the example above given commerce would not prevent it, because the shipments of our own products and sale of national bonds abroad would balance the cost of our imports. But the sales of $140,000,000, for foreign account, of these shipments, would be made at prices fifty per cent. higher than they could be under a gold currency. This fifty per cent. would be upon their foreign value, and would amount to $70,000,000. And this amount, being almost equal to the entire annual product of our bullion, would go from us in total loss. Such is the annual tribute which we pay to foreigners to gratify the avarice of bank shareholders, and to support the system of debt currency.

In treating of currency, some writers use the term "debt-currency," while others prefer the term "credit currency." Any currency, like that of the National banks, which is made by organizing debt into the circulating medium of exchange, may be properly called debt-currency. The circulation of the banks is strictly debt-currency; but their deposits, except those in coin, and the legal tender notes of the Government are credit-currency. Each of these forms of currency is pernicious in the extreme, excepting deposits in coin, which are proper to any extent.

It is nearly six years since Congress passed the first of the Legal Tender Acts—making the printed promises of the Government legal tender. When this unjust experiment was inflicted upon the country, it was thought that the coercive power of the federal government, making such issues tender, would be sufficient to keep them nearly at the par of gold. But the result proved that legislation could not galvanize them with any such vitality.

An astute writer thus treats the subject:

"Directly to alter the terms of the contracts between individuals, would be too barefaced and tyrannical an interference with the rights of property to be tolerated. Those, therefore, who endeavor to enrich one part of society at the expense of another, find it necessary to act with caution and reserve. Instead of changing the stipulation in contracts, they have resorted to the ingenious device of changing the standard by which these stipulations are adjusted. They have not said, in so many words, that ten or twenty per cent. should be added to, or deducted from, the debts and obligations of society; but they have, nevertheless, effected this by making a proportional change in the value of money. Men, in their bargains, do not stipulate for signs or measures of value, but for real equivalents. Money is not merely the standard by a comparison with which the values of commodities are ascertained; it is also the equivalent, by the delivery of a specified amount of which the stipulations in most contracts and engagements may be discharged. It is plain, therefore, that it cannot vary without affecting these stipulations. Every addition to its value makes a corresponding addition to the debts of the State, and of individuals; whereas every diminution of its value makes a corresponding diminution of these debts."

The economist, J. Stuart Mill, makes the following illustration of the subject:

"Profligate governments have, until a very late period, never scrupled, for the sake of robbing their creditors, to confer upon all other debtors a license to rob theirs, by the shallow and impudent artifice of lowering the standard; that least covert of all modes of knavery, which consists in calling a shilling a pound, that the debt of one hundred pounds may be canceled by the payment of one hundred shillings. It would have been as simple a plan, and would have answered the purpose as well, to have enacted that 'a hundred' should always be interpreted to mean five, which would have effected the same reduction in all pecuniary contracts, and would not have been at all more shameless. Such strokes of policy have not wholly ceased to be recommended, but they have ceased to be practiced, except occasionally through the medium of paper money; in which case, the character of the transaction, from the greater obscurity of the subject, is a little less barefaced."

And how much less "barefaced" is it than the Acts of our Government—making greenbacks legal tenders on all debts? We have been moving on for nearly six years under these laws, and although it was thought (when we digressed so far from probity and justice as to pass them) that they would not be needed for more than a year, or two at the longest, we do not seem to have made the first step towards returning to correct principles. The question of paying the debt in legal tenders is opening the eyes of the public to the injury which these laws impose upon us. If they are really constitutional issues, and legal tender upon all debts, they are good enough to pay Government debts in all cases, except where coin payment is specified. They are also good payment upon State indebtedness, if they are constitutional; for the Act authorizing their issue declares that they "shall also be lawful money and a legal tender in payment of all debts, public and private, within the United States, except duties on imports and interest" on the public debt. Now, if they are legal tender upon all debts, public and private, they are legal tender upon State debts as well as federal debts. But, most clearly, they cannot be a tender upon State debts; for the Constitution declares that "no State shall make *anything* but gold and silver coin a tender in payment of debts." If they are a legal tender for all debts, public and private, they must be a tender upon all State indebtedness, as well as individual. To make them a tender upon State indebtedness is flatly against the Constitution. *Ergo*, the laws themselves are unconstitutional; and the sooner we recognize it, and repeal them, the sooner shall we dispose of this contention as to the right or wrong of paying the public debt in legal tenders. With these laws repealed, no man, who has the least regard for the national honor, would ever think of discharging the public debt in any form of currency of less value than the coin of our mints. It would be amply sufficient for all the requirements of our ordinary business if the legal tender notes were immediately shorn of all qualities of tender further than the National bank notes are made tenders.

Through the medium of paper money our own Government has made itself obnoxious to the "shameless and barefaced" transaction, to the "shallow and impudent artifice" of calling what was equivalent to half a dollar, or two-thirds of a dollar, or three-quarters of a dollar, the full equivalent of a whole dollar. Tried by Mr. Mill—and the question is not one which would puzzle the most ordinary understanding—the Legal Tender Acts would be ruled as "shallow and impudent artifices" to rob all creditors, in order that the Government might be able to pay in legal tenders.

The issue of notes for circulation upon Government debt was instituted by the Bank of England. Sir Robt. Peel assumed that the circulation of the Bank of England could never be less than fourteen millions sterling. The total amount allowed to be issued upon securities is £14,475,000. "For every other note which the issue department may at any time issue over and above the maximum amount (£14,475,000) issued on securities, an equal amount of coin or bullion must be paid into its coffers." It was upon the principle that the circulation of the bank could never go below that amount, that induced this statesman to allow of such an amount to be issued upon the debt of the kingdom.

This pernicious example of the Bank of England has been the grand authority cited by our currency makers for all the mischief which our inflated circulation has imposed upon our progress and prosperity. The debt of the Government to the bank was £11,015,100. If the United States had assumed and paid this debt to Great Britain, upon the condition that she should never allow of banking upon the public debt, it would have been but a small damage to the country compared with that of following this mischievous example, thereby imposing upon us a ruinous system of finance, the loss of our bullion product since 1848, and doubling the debt of the civil war. The Americans, as a people, must always go in advance of others. If the Bank of England can issue £14,000,000 on securities, they can issue £60,000,000 by the National banks, and £80,000,000 of legal tenders. Thus, with the population of the United States and the United Kingdom about equal, one country issues about £140,000,000, the other about one-tenth, or £14,000,000. Notwithstanding our circulation is so much larger than theirs, the debt of Great Britain is much larger than that of the United States. Hence we must reform our currency, or admit that the English are incomparably our superiors in matters of finance, and continue to aid them in maintaining their superiority. We judge ourselves by a fallacious criterion if we suppose that we can circulate, upon a basis of debt, such an immense amount of currency without ruinous consequences to our material interests.

But, admitting that Sir Robert Peel reasoned correctly in assuming that the circulation of the bank would never be less than fourteen millions, it does not follow that it was a wise measure, in practice, to allow of this increase of currency; for it must be either an increase of the currency to that amount, or it must drive an equal amount of coin to the arts or to other countries. If it were an increase of the currency, it increased prices in a corresponding ratio; if it were not an increase of the currency—but a simple coercing from the circulation an equal amount of coin to the issue, compelling that coin to seek a market in other countries, or to resort to the arts in its use—it was of no benefit to the country in general. If it displaced an equal amount of coin—and it must have done this or made prices upon an inflated basis—it was useless. Again: if it forced an amount of coin from circulation into the arts, it did not render any national advantage; for it were as well for the nation to have their entire paper circulation represent gold coin on hand, as to have bullion locked up in the form of plate, to be used once or twice in a century on some extraordinary festive occasion. If it forced the coin from the country to other nations, it weakened the monetary strength of the realm *pro rata;* and, although the country imported other forms of wealth for this bullion, these representatives were not money; and the damage to a country of not possessing a sufficiency of real cash, in times of distress and commercial crises, is not the amount of such deficiency, but *ten times* the amount of it. Every dollar of the currency supports ten dollars of the general credits; and every dollar of the currency which fails, or is impotent to help in times of distress, carries down with it ten dollars of the general credits. Is it not plain enough, then, how a sound currency—one of intrinsic value which never needs redemption—sustains general credits, in times of panic and commercial revulsions?

When every other business needs the monetary interest to support it, at such times a parasite currency is seeking all the coin of the country to support its own credit, or for its own redemption; thereby rendering all commercial crises disastrous in multiplied proportions.

The currency is the foundation upon which all our prosperity rests. It is this which sustains the entire fabric of commercial and mercantile credits, and all other credits. It is estimated that every dollar of currency sustains ten dollars of the general credits. If this be so, then every dollar of currency which fails, or which has to be withdrawn from circulation by redemption, in times of panic and commercial distress, must make ten dollars of failures or bankruptcy. It results, that every gold dollar we send out of the country, by substituting a "paper dollar" to do its offices at home, cripples our means of sustaining a panic in a ten-fold proportion. It is exactly analogous to founding a valuable and durable edifice upon bass-wood, instead of the granite of our mountains. The granite will last for thousands of years—the wood may last for one thousand days. Until the entire volume of currency is filled, which our people need to move their industries in the most efficient manner, with the gold coin of our mints, every dollar in coin or bullion which leaves the country weakens its normal power of product in a ten-fold proportion to the value of such coin. The coin of the country is like the seeds we strew upon our lands. A bushel of wheat may produce twenty or thirty times its amount, if we sow it on good soil; but a bushel of chaff will produce nothing. If we would reap good crops, we must plant good seed; for such as we strew we must expect to harvest. If we would have our money valuable, and receive continued valuable returns for its uses, we must make it intrinsically valuable in its inception. These principles apply alike to our individual and national progress and prosperity. We cheat ourselves, in doing business upon a currency worth less than it purports to be, as much as the husbandman cheats himself by sowing poor grain upon his fields.

It is not probable that a return to specie payments, upon the basis that gold coin shall measure the value of property, will be achieved for some time to come. During this period, the gold of our mines will be depressed by the force of unjust and unequal legislation acting against its normal value. This action is inequitable, and onerous in the extreme, upon the population of the Pacific States. If it is impossible to avoid it—if California, and all the mining States and territories west of the Rocky Mountains, must submit to the condition that they shall not use their money in the markets of the world, without paying such enormous duties upon the goods which they purchase and bring to the United States—thereby reducing the value of gold some forty or fifty per cent. for uses abroad—and must further pay some fifty or sixty per cent. more for domestic manufactures, on account of their being advanced that much by reason of the high tariff on foreign goods; and must lose still further by reason of gold not standing at its just relative value to currency, which makes prices for all goods; this abnormal condition of gold, not taking its proper rank when measured by legal tenders and National bank circulation, resulting from the Acts of Congress in making the greenbacks legal tenders, and chartering the National banks upon the basis of making the public debt the security for the issue of currency—if the Pacific States must submit to such onerous exactions upon their staple product—gold—it is the bounden duty of Congress to take an intelligent view of these losses, and to aid the Pacific Coast by special legislation as far as possible.

For the losses in the past twenty years, it would not be unreasonable for the Government to aid the railroads across the continent, and the railroads in California and Oregon to the amount of two hundred millions of dollars in lands and government bonds, always bearing in mind, that these are great national improvements—as needful for defense as the army and navy—and that the national power and prowess will be enlarged in a direct proportion as these improvements progress. These subsidies should be rendered by Government, then, (1.) because they are needed for national defense; (2.) in making them the nation will advance in power many times over their cost; (3.) as an act of justice, to return to the Pacific States a small part of the losses sustained upon their staple—gold—during the past twenty years. So far as this the Federal Government ought to give us reclamation for the past. And for the future what should be done? The currency should be brought up to the specie equivalent as soon as possible; and debt currency should be annihilated by the whole force of Congress, the judiciary of the Federal and State Governments, and the fiat of the people. But even after the currency shall be brought up to the gold standard, the tariff will bear upon the Pacific Coast more onerously than any other portion of the country; and for this reason: that while it acts against the sale of commodities abroad, it does not act against them uniformly and constantly as it does against gold. Our commodities are sometimes in demand abroad ; at others there is no sale for them. But gold is uniformly and always in demand. When commodities are in demand abroad we send them ; and when sold they pay for imports as well as gold ; but when commodities are not in demand, we send gold, and are always sure of the price which it will bring. The gold of the Pacific States is paid for in domestic products and manufactures which are advanced largely in price on account of duties upon foreign goods. Thus, when our commodities are not in demand abroad, we send gold, and in this manner the losses on trade are thrown disproportionately upon California's staple—our bullion—for bullion always brings its value abroad.

Interest is the ruling principle which must permanently bind a nation together. We may talk about the glory of the country, brotherly love, the pride of the nation, the beauty of our flag, and other patriotic motives which ought to inspire our hearts ; but our interest, in the long run, will outweigh all these.

In consideration of the onerous and unequal action of the tariff upon the Pacific States—thereby subjecting them to much greater losses upon their gold than the tariff imposes on any other State east of the Rocky Mountains—gold being always marketable abroad at its full value, while commodities are often unsaleable—and, although commodities are unsaleable abroad, the tariff advances domestic goods and manufactures equal to its full rate of impost, so that gold cannot bring its value in domestic markets; and although it brings its value in foreign markets, if this value is brought to the United States it is subject to an impost of sixty per cent. or more upon the foreign price, thereby rendering it impossible for the owner of gold to get its value at home or abroad (unless he lives abroad to use it); in consideration of these onerous legal exactions against the value of gold, it would not be inequitable or unjust for the Federal Government to grant a special boon in future to the commerce of the Pacific States and Territories. Suppose, for example, that Congress should grant a drawback upon all goods imported from European ports into any of the American ports upon the Pacific the drawback to equal the difference in freight between such foreign ports and the freights to the Atlantic and Pacific ports. Illustrated thus: If the freight from Liverpool to New York, per ton, was five dollars, and from Liverpool to San Francisco twenty dollars, then the San Francisco freight should be allowed a drawback of fifteen dollars at the Custom House in San Francisco. But if the duty on the goods was not enough to pay fifteen dollars per ton drawback, or whatever the difference on freight between European ports and Atlantic and Pacific ports might amount to, then that such freight should not be allowed any drawback, but instead thereof should be admitted free of duty. There would be no danger of smuggling from the Pacific side of the continent to the Atlantic, because the imports would cost as much to the importer on this side as on the other. This would be a boon to the Pacific States, but a very small one in return for the unequal action of the tariff laws. It would not be giving any preference to the ports of the Pacific over those of the Atlantic, because goods would cost as high, under such a provision, on the west as on the east side of the continent. If, however, the Courts should hold that it con flicted with Article I, Section VIII, paragraph I, or with Section IX, paragraph 5 of the Constitution, then the Pacific States have a right to demand an amendment of the supreme law. When our forefathers made the Constitution, it is not probable that one of them thought that the American Republic would ever extend to the shores of the Pacific. Consequently, regulations of commerce which would act very justly upon the Atlantic States might be extremely onerous when applied to our new possessions upon the Pacific. These possessions might require changes in the organic law of the republic. If the American Republic is to take in all of North America, there is nothing plainer than that laws adapted for one section of the country may be unwise and onerous upon another. Laws which may be imperatively necessary in Alaska might be oppressive and unjust in Florida. The matter of interest must be studied by our legislators, for nothing will ever be so great a national pacificator as interest. Make it for the interest of the people to be united, and you will bind them together for cycles and centuries.

The subjects of tariff and currency are so closely connected, when considered from a California standpoint, that they are constantly running into each other. This policy of discriminating duties upon the Atlantic and Pacific sides of the continent, has been only opened. It would require a lengthy argument to prove its advantages to the Union at large, but it is matter of certainty that these advantages would result from legislation which might concede such boon to the Pacific States.

In relation to the currency, it is not too late to forfend an almost universal bankruptcy of the Government and people. But the time for action is rapidly passing, and the longer we defer coming to the just standards of value and measuring by these, the more difficulty shall we find in reforming our errors, and the more hopeless will our condition become at last. Let us adopt the teachings of truth, justice, equity, right, science, experience, probity, wisdom, philosophy, political economy, law, history, the Constitution of our country, and every other motive which should inspire the conduct of good citizens; apply these to our actions, and in so doing all will yet be well with the American people.

J. A. F.

SAN FRANCISCO, Cal., January, 1868.

The preceding arguments are submitted to all to whom these Presents may come,

With Compliments of

The Author.

ERRATUM.

On page 30, thirteen lines from the bottom, for "imports" read imposts.

www.ingramcontent.com/pod-product-compliance
Lightning Source LLC
LaVergne TN
LVHW021146110826
845150LV00005B/1135

* 9 7 8 1 4 2 5 5 4 7 3 4 9 *